campir
sites 2004

‖‖‖‖‖‖‖‖‖‖‖‖‖‖‖‖‖‖
CW00521120

CONTENTS

LOCATING YOUR SITE could not be
simpler. The sites are listed county by county
and then under the headings of the cities,
towns or villages nearest to them. Usually the
town or city forms part of the site's address.
Where possible we have included directions to
the site and given its exact location.

We have pulled out all the stops to ensure
that this guide is as accurate as it can possibly
be. However, we accept no responsibility for
information given in error to us by any of the
listed sites. We do not guarantee that every
site in the UK and Ireland is included.

> **Front cover** Peaceful relaxation can be
> enjoyed at the Camping & Caravanning Club
> Site, Tregurrian, Newquay, Cornwall, where there
> are 90 pitches accepting all types of units.

Welcome to the latest, updated edition
of *Camping Sites*, which contains
details of 1,991 touring parks in Britain
and Ireland. It may have what seems to be a
generic title but it is far from being non-specific.

Published in association with *Motor Caravan
Magazine*, it is an essential accompaniment to
everyone who enjoys motor caravanning and
camping in tents or trailer tents. It is produced
specifically with their needs in mind. A small
minority of the sites do not accept tents, and
a handful of them do not take motor caravans
or touring caravans, so you are advised to
check on facilities in advance of arrival.

Standards and facilities vary from site to
site, but increased competition and the
demands of motor caravanners and campers,
local authorities, tourist associations and
industry organisations ensure that site owners
should be kept fully aware of their obligations.

camping
sites 2004

**An IPC Focus Network publication, published by
IPC Country & Leisure Media Ltd, part of IPC
Media Ltd.** © *Copyright 2003 IPC Media Ltd.*

Editor Roger White
Database manager Martine Derwish
Production editor Beverly Winram
Front cover design Sam Dorrington
Group advertisement manager Chris Williams
Advertisement sales Jill Kelf
Advertisement production manager Gina Mitchell
Publisher Ilka Schmitt

Editorial and advertisement departments
Camping Sites, Focus House, Dingwall Avenue,
Croydon, Surrey CR9 2TA
☎ 020 8774 0600 fax 020 8774 0939

Origination CTT, Units C/D, Sutherland House,
Sutherland Road, London E14 6BU

Printer Acorn Web Offset, Loscoe Close,
Normanton Industrial Estate, Normanton, West
Yorkshire WF6 1TW

How to use your guide

WHAT THE SYMBOLS MEAN AND MAKING THE RIGHT CHOICE

KEY TO SYMBOLS

Site facilities
Motor caravans accepted 🚐
Flush toilets [WC]
Chemical toilets or earth type 🝙
Some facilities for disabled visitors ♿
Site open all year ✱
Mains electric hook-ups on site 🔌
No dogs allowed ✗
Takeaway service ⊎
Swimming pool on site ≋
Food shop (either on site or nearby) 🛒
Café on or near site ✕
Electric shaver points ⊙
Bottled gas supplies ♃
Hot water supply ⊾
Clothes-washing and drying facilities ▣
Recreation room ♠
Showers or baths available 🜄
Frequent bus service nearby ⊟
Railway station nearby ⇌
Site licensed by local authority *L*
(or equivalent body)
Organised site on a farm ⤾
Farm produce available ♀
(on the spot or nearby)
Tradesmen call fairly frequently [T]
(usually a mobile shop)

Sporting activities
Boating ◭
Rock climbing area ⚐
Fishing (not necessarily free) ⇗
Golf course or putting green nearby ⚑
Horse or pony riding ℧
Water suitable for swimming ⇗
Tennis courts nearby ⚲
Underwater swimming or skin-diving ⚐
(suitable location nearby)
Water-skiing facilities ⤔
Pot-holing ⚇

Advance bookings
After the address of each site, the name of
the person responsible for the running of
the site is normally given. In many cases it
is unnecessary to book in advance when
touring, but some sites in popular areas do
get full at peak times. If you are unsure it is
worth a telephone call to check. Some
camping sites do not accept bookings.

You are also advised to check exactly what
facilities are available for caravans and tents.

Want to take your dog?
As you'll see from the key, those sites where
dogs are NOT allowed are clearly marked. All
other sites will welcome your pet. But do
check the entry of your chosen site for any
restrictions, even where the ✗ symbol is
absent. For example, some sites may not
allow dogs at certain times of the year, or
may specify what types of dog are allowed.
If you're still in any doubt, just pick up the
phone and ask before you book or arrive.

About our listings
As always, we have taken every care in the
preparation of this guide, but we cannot
accept responsibility for any errors or
omissions that may have occurred.

Please remember also that a listing in
this guide is not a recommendation.

If you have any comments about any
listed site, you should make your views
known to the proprietor at the time of
your visit.

If you have any suggestions as to how
our guide could be improved, please write
to us at :
Camping Sites, IPC Focus Network,
Focus House, Dingwall Avenue, Croydon,
Surrey CR9 2TA.

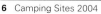

ENGLAND

BATH

Bath

Bury View Farm, Corston Fields, Bath BA2 9HD. *01225 873672*. salbowd@btinternet.com. Mr & Mrs J A Bowden. On the A39 Bath to Wells road. Midway between Wheatsheaf Inn and Corston Car Sales. Quiet farm site, five miles from Bath. Park and Ride to Bath two miles. Rural surroundings.

🚐 🚂 📺 ⊙ 🕭 🔥 🏕 × 🚻 ❄ ♨ 🅛 ⚓ ⤸ �/ ↺

Newton Mill Camping Park, Newton Road, Bath BA2 9JF. *01225 333909*. newtonmill@hot-mail.com. www.campinginbath.co.uk. Keith & Louise Davies. A4 towards Bristol, left at round-about by Globe public house take exit signposted Newton St Loe, park is one mile on left. 100 tent pitches. Situated in a hidden valley, the park is a suitable touring centre with a nearby frequent bus service and level-free cycle path to the centre. Graded: 4 stars. AA 4 pennant.

🚐 🚂 📺 🅛 🛢 × ⊙ 🕭 🔥 🏕 🍴 🚻 ❄ ⚓ ⤸ �/ ↺ ⟲ 🔌

BEDFORDSHIRE

Leighton Buzzard

The Silver Birch Cafe, Ivinghoe, Leighton Buzzard, Bedfordshire. *01296 668348*. Mr S J Newman & Mrs J M Rance. Off the A41 at Tring to B488 Tring/Luton road. Site is on the B488. Within easy reach of Whipsnade Zoo, Woburn Abbey and the Chiltern Hills. Fees on application. Open March-November.

🚐 📺 ⊙ 🚻 🍴 🅛 ⤸ 🔌

Woburn

Rose & Crown, Ridgmont, Woburn, Bedfordshire MK43 0TY. *01525 280245*. Mr N C McGregor. 3m NE of Woburn on A507, 3m from jct 13 on M1. Flat, well-drained site close to Woburn Abbey and Safari Park. 5 miles from Milton Keynes. Open all year.

🚐 🚂 🚴 📺 🅛 × ⊙ 🔥 🍴 🚻 🍴 ❄ 🅛 ⚓ �/ ↺ ⟲ 🔌 🎣

BERKSHIRE

Maidenhead

Amerden Caravan Site, Old Marsh Lane, Dorney Reach, Maidenhead, Berkshire SL6 0EE. *01628 627461*. B Hakesley. Leave M4 at Junction 7 (Slough west), and turn left along A4 towards Maidenhead, third turn left into Marsh Lane, first right into Old Marsh Lane. A small, quiet riverside site with motorway and railway links to London. Open April 1-October 31.

🚐 🚂 📺 🛢 🅛 🛢 ⊙ 🕭 🔥 🚻 🏕 🍴 ⤸ 🅛 🌢 �/ ↺ 🔌 🔌

Hurley Riverside Park, Hurley, Maidenhead, Berkshire SL6 5NE. *01628 824493/823501*. info@hurleyriversidepark.co.uk. www.hurleyriversidepark.co.uk. Situated off the A4130 midway between Henley on Thames and Maidenhead. Entry is via Shepherds Lane, one mile west of Hurley village. On the river Thames. Fishing and slipway. Disabled toilet facilities. David Bellamy Gold Conservation Award. Graded: 3 stars. Open March-October.

🚐 🚂 📺 🅛 🛢 × ⊙ 🕭 🔥 🍴 🏕 🚻 ❄ 🅛 ⚓ �/ ↺ 🔌

Newbury

Oakley Farm Caravan Park, Wash Water, Newbury, Berkshire RG20 0LP. *01635 36581*. info@oakleyfarm.co.uk www.oakleyfarm.co.uk Mr Hall. 2.5 miles south of Newbury off A343. From A34 Newbury by pass, take exit marked Highclere/Wash Common. Turn left towards Newbury on A343. After 400 metres turn right into Penwood Road. Open March 1-October 31.

🚐 🚂 📺 🛢 ⊙ 🕭 🔥 🍴 🏕 🚻 ❄ 🅛 🔌 🔌

Reading

Loddon Court Farm, Beech Hill Road, Spencers Wood, Reading, Berkshire RG7 1HT. *01189 883153*. Executor of D M Morgan (Decd). 2m S of Reading. Travel south on the A33 from junction 11 of the M4. At first roundabout take left exit to Spencers Wood, then turn right at Doubles garage to site 0.5 mile on left. Flat site with made-up roads.

🚐 📺 🅛 ⊙ 🕭 🔥 🏕 ❄ ♨ 🅛 🆃 ⤸ ↺

Wellington Country Park, Riseley, Reading, Berkshire RG7 1SP. *01189 326444*. www.wellington-country-park.co.uk. Off A33 4m S of M4 junction 11. 350-acre country park with woodland glades and nature trails. Adventure playground. Row boats and pedaloes on large lake. Crazy golf. Miniature steam railway. Sandpit and animal farm. Graded: 3 stars. Open March 1-October 31.

🚐 🚂 📺 🅛 × ⊙ 🔥 🏕 🚻 ❄ 🅛 🌢 ⤸ ᶜ/ ↺

Wokingham

California Chalet & Touring Park, Nine-Mile-Ride, Finchampstead, Wokingham, Berkshire RG11 3NY. *01734 733928*. Mr R & P Morris. Lake with coarse fishing. Tennis. Nature trail. Paddling pool. Play area adjacent to country park. Dogs allowed. Graded: 3 stars. Open March 1-October 31.

BRISTOL

Bristol

Brook Lodge Country Caravan & Tent Park, Brook Lodge, Cowslip Green, Bristol, Bristol BS40 5RD. *01934 862311*Mrs J House. From Bristol take A38 south-west 7 miles. Park signed on left. Small, unique family-run park, surrounded by trees. Also Caravan hire. Cycle/mountain bikes hire. Suitable for touring Bristol, Bath, Cheddar and Wells. Bus service to Bristol. Dogs on leads allowed. Cowslip Green, most historic hamlet connected with abolition slavery (Wilberforce/Hannah More 1745-1833). Open March 1-October 31.

Oak Farm Touring Park, Weston Road, Congresbury, Bristol, Bristol BS49 5EB. *01934 833246/07989 319686 (m)*. Mr B A Sweet. 4m from junction 21 off M5 on A370 mid-way between Bristol and Weston-super-Mare. Nice quiet orchard site with easy access. Events field available. Open April 1-October 31.

BUCKINGHAMSHIRE

Beaconsfield

Highclere Farm Country Touring Park, Newbarn Lane, Seer Green, Beaconsfield, Buckinghamshire HP9 2QZ. *01494 874505*. M J Penfold. M40 Junction 2 to Beaconsfield. A355, 1 mile right to Seer Green. Peaceful site well situated for South Bucks. Just off A40, M40 and M25. 20 miles from London. Graded: 3 stars. Open March-January.

Olney

Emberton Country Park, Emberton, Olney, Buckinghamshire MK46 5DB. *01234 711575*. emberton park@milton-keynes.gov.uk www.mkwes.co.uk/embertonpark Milton Keynes Borough Council. On A509 Newport Pagnell to Olney. Open April-October.

CAMBRIDGESHIRE

Cambridge

Highfield Farm Touring Park, Long Road, Comberton, Cambridge, Cambridgeshire CB3 7DG. *01223 262308*. enquiries@highfieldfarmtouringpark.co.uk. www.highfieldfarm touringpark.co.uk. Mr & Mrs B H Chapman. 5m W of Cambridge (A428 Bedford). After 3m follow international camping signs. From M11 leave jct 12 and take A603 (Sandy) for 0.5m then B1046 to Comberton. Fairly flat, well-maintained site with made-up roads. Hardstandings. Post box. Graded: 5 stars. BH&HPA member. Open April-October.

Roseberry Tourist Park, Earith Road, Willingham, Cambridge, Cambridgeshire CB4 5LT. *01954 260346*. Isobel Cuthbert. From A14 take B1050 at Bar Hill. Site 1m N of Willingham on left of B1050. 9-acre orchard site, ideal for touring Cambridge, Ely or St Ives on route Felixstowe or Harwich Ferry. Open all year.

Stanford Park, Weirs Road, Cambridge, Cambridgeshire CB5 0BP. *01638 741547/07802 439997*. www.stanfordcaravan park.co.uk. Mr J Stanford. In Burwell 4m NW of Newmarket. Overnight stop route to London to east coast, or touring centre. Quiet site with excellent facilities. Ideally sited for exploring Cambridge and Newmarket. AA 4 Pennant. RAC appointed. Fees on application. Open all year.

Toad Acre Caravan Park, Mills Lane, Longstanton, Cambridge, Cambridgeshire CB4 5DG. *01954 780939/01353 720661*. K Dorling. From Cambridge A604 towards Huntingdon. Turn on B1050. 2nd right opposite church. 4.5-acre grassy, level site.

Fenstanton

Crystal Lakes Touring Caravan, Tent & Fishing Park, Low Road, Fenstanton, Cambridgeshire PE18 9VV. *01480 497728*. crystalleisure@msn.com. J E Smith. 20 acres of meadowland and small fishing lakes. Bordered by mature trees and hedgerows. Close to Fenstanton village with shops and 5 pubs. Cambridge, St Ives and Huntingdon within easy reach. Graded: 1 star. Open March-October.

Great Shelford

Camping & Caravanning Club Site - Cambridge, 19 Cabbage Moor, Great Shelford, Cambridgeshire CB2 5NB. *01223 841185*. www.campingandcaravanningclub.co.uk. The Camping

& Caravanning Club Ltd. 12-acre site with 120 pitches. Signposted on the A1301. Non-members welcome. Site is on the outskirts of the city of Cambridge. Caravans, motorcaravans and tents accepted. Open March-October.

🏕🅿🖃🛉♿🎣☉🛂🔥🗎🏠🛋⇌🗘🗘🗘

Huntingdon

Old Manor Caravan Park, Church Road, Grafham, Huntingdon, Cambridgeshire PE28 0BB. *01480 810264.* camping@old-manor.co.uk. www.old-manor.co.uk. D P & C G Howes. From A1 follow international camping sign at Buckden roundabout (B661), or turn S to Grafham off A14. Seven new hardstanding pitches. Children's playground. Deep freeze facilities. Dishwashing room. Graded: 4 stars. Open March 1-October 31.

🏕🅿♿🛂🎣☉🛂🔥🗎🥡🏠♨🏘🞔🗘🗘🗘🗘🗘🗘

Park Lane (Touring) Camping Park, Godmanchester, Huntingdon, Cambridgeshire PE18 8AF. *01480 453740.* Mr A J & K M Mills. From the A14 westbound, turn off at large sign Huntingdon/Godmanchester. Follow signs to Godmanchester. Camp signs on lamp post. Turn at Black Bull pub and memorial. Well-signed entrance. Graded: 4 stars. Open March-October.

🏕🅿♿🛂✕☉🛂🔥🗎🏠⇌🗘🗘🗘🗘🗘

Quiet Waters Caravan Park, Hemingford Abbots, Huntingdon, Cambridgeshire PE28 9AJ. *01480 463405.* www.quietwaterscaravanpark.co.uk W H Hutson & Son Ltd. From Huntingdon, take A14 towards Cambridge. 2m past Godmanchester J25, turn N for 1m. 4m E of Huntingdon. Graded: 4 stars. Open April-October.

🏕🅿🖃🛂☉🛂🔥🗎🏠⇌🗘🗘🗘🗘🗘🗘

The Willows Caravan Park, Bromholme Lane, Brampton, Huntingdon, Cambridgeshire PE18 8NE. *01480 437566.* willow@willows33.freeserve.co.uk. Stephen A Carter. Brampton is situated on the A1 and A14 (formerly A604). Follow B1514 through Brampton towards Huntingdon, taking right hand turning (signposted) into Bromholme Lane. On the Ouse Valley Way with attractive walks and launching area for boats and canoes.

🏕🅿⛵🖃🛉♿✕☉🛂🔥🗎🏠⇌✲🗘🗘🗘🗘🗘🗘

Wyton Lakes Holiday Park, Banks End, Wyton, Huntingdon, Cambridgeshire PE28 2AA. *01480 412715.* holidaypark@ wytonhuntingdon.fslife.com. www.wyton lakes.com. Head for A14. Take exit 23 off, follow A141 to March. After four roundabouts take A1123 St Ives. One mile down pass Hartford Marina. Wyton Lakes is next door. Cafe/restaurant available nearby. Open April 1-October 31.

🏕🅿🖃🛉♿🛂🛋🏠⇌🗘🗘🗘🗘🗘🗘🗘

Peterborough

Sacrewell Farm & Country Centre, Thornhaugh, Peterborough, Cambridgeshire PE8 6HJ. *01780 782254.* wsatrust@supanet.com. www.sacrewell.org.uk. William Scott Abbott Trust. Access off A47. 9 miles West of Peterborough and 400 metres east of A1/A47 interchange.

🏕🅿🖃✕☉🏠✿♨🗘🗘☉

Yarwell Mill Caravan Park, Mill Lane, Peterborough Cambridgeshire PE8 6PS. *01780 782344.* Mr & Mrs K Usher. Fishing available on site in river Nene/lake. Many small stone villages nearby. The main towns of Stamford and Peterborough are within six miles north and south. Open March 1-October 31.

🏕🅿🖃🛉♿🛂☉🛂🔥🗎🏠⇌🜄🗘🗘🗘☉

St Neots

Camping & Caravanning Club Site - St Neots, Rush Meadow, Hardwick Road, Eynesbury, St Neots, Cambridgeshire PE19 2PR. *01480 474404.* www.campingand caravanningclub.co.uk. The Camping & Caravanning Club Ltd. 10-acre site with 180 pitches. Next to Riverside Park on the banks of the Great Ouse. At St Neots, on the A45 turn on to the B1043. At Eynesbury fork right. Fishing from site. Non-members welcome. Caravans, motor caravans and tents accepted. Open March-October.

🏕🅿🖃♿🛂☉🛂🔥🗎🏠⇌🗘🜄🗘🗘🗘🗘

CHANNEL ISLANDS

Guernsey

Fauxquets Valley Farm Camp Site, Castel, St Peter Port, Guernsey, Channel Islands. *01481 255460.* info@ fauxquets.co.uk. www.fauxquets.co.uk. Mr R O Guille. 3m W of St Peter Port. Right from main road at the sign for the German underground hospital, then fourth left. Families and couples only. Fully-equipped tents available for hire. Open May-September.

🅿⛵🖃🛉🛋✕☉🛂🔥🗎🥡🍴🏠♨🗘🗘🗘🗘🗘🗘🗘🗘

La Bailloterie Camp Site, Vale, Guernsey, Channel Islands GY3 5HA. *01481 43636.* Mr Richard A Collas. From St Peter Port 2.5 miles north via Halfway, left to Crossways. Then right and first left to site. Landscaped areas with plenty of room. Within easy reach of beaches. Fully-equipped sites available. Dogs welcome at park owner's discretion. Open May-September.

🅿⛵🖃🛉🛋✕☉🛂🔥🗎🥡🏠🗘🏠🞔🗘🗘🗘🗘🗘🗘🗘🗘

Herm

Seagull Campsite, Herm, Channel Islands GY1 3HR. *01481 722377.* camping@herm-island.com. www.herm-island.com. Wood of Herm Island Ltd. By launch from St Peter Port, Guernsey. An isolated peaceful site. Lovely beaches. Camping gear and fully equipped tents can be hired. Modern toilet and shower facilities. Open May-September.

🖃🛋✕☉🛂🔥🗎🏠🞔🗘🗘🗘🗘

Jersey

Beuvelande Camping Site, Beuvel ande, St Martin, Jersey, Channel Islands JE3 6EZ. *01534 85375/852223/ 851156.* S J de la Haye. A flat, secluded, family-run site suitable for trailer tents. Near St Martin's Church. Free parking alongside tents. TV room. Children's recreation room. Open May 1-September 15.

🅿⛵🖃🛉♿🛋✕☉🛂🔥🗎🏠🍴🗎🏠🗘🗘🗘☉🗘

CHANNEL ISLANDS/CO DURHAM

Rozel Camping Park, St Martin, Jersey, Channel Islands JE3 6AX. *01534 856797.* rozelcamping@jerseyhols.com. www.jerseyhols.com/rozel. Messrs John & David Germain. 5m from St Helier on the A6. 0.5m from beach. Children's play area. Package tents and own tents welcome. Free parking near tents. Fees on application. Open early May-mid September.
📞 🏠 🚮 🖂 🗐 🔥 🕯 ⊙ 🗗 🔥 🗐 ≋ 🔦 🍴 ✕ 🗓 💡 🛆 🏸 ⅃ 🌙 ✓ 🌙 ✓ ↺ 🔧 ⚓

CHESHIRE

Chester

Birch Bank Farm, Stamford Lane, Christleton, Chester, Cheshire CH3 7QD. *01244 335233.* Mr A W Mitchell. Turn right off A51 Chester to Nantwich road after Little Chef into Stamford Lane. 2nd farm on left. A small site on a working farm in the green Cheshire countryside, free of traffic noise. Open May 1-October 31.
📞 🏠 🖂 ⊙ 🔥 🕯 🐾 ⅃ ✓

Chester Fairoaks Caravan Club Site, Rake Lane, Little Stanney, Chester, Cheshire CH2 4HS. *01513 551600.* www.caravanclub.co.uk The Caravan Club. Operated by the Caravan Club. Non-members welcome. Leave M53 at junction 10 on to A5117. In 0.3m turn left into Little Stanney. Advance booking essential for weekends, bank holidays and peak periods. Peaceful off peak. 99 pitches—suitable family site. Graded: 5 stars.
📞 🏠 🖂 🗐 🔥 💡 ⊙ 🗗 🔥 🕯 ⅃ ✓

Chester Southerly Caravan Park, Balderton Lane, Marlston-cum-Lache, Chester, Cheshire CH4 9LF. *01244 671308/0976 743888.* Mr & Mrs Tony McArdle. Level, attractive site. Suitable touring base and close to leisure facilities. Dogs allowed on leads. Rallies by arrangement. Fees on application. Advance booking for periods of one week or more and bank holidays.
📞 🏠 🖂 🗐 🔥 💡 ⊙ � 🗗 🔥 🗐 🕯 ✕ 🕯 ⊙ ⅃ 🔧 🛆 ✓ ↺ 🔧 🔦

Northwood Hall Country Touring Park, Frodsham Street, Kelsall, Chester, Cheshire CW6 0RP. *01829 752569.* enquiries@northwood-hall.co.uk. www.northwood-hall.co.uk. Mr & Mrs Nock. Off A54 in Kelsall village. 6m E of Chester adjacent Delemare Forest. Set among mature oak and chestnut trees, this is a small, family-run park.
📞 🏠 🖂 🗐 🔥 💡 ⊙ 🗗 🔥 🗐 🕯 🗐 🔧 🛆 ⅃ ✓ ↺ 🔧 🔦

Glossop

Camping & Caravanning Club Site - Crowden, Glossop, Cheshire SK13 1HZ. *01457 866057.* www.campingandcaravanningclub.co.uk The Camping & Caravanning Club Ltd. Two-acre site with 45 pitches. Adjoining Crowden Brook overlooked by the moors. Site on the Pennine Way. East of Tintwistle on the A628. Dogs allowed. Non-members welcome. No caravans or motor caravans. Open April-September.
🖂 🗐 💡 ⊙ 🗗 🔥 🕯 🗐 ⅃ 🛆

Nantwich

Brookfield Caravan Park, Shrewsbury Road, Nantwich, Cheshire CW5 7AD. *01270 537841.* Crewe & Nantwich Borough Council. Situated on public park close to the river Weaver. Children's play area. Open Easter-end September.
📞 🏠 🚮 🖂 💡 ✕ ⊙ 🔥 🗐 🔥 🗐 🗐 ≋ ⅃ ✓ ↺ 🔧 🔦

Northwich

Lamb Cottage, Daleford's Lane, Whitegate, Northwich, Cheshire CW8 2BN. *01606 882302/888491.* Mr R Walker & Mr A Walker. Leave M6 at Exit 19 on to A556 (Chester). Site is 4m W of Northwich, turn at traffic lights into Daleford's Lane at Sandaway. Pub nearby. Route to north England and Wales. Dogs allowed. Fees on application. Open March-October.
📞 🏠 🖂 🗐 🔥 ⊙ 🗗 🔥 🕯 🗐 ≋ ⅃ 🗓 ⅃ ✓ ↺ 🔧

Woodbine Cottage Caravan Park, Warrington Road, Acton Bridge, Northwich, Cheshire CW8 3QB. *01606 852319/77900.* Mr & Mrs Done. On A49 8m S of Warrington. Within easy reach of Chester, Manchester, Liverpool and North Wales coast. Rural riverside site. Advance booking at peak periods. Open March-October.
📞 🏠 🖂 🗐 🔥 ✕ ⊙ � 🔥 🗐 🔥 🗐 ≋ ⅃ 🛆 ⅃ ✓ ↺ 🔧 🔦

Warrington

Holly Bank Caravan Park, Warburton Bridge Road, Rixton, Warrington, Cheshire WA3 6HU. *01617 752842.* Mr J O Walsh. 2m from M6 jctn 21. On A57 (Irlam), turn right at lights into Warburton Bridge Road, entry on left. 8 acres grassy, level site. AA 3 pennants, RAC appointed. Booking advisable. SAE for brochure. Graded: 4 stars.
📞 🏠 🖂 🗐 🔥 💡 ⊙ 🗗 🔥 🗐 🕯 🔥 🗐 ≋ 🔧 ⅃ ⅃ ✓ ↺ 🔧 🔦

CO DURHAM

Barnard Castle

Camping & Caravanning Club Site - Barnard Castle, Dockenflatts Lane, Lartington, Barnard Castle, Co Durham DL12 9DG. *01833 630228.* www.campingandcaravanningclub.co.uk Camping & Caravanning Club. Take A67 at Barnard Castle, then B6277 for 1 mile towards Middleton, site is on the left. Non members welcome. Well placed for exploring the Pennines and the city of Durham. Open March-October.
📞 🏠 🖂 🗐 🔥 💡 ⊙ 🗗 🔥 🗐 🔥 🗐 ⅃ ⅃ ↺ 🔧 🔦

Westgate-in-Weardale

Westgate Camping Site, Westgate-in-Weardale, Co Durham DL13 1LN. *01388 517309.* Mrs M Pears. 7m W of Stanhope via A689 in Westgate village. Flat, well-drained site close to river Wear. Open March-October.

🚐 ⛽ 📺 🏧 ⊙ 🚿 🔥 ⛺ 🅿 🗑 𝐿 ✈ ⛵ ♒

CORNWALL

Bodmin

Camping & Caravanning Club Site - Bodmin, Old Callywith Road, Bodmin, Cornwall PL3I 2DZ. *01208 73834.* www.campingandcaravanningclub.co.uk The Camping & Caravanning Club Ltd. 10.5-acre site with 175 pitches accepting all units. From Launceston A30, take Bodmin turn off from dual carriageway A389 to Liskeard A38. Immediately after leaving dual carriageway turn right. Site is 500 yards. Children's play area. Bodmin 0.75m. On the edge of Bodmin Moor near coast. Dogs allowed. Caravans, motor caravans and tents accepted. Non-members welcome. Open April-November.

🚐 ⛽ 📺 🏧 ⊙ 🚿 🔥 ⛺ 🅿 🗑 ⛵ 🛒 ♒

Croft Farm Holiday Park, Luxulyan, Bodmin, Cornwall PL30 5EQ. *01726 850228.* lynpick@ukonline.co.uk. www.croftfarm. co.uk. C H & L V H Pickering. Secluded park suitable for walking, beaches and attractions. Family-owned and friendly. Dogs welcome. Wooded walk available. One mile from Eden Project. Open March-January.

🚐 ⛽ 📺 🏧 ⊙ 🚿 🔥 ⛺ 🅿 🗑 𝐿 ✈ ⛵ ⌃ ♒ ⛳

Wooda Farm Park

The Best of British

AA ✦✦✦✦✦ PREMIER PARK

Amidst some of the finest coastal scenery and sandy beaches on Devon and Cornwall's borders.

A real Cornish welcome awaits you from the Colwill family. Enjoy a farm and seaside holiday with us. We offer luxury holiday homes and excellent facilities for touring and camping. Shop and laundry room. Activities include playground, course fishing, short golf course. In main season – indoor archery, tractor and trailer rides and clay pigeon shooting. Down at the farm there is a restaurant and beer garden. Also farmyard friends. Sandy beaches 1¼ miles. 'Splash' indoor play pool is nearby. Local village inn 5 mins walk.

Write, phone or fax for brochure and tariff to:

Mrs G. Colwill, Wooda Farm Park, Poughill, Bude Cornwall EX23 9HJ.

Telephone: 01288 352069   Fax: 01288 355258

E-mail: enquiries@wooda.co.uk   www: wooda.co.uk

Glenmorris Park, Longstone Road, St Mabyn, Bodmin, Cornwall PL30 3BY. *01208 841677.* gmpark@ditcon.co.uk. Michael & Leslie-Ann. Take B3266 Bodmin/Camelford road. Site situated 0.25-mile from road at Longstone Cross towards St Mabyn. 10 level acres on quiet, secluded, family park. Centrally situated. Children's play area. Heated pool. AA 3-pennant. Graded: 3 stars. Open Easter-October inclusive.

🚐 ⛽ 🏧 📺 ⊙ 🚿 🔥 ⛺ 🅿 🗑 𝐿 ✈ ⛵ ♒

Lanarth Hotel and Caravan Park, St Kew Highway, Bodmin, Cornwall PL30 3EE. *01208 841215.* Mrs Buckley. On A39 between Wadebridge, 4 miles, and Camelford, 7 miles. Quiet rural park, beautiful views and gardens. No children's facilities. Licenced bar. Dog exercise meadow. 4 miles to beach. Bed and breakfast also available. Open April 1-October 31.

🚐 ⛽ 📺 🏧 ⊙ ✕ 🚿 🔥 ⛺ 🅿 𝐿 ✈ ⛵ ♒

Ruthern Valley Holidays, Ruthern Bridge, Bodmin, Cornwall PL30 5LU. *01208 831395.* enquiries@ruthernvalley.fsnet.co.uk. www.self-catering-ruthern.co.uk. Mr & Mrs T I Zair. From Bodmin leave on A391. Take 2nd right for Nanstallon. Then 2nd left to Ruthern Bridge. Left at bridge 400yds to site. Secluded site in unspoilt valley. Touring centre or overnight stop London and south-west. Fees on application. Open April-October.

🚐 ⛽ 📺 🏧 ⊙ 🚿 🔥 ⛺ 🅿 ✈ ⛵ ♒

Boscastle

Lower Pennycrocker Farm, St Juliot, Boscastle, Cornwall PL35 0BY. *01840 250257.* pennycrocker.co.uk. Mr B Heard. B3263 to Bude then Pennycrocker turning 2m NE of Boscastle. Beautiful country near coast. Open Easter-September.

🚐 ⛽ 🏧 🍴 🏧 ⊙ 🔥 ⛺ 🅿 🛒 𝐿 ✈ ⛵ ♒

Bude

Bude Holiday Park, Maer Lane, Bude, Cornwall EX23 9EE. *01288 355955.* Mr M Hyde. Im N of Bude. Take A39 through town to Crooklets Beach. Then follow signs. Family holiday park with tarmac roads and car parking. Level pitches. Beach 0.25m away. Club and entertainment. Open April-September.

🚐 ⛽ 📺 🏧 🍴 🏧 ✕ ⊙ 🚿 🔥 ⛺ 🅿 𝐿 ⌃ ✈ ⛵ ♒

Camping & Caravanning Club Site - Bude, Gillards Moor, St Gennys, Bude, Cornwall EX23 0BG. *01840 230650.* www.campingandcaravanningclub.co.uk. The Camping & Caravanning Club Ltd. 8m S of Bude on the A39 0.5m past Wainhouse Corner, off large lay by. 100 pitches in 6 acres of quiet, level, grassy parkland overlooking the valley towards Crackington Haven and sea beyond. Easy access to all of north Cornwall coastline and moors. Dogs allowed. Caravans, motor caravans and tents accepted. Non-members welcome. Open May-September.

🚐 ⛽ 📺 🏧 ⊙ 🚿 🔥 ⛺ 🅿 𝐿

Cornish Coasts Caravan & Camping Park, Middle Penlean, Poundstock, Widemouth Bay, Bude, Cornwall EX23 0EE. *01288 361380.* info.1@cornishcoasts.co.uk. www.cornish coasts.co.uk. Mrs J Woods. On A39, 5m S of Bude. Quiet, friendly, touring holiday site with good views, near sandy,

surfing beaches and coastal path. Suitable base for touring Cornwall and north Devon. Holiday caravans to let. Open Easter-October.

🚐🔌📷✇🛠🔥⊙🖒🛠🔥🌂🏚♿🛁 *L* ♀💧✂🍴🚻⛱

Coxford Meadow, Crackington Haven, Bude, Cornwall EX23 0NS. *01840 230707.* Mrs J Onions. Crackington Haven 1m. 1-acre field with easy access. Shops, cafe 1m away. Above quiet wooded valley leading to sea. Open Easter-September 30.

🚐📶🛠✖⊙🔥🍴 ⛱🍴

East Caravan & Camping Park, Kilkhampton, Bude, Cornwall EX23 9RY. *01288 321654.* keith.ovenden@btopenworld.com. Mr & Mrs Ovenden. 5m north of Bude on A39 trunk road. Park 0.5m from village on B3254. Small family-run park set in quiet farmland on the outskirts of Kilkhampton village.

🚐🔌📷⊙🖒🛠🔥♿🍴 *L* ♿✂🍴⊙

Hentervene Caravan & Camping Park, Crackington Haven, nr Bude, Cornwall EX23 0LF. *01840 230365.* contact@hentervene.co.uk. www.hentervene.co.uk. Mrs S Weller. Secluded attractive park. Area of Outstanding Natural Beauty. Two miles from sandy surfing cove, coastal footpaths, pub/restaurant. TV/pool rooms, free microwave, pets welcome. Tourer parking, caravan sales. (OS grid SX155944). Open Easter-end October.

🚐🔌📷🛠⊙🖒🛠🔥♿🍴 *L* ♿✂🍴⛱

Ivy Leaf Camping Site, Ivy Leaf Hill, Bush, Bude, Cornwall EX23 9LD. *01288 321442.* N A Butchers. North of Bude on A39. Turn right at Willow Camping Site, up Ivy Leaf Hill. Site halfway up hill on right. Small sheltered site with beautiful views.

🚐🔌📶🛠✖⊙🖒🛠🔥🍴🔲✂🍴✂🍴⛱⛱🚩

Keywood Caravan Park Ltd, Whitstone, Bude, Cornwall EX22 6TW. *01288 341338.* Mr D Chapman. From Launceston on B3254 to Bude. After Whitstone turn left at second country lane signposted Keywood. Open April-October.

🚐🔌⛲📶🛠🔥✖⊙🔥🛠🔥🍴♀🔲🍴🍴✂🍴⊙⛱🍴

Penhalt Farm Holiday Park, Widemouth Bay, Bude, Cornwall EX23 0DG. *01288 361210.* denandjennie@penholtfarm.fsnet.co.uk. www.holidaybank.co.uk/penhaltfarmholiday park. Mr D Marks. 4m S of Bude take 2nd right for Widemouth bay, turn left at bottom. Site 0.75m on left. Family camp site on working farm, overlooking Widemouth Bay. Panoramic sea views. Watersports centre 0.5-mile away. Widemouth is great surfing beach. Two holiday caravans for hire. Open Easter-October.

🚐🔌📷🛠♿⊙🖒🛠🔥🍴🍴🛁♿✂🍴⊙⛱🍴

Red Post Inn, Launcells, Bude, Cornwall EX23 9NW. *01288 381305.* Mr M Hinks & Mrs Hinks. Off the A3072, 3 miles east of Bude. Level, family site. Ideal base for touring north Devon

and Cornwall. Dogs allowed. Children's playground. Sports and surfing nearby. Pub and restaurant. Open Easter-October.

🚐🔌⛲📶🛠♿✖⊙🔥🛠🔥🍴 *L* ♀🍴✂🍴⊙⛱🍴

Red Post Meadows, Launcells, Bude, Cornwall EX23 9NW. *01288 381306.* Mr & Mrs Parnell. 3m E of Bude off A3072. Level, well sheltered site. Good family site, ideal base touring north Devon and Cornwall. Open Easter-October.

🚐🔌⛲📶🛠✖⊙⌀🛠🔥🍴 *L* ♀🔲♿✂🍴✂🍴⊙⛱

Sandymouth Bay Holiday Park, Sandymouth Bay, Bude, Cornwall EX23 9HW. *01288 352563.* sandymouthbay @aol.com. www.sandymouthbay.co.uk. Mr Joce. Take A39, through Kilkhampton towards Bude. 1st right signposted Stibb, Sandymouth. Through village of Stibb, left at sign Sandymouth Bay. Site on left after 0.5-mile. Open April-November.

🚐🔌⛲📶🛠✖⊙🖒🛠🔥〰🍴🔥 *L* 🍴✂⊙⛱🍴

Upper Lynstone Camping & Caravan Park, Bude, Cornwall EX23 0LF. *01288 352017.* reception@upperlynstone.co.uk. www.upperlynstone.co.uk. Mr & Mrs J Cloke. From Bude take road S to Widemouth Bay and Lynstone. Site is about half mile S of Bude. Within easy reach of surfing beaches. Fees by arrangement. Open Easter-September.

🚐🔌📶🛠♿🛠⊙🖒🛠🔥🛠🔥🍴 *L* ♿✂🍴⊙⛱🍴

Willow Valley Holiday Park, Bush, Bude, Cornwall EX23 9LB. *01288 353104.* John & Janet Holden. 2m N of Bude on A39. 3m S of Kilkhampton. Small sheltered touring site in Strat Valley. Fees on application. Send for colour brochure. Open March-December.

🚐🔌📷🛠🛠⊙🖒🛠🔥🍴 *L* ♀♿✂⊙⛱🍴

Wooda Farm Park, Poughill, Bude, Cornwall EX23 9HJ. *01288 352069.* enquiries@wooda.co.uk. www.wooda. co.uk. Mr G Colwill. 2m NE of Bude. Approach via road signposted for Poughill or Stibb off A39 N of Stratton. Family-run park 1.25 miles from sandy beaches. Coarse fishing. Woodland walks. Licensed restaurant. Open April-October.

🚐🔌📶🛠♿✖⊙🖒🛠🔥🍴🛁🔥 *L* ♿🍴✂🍴✂🍴⊙⛱🍴

Camborne

Magor Farm Caravan Site, Tehidy, Camborne, Cornwall TR14 0JF. *01209 713367.* www.magorfarm.co.uk. Mr H Williams & Son. Flat, sheltered, large country park, convenient for beaches and leisure centre. Free hot water and showers. Dogs allowed. Open March-October.

🚐🔌📶🛠⊙🖒🛠🔥🍴⇄🛠🍴 *L* 🍴✂🍴✂⊙⛱🍴⛵

CORNWALL

Camelford

Juliot's Well Holiday Park, Camelford, Cornwall PL32 9RF. *01840 213302.* Mr J C Watkins. 1m W of Camelford via A39 Wadebridge Road. Out of Camelford, 2nd right, then 1st left. Site 400yds down lane on right. Picturesque setting 3m from beach and close to Bodmin Moor. Licensed bar. Restaurant on site. Extensive range of static caravans. Graded: 3 stars. Open March-October.

🏕🏠⚡📺🛁♿✕☉◐♨🔥🔆❄♦📻♠ℓ🚲♣◭✳♪♫✠∪↻☂♣✿

Lakefield Caravan Park & Equestrian Centre, Lower Pendavey Farm, Camelford, Cornwall PL32 9TX. *01840 213279.* Mr D E Perring. On B3266, 1 mile north of Camelford. Quiet, secluded site set in 5 acres on a 25 acre farm. Full riding school on site with lessons and hacks available. Open April 1-October 31.

🏕🏠📺⚡🛁✕☉◐🔥🔆♦📻♨ℓ♣♪✠∪↻

West End Farm, Tresparrett, Camelford, Cornwall PL32 9SX. *01840 261612.* Mr D Routly. 2 miles to Boscastle. Turn left on A39. Between Camelford and Bude. Open Easter-September.

🏕📺⚡🛁♿📻🔥∪↻

Delabole

Planet Caravan Park, Delabole, Cornwall PL33 9BQ. *01840 213361.* Mr & Mrs R W Round. 4m W of Camelford and 6m S of Tintagel. SW end of village on B3314, off A39. Quiet park with wonderful views. Shop 33yd. Touring centre. Fees on application.

🏕🏠📺⚡🛁☉🍴🔥🔆♠♦📻✿ℓ📺♪✠∪↻

Falmouth

Goonreath, Broads Lane, Mylor Downs, Falmouth, Cornwall TR11 5UL. *01872 863670.* Mr & Mrs D J Mawby. 5m N of Falmouth. From Truro towards Falmouth turn E about 1m beyond Norway Inn, follow sign to Comfort, then 2nd lane on right, 0.5m to site. Last 400yd of lane is rough. Quiet and sheltered in beautiful area. No sanitation. Open April-October.

🏕🅿♿🏠♨🛁📺⚡♪✠∪↻♣✠

Maen Valley Holiday Park, Falmouth, Cornwall TR11 5BJ. *01326 312190.* John Hick. Follow A39 ring road into Falmouth at Hillhead roundabout. Turn right and follow international camping signs, straight on for 1.5 miles. Maen Valley is situated in lovely sheltered, wooded valley. Family-run park for families. 1 mile from safe, sandy beaches. Touring centre. Graded: 3 stars. Open Easter-November 1.

🏕🏠⚡🛁📺✕☉◐🔥🔆♠♦📻♨≈ℓ♣◭♪✠✳✠↻♣☂✠

Menallack Farm, Treverva, Penryn, Falmouth, Cornwall TR10 9BP. *01326 340333.* menallack@fsbdial.co.uk. Caryl & John Minson. Half mile beyond Treveva village. From Penryn, Falmouth take road to Gweek. Good centre for touring, 4m from sea in unspoilt countryside. Fees on application. Open Easter-October.

🏕🏠📺⚡🛁☉◐🔥🔆📻♠♣◭♪✠∪↻♣✠

Pennance Mill Farm, Maenporth, Falmouth, Cornwall TR11 5HJ. *01326 312616/317431.* Mr A J Jewell. Approach Falmouth via A39 continue to Maenporth. Along road for 2 miles. Pennance Mill is on your left at bottom of hill. Open April-October.

🏕🏠📺⚡🛁♿☉◐🔥🔆♠📻♨≈♦🔥ℓ♣◭♪✠✳∪↻♣☂✠

Tremorvah Tent Park, Swanpool, Falmouth, Cornwall TR11 5BE. *01326 318311.* Mr S P Bishop. 400yd past Swanpool Beach. 1m SW of Falmouth. Terraced holiday site on hillside overlooking Falmouth Bay. Near beach. Open mid-May to mid-October.

🏕📺♿☉🔥🔆♠📻♨≈ℓ♣◭✳♣☂✠✠

Stephen. On A387 3.5m from Looe turn left at s/post for Killigarth. Site about 400yd farther on, 1m E of Looe. 1m from beach. Fees on application. Open Easter-October.

Polborder House Caravan & Camping Park, Bucklawren Road, St Martins by Looe, Looe, Cornwall PL13 1QR. *01503 240265.* rlf.polborder@virgin.net. www.peaceful-polborder. co.uk. Mr & Mrs R Frankland. 2.5 miles east of Looe off the B3253 road, follow signs for Polborder and monkey sanctuary. Small, peaceful, select site. Fees available on application. Cafe/restaurant nearby. Open April-October.

St Martins Holiday Park, St Martins, Looe, Cornwall PL13 1NX. *01326 240969/01503 263737.* Westar Holidays. On B3253 Plymouth to Looe road. Family park with all amenities. Licensed club. Open Easter-end September.

Talland Caravan Park, Talland Bay, Looe, Cornwall PL13 2JA. *01503 272715.* Mr & Mrs R S Haywood. Take the 'B' road from Looe to Polperro. 1 mile out of Looe, turn left by signposts and follow left-hand road for 1.25m. Site is next to Talland Church. Open April 1-October 31.

Tencreek Caravan & Camping Park, Looe, Cornwall PL13 2JR. *01503 262447.* Dolphin Holidays. 1m W of Looe, on Looe to Polperro road. Level, family site, overlooking sea. Good facilities: self-service shop, play area, amusement arcade, indoor pool. 45m water flume. Tarmac roads with street lighting.

Tregoad Farm Touring Caravan & Camping Park, St Martins, Looe, Cornwall PL13 1PB. *01503 262718.* tregoadfarmtccp@aol.com. www.cornwall-online.co.uk/ tregoad. Mr Werkmeister. 1.5m E of Looe on B3253 Plymouth to Looe. Well-drained site with scenic views, easy access to beaches and moors. Free hot showers. Laundrette. Bottle gas. 3 coarse fishing lakes. Bar/Bistro. Fees on application. Open April-October.

Trelawne Manor Holiday Village, Looe, Cornwall PL13 2NA. *01503 272151.* Parkworld Holidays Ltd. Holiday Village is well signposted midway between Looe and Polperro. One of Haven's 29 tenting and touring parks around the coast. All the facilities are free. Graded: 4 stars. Open April-September.

Trelay Farm Park, Pelynt, Looe, Cornwall PL13 2JX. *01503 220900.* stay@trelay.co.uk. www.trelay.co.uk. Graham & Heather Veale. Park is 0.5-mile south of Pelynt on the B3359. Looe/Polperro both three miles away. Small, friendly, family-run park surrounded by farmland with superb new washing facilities. Pub, shop and restaurant 10-minute walk. BH&HPA member. Graded: 4 stars. Open Easter to end-October.

Lostwithiel

Downend Camp Site, Downend Garage, Lostwithiel, Cornwall PL22 0RB. *01208 872363.* Mr J Hawke. 0.5 mile east of town on the Liskeard road (A390). Overnight or touring centre.

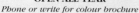

CORNWALL

Powderham Castle Tourist Park, Lanlivery, Lostwithiel, Cornwall PL30 5BU. *01208 872277.* J D B Evans. On the A390 from Lostwithiel to St Austell road. Signposted Powderham Castle. One and a half miles west of Lostwithiel. On the London to Land's End route. Quiet, uncommercialised award winning park in ideal location for touring all of Cornwall and near the Eden project. Battery charging. Ice-pack service. TV and gas. Storage and seasonal pitches. Open Easter-October.

🚐🚉📧🍴👍🍳⊙🚲🔥🗐🏠♿⇄ᴸ♦ɟɟ✓∪ᗐ९🐕🅿🛝

Marazion

Wheal Rodney, Gwallon, Marazion, Cornwall TR1 0HL. *01736 710605.* reception@whealrodney.co.uk. www.wheal rodney.co.uk. Steve & Sian Lugg. 0.25 mile north of Marazion. Flat, well-drained, clean and quiet. Sauna, solarium, spa bath in individual rooms on site. Heated indoor swimming pool. Chalets available. Open April-October.

🚐🚉📧🍴👍🍳⊙🚲🔥🗐≋📧ᴸɟɟ✓∪🅿🛝

Mevagissey

Heligan Woods Holiday Park, St Ewe, Mevagissey, Cornwall PL26 6EL. *01726 843485.* info@pentewan.co.uk. www.pentewan.co.uk. Pentewan Sands Ltd. Six miles south of St Austell, west off the B3273 (Gorran) road. 12 acres, grassy with mature trees and bushes. Part sloping and sheltered overlooking Mevagissey Bay. Shop, children's adventure playground. Next door to The Lost Gardens of Heligan. Open April 1-October 31.

🚐🚉📧🍴👍🍳⊙🚲🔥🗐🏠♿⇄♦९🐕🅿🛝

Newquay

Camping & Caravanning Club Site -Tregurrian, Newquay, Cornwall TR8 4AE. *01637 860448.* www.campingandcaravanning club.co.uk. The Camping & Caravanning Club Ltd. 4.2-acre site with 90 pitches accepting all units. 3m from Newquay. Follow B3276 to Watergate Bay, look for club signs. Non-members welcome. Caravans, motor caravans and tents accepted. 4 star rated. Open May-September.

🚐🚉📧🍴👍🍳⊙🚲🔥🗐🏠ᴸ♦ɟ∪🅿

Cottage Farm Touring Park, Treworgans, Cubert, Newquay, Cornwall TR8 5HH. *01637 831083.* Steve & Muriel Jenkins. 5m SW of Newquay. South from Newquay on the A3075. At Rejerrah crossroads, turn west for Cubert, then north towards Crantock for 0.75m. Small, quiet family site. Open Good Friday-September 30.

🚐🚉📧🍴👍🍳⊙🚲🔥🗐📧×🏠⇄ᴸ♦ɟɟ✓∪ᗐ९🐕🅿🛝

Crantock Plains Touring Park, Crantock, Newquay, Cornwall TR8 5PH. *01637 831273/830955.* www.crantock-plains.co.uk. John & Katherine Gibbes. 2.5m S of Newquay via A3075 Redruth. After lake on right, garage on left. Continue over mini roundabout. Site is 0.5m down 2nd posted lane to Crantock on right. 1.5m to beach and Crantock. Flat, spacious pitches. No single-sex groups. Open Easter-September 30.

🚐🚉📧🍳⊙🚲🔥🗐🍴🏠⇄🕑🍴♦ɟ✓∪ᗐ९🐕

Hendra Holiday Park, Newquay, Cornwall TR8 4NY. *01637 875778.* Mr & Mrs R Hyatt. Two miles SSE of Newquay. Signposted from main road. Well-equipped within easy reach of beaches. Booking advised at peak periods. Family site with entertainment and children's club. Brochure Line, Freephone 0500 242523. Open February-October.

🚐🚉👍🍳👍🏠🍴✖⊙🚲🔥🗐≋🍴🏠⇄ᴸ🅿♦ɟɟ✓∪ᗐ९🐕🛝

CORNWALL

Holywell Bay Holiday Park, Holywell Bay, Newquay, Cornwall TR8 5PR. *01637 871111/0191 2759098.* parkdean enquiries@parkdean.com. www.parkdean.com. Parkdean Holidays Plc. Six miles west of Newquay off the A3075 signposted Cubert and Holywell Bay. Peaceful valley with sandy, family beach a short walk away. Children club, free nightly entertainment, heated pool with 300 ft slide, amusements. Open March-October.

Magic Cove Touring Park, Mawgan Porth, Newquay, Cornwall TR8 4BZ. *01637 860263.* magic@redcove.co.uk. www.redcove.co.uk. Lesley Campbell. Halfway between Newquay and Padstow on north Cornish coast. 26 pitches on level site, 300yd from beach. Tap and drain adjacent to each pitch. Open Easter-October.

Marver Site, Mawgan Porth, Newquay, Cornwall TR8 4BB. *01637 860493.* John Lennon Ltd. 200yd from beach at Mawgan Porth.

Monkey Tree Holiday Park, Rejerrah, Newquay, Cornwall TR8 5QL. *01872 572032.* walker.group@virgin.net. www.chycor.co.uk/monkey-tree. Walker Leisure (Mr R Walker). 4m SW on A3075 from Newquay towards Redruth. Site signposted on right, immediately after passing Rejerrah, signpost left off main road, signposted Zelah, site 800yd on right. Sauna. Lounge bar. Luxury caravans and ready erected tents. Dogs allowed on leads. Open April 1-October 31.

Newquay Holiday Park, Newquay, Cornwall TR8 4HS. *01637 871111.* parkdeanenquiries@parkdean.com. www. parkdean.com. Parkdean Holidays Plc. Off A3059 2m from Newquay. Club. Free nightly entertainment. 3 heated swimming pools, 200ft water slide. Amusements. TV lounge. Snooker. Pool. Pitch and putt, crazy golf. Children's club and playground. Restaurant/take-away. Free brochure. AA holiday centre. Open March-October.

Perran Quay Tourist Park, Hendra Croft, Rejerrah, Newquay, Cornwall TR8 5QP. *01872 572561.* Mr & Mrs Harwood & Mrs L Mayer. On main road halfway between Newquay & Perranporth. Close to some of the finest beaches in Europe. Brochure on application. Open Easter-October.

CORNWALL

Resparva House Touring Park, Summercourt, Newquay, Cornwall TR8 5AH. *01872 510332.* Dave & Miranda Knight. From A30 take exit signposted Chapel Town & Summercourt. entrance nearby on right. 12 secluded pitches. Farm meadows adjacent. At centre of Cornwall. Adults only. Graded: 4 stars. Open Spring Bank Holiday-September.
🚐🏠♿🎦⊙🅿🍴🛁⛺🚾L

Riverside Holiday Park, Newquay, Cornwall TR8 4PE. *01637 873617.* info@riversideholidaypark.co.uk. www.riversideholiday park.co.uk. Paul Miller. From A30 at Indian Queens, take the A392 to Newquay. At roundabout at Quintrell Downs, go straight across then take 2nd left and next right. Peaceful, riverside family park with level sheltered touring and camping pitches. Open Easter-October 31.
🚐🏠♿🍴🎦♿⊠✕⊙🅿🍴🛁⛺≋♦🏡🚾⇌L🎦🍴♨♿🚿∪🔾🎣

Rosecliston Tourist Park, Trevemper, Newquay, Cornwall TR8 5JT. *01637 830326.* Mr K Gregory. Good recreational facilities in a pleasantly designed park. Singles and couples welcome. Open Whitsun-mid September.
🚐🏠♿🍴🛁🅿⊙🅿🎦🔥≋♿🏡🚾⇌L♨♿♨🚿∪🔾🎣

Summer Lodge, White Cross, Newquay, Cornwall TR8 4LW. *01726 860415.* reservations@summerlodge.co.uk. www.summer lodge.co.uk. B T Miller & Mr D F Hall. 2m S of St Columb. 5m E of Newquay on A392 at White Cross. Good central touring base. 5m from beaches. Rural site, well-lit at night, with licensed club and nightly entertainment. Open April-October.
🚐🏠♿🍴🛁♿🍴✕⊙🅿🔥🎦≋♿🏡✕🚾L♨♿♨🚿∪🔾

Sun Haven Valley Caravan & Camping Park, Mawgan Porth, Newquay, Cornwall TR8 4BQ. *01637 860373.* traceyhealey@hotmail.com. www.sunhavenvalley.co.uk. Tracey & Keith Healey.

From Newquay B3276 to Mawgan Porth, turn R at beach. 6m N of Newquay. Quiet park in unspoilt Vale of Lanherne, 0.75m from sandy beach. 5 star rating. Open April-October.
🚐🏠♿🍴🛁♿⊙🅿🔥♿🏡🚾♿🌸L🎦🍴∪

Sunnyside Holiday Park, Quintrell Downs, Newquay, Cornwall TR8 4PD. *01637 873338.* info@sunnyside.co.uk. www.sunnyside.co.uk. Mr D A Gamble. Situated off the A392 to Newquay. Three miles from the beach and town centre. Cornwall's premier 18-30's holiday park. Nightclub. Not suitable for families with children. Open March 1-December 31.
🚐♿🏠♿✕⊙🅿🔥🍴≋♿🏡🚾⇌L♨🎦🛁♿🚿∪🔾🎣🎣

Treago Farm, Crantock, Newquay, Cornwall TR8 5QS. *01637 830277.* J A & P A Eastlake. On the A3075 1.5m south of Newquay, turn west on minor road. Through Crantock towards West Pentire and turn south on the farm road 0.75m from Crantock. 5m SW of Newquay. Site is in sheltered valley 0.5m from the sea and surrounded by National Trust land. Open Easter-October.
🚐🏠♿🛁♿⊙🅿🔥♿🏡🚾⇌🔥L♿♨♨🚿∪🔾🎣🎣🎣

Trebarber Farm Camping Park, St Columb Minor, Newquay, Cornwall TR8 4JT. *01637 873007.* Mr & Mrs Shipton. 3m E from Newquay off A3059 Newquay to St Columb road. Level site 3m from beach. Coarse fishing and golf nearby. Open May-October.
🚐🏠♿🍴🛁♿🔥♿🏡🚾🌸♨♨🎣🎣

Trekenning Tourist Park, Trekenning, Newquay, Cornwall TR8 4JF. *01637 880462.* holidays@trekenning.co.uk .www.trekenning.co.uk. Mr & Mrs B Thomas. Just off the A39, 0.5m south of St Columb Major, 10 minutes from Newquay.

TYNLLWYN CARAVAN & CAMPING PARK

Tynllwyn is a small family run site situated in the picturesque hamlet of Rhdyronnen, with the Talyllyn Railway running gently alongside the site, and Rhdyronnen Station only 50 yards away.
We have a level sheltered camping field with electric hook-ups and water points. Good, clean Shower/Toilet block - free showers - washing-up and laundry facilities, small site shop, childrens' play area and chemical toilet disposal point.
Approximately 2.5 miles Tywyn on the A493, then take a right turn to B4405, then first right by grass island.
Tents, tourers and motor homes all welcome. Also luxury static caravans for hire. Excellent base for walking, climbing, cycling, fishing and all watersports.

Tynllwyn Caravan & Camping Park
Bryncrug, Tywyn
Gwynedd LL36 9RD
Tel/Fax: 01654 710370
E-mail: ppspsmc@aol.com
www.tynllwyncaravanpark.co.uk

PARC GWYLIAU
★★★
HOLIDAY PARK

CORNWALL

Four miles Watergate and Mawgan Porth beaches. Family bathrooms, free showers. Exclusive tourist park with large individual pitches. Licensed bar, TV and games room. Hot and cold washing-up basins.

🚐🔌♨️📺🎣🛢️🍴✕☉🌣🔥🛢️≈🏇🏕️✿🧺♨️🛶⚓🚲🏊🛶🔒🏕️🏖️

Treloy Tourist Park, Newquay, Cornwall TR8 4JN. *01637 872063/876279.* holidays@treloy.co.uk. www.treloy.co.uk. W J & P M Paull. Just off the A3059 Newquay road. Heated swimming pool. Licensed bar and family room. Entertainment. Cafe and takeaway. Own golf course, concessionary green fees for guests. Free showers. Electric hook-ups. Serviced pitches. Open April-end September.

🚐🔌♨️📺🎣🛢️✕☉🌣🔥🛢️≈🏇🏕️🏖️≈🛶⚓⚓🛶🔒🏕️🏖️🛶

Trencreek Holiday Park, Newquay, Cornwall TR8 4NS. *01637 874210.* enquiries@trencreekholidaypark.co.uk. www.trencreekholidaypark.co.uk. Mr G N Hautot. Entering Newquay from St Columb (A3059) direction. Turn left at Trevenson Road, Trencreek. 1m N of Newquay. Outskirts of town and 1m from beaches. Coarse fishing on site. Open April-September.

🚐🔌♨️📺🎣🛢️🛢️✕☉🌣🔥🛢️≈🏇🏕️✕🏕️🏖️≈🛶⚓🛶🛶🔒🛶🏕️🏖️🛶

Trethiggey Touring Park, Quintrell Downs, Newquay, Cornwall TR8 4LG. *01637 877672.* enquiries@trethiggey.co.uk. www.trethiggey.co.uk. M5 to Exeter, then A30 to Okehampton, Bodmin to Indian Queens, turn right on the A392, and follow this road for about five miles to Quintrell downs roundabout. Turn left to site half mile. Good access to site on this road (A3058 Newquay to St Austell). Open March 1-January 2.

🚐🔌♨️📺🎣🛢️✕☉🌣🔥🛢️🏇🏕️🏖️≈🛶⚓⚓🛶🔒🏕️🏖️🛶

Trevarrian Holiday Park, Trevarrian, Mawgan Porth, Newquay, Cornwall TR8 4AQ. *01637 860381.* Mr Dave Phillips. 4.5m N of Newquay via B276 Padstow. Flat, well-drained site with fine views; approx 1m from beach. Open Easter-September.

🚐🔌♨️📺🎣🛢️☉⚓🔥🛢️≈🏇🏕️🏖️≈🛶⚓♨️🛶🔒🏕️🏖️🛶

Trevella Caravan & Camping Park, Crantock, Newquay, Cornwall TR8 5EW. *01637 830308.* trevellapark@aol.com. www.trevella.co.uk. On Crantock road, just off A3075 Newquay to Redruth, 1.5m SW of Newquay. Sheltered parkland. Crazy golf. Own fishing lake. Fees on application. Open Easter-October.

🚐🔌♨️📺🎣🛢️🛢️✕☉🌣🔥🛢️≈🏇🏕️🏖️≈🛶⚓♨️🛶🔒🏕️🏖️🛶⚓🛶🔒🏕️

Trevornick Holiday Park, Holywell Bay, Newquay, Cornwall TR8 3PN. *01637 830531.* bookings@trevornick.co.uk. www.trevornick.co.uk. Mr R Hartley. A3075 from Newquay to sign for Cubert. Through village .5m on right. 4m SW of Newquay. Near Holywell Beach. Full entertainment programme, children's club, pool, fishing and golf course. Open May-September.

🚐🔌♨️📺🎣🛢️✕☉🌣🔥🛢️≈🏇🏕️🏖️≈🛶⚓♨️🛶🔒🏕️🏖️🛶🔒🏕️

Watergate Bay Touring Park, Watergate Bay, Tregurrian, Newquay, Cornwall TR8 4AD. *01637 860387.* watergatebay@email.com. www.watergatebaytouringpark.co.uk. Mr B Jennings. 4m N of Newquay on B3276 off A39 on E outskirts of Newquay. 0.5m from Watergate Bay. Easy reach of Eden Project. Roomy site. Open March 1-October 31.

🚐🔌♨️📺🎣🛢️🛢️✕☉🌣🔥🛢️≈🏇🏕️🏖️≈🛶⚓♨️🛶🔒🏕️🏖️🛶

CORNWALL

White Acres Holiday Park, Whitecross, Newquay, Cornwall TR8 4LW. 0845 4580065. reception@whiteacres.co.uk. www.whiteacres.co.uk. The Seery Family. Come off A30 at High Gate Hill slip road. Follow sign to Newquay. Join A392 3m come to White Acres at Whitecross junction. Open end March-November.

Padstow

Carnevas Farm Holiday Park, Carnevas Farm, St Merryn, Padstow, Cornwall PL28 8PN. 01841 520230. The Brewer Family. 4m SW of Padstow via B3276. Central for touring Cornwall, 0.5m from Porthcothan beach. Rose Award Park 2003. Family-run site. Showers, laundry, children's play area. Bar, shop. Open April-October.

Dennis Cove Camping, Dennis Lane, Padstow, Cornwall PL28 8DR. 01841 532349. Simon Zeal. At south side of town. Approaching on A389, turn right at Tesco supermarket. Holiday site on river Camel estuary. Boating lake. Ten minutes' walk to Padstow harbour. Supermarkets, cafes and restaurants nearby. Open April-September.

Harlyn Sands Holiday Park, Lighthouse Road, Trevose Head, St Merryn, Padstow, Cornwall PL28 8SQ. 01841 520720. harlyn@freenet.co.uk. www.harlynsands.free-online.co.uk. Mr J Richards. Licensed bar. Reception area. Play park. Holiday caravans for hire. 300yd from superb beaches. Families only. Shop, restaurant, childrens' games room.

Higher Harlyn Caravan Site, St Merryn, Padstow, Cornwall PL28 8SG. 01841 520022. Mr P H Bennett. 3m W of Padstow via B3276, local road S of St Merryn. 1m to beach. Licensed bar and diner. Outdoor heated swimming pool. Open Easter-September 30.

Maribou Holiday Park, St Merryn, Padstow, Cornwall PL28 8QA. 01841 520520. T J Orriss, Maribou (Holidays) Ltd. 3.5m SW of Padstow. Take A389 from Wadebridge to St Merryn. Site is signposted. Open site within reach of surfing beach. Fees on application. Open Easter-October.

Mother Ivey's Bay Caravan Park, Trevose Head, Padstow, Cornwall PL28 8SL. 01841 520990. www.motheriveysbay.com. Patrick & Caroline Langmaid. 4m from Padstow signed off the B3276 Padstow to Newquay coast road (Trevose Head). Graded: 4 stars. Open Easter-October 31.

Old MacDonald's Farm, Porthcothan Bay, Padstow, Cornwall PL28 8LW. 01841 540829. oldmacdonaldsfarm@tinyworld.co.uk. www.old-macdonalds-farm.co.uk. John & Karen Nederpel. On B3276 coast road between Padstow and Newquay, look for signs. Quiet park ideal for families. Free entrance to farm park, during stay children can help with feeding the animals. 1m from safe beach and surfing. Children's play area. Pets welcome.

Seagull Tourist Park, St Merryn, Padstow, Cornwall PL28 8PT. 01841 520117. Mrs Wendy Pollard. B3274 via St Columb bypass. Approximately 4 miles past Bogee Farm. At crossroads, take left sign St Merryn. Follow signs until go-karts on right. Seagull Park 100yd on left. Quiet family site with coastal views. 10 minutes to seven sandy beaches to St Merryn village. Indoor storage facilities. Open April 1-end October.

Tregavone Touring Park, Tregavone Touring Farm, St Merryn, Padstow, Cornwall PL28 8JZ. 01841 520148. Mr & Mrs J Dennis. On A389 Padstow see Padstow Park on R, turn L just past Padstow Park. Farm entrance after 0.75m on left. Clean, quiet family-run site, unspoilt country views. Suitable for beach and touring base. Open March-October.

Tregidier Caravan Park, Trevean Lane, St Merryn, Padstow, Cornwall PL28 8PR. 01841 520264. Brian & Jean Parker. Situated 1.75m from Treyarnon Bay, which has one of the betssurfing beaches in the country and a natural swimming

CORNWALL

pool. Other beaches within easy distance. 3.75m from Padstow, 11m from Newquay. Small friendly site with sea views. High stand Open April 1-September 30.

⊞ ✢ ⊡ ⛟ ⛟ ✕ ☺ ☺ ⛟ ⛟ ⛟ ⛟ ⌇ ⛟ ⛟ ⛟ ⛟ ⛟ ⎎ ⛟

Trerethern Touring Park, Padstow, Cornwall PL28 8LE. *01841 532061.* camping.trerethern@btinternet.com. www.trerethern. co.uk. Mr P Denton. On A389 Wadebridge to Padstow road. Quiet, rural setting with panoramic views. Extra large pitches on 13.5 acres. Footpath to Padstow. Cafe/restaurant nearby. Several sandy beaches within 3 miles. Graded: 4 stars. Open April-mid October.

⊞ ⊡ ⛟ ⛟ ⛟ ⛟ ☺ ☺ ⛟ ⛟ ⛟ ⛟ ⌇ ⛟ ⛟ ⛟ ⛟ ⎎ ⛟ ⛟

Trethias Farm Caravan Park, Treyarnon Bay, Padstow, Cornwall PL28 8PL. 01841 520323. David & Sandi Chandler. From Wadebridge, signs to St Merryn, go past Farmer's Arms pub, 3rd turning on right. Quiet, family park near beach and lovely cliff walks. Suitable for families and couples. BH&HPA. Open April 1-September 30.

⊞ ⊡ ⛟ ⛟ ⛟ ☺ ☺ ⛟ ⛟ ⛟ ⛟ ⌇ ⛟ ⛟ ⛟ ⛟ ⎎ ⛟

Trevean Caravan & Camping Park, St Merryn, Padstow, Cornwall PL28 8PR. 01841 520772. Mrs M J Raymont. From St Merryn village take the B3276 Newquay road for one mile, then turn left for Rumford.The site is 0.25 mile on the right hand side. Suitable family site situated near to sandy, surfing beaches. Explore coastal footpaths with spectacular scenery of the north Cornwall coast. Graded: 3 stars. Open April 1-October 31.

⊞ ⊡ ⛟ ⛟ ⛟ ☺ ☺ ⛟ ⛟ ⛟ ⛟ ⌇ ⛟ ⛟ ⛟ ⛟ ⎎ ⛟ ⛟

Treyarnon Bay Caravan Park, Treyarnon Bay, Padstow, Cornwall PL28 8JR. 01841 520681. www.treyarnonbay.co.uk. Old & Partridge. Off the B3276 Newquay to Padstow road. Turn off for Treyarnon Bay, follow lane into beach car park. Holiday park adjacent. Suitable family site, 200yd from beach, overlooking Treyarnon Bay. Coastal walks and surfing. No dogs during peak season. Site wardens: Brian and Yvonne Hinsley. Open April 1-September 30.

⊞ ✢ ⊡ ⛟ ⛟ ✕ ☺ ☺ ⛟ ⛟ ⛟ ⌇ ⛟ ⛟ ⛟ ⛟ ⎎ ⛟

Penryn

Calamankey Farm, Longdowns, Penryn, Cornwall TR10 9DL. *01209 860314.* calamankey@cwcom.net. www.calamankey. cwc.net. Mr C Davidson. Two and a half miles west of Penryn on the A394 opposite Texaco filling station. Small touring centre or overnight stop. Route to south Cornwall coast. Nine miles from Truro, nine miles from Helston and three miles from Falmouth. No touring caravans. Ideal for exploring Helford river and the Lizard Peninsular. Open Easter-October.

⊞ ⊡ ⛟ ⛟ ☺ ⛟ ⛟ ⛟ ⛟ ⛟ ⌇ ⛟ ⛟ ⛟ ⎎ ⛟ ⛟

Penzance

Boleigh Farm Site, Lamorna, Penzance, Cornwall. *01736 810305.* Mr D Eddy. B3315 south through Newlyn from Penzance, four miles to Lamorna Cove. First right after Lamorna Cove turning. On site of ancient battle and within easy reach of beaches and places of interest in the Land's End peninsula. Friendly, small farm site. Fees on application. Open March-October.

⊞ ⊡ ⛟ ⛟ ☺ ☺ ⛟ ⛟ ⛟ ⌇ ⛟ ⛟ ⛟ ⎎ ⛟

Bone Valley Caravan & Camping Park, Heamoor, Penzance, Cornwall TR20 8UJ. *01736 360313.* www.cornwalltourist board.co.uk/bonevalley. Bob & Margaret Maddock. From Penzance follow signs for hospital, proceed past hospital and fire depot and continue straight through village, or follow A30 (Penzance by pass) turn off for Heamoor through village to camp sign on right to next sign left signposted Bone Valley. TV room and baby changing facilities. Open March 1-January 7.

⊞ ⊡ ✢ ⛟ ⛟ ☺ ☺ ⛟ ⛟ ⛟ ⛟ ⛟ ⌇ ⛟ ⛟ ⛟ ⎎ ⛟ ⛟

Camping & Caravanning Club Site - Sennen Cove, Higher Tregiffian Farm, St Buryan, Penzance, Cornwall TR19 6JB. *01736 871588.* www.campingandcaravanningclub.co.uk. The Camping & Caravanning Club Ltd. 4-acre site with 75 pitches accepting all units. Take the A30 from Penzance to junction with B3306 (St Just road). Turn sharp right, site on left 300yds. Non-members welcome. Caravans, motorcaravans and tents accepted. Play field available. Open May-September.

⊞ ⊡ ⛟ ⛟ ⛟ ☺ ☺ ⛟ ⛟ ⛟ ⛟ ⌇ ⛟ ⛟ ⛟ ⎎

CORNWALL

Garris Farm, Gulval, Penzance, Cornwall TR20 8XD. *01736 365806.* Mr I A Philips. 2.5m N of Penzance. Leave A30 Crowlas to Castle Gate. Follow signs to Chysauster ancient village. Quiet site. Open May-October.

Kelynack Caravan & Camping Park, Kelynack, St Just, Penzance, Cornwall TR19 7RE. *01736 787633.* steve@ kelynackholidays.co.uk. www.kelynackcaravans.co.uk. Mr S J Edwards. 7m W of Penzance via A3071 to St Just, S on B3306. 0.5m to site signposted to left. From Land's End on A30, 3m N on B3306, 2m to site. Alongside stream in secluded valley. David Bellamy Gold Conservation Award. Open Easter-October.

Kenneggy Cove Holiday Park, Higher Kenneggy, Rosudgeon, Penzance, Cornwall TR20 9AU. *01736 763453.* enquiries@ kenneggycove.co.uk. www.kenneggycove.co.uk. Mr & Mrs M E Garthwaite. On A394. 2.5m E of Marazion, between Penzance and Helston. Quiet, level, family site with spectacular sea views. Safe, sandy, secluded beaches and SW coastal path—10 mins walk. Children's play area. Shop on site. Freezer facilities. Hair-dryers. Graded: 3 stars. Open April-October.

Levant House, Levant Road, Pendeen, Penzance, Cornwall TR19 7SX. *01736 788795.* Mr J H A Boyns. From Penzance go W on A30, fork N on A3071 to St Just. After 4m fork N on to B3318 to Pendeen. After 2m take Trewellard road. At Trewellard hotel turn left, then right to site 300yd on left. Pleasant small site near beautiful scenery. 0.25m from cliff path. Dogs allowed. Open April-October.

Lower Treave Caravan & Camping Park, Crows-an-Wra, St Buryan, Penzance, Cornwall TR19 6HZ. *01736 810559.* camping @lowertreave.demon.co.uk. www.lowertreave.co.uk. Mr & Mrs N A Bliss. Located on A30 six miles west of Penzance. A quiet, family site at heart of the Land's End peninsula with panoramic rural views to the sea. Sheltered grass terraces. Sennen Blue Flag beach 2.5m. Open April-October.

River Valley Country Park, Relubbus, Penzance, Cornwall TR20 9ER. *01736 763398.* www.rivervalley.co.uk. J E & M J Taylor. 3m NE of Marazion. From Hayle B3302 to Leedstown turn right onto B3280 to Townsend and straight on to Relubbus. Quiet, rural family site on banks of trout stream. Exceptionally large, level pitches. Short or long stays welcome. Open March 4-January 2.

Roselands Caravan Park, Dowran, St Just, Penzance, Cornwall TR19 7RS. *01736 788571.* camping@roseland84. freeserve.co.uk. www.roselands.co.uk. Peter & Jane Hall. From Penzance on A3071 to St Just—6m, signposted on right 800yd. Licenced, bar meals. New toilet block, laundrette and games room. Sea views. Level pitches. Suitable base for walking, water activities and local attractions. Open January-October 31.

Tower Park (FCS), St Buryan, Penzance, Cornwall TR19 6BZ. *01736 810286.* enquiries@towerparkcamping.co.uk. www. towerparkcamping.co.uk. Dave & Joyce Green. A30 west from Penzance then fork left on B3283. Fork right at church. Site is 200yd on right. Near many places of interest in SW Cornwall. Write or phone for free brochure. Open March 7-January 7.

Trevair, South Treveneague, St Hilary, Penzance, Cornwall TR20 9BY. *01736 740647.* Mr & Mrs P J Luxford. 2 miles NE of Marazion on B3280. Set in 3 secluded acres surrounded by fields and woodland. Well-maintained, friendly family site. Good facilities. Caravans to let. Cornwall Tourist Board approved. Open April-October.

Trevaylor Caravan Park, Truthwall, St Just, Penzance, Cornwall TR19 7PU. *01736 787016.* www.bookings@trevaylor. com. www.trevaylor.com. R & P Eachus. Located 0.5 mile north of St Just off B3306. Surfing beaches and many places of interest all within easy reach. Bar on site. Open Easter-October.

Treverven Touring Caravan & Camping Site, St Buryan, Penzance, Cornwall TR19 6DL. *01736 810200.* skewjack@aol.com. www.chycor.co.uk/camping. Mrs H M Gwennap. From Penzance through Newlyn on to B3315. Site is on this road six miles from Penzance. Within easy walking distance of coast and coves. Open Easter-October.

Wayfarers Caravan & Camping Park, St Hilary, Penzance, Cornwall TR20 9EF. *01736 763326.* wayfarers@eurobell.co.uk. Steve & Elaine Holding. From Penzance A30 left on to A394. First roundabout left on to B3280 for 1.5m. Adult-only park. Tranquil award-winning park beautifully landscaped. Marked, level pitches. Good facilities. Shop. Launderette. Open March-November.

CORNWALL

Perranporth

Perran Springs Touring Park, Goonhavern, Perranporth, Cornwall TR4 9QG. *01872 540568.* perransprings@cwcom.net. www.perransprings.co.uk. T Howard & M Thomas. Leave A30 on to B3285 'Perranporth'. Follow 'Perran Springs' signs for 1.5 miles. Award-winning family park, 21 acres. Hook-ups, Eurotents, caravan holiday-homes. Free fishing on our coarse fishing lake. Panoramic countryside views. Open April-October.

Polzeath

Gunvenna Touring Caravan & Camping Park, St Minver, Wadebridge, Polzeath, Cornwall PL27 6QN. *01208 862405.* Mr & Mrs P Diamond. 4m from Wadebridge on B3314 Port Isaac to Delabole. 10 acres. Licensed restaurant and indoor tea garden, heated indoor swimming pool. Open Easter-October.

Porthtowan

Rose Hill Touring Park, Porthtowan, Cornwall TR4 8AR. *01209 890802.* reception@rosehillcamping.co.uk. www.rosehillcamping.co.uk. Mr & Mrs J E Barrow. From A30 follow B3277 signposted Porthtowan, brown tourism signs to Rosehill. Sheltered site 4 minutes' level walk to beach, pubs, restaurants. Fresh crusty bread, croissants baked daily. 5 star toilet block. Open April-October.

Portreath

Tehidy Holiday Park, Harris Mill, Illogan, Portreath, Cornwall TR16 4JQ. *01209 216489/314558.* holiday@tehidy.co.uk. www.tehidy.co.uk. Mr & Mrs R Corbett. 2.5m south east of Portreath. A30 Penzance Redruth to Porthtowan road. Turn right to Porthtowan at first roundabout then first left, continue straight over two crossroads. Site 300yd on left past 'Cornish Arms'. Good touring site. Open April-October.

Redruth

Cambrose Touring Park, Portreath Road, Redruth, Cornwall TR16 4HT. *01209 890747.* cambrosetouringpark@supanet.com. www.cambrosetouringpark.co.uk. Mr & Mrs Fitton. 2m NW from Redruth on B3300. Site is posted on right. Sheltered site 2m from sea. Wet weather room. Heated outdoor pool from May-September. Dogs allowed. Fees on application. Graded: 3 stars. Open March-October.

Lanyon Holiday Park, Loscombe Lane, Four Lanes, Redruth, Cornwall TR16 6LP. *01209 313474.* jamierielly@supanet.com. www.lanyoncaravanandcampingpark.co.uk. Mr & Mrs J Rielly. Take A30 to Redruth then A393 towards Falmouth. Turn right onto Helston road (B3297) for 1.5 miles to Four Lanes. Secluded, family park central to beaches and tourist attractions, well worth a visit. ETC: 4 stars. Open April-October.

Tresaddern Holiday Park, St Day, Redruth, Cornwall TR16 5JR. *01209 820459.* gillroberts53@yahoo.com. Roy & Gill Roberts. 2m E of Redruth on B3298, site signposted. Small, quiet site central for south Cornwall. Open, close-mown meadow screened by hedging. Freezer service. Booking advisable August only. Open April 1-October 31.

Saltash

Dolbeare Caravan & Camping Park, St Ive Road, Landrake, Saltash, Cornwall PL12 5AF. *01752 851332.* dolbeare@btopenworld.com. www.dolbeare.co.uk. Mark

CORNWALL

Woodason & John Taylor. 4m W of Saltash via A38 to Landrake. Then N to Blunts and Quethiock to site, 1m approx on right. Flat, gently sloping, hard standings. Well-drained, in reach of many places of interest. 6m from beach. Discounts at the St Mellion Golf and Country Club for visitors at Dolbeare.

🚐🏕🖳🔌🔥☉🅿🔥🛒🏪🍴♿❄💧♨️⛵♨️🎣↘🔍

Notter Bridge Caravan & Camping Park, Notter Bridge, Saltash, Cornwall PL12 4RW. *01752 842318.* holiday@notterbridge.co.uk. www.notterbridge.co.uk. David & Beryl Hacking. On the A38, 3.5 miles west of Tamar Bridge. sheltered, level site in picturesque wooded valley with river frontage. Fishing. Pub food opposite. Open Easter/September 30.

🚐🏕🖳♿🔌☉🅿🔥🛒🏪🍴♨️💧♨️🎣↘🔍

St Agnes

Beacon Cottage Farm, Beacon Drive, St Agnes, Cornwall TR5 0NU. *01872 552347/553381.* beaconcottagefarm@lineone.net. Mr & Mrs J Sawle. B3277 off A3075 or A30, or B3285 from Perranporth. Secluded holiday site on working farm. 50 level and grassy pitches. Graded: 4 stars. Open May-October.

🚐🏕🖳♿🔌☉🅿🔥🛒🏪🍴♨️💧📞♿💧♨️♨️↘🔍🔧↗

Pressingoll Farm Caravan & Camp Site, Pressingoll Farm, St Agnes, Cornwall TR5 0PB. *01872 552333.* pam@presingollfarm.fsbusiness.co.uk. www.presingollfarm.fsbusiness.co.uk. Mrs P Williams. Leave A30 at Chyverton Cross Garage and take B3277. 1m S of St Agnes. On main North Cornwall coast route. Holiday site near surfing coast. Fees on application. Open April-October.

🚐🏕🖳♿🔌☉🅿🔥🛒🏪🍴♨️💧📞🎰♨️↘🔍

Nine acre beautifully maintained site and facilities, one mile from sandy beaches, cliff walks and rolling surf of Widemouth Bay. Individual pitches and no overcrowding. Fully licensed bar. All hot water is free and we make no charge for awnings and additional tents. 3 miles south of Bude. Facilities for the disabled.
**Budemeadows Touring Holiday Park
Poundstock, Bude, Cornwall EX23 0NA
Tel: 01288 361646**
"Find us at http://www.budemeadows.com"

St Austell

Carlyon Bay Camping & Caravan Park, St Austell, Cornwall PL25 3RE. *01726 812735.* holidays@carlyonbay.net. www.carlyonbay.net. Mrs Shirley Taylor-Grose. 2m E of St Austell. Turn S off A390 at Britannia Inn. On A3082 follow signs to Carlyon Bay. Level grassy pitches. Footpath to golf course and sandy beach. Open April-October.

🚐🏕🚿♿🔌☉🅿🔥🌊♨️🍴♨️↘♨️♨️↻♿↗⚡

Par Sands Holiday Park, Par Beach, St Austell Bay, Cornwall PL24 2AS. *01726 812868.* holidays@parsands.co.uk. www.parsands.co.uk. Mr G Bass. Half mile E of Par off A3082. Level site by large safe sandy beach. Crazy golf and children's playground. Indoor heated pool with aquaslide. Tennis. Bowls. Pets welcome. Takeaway meals, cafe/restaurant available nearby. 4 Star. Rose Award park. Open Good Friday or April 1-October 31.

🚐🏕🖳🏕✖☉🅿🔥🌊♨️♿🍴♨️↘🔥♨️♨️↻♿↗

Penhaven Touring Park, Pentewan Road, St Austell, Cornwall PL26 6DL. *01726 843687.* enquiries@penhaventouring.co.uk. www.penhaventouring.co.uk. Ian & Angela Hackwell. South of St Austell on B3273 Mevagissey. Level pitches in sheltered valley. Riverside walk to village and beach. Gardens of Heligan and Eden Project nearby. Brochure on application. Open April 1-October 31.

🚐🏕🚿🏕♿🔌🖳☉🅿🔥🌊♨️🍴♨️↘♨️♨️↗♿♨️↘↗⚡

Pentewan Sands Holiday Park, Pentewan, St Austell, Cornwall PL26 6BT. *01726 843485.* info@pentewan.co.uk. www.pentewan.co.uk. Pentewan Sands Ltd. 4 miles from St Austell on B3273. Large, safe, sandy beach, boat launching facilities. No jet-skis. Advance booking advised in high season. Open March 21-October 31.

🚐🏕🚿🏕♿🔌🖳✖☉🅿🔥🌊♨️♨️🍴♨️↘🔥♨️♨️↻♿↗⚡

River Valley Holiday Park, London Apprentice, St Austell, Cornwall PL26 7AP. *01726 73533.* johnclemo@aol.com. www.cornwall-holidays.co.uk. Mr & Mrs John Clemo. 1.5 miles south of St Austell on the B3273 towards Mevagissey. Small touring centre. Graded: 4 stars. A small family-owned park in a woodland setting. Open Easter-October.

🚐🏕🖳♿🔌☉🅿🔥🌊♨️🍴♨️↘♨️↗🔍

Sea View International Caravan & Camping Park, Boswinger, Gorran, St Austell, Cornwall PL26 6LL. *01726 843425.* enquiries@seaviewinternational.com . www.seaviewinternational.com . Mr & Mrs C J Royden. S from St Austell on B3273. Follow signs to Gorran Boswinger. 3.5m SW of Mevagissey, 10m S of St Austell. 0.5m from sandy beach. Booking advised. Telephone for brochure. Eden Project close

by. AA 5 Pennant. Graded: 5 stars. Open Easter-end September.
♨🚫🛢🍴🔥🛒☺☉🚐🛢❄♦🏠🚻🌙🚿🚽∪⚓

Sun Valley Holiday Park, Pentewan Road, St Austell, Cornwall PL26 6DJ. 01726 843266. reception@sunvalley holidays.co.uk. www.sunvalleyholidays.co.uk. Mr C Mynard. From St Austell take the B3273 to Mevagissey. Park is 2.5 miles on right. Ideal touring centre, in wooded valley 1m from sea. Licensed club and indoor pool. Graded: 5 stars. Open April-October.
♨🚫🛢🍴🛢🗙☉🚐🛢❄♦🏠🚻≋♦🌙🚿🚽🚿⚓🛴

Tregarton Park, Gorran, Nr Mevagissey, St Austell, Cornwall PL26 6NF. 01726 843666. holidays@ tregarton.co.uk. www.tregarton.co.uk. The Hicks Family. From St Austell take the B3273 towards Mevagissey. Top of Pentewan Hill turn right to Gorran, and follow the brown tourist signs. Large hedged pitches, grass or hard standings, in a sheltered park with glimpses of the sea. Open April 1-October 31.
♨🚫🛢🍴🛢🛢☺☉🚐🛢❄♦🏠🚻🌙🚿🚽🚿∪⚓🛴

Trelispen Camping Park, Gorran Haven, St Austell, Cornwall PL26 6HT. 01726 843501. trelispen@care4free.net. Dr James Whetter. 0.75m NW of Gorran Haven. From St Austell on B3273, nearing Mevagissey, follow signs for Gorran Haven, then watch for signs to camp. Beautiful countryside near fine beaches. Open April-October.
♨🚫🛢🍴🛢☺☉🛒🏠🚻🌙🚿🚽∪⚓🛴

Treveor Farm Caravan & Camping Park, Gorran, St Austell, Cornwall PL26 6LW. 01726 842387. Mrs M Parkhouse. B3273 from St Austell. After Pentewan beach, turn right to Gorran. After four miles follow signs for Park. Close to beaches, coastal walks, Eden Project and Lost Gardens of Heligan. Working dairy farm. Open Easter-October.
♨🚫🗙🛢☺🛒🛢🏠🚻🚿🌙🚿⚓

Trewhiddle Holiday Estate, Pentewan Road, St Austell, Cornwall PL26 7AD. 01726 879420. dmcclelland@ btconnect. com. www.trewhiddle.co.uk. Mr D McClelland. From A390 in St Austell, take Pentewan road towards Mevagissey, the B3273.

Entrance is 0.75 mile on the right hand side. Good facilities and well situated for touring Cornwall. 15 minutes away from the Eden Project.
♨🚫🗙🛢🗙☉🚐🛢☺❄♦🏠🚻❄🌙🚿🚽

St Columb Major

Trewan Hall Camping Site, St Columb Major, Cornwall TR9 6DB. 01637 880261. trewan-hall@fsbdial.co.uk. www.trewan-hall. co.uk. Trewan Hall Ltd. 0.75m N of St Columb Major. The Camping & Caravanning Club. Members only. Open mid May-mid September.
♨🚫🗙🛢🗙☉🚐🛢❄♦🏠🚻≋🌙🚿🚽∪

St Ives

Ayr Holiday Park, Ayr, St Ives, Cornwall TR26 1EJ. 01736 795855. Mr R D Baragwanath. Off Land's End road B3306 at Bullans Lane Hill or Carnellis Road. 0.5m W of St Ives. Open April-October.
♨🚫🗙🛢🗙☉🚐🛢❄♦🏠🚻🌙🚿🔥❄🌙🚿🚽∪⚓🛴🛴

Balnoon Camp Site, Nr Halsetown, St Ives, Cornwall TR26 3JA. 01736 795431. nat@balnoon.fsnet.co.uk. Mrs J M Long. From the A30 take the A3074 to St Ives, first left at second roundabout and second right signposted (Balnoon) about three miles from A30. Sheltered site two miles from the sea. Dogs allowed on leads. Fees on application. Open Easter-October.
♨🚫🛢🛢☺☉🚐🏠🚻≋🌙🚿🔥🚽🚿∪⚓🛴

Little Trevarrack Tourist Park, Laity Lane, Carbis Bay, St Ives, Cornwall TR26 3HW. 01736 797580. www.littletrevarrack. co.uk . Mr Neil Osborne. Take A3074 to St Ives from A30. After 3m at Carbis Bay, site is signposted left opposite junction to beach. Turn and follow for 150yds to crossroads. Go straight across and the site is on the right. Open May 1-September 7.
♨🚫🛢🛢☺☉🛒🛢🏠🚻≋🌙🚿∪⚓🛴

Penderleath Caravan & Camping Park, Towednack, St Ives, Cornwall TR26 3AF. 01736 798403. www.penderleath.co.uk. Scott & Denise Stevens. Off B3311 from St Ives to Penzance;

CORNWALL

take first right after Halsetown, after 0.25m take left fork. Set in classified area of outstanding natural beauty with unrivalled views. Family-run and supervised park. Licensed bar with no disco or noisy clubhouse. Open Spring Bank Holiday-October.

🚐🏕♿🖰🏧🖲✕☉🏕🕭🚲🏕🕿🏠⇌ℓ♀♦⅄♉↯⤳∪⏁⚡↝⤙⟟

Polmanter Tourist Park, Halsetown, St Ives, Cornwall TR26 3LX. *01736 795640.* reception@polmanter.com. www.polmanter.com. Mr P J Osborne. A30 to St Erth roundabout. Right to St Ives, follow HR. Left up hill, signposted Halsetown. Right at inn then left by chapel. From St Ives B3306, then left on B3311, pass inn and turn left. 1.5m S of St Ives. Two tennis courts on site. Fees on application. Graded: 5 stars. Open April-October.

🚐🏕♿🖰🖲✕☉🏕🕭🚲🏕🕿🏠⇌ℓ♀♦⅄♉↯⤳∪⏁⚡↝⤙⟟

> **St Ives Bay Holiday Park, 73 Loggans Road, Upton Towans, Hayle, St Ives, Cornwall TR26 5BH.** *01736 752274.* stivesbay@dial.piper.com. www.stivesbay.co.uk. Take Hayle exit off A30, R at mini-roundabout onto B3301. Half a mile on enter our park. Good touring centre adjoining own sandy beach. Hire shop. Pub and club. Pets welcome. Brochure. Graded: 4 stars. Open May-September.
>
> 🚐🏕♿🖰🏧🖲☉🏕🕭🚲≋🕭🏠ℓ⅄♉⤳∪⏁⚡

Trevalgan Holiday Farm, St Ives, Cornwall TR26 3BJ. *01736 796433.* trevalgan@aol.com www.trevalganholidayfarm.co.uk The Osborne Family. Two miles west of St Ives on the coast road to Land's End. Roomy site with sea views. Friendly family site. Farm trails. Coast path walking. Cliff picnic tables. Farm pets. Open Easter-October.

🚐🏕♿🖰🏧🖲🏧🖲☉🏕🕭🏠⇌🖾ℓ♦↯⅄♉↯⤳∪⏁⚡↝⤙⟟

St Mawes

Trethem Mill Touring Park, St Just in Roseland, St Mawes, Cornwall TR2 5JF. *01872 580504.* reception@trethem-mill.co.uk. www.trethem-mill.co.uk. D & I Akeroyd. Follow brown tourism signs on the A3078, three miles north of St Mawes. Small, clean family park. Suitable location for exploring beaches and country walks. Caravan Park of the Year Cornwall Tourism Award 2002. Graded: 5 stars. Open April 1-mid October.

🚐🏕♿🖰🏧🏧🖲☉🏕🕭🚲🏕🕭🏠ℓ♀♦⅄♉⤳∪⏁⚡↝⤙⟟

Tintagel

Bossiney Farm Caravan Park, Tintagel, Cornwall PL34 0AY. *01840 770481.* www.bossineyfarm.co.uk. Mr R L Wickett. 1m E of Tintagel on B3263 towards Boscastle. Flat, sheltered pitches on coast. Near beach. Hook-ups. Walking and touring centre. Pets welcome. Free colour brochure available. Open April-October.

🚐🏕♿🏧🖲☉🏕🕭🚲🕭🏠ℓ⅄♉⤳∪⏁⚡

The Headland Camping Site, Atlantic Road, Tintagel, Cornwall PL34 0DE. *01840 770239.* max.francis@virgin.net. www.headlandcp-tintagel.co.uk. Mr & Mrs M Francis. Follow signs from the B3263 through village to Headland. Close to coastal path for walkers. Open April-October.

🚐🏕♿🖰🖲☉🏕🕭🏕🕿🏠ℓ♀♦↯⅄♉↯⤳∪⏁⚡↝

Torpoint

Whitsand Bay Holiday Park, Millbrook, Torpoint, Cornwall PL10 1JE. *01752 822597.* Rob Wintle. 8m from Plymouth with good views spanning 30 miles over Tamer Estuary, Plymouth and the moors. South east Cornwall's award-winning park. Full range of facilities, including heated pool and club with entertainment. Free colour brochure. Open March 1-December 31.

🚐🏕♿🖰🏧♿🖲✕☉♦🏕🕭🚲🕭🏠ℓ♦⅄♉↯⤳∪⏁⚡↝⤙⟟

CORNWALL

Truro

Camping & Caravanning Club Site - Veryan, Tretheake Manor, Veryan, Truro, Cornwall TR2 5PP. *01872 501658.* www.campingandcaravanningclub.co.uk. The Camping & Caravanning Club. Truro 11m. Two miles south of Tregony on the A3078 turn left for Veryan after petrol station and follow international signs. Ideal for exploring the beaches and coves of the Cornish coast. 150 pitches set in 9 acres. Non-members welcome. Caravans, motorcaravans and tents accepted. Holiday lodge available to let (sleeps ten) all year. Open March-November.

🚐🏕📶🎣🕭⊙🕒🔥🔌❀🍴🚻🌊 *L* *J* U

Carnon Downs Caravan & Camping Park, Carnon Downs, Truro, Cornwall TR3 6JJ. *01872 862283.* park@carnon-downs-caravanpark.co.uk. www.carnon-downs-caravanpark.co.uk. Markrun Ltd. Between Truro and Falmouth off A39 at Carnon downs roundabout. Very easy access. Restaurant nearby. David Bellamy Gold Conservation Award. Graded: 5 stars.

🚐🏕📶🎣🕭⊙🕒🔥🔌❀🍴🚻🌊✿ *L* 🅃🔺 *J* ✒🌊 U ◔🎾☂🚲🎿

Chacewater Park, Cox Hill, Chacewater, Truro, Cornwall TR4 8LY. *01209 820762.* enquiries@chacewaterpark.co.uk. www.chacewaterpark.co.uk. R & D Peterken. From A30 take A3047 to Scorrier, left at Crossroads Hotel take B3298 1.25 miles left to Chacewater then after 0.75-mile sign directs you to park. Flat, grassy, quiet park central for touring west Cornwall. Exclusively for adults over 30. Graded: 4 stars. Open May 1-September 30.

🚐🏕📶🎣🕭⊙🕒🔥🔌🍴🚻🌊 *L* ♀✒🌊 U ◔

Chiverton Caravan & Touring Park, Blackwater, Truro, Cornwall TR4 8HS. *01872 560667.* chivertonpark@btopen-world.com. Mr & Mrs Ford-Dunn. From A30(T) Chiverton roundabout, take B3277 signed to St Agnes. In 0.5m turn left, in 200yd turn left into park. Quiet, grass, family park well situated for beaches and tourist attractions. Dogs allowed. Open April 1-October 31.

🚐🏕📶🎣🕭⊙🕒🔥🔌❀🍴🚻🌊♀🔺 *J* ✒🌊 U ◔🎾🚲🎿

Cosawes Caravan Parks Ltd, Perranarworthal, Truro, Cornwall TR3 7QS. *01872 863724.* A & I Fraser. Take A39 towards Falmouth, first turn right. 400yds SW of Perranarworthal. 4m NW of Falmouth. Sheltered valley. Quiet site. Squash court. Route London to Penzance. Dogs allowed. Fees on application.

🚐🏕📶🎣🕭⊙🕒🔥🔌🍴🚻🌊✿ *L* 🅃🔺 *J* ✒🌊 U ◔🎾🚲🎿

Liskey Holiday Park, Greenbottom, Truro, Cornwall TR4 8QN. *01872 560274.* enquiries@liskeyholidaypark.co.uk. www.liskeyholidaypark.co.uk. Martyn Osborne. 3.5 miles west of Truro off the A390 between Threemilestone and Chacewater. A small, family-run site central for touring. Ten minutes to the coast. Heated toilet block. Family bathroom. Dish-washing facilities. Hard standings. Children's adventure playgrounds. Games field. Graded: 5 stars. Open March-October.

🚐🏕📶🎣🕭⊙🕒🔥🔌❀🍴🚻🌊 *J* ✒🌊 U ◔

Penrose Farm Touring Park, Goonhavern, Truro, Cornwall TR4 9QF. *01872 573185.* C J Stobbs. From A30, turn R on to B3285 to Perranporth. Site 1.5m on left. Just 2.5m from Perranporth beach. Quiet, level, sheltered family park. Animal centre and adventure playground. No club or bar. Award-winning private

CORNWALL

'Superloos'. Families and couples only. Graded: 4 stars. Open April 1-October 7.
🚐 🚉 🏪 ⚿ 🛁 ⊙ ⌀ ♨ 🞒 ♜ 🏕 🏵 ⚐ ⚴ 🍴 🥤 ✓ ∪ ⚲ ⚲ ⛵

Porthtowan Tourist Park, Mile Hill, Porthtowan, Truro, Cornwall TR4 8TY. *01209 890256.* admin@porthtowantourist park.co.uk. www.porthtowantouristpark.co.uk. Mr & Mrs Jonas. Along A30 to Redruth/Porthtowan exit. Cross A30 and continue through North Country to T junction, turn right up hill. After half mile park entance on left. Level site ideal for families. Beautiful surroundings and play areas for children. Open Easter-October.
🚐 🚉 🏪 ⚿ 🛁 ⊙ ⌀ ⛱ 🞒 ♜ 🏕 ≋ 🍴 🥤 🏵 ⚴ 🍴 ✓ ∪ ⚲ ⚲ ⛵ 🏄

Ringwell Valley Holiday Park, Bissoe Road, Carnon Downs, Truro, Cornwall TR3 6LQ. *01872 862194.* keith@ringwell.co.uk. www.ringwell.co.uk. Julie & Keith Horsfall. Pretty, relaxing 12- acre site, well positioned for easy access to north and south coasts. Signposted from main A39 Truro to Falmouth. Full facilities; uncrowded. Graded: 5 stars. Open April-September.
🚐 🚉 ⚐ 🏪 ⚿ 🛁 ✕ ⊙ ⌀ ⛱ 🞒 ≋ ♜ 🏕 ≋ 🍴 🥤 ⚴ ✓ ∪ ⚲ ⛵

Silverbow Park, Goonhavern, Truro, Cornwall TR4 9NX. *01872 572347.* Mr Geoff Taylor. Leave A30 W on B3285 sign-posted for Perranporth. At A3075 crossing turn left towards Redruth, 0.5m to park. 2m E of Perranporth. Touring centre. Small, quality park in beautiful countryside, catering for the more discerning. Open April-October.
🚐 🚉 ⚐ 🏪 ⚿ 🛁 ⊙ ⌀ ⛱ 🞒 ≋ ♜ 🍴 🥤 ⚴ 🍴 ✓ ∪ ⚲ ⚲

Summer Valley Touring Park, Shortlanesend, Truro, Cornwall TR4 9DW. *01872 277878.* res@summervalley.co.uk. www. summervalley.co.uk. Mr & Mrs C R Simpkins. Siignposted on B3284 2.5m from Truro, 1.5m from A30. Quiet, family-run site, new facilities. AA Environmental Award. David Bellamy Silver Conservation Award. Countryside Discovery members. Open Easter-October.
🚐 🚉 🏪 ⚿ 🛁 ⊙ ⌀ ⛱ 🞒 ♜ 🏕 ≂ 🍴 🥤 ✓ ✓ ⚲ 🏄

Treloan Coastal Farm Holiday Park, Treloan Lane, Portscatho, The Roseland, Truro, Cornwall TR2 5EF. *01872 580899.* holidays@treloan.freeserve.co.uk. www.coastalfarm holidays.co.uk. Treloan Farm Holidays Ltd. From A30, take A3076 to Truro then A390 towards St Austell. Take A3078 to St Mawes at Trewithian, turn to Gerrans/Portscatho until church where Treloan Lane runs alongside pub. Family site with friendly atmosphere. Only 3 min walk to church, shops, pub, playground etc. Phone for brochure.
🚐 🚉 🏪 ⚿ 🛁 ⊙ ⌀ ⛱ 🞒 ♜ 🏕 ❋ 🔥 ⚴ 🍴 ∪ ⚲ ⚲ ⛵ 🏄

Trevarth Holiday Park, Blackwater, Truro, Cornwall TR4 8HR. *01872 560266.* trevarth@lineone.net. Mrs Sandra Goldring. From Chiverton roundabout on A30 take Blackwater exit. 5m W of Truro and 5m S of Perranporth. 4m NE of Redruth. Touring centre. Graded: 4 stars. Open Easter-October.
🚐 🚉 🏪 ⚐ ⚿ ✕ ⊙ ⌀ ⛱ 🞒 ♜ 🏕 🍴 ∪

Wadebridge

Dinham Farm Caravan & Camping Park, St Minver, Wadebridge, Cornwall PL27 6RH. *01208 812878.* info@dinham farm.co.uk. www.dinhamfarm.co.uk. Mr & Mrs Mably. From Wadebridge off B3314. Level, sheltered site overlooking River Camel. Free use of hot water and showers. New super- pitches with hook-ups. Heated swimming pool. Open week before Easter-end October.
🚐 🚉 🏪 ⚐ ⊙ ⌀ ⛱ 🞒 ≋ ♜ 🏕 🍴 🥤 ⚴ 🍴 ✓ ∪ ⚲ ⚲ ⛵ 🏄

Little Bodieve Holiday Park, Bodieve Road, Wadebridge, Cornwall PL27 6EG. *01208 812323.* berry@littlebodieve holidaypark.fsnet.co.uk. www.littlebodieve.co.uk. Karen & Chris Berry, Barbara & Dennis Hills. One mile north of Wadebridge. Take the A39 at Camelford. Turn north at 2nd roundabout in Wadebridge on B3314. Signed 600yd right. Nearest to Camel Trail. Well-drained site 4m from beach. Crazy golf. Heated outdoor swimming pool, water-slide. Club house, live entertainment in high season. 25-minute car ride from Eden Project. Open April-October.
🚐 🚉 ⚐ 🏪 ⚿ ✕ ⊙ ⌀ ⛱ 🞒 ≋ ♜ 🏕 🍴 🥤 ⚴ 🍴 ✓ ⚲ ⚲ ⛵ 🏄

CORNWALL/CUMBRIA

Music-Water Touring Site, Rumford, Wadebridge, Cornwall PL27 7SJ. *01841 540257.* Mr & Mrs Mabbley. 4m S of Padstow. From A39 Wadebridge to St Columb road. Turn N on B3274 for 2m then W for 500yd to site. Holiday centre 3m from sea. Fees on application. Open Easter-October.

South Winds, off Polzeath Road, Polzeath, Wadebridge, Cornwall PL27 6QU. *01208 863267.* www.rockinfo.co.uk. Mr R R & B Harris. 7m N of Wadebridge via B3314 and roads to Polzeath. Well-drained site with bay and country views. 0.5m to beach. Dogs allowed on leads. Fees on application. Booking advisable in school holidays. Open Easter-October.

St Minver Holiday Park, St Minver, Wadebridge, Cornwall PL27 6RR. *01208 862305.* parkdeanenquiries@parkdean.com. www.parkdean.com. Parkdean Holidays Plc. Take B3314 from Wadebridge. Head for Port Isaac, after 3.5m turn left at signpost to Rock. St Minver 250yds on right. All-round entertainment absolutely free. Dogs allowed. Graded: 4 stars. Open March-October.

The Laurels Holiday Park, Padstow Road, Whitecross, Wadebridge, Cornwall PL27 7JQ. *01208 813341.* anicholson@thelaurelsholidaypark.co.uk. www.thelaurelsholiday park.co.uk. Mr & Mrs A Nicholson. Near A39 and A389 junc. with entrance on A389 (Padstow road). Level 2.5-acre site with individual pitches. Designated area of outstanding natural beauty. Suitable for touring Cornwall and north Devon. Graded: 4 stars. AA 3 pennants. Colour brochure. Open Easter-October 31.

Trenant Steading Touring Park, New Polzeath, St Minver, Wadebridge, Cornwall PL27 6SA. *01208 869091.* Mr Robert Love, Miss J M King. Off B3314, 5m NW of Wadebridge. Quiet, family site near safe, sandy beaches. Level terraces. Safe for children. 10-minute walk to Polzeath beach and shops. Open April-September.

Trewince Farm Holiday Park, St Issey, Wadebridge, Cornwall PL27 7RL. *01208 812830.* From A39 take the A389 signposted Padstow. Quiet, rural, family site within easy reach of all beaches in north Cornwall, the nearest being 4m. Crazy golf. Children's play area. Dish-washing facilities. Dogs on lead only. Children's bathroom. ETB Rose Award park. AA 5 Pennant. RAC listed.

Tristram Camping & Caravan Park, Polzeath, Wadebridge, Cornwall PL27 6SR. *01208 862215.* paul@tristram freeserve.co.uk. www.rockinfo.co.uk. Mr R R & Mrs B Harris. 7m N of Wadebridge via B3314 to Polzeath. Clifftop site overlooking Polzeath beach. Own private access onto beach. Site fenced off for safety. Booking advisable in school holidays. Fees on application.

CUMBRIA

Alston

Horse & Wagon Caravan Park, Nentsberry, Alston, Cumbria CA9 3LH. *01434 382805.* William Patterson. 2 miles SE Alston on A689. Quiet, country location in area of outstanding natural beauty. Open March-October.

Ambleside

Chapel Stile Campsite, Bayesbrown Farm, Great Langdale, Ambleside, Cumbria LA22 9JZ. *01539 437300.* Mr David Rowand. From Ambleside follow signs for Great Langdale to Elterwater. Carry on to Chapel Stile, go through Chapel Stile, about 300yd on left past school. Set at beginning of Langdale Valley. Central to most attractions. Open February-November.

Hawkshead Hall Farm, Hawkshead, Ambleside, Cumbria LA22 0NN. *01539 436221.* M T Brass. 0.5m from Hawkshead. 5m SW Ambleside. Fees by arrangement. Open March-November.

Low Wray Campsite, Low Wray, Ambleside, Cumbria LA22 0JA. *01539 432810.* rlwcam@smtp.ntrust.org.uk. www.national trust.org.uk/campsites/lakedistrict. Signed from B5286 Ambleside to Hawkshead road. Small campervans welcome. No power boats. No cars on grass. No caravans. Open Easter-end October.

National Trust Camp Site, Great Langdale, Ambleside, Cumbria LA22 9JU. *01539 437668.* National Trust. 8m W of Ambleside via B5343. Stunning setting amid mountains. Walks from site—easy to very strenuous. 3 areas: general, families, groups. Family and group fields can be booked. SAE.

Appleby

Hawkrigg Farm, Colby, Appleby, Cumbria CA16 6BB. *01768 351046.* F A Atkinson & Sons. In Colby, take the Kings Meaburn road. Halfway up first hill, turn right, this brings you to farm. Cafe/restaurant, laundry facilities nearby.

Roman Road Campsite, Appleby, Cumbria CA16 6JH. *01768 351681.* Mr & Mrs W Robson. Small, private rural site (20 tents). 0.5m from historic, picturesque town. Panoramic views of Pennine Hills, Lakeland Mountains and Eden Valley. Suitable centre for touring these areas and Dales. Open Easter-September.

Wild Rose Park, Ormside, Appleby in Westmorland, Cumbria CA16 6EJ. *01768 351077.* hs@wildrose.co.uk. www.wildrose.co.uk. D A & M Stephenson. 3.5m SE of Appleby. From Appleby on B6260 to Orton. In 1.5m turn E on Ormside and Soulby road. At first crossroad turn left to Ormside. After 600yds turn right into lane, then a further 600yd into drive to site. Quiet, family park with superb mountain views.

Askam-in-Furness

Marsh Farm Caravan Site, Askam-in-Furness, Cumbria LA16 7AW. *01229 462321.* T Johnson. Over railway crossing of A595 Askam. Straight down to shore, right at sign. Grassy, level, sheltered by hedges. Adjacent to golf course. Open March-October.

Barrow-in-Furness

South End Caravan Park, Walney Island, Barrow-in-Furness, Cumbria LA14 3YQ. *01229 472823/471556.* enquiries@ walney-island-caravanpark. www.walney-island-caravan park.co.uk. Michael Mulgrew. M6 exit 36, follow A590 to Barrow then signs for Walney Island. Left on promenade. Park 4 miles. Close to Lakes. Mostly level, grassy site. Open March 1-October 31.

Beckermet

Tarnside Caravan Park, Braystones, Beckermet, Cumbria CA21 2YL. *01946 841308.* ann@hotmail.com. www.ukparks. co/uk/tarnside. Mrs A Lockhart. A595 south of Egremont. 2 miles south of Egremont follow tourist signs on B5345. Overlooking the sea, close to Lake District. Club house and restaurant on site. Coarse fishing available.

Bothel

Skiddaw View Caravan Park, Bothel, Cumbria CA5 2JG. *01697 320919.* www.skiddawview.co.uk. Mr P Carr. 7m NE of Cockermouth. Take A591 N from Keswick. After 12m turn left on to minor road towards Sunderland to site 0.25m. Flat, elevated site with view of Lakeland Fells. Beach 8m. Wordsworth House 7m. Open March-November.

Brampton

Irthing Vale Caravan Park, Old Church Lane, Brampton, Cumbria CA8 2AA. *01697 73600.* Mrs O R Campbell. 0.5m N of Brampton off A6071. Flat, well-drained site. Near Hadrian's Wall and 9m NE from cathedral city of Carlisle. Lake District, Solway coast and Scotland within easy reach. Open March 1-October 31.

Carlisle

Cottage Caravan Park, Port Carlisle, Carlisle, Cumbria CA5 5DJ. *01697 351317.* Wyreside Caravans. 2m E of Bowness-on-Solway and 11.5m W of Carlisle. On coast road. Sign to site 0.5m E of Port Carlisle. Near sea and site of Roman wall. Fees on application. Open March-November.

Dalston Hall Caravan Park, Dalston, Carlisle, Cumbria CA5 7JX. *01228 710165/25014.* Mrs D Leslie & Mrs J Simpson. Off M6 exit 42. On the B5299. 60 pitches, four acres. Dogs on leads only. Small, well-maintained, family-run park set in beautiful surroundings and within easy reach of Lake District, Solway Firth and Border counties. Graded: 4 stars. Open March 1-October 31.

Dandy Dinmont Caravan & Camping Park, Blackford, Carlisle, Cumbria CA6 4EA. *01228 674611.* dandydinmont @btopenworld.com. www.caravan-carlisle.itgo.com. Mrs B Inglis. Just N of Carlisle. M6 J44 to A7 (Galashiels Road). From here park is about 1.5m on right. after Blackford village sign, follow road directional signs to park. Overnight route Carlisle to Edinburgh. Good base for visiting Roman Wall,

IRTHING VALE CARAVAN PARK

OLD CHURCH LANE, BRAMPTON, CUMBRIA CA8 2AA
Telephone: (016977) 3600

This Park is for the discerning holidaymaker. We have no beer, no bingo, no disco, no swimming pool and no hooligans. If you require these things we can direct you to a park or two that have these on offer and it will cost you much more than what it will cost you to stay with us. We are the park you have been looking for if you do not require any of the above.

Scottish Border country, historic Carlisle. Dogs allowed. Open March-October.

Glendale Caravan Park, Port Carlisle, Carlisle, Cumbria. *01697 351317.* Wyreside Caravans. 1.5m E of Bowness-on-Sea on minor road through Burgh-by-Sands. Site 200yd from beach. Licensed club. Fees on application. Open Easter-November 1.

Oakbank Lakes, Longtown, Carlisle, Cumbria CA6 5NA. *01228 791108.* oakbank@nlaq.globalnet.co.uk. S H & M H Boulter. One mile north of Longtown on the A7. 56-acre site with three lakes with carp, roach, tench, etc. Wildlife, bird-watching, very peaceful.

Orton Grange Caravan & Camping Site, Wigton Road, Carlisle, Cumbria CA5 6LA. *01228 710252.* chris@orton grange.flyer.co.uk. Mr Chris Veevers. 4m W on A595 on S side of road. Flat, grassy, wooded site. Ideal touring base. TV lounge. Outdoor swimming pool. Accessory shop. Shop with off-licence on site. Takeaway,cafe and outdoor pool only available during Summer. Fully-equipped holiday caravans for hire.

Cockermouth

Inglenook Caravan Park, Lamplugh, Cockermouth, Cumbria CA14 4SH. *01946 861240.* mesicp@fsbdial.co.uk www.inglenook caravanpark.co.uk Mr B Simpson. A5086 from Cockermouth for 6m. Left past The Lamplugh Tip pub. Site is 0.5m. Flat site with tarmac and gravel roads in beautiful surroundings. Play area. Beach 10m. Wordsworth House 6m.

Violet Bank Holiday Home Park, Simonscales Lane, off Lorton Road, Cockermouth, Cumbria CA13 9TG. *01900 822169.* www.violetbank.co.uk. Mr John Harrold. Approach by way of the A5292 Lorton Road via town centre. Family-run park in area of outstanding natural beauty. Well maintained, grassy site with full facilities. Children's play area. SAE for illustrated brochure. Open March-November.

Whinfell Hall Farm, Lorton, Cockermouth, Cumbria CA13 0RQ. *01900 85260.* Mr R E McClellan. 4.5m SE of Cockermouth off B5289. Dish-washing facilities. Hair-dryers. Open March 1-November 15.

Wyndham Holiday Park, Old Keswick Road, Cockermouth, Cumbria CA13 9SF. *01900 822571/825238.* www.wyndham holidaypark.co.uk . Signposted on the A66. Turn right at Castle Inn sign at the end of Bassenthwaite Lake. Bear left to Embleton/Cockermouth. Entrance on left. Swimming pool nearby. Open March 1-November 1.

Coniston

Coniston Hall Campsite, Hawes Bank, Coniston, Cumbria LA21 8AS. *01539 441223.* Mr Wilson. 1m S of Coniston village centre. Turn off the A593 at Hawes Bank towards the lake. Size of site: 20 acres. Open March-October.

Cook Farm Camping Site, Torver, Coniston, Cumbria LA21 8BP. *01539 441453.* Mrs J Leeson. 3m S of Coniston via A593. Very quiet site close to Lake Coniston and surrounding countryside. Cold water tap only. Snacks on request. Breakfast cooked on request. Guesthouse for B&B on site.

CUMBRIA

Hoathwaite Farm Camping & Caravan Park, Hoathwaite Farm, Torver, Coniston, Cumbria LA21 8AX. 01539 441349. Mrs Joan Wilson. 3m S of Coniston via A593. Then turn east at green railings. Left again to site over first cattle grid. Naturally screened site with easy access to lakes and mountains. Good walking, orienteering and windsurfing. touring vans and tents require own chemical toilets. Seasonal flush toilet and showers.
🏕🌣🏕🛉🛆🏕🗲🔾↴🗲

Eskdale

Fisherground Farm Campsite, Eskdale, Cumbria CA19 1TF. 01946 723349. camping@fishergroundcampsite.co.uk. www.fishergroundcampingsite.co.uk. Mr Hall. Camp fires allowed. Hard access road. Member of Cumbria Tourist Board. Adventure playground. Miniature railway. Pets welcome. AA 3 pennant. AA 'Award for Excellence'. Graded: 2 stars. Open March-October.
🏕🚃🖛🖩🛱🔾🏕🗲➔🛉🗲

Hollins Farm, Boot, Holmrook, Eskdale, Cumbria CA19 1TH. 01946 723253. Rosemary Bogg. In valley of Eskdale approached via unclassified road. Via Ambleside and Langdale to Boot in Eskdale Valley. Site is at a farm through gate on right just before passing crossroads in Boot. Walking country.
🏕🖩🛆🛉✕🔾🏕🖩✕➔🌣🖛L🛉🗲

Grange-over-Sands

Greaves Farm Caravan Park, Field Broughton, Grange-over-Sands, Cumbria LA11 6HU. 01539 536329/536587. Mrs Eunice Rigg. On the Cartmel/Newby Bridge Road. Quarter mile north of Field Broughton Church. Small, quiet, family-run site. Graded: 4 stars. Open March-October.
🏕🚐🖩🛎🔾🔾🏕🖩🗲➔L🛉🛆🗲🗲🔾🔾🛪

Lakeland Caravan Park, Moor Lane, Flookburgh, Grange-over-Sands, Cumbria LA11 7LT. 01539 558556. www.british-holidays.co.uk. British Holidays. Take exit 36 from M6 on to A590. Turn left on to A6/A590 for Barrow in Furness, through Grange over Sands. 1 mile from Flookborough. Indoor and outdoor swimming pools. Sports and leisure facilities. Kids' clubs. Rose award and David Bellamy Conservation Award. Graded: 4 stars. Open March-October 31.
🏕🚐🚲🖛🛆✕🔾🖛🖩🏕🖛🗲LU

Oak Head Caravan Site, Ayside, Grange-over-Sands, Cumbria LA11 6JA. 01539 531475. Mr A S N Scott. M6 junction 36 then A590 to Newby Bridge, about 14m. Site signposted on left-hand side of A590, two miles south of Newby Bridge. Dry, clean site. Open March-October.
🏕🚐🖩🛆🛎🔾🔾🏕🖩🖩🛆🗲🗲🔾🔾🛪

Hawkshead

The Croft Caravan & Campsite, North Lonsdale Road, Hawkshead, Cumbria LA22 0NX. 01539 436374. enquiries@hawkshead-croft.com. www.hawkshead-croft.com. Ruth E Barr. In Hawkshead on B5285. At N end of Esthwaite Water. Between Windermere and Coniston. Fees on application. Touring caravans and holiday caravans for hire. Open March-November.
🏕🚐🖩🛆🛎🔾🔾🏕🖩🏕🗲L🛉🖩🛆🗲

Holmrook

Seven Acres Caravan and Camping Site, Holmrook, Cumbria CA19 1YD. 01946 725480. John Temple. One mile south of Gosforth on the A595 Cumbria-West Coast Road. Flat, grassy, sheltered site in western Lake District. Two miles to

coast, eight miles to Wasdale/Scafell. Dish-washing room. BH&HPA. Open March-mid November.
🏕🚐🖩🔾🔾🏕🖛🖩🗲➔L🛆🛉🗲🗲🔾🔾🛪🗲

The Old Post Office Camp Site, Santon Bridge, Santon Bridge, Holmrook, Cumbria CA19 1UY. 01946 726286. BJ & MAF Thwaites. 2.5 miles from Holmrook on the A595. Small level touring site beside the river Irt. Bridge Inn/Hotel nearby. Close to miniature railway and ancient castle. 2.5 miles from Wasdale Lake, 5 miles from sea. Open: April 1-October 31.
🏕🚐🖩🛆🛎🔾🏕🖛🗲L🛉🗲🗲🔾U🗲

Kendal

Camping & Caravaning Park - Windermere, Ashes Lane, Staveley, Kendal, Cumbria LA8 9JS. 01539 821119. www.campingandcaravanningclub.co.uk. The Camping & Caravanning Club. Five miles south of Windermere close to the village of Staveley. Situated in an unrivalled rural location of the Lake District. Backpacker facilities available. Open March-January.
🏕🚐🚲🖩🛆🛎🔾🔾🏕🖛🖩L🗲🗲🔾🔾🛪

Camping & Caravanning Club Site - Kendal, Millcrest, Skelsmergh, Shap Road, Kendal, Cumbria LA9 6NY. 01539 741363. www.campingandcaravanningclub.co.uk. The Camping & Caravanning Club Ltd. 1.5 miles north of Kendal on the right-hand side of the A6. Good base for touring the Lake District. Kendal is ideal for shopping trips and has a factory shopping centre. All units accepted. Non-members welcome. 50 pitches set in 3.5 acres. Motorcaravans, caravan and tents accepted. Open end March-October.
🏕🚐🖩🛆🛎🔾🔾🏕🖛🖩🗲L🗲🗲🔾🔾🛪🛪

Pound Farm Caravan Park, Crook, Kendal, Cumbria LA8 8JZ. 01539 821220. E & M Lister. Leave M6 at junction 36 and follow dual A591 for 10 miles to roundabout. Exit on B5284 (Crook). Pound Farm is 2.5m on left. Small, quiet site, 5 miles from Lake Windermere. Easy driving distance from lakes and coast. Open March 1-November 14.
🏕🚐🖩🔾🏕🖛🖩🗲🗲🛪

Ratherheath Lane Camping & Caravan Park, Chain House, Bonningate, Kendal, Cumbria LA8 8JU. 01539 821154. ratherheath@lakedistrictcaravans.co.uk. www.lakedistrictcaravans.co.uk. David Wilson. Leave M6, exit Junction 36 towards Windermere. Take the B5284 for Hawkshead. Small family site. Advance booking advised. Graded: 4 stars. Open March 1-November 15.
🏕🚐🖩🛎L🗲✕🔾🏕🛆🖛L🛆🛉🗲🗲🔾🔾🛪🛪

Waters Edge Caravan Park, Crooklands, Nr Milnthorpe, Kendal, Cumbria LA7 7NN. 01539 567708. www.watersedge.co.uk. Waters Edge Caravan Park Ltd. Three quarters of a mile from the M6 Junction 36 (follow A65 Kirkby Lonsdale and then A65 Crooklands at roundabout). Site on right hand side before Crooklands Hotel. Idyllic surroundings with all new facilities, including toilet block. Toilet emptying point. Solarium. Reception lounge and licensed bar. Cafe/restaurant within 300yd. Graded: 4 stars. Open March-November.
🏕🚐🖩🛆🛎✕🔾🔾🏕🖛🖩L🛉🗲🔾🛪

Keswick

Ashness Farm, Borrowdale, Keswick, Cumbria CA12 5UN. 01768 777361. www.ashnessfarm.co.uk. Mr & Mrs M Cornthwaite. Take Borrowdale road B5289 for one and half miles, then Watendlath road for one mile. Three miles south of Keswick. Situated a short walk from Ashness Bridge and Suprise View. Open March-November.
🏕🖩🛎✕🔾🏕🖩🖩L🛉🛆🛉🗲🔾🛪

CUMBRIA

Burns Farm Caravan & Camping Site, St John's in the Vale, Keswick, Cumbria CA12 4RR. *01768 7 79225.* info@burns farmcamping.co.uk. www.burnsfarmcamping.co.uk. Mrs Linda Lamb. From A66, take first left past Threkeld signpost for 'Youth Centre' and Castlerigg Stone circle. Quiet, family-run site. Beautiful views, 2.5m from Keswick. Perfect walking country. Open Easter-October.

Camping & Caravanning Club Site - Derwentwater, Crow Park Road, Keswick, Cumbria CA12 5EN. *01768 772392.* www.campingandcaravanningclub.co.uk. The Camping & Caravanning Club Ltd. 14-acre site with 250 pitches. Take the A66 to Keswick, turn on to A5271 to T junction, turn left then right at bus station. Turn right at Tithebarn Street Church. Fork right at new flats and first right after Rugby Club. On banks of Lake Derwent Water. Non-members welcome. Please phone warden to check availability. Caravans, motor caravans accepted but no tents permitted. Open March-November.

Castlerigg Hall Camping & Caravan Park, Keswick, Cumbria CA12 4TE. *01768 772437.* www.castlerigg.co.uk . Mrs B & Mr D D Jackson. 1.5m SE of Keswick off A591 to Ambleside. Northern Lake District with good scenery. Last arrivals 9pm. Fees on application. Graded: 4 stars. Open Easter to mid-November.

Dale Bottom Farm, Naddle, Keswick, Cumbria CA12 4TF. *01768 772176.* Messrs. Kitching. Off A591, 2.5 miles SE of Keswick. Heart of the Lake District. Open March-October.

North Lakes Caravan & Camping Park, Bewaldeth, Bassenthwaite Lake, Keswick, Cumbria CA13 9SY. *017687 76510.* info@northlakesholidays.co.uk. www.northlakes holidays.co.uk. Mr & Mrs J & P R Frew. 9m N of Keswick on A591. Park entrance off large layby on on left-hand side. 30 acre park in quiet surroundings. Coarse fishing on park. Cafe/restaurant nearby. Open March-November.

Scotgate Caravan & Camping Site, Braithwaite, Keswick, Cumbria CA12 5TF. *01768 778343.* Stuart Bros. Two miles west of Keswick on the A66 at junction with the B5292. Near north end of Derwentwater. Dogs allowed on leads. Fees on application. Open March-October.

Seatoller Farm, Borrowdale, Keswick, Cumbria CA12 5XN. Mr R Cubby. Eight miles west of Keswick on road through

DALEBOTTOM FARM
CARAVAN & CAMPING PARK
NADDLE KESWICK
CUMBRIA CA12 4TF
Tel: 017687 72176

"HEART OF LAKELAND"
Peacefully situated in the picturesque Naddle Valley two miles south of Keswick on A591 Windermere road. Touring & Tenting pitches. Electric hook up. Toilet & Shower Facilities. Static Caravans & Country Cottages to let. Colour TV Toilet & Shower Facilities in all units. Static Caravans Tourers Tents March 1st to November 1st. County Cottaages available all year.
S.A.E. for brochure to:
Proprietors: Messrs Kitching

Borrowdale. Among fells and mountains. On left at the foot of Honister pass going to Buttermear on right coming from Buttermear. Open March-November.

Stonethwaite Farm, Borrowdale, Keswick, Cumbria. *01768 777234.* Mr V B Brownlee. In Stonethwaite village. Through village, along track for half mile. Campsite alongside stream on left. Open March-October.

Kirkby Lonsdale
Cragside, Hutton Roof, Kirkby Lonsdale, Cumbria. *01524 271415.* Mr J Dixon. 6m from M6 at Carnforth, turn off A6 for Burton. Hutton Roof is three miles west of Kirkby Lonsdale, off A65 or W off B6254 at Whittington. Quiet situation in countryside. Shops and buses 3m away. Fees on application. Advance booking advised.

Kirkby Stephen
Bowber Head Camping Site, Ravenstonedale, Kirkby Stephen, Cumbria CA17 4NL. *01539 623254.* enquiries@bowberhead.co.uk. www.bowberhead.co.uk. Mr & Mrs W Hamer. 10m NE of Sedbergh. From M6 junction 38 to Ravenstonedale (A685). Or from junction 37 to Sedbergh. Then A683. Site is on A683 two miles south east of Ravenstonedale and four miles south of Kirkby Stephen. Site has open aspect with beautiful views. Walking country, within reach of the Lake District and the Dales. Classic coach services from site.

Longtown
Camelot Caravan Park, Longtown, Cumbria CA6 5SZ. *01228 791248.* Mrs M Fyles-Lee. 1.5m south of Longtown on the A7. From south join the A7 at last junction of M6 and travel north for four miles to site on right. Quiet, secluded site near Solway coast, Hadrian's Wall, SW Scotland. Route Carlisle to Edinburgh. Dog exercising field. Hard standing. Storage. Open March-October.

Maryport
Manor House Caravan Park, Edderside Road, Allonby, Maryport, Cumbria CA15 6RA. *01900 881236.* holidays@manorhousepark.co.uk. J M Brooks. E off B5300, 1m N of Allonby and 6m N of Maryport. Signpost to Edderside. Site 0.75m. Large caravan site with space for tents. Sauna, gym. Club. Fees on application. Graded: 3 stars. Open March-October.

Spring Lea Caravan Centre, Allonby, Maryport, Cumbria CA15 6QF. *01900 881331.* mail@springlea.co.uk. www. springlea.co.uk. John Williamson. On the B5300—five miles north of Maryport. Family run park with all amenities including indoor leisure facilities. Graded: 4 stars. Open March-October.

Millom
Butterflowers Holiday Homes, Port Haverigg, Millom, Cumbria LA18 4HB. *01229 772880.* office@butterflowers.net. www.butterflowers.net. Mr R P & R J Attwood. 1.5m SW of Millom via A5093, follow beach road to Haverigg. Level site with made-up roads adjacent to beach. Fees on application.

CUMBRIA

Milnthorpe

Fell End Caravan Park, Hale, Milnthorpe, Cumbria LA7 7BS. *01539 562122.* South Lakeland Caravans. From junction 35 on the M6. Head north up A6 for 3.5 miles. Take first left after Cumbria border. Follow signs for 0.75 mile. TV and satellite. AA Pennant. Open March 1-January 14 for statics; all year for tourers.
⊞ ⊡ ⌖ ⊠ ⌀ ⌱ ⌂ ⊙ ⊛ ⚑⊟ ⌘ ⊹ *L* ♪ ⌇ ∪

Hall More Farm, Hale, Milnthorpe, Cumbria LA7 7BP. *01539 564163.* South Lakeland Caravans. 2m SW of Milnthorpe, and 9m S of Kendal. Leave motorway at Carnforth, take A6 4m N, take first turn left after Mossdale Filling Station. Area of outstanding natural beauty 2.5m from sea. Trout fishing and pony trekking on site. Dogs allowed. Open March-October.
⊞ ⊡ ⌀ ⌱ ⌂ ⚑ ⊠ × ⊙ ⊛ ⚑ ⊟ ⌘ ⇌ *L* ♪ ⌇ ⊟ ∪ ⤸

Hazelslack Caravan Site, Carr Bank House, Carr Bank, Milnthorpe, Cumbria LA7 7LG. *01524 761974.* Mr Alf Barber. 3m SW of Milnthorpe. From Milnthorpe follow Arnside road. Go almost to Arnside then at signpost for Carr Bank and bear right along this road, turning left after 0.5m along narrow lane. Site 200yd on right. Edge of Lake District and near coast. Open March-October.
⌀ ⌀ ⊟ ⇌ ⚑ *L* ♀ ♪ ⌇ ⚲

Millness Hill Holiday Park, Crooklands, Milnthorpe, Cumbria LA7 7NU. *01539 567306.* K I & E J Fairall. Leave M6 junction 36, turn east on to A65 (Kirkby Lonsdale). Turn left at next roundabout signed Endmoor and Crooklands. Site is 100 metres on left. Kendal 6m. Windermere 13m. Gateway to Lakes and Dales. Restaurant nearby. Graded: 4 stars. Open March-November 14.
⊞ ⊡ ⊠ ⊙ ⌀ ⌀ ⚑ ⊟ ⌘ ⊟ *L* ⌀ ♪ ⌇ ∪ ⤸ ⚲

Newby Bridge

Black Beck Caravan Park, Bouth, Newby Bridge, Cumbria LA12 8JN. *01229 861274.* reception@blackbeck.net. Ribble Estates Ltd. 2.5m W of Newby Bridge; take A590 towards Ulverston. After 2.5m turn right and follow Bouth signposts to site. Owners: Ribble Estates (Clifton) Ltd. Touring centre for Lake District. Graded: 5 stars. Open March-November.
⊞ ⊡ ⌀ ⌱ ⌂ ⊙ ⊛ ⚑ ⊟ ⌘ ⊟ *L* ♀ ⊤ ⌀ ♪ ⌇ ∪ ⤸ ⚲

Penrith

Beckses Caravan Park, Penruddock, Penrith, Cumbria CA11 0RX. *01768 483224.* Mr J Teasdale. About 6m W of Penrith on A66 to Keswick, turn right on B5288. Site within a few hundred yards. Small touring site, easy reach of Lake District. Fees on application. Open Easter-October.
⊞ ⊡ ⊠ ⌱ ⌂ ⊙ ⊛ ⚑ ⊟ *L* ⌀ ♀ ♪ ⌇ ∪ ⤸

Cove Camping Park, Lake Ullswater, Watermillock, Penrith, Cumbria CA10 0LS. *01768 486549.* Mr L Wride. From M6 exit 40, go W following signs for A592 Ullswater. At lake T-junction turn right, then right again at Brackenrigg Hotel. Keep left for I.5m. Peaceful park surrounded by fells overlooking Lake Ullswater. Excellent, modern facilities. Children's play area. Freezer for ice-packs. Graded: 5 stars. Open March-October 31.
⊞ ⊡ ⊠ ⌀ ⌱ ⌂ ⊙ ⊛ ⚑ ⊟ ⌘ ⊟ ♀ ⌀ ♪ ⌇ ∪ ⤸ ⚲

Cross Fell Caravan & Camping Park, The Fox Inn, Ousby, Penrith, Cumbria CA10 1QA. *01768 881374.* sue@fox-ousby.co.uk. www.fox-ousby.co.uk. Mr & Mrs R G Thomas. 9m NE of Penrith. Leave M6 jct 40 on to A686 Alston. Take 2nd right, 1.5m beyond Langwathby. Site is 2m at Ousby. Flat, well-drained site with limited space for tents. Open March 1-January 10.
⊞ ⊡ ⌖ ⊠ ⊠ × ⊙ ⊛ ⚑ ⌂ ⌘ *L* ♪ ⌇ ⤸

Gill Head Farm, Troutbeck, Penrith, Cumbria CA11 0ST.
01768 779652. enquiries@gillheadfarm.co.uk. www.gillhead farm.co.uk. Mr W J Wilson. Quiet site in the Lake District, ideal for touring northern lakes. sheltered with views of northern fells. Fees on application. Open March 1-end October.
⊞ ⊡ ⊠ ⌱ × ⊙ ⊛ ⚑ ⌂ ⚑ ⚑ ⊟ ⌀ ⌀ ⌇ ∪ ⤸

Hillcroft Park, Roe Head Lane, Pooley Bridge, Penrith, Cumbria CA10 2LT. *01768 486363.* Mr P T Morgan. 400yd from Ullswater, on outskirts of Pooley Bridge. Elevated location with magnificent views. Suitable for fell walking. Open March-October.
⊞ ⊡ ⊠ ⌀ ⌱ ⌂ ⊙ ⊛ ⚑ ⊟ ⌘ ⊟ *L* ♀ ⌀ ♀ ⌇ ∪ ⤸

'Hopkinsons', Whitbarrow Hall Caravan Park, Berrier, Penrith, Cumbria CA11 0XB. *01768 483456.* T A & M Hopkinson. Junction 40, M6 take A66 towards Keswick, after 8 miles turn right at Sportsman's Inn, signposted Hutton Roof. Site 0.5m from A66. Open March 1-October 31.
⊞ ⊡ ⊠ ⌀ ⌱ ⊙ ⊛ ⌀ ⚑ ⌂ *L* ♀ ⌇ ∪

Hutton Moor End Caravan & Camping Site, Troutbeck, Penrith, Cumbria CA11 0SX. *01768 779615.* Mr & Mrs J Bennett. On A66 between Penrith & Keswick. Turn opposite Mungrisdale turn. 8m E of Keswick. Lake District, Roman and Druid remains. Fees on application. Open Easter-October.
⊞ ⊡ ⊠ ⌀ ⌱ ⌂ ⊙ ⊛ ⚑ ⌂ ⚑ ⚑ *L* ♀ ♀ ♪ ⌇ ∪

Low Moor Farm, Kirkby Thore, Penrith, Cumbria. *01768 361231.* Mr Farrell. 7m SE of Penrith on A66. 5m NW Appleby on A66. Overnight stop route London to Glasgow. 7m J40 M6. Open April-October.
⊞ ⊡ ⌖ ⊠ ⌀ × ⊙ ⊛ ⌂ ⚑ *L* ♀ ⊤

Lowther Holiday Park, Eamont Bridge, Penrith, Cumbria CA10 2JB. *01768 863631.* 1m S on A6. From M6 leave exit 40 and follow Lowther signs. Quiet wooded parkland. Fees on application. AA 4 pennants. Open March-November.
⊞ ⊡ ⌖ ⊠ ⌀ ⌱ ⌂ × ⊙ ⊛ ⌂ ⚑ ⌂ ⚑ ⊟ ⇌ *L* ♀ ⌀ ♀ ⌇ ∪ ⤸ ⚲

Park Foot Caravan & Camping Park, Howtown Road, Pooley Bridge, Penrith, Cumbria CA10 2NA. *01768 486309.* park.foot@talk21.com. www.parkfootullswater.co.uk. Mrs Bell & Miss Allen. Take A592 for Ullswater. 1m from Pooley Bridge on Howtown Road. Licensed bar. Lake access. Children's playground. Mountain bike hire. Pony trekking. Shop, restaurant, takeaway, laundry, tennis. Self catering available. Open March-October.
⊞ ⊡ ⌖ ⊠ ⌀ ⌱ ⌂ × ⊙ ⊛ ⌂ ⚑ ⌂ ⚑ ⊟ ⇌ *L* ♀ ⌀ ♀ ⌇ ∪ ⤸ ⚲

Stonefold, Newbiggin, Stainton, Penrith, Cumbria CA11 0HP. *01768 866383.* gill@stonefold.co.uk. www.stonefold. co.uk Mrs Gill Harrington. Leave M6 at junction 40 on to A66 Keswick road. After 2m turn right at signpost Newbiggin. Site 0.2 miles on left. Small, level touring site set in a beautiful panoramic position overlooking Eden Valley with majestic Pennine hills in background. Open April-November.
⊞ ⊡ ⊠ ⌀ ⌱ ⊙ ⚑ × ⊟ ⇌ ⚑ *L* ⌀ ♪ ⌇ ∪ ⤸ ⚲

Thanet Well Caravan Park, Greystoke, Penrith, Cumbria CA11 0XX. *01768 484262.* G & S Cannon. Leave M6 junction 41 take B5305 to Wigton for 6m turning left for Lamonby then follow caravan signposts. Sporting facilities within a 12m radius. Open March 1-October 31.
⊞ ⊡ ⊠ ⌀ ⌱ ⊙ ⊛ ⚑ ⌂ ⇌ *L* ♀ ♀ ∪ ⤸

The Quiet Site, Ullswater, Penrith, Cumbria CA11 0LS. *01768 486337.* info@thequietsite.co.uk. www.thequietsite.co.uk. Daniel Holder. Family-run site in idyllic location. Voted 'Best Site in Britain' by Camping Magazine. Awarded AA Northern

CUMBRIA

Campsite of the Year. Calor Campsite of the Year, national runner up. Large adventure playground. Graded 'exceptional' (5 stars). Open March 1-November 14.

Ullswater Caravan Camping & Marine Park, Watermillock, Penrith, Cumbria CA11 0LR. *01768 486666.* info@uccmp.co.uk. www.uccmp.co.uk. Mr Dobinson. M6 Junction 40. 0.5m off A592. Turn at signpost 'Watermillock Church, Longthwaite'. Ullswater, 1m. Playground. Lake access (1m). Licensed bar. Fees on application. Open March-November.

Waterside House, Howtown Road, Pooley Bridge, Penrith, Cumbria CA10 2NA. *01768 486332.* www.watersidefarm-campsite.co.uk. C R & J Lewis. Leave M6 at Junc 40. A66 1 mile then A592 to Pooley Bridge. 1m from village on Howtown Road. Tents and caravanettes only. Canoe, rowing boats and cycle hire. Separate field for large groups. Graded: 4 stars. Open March-October.

Ravenglass

Walls Caravan & Camping Park, Ravenglass, Cumbria CA18 1SR. *01229 717250.* wallscaravanpark@ravenglass98. freeserve.co.uk. www.ravenglass98.freeserve.co.uk. Keith & Stephanie Bridges. Dogs on leads allowed. Open March-October.

Seascale

Church Stile Farm, Wasdale, Seascale, Cumbria CA20 1ET. *01946 726252.* Mr A J Knight & Mrs R Knight. 4m E of Gosforth via minor unclassified roads to Nether Wasdale village. Site is by church. Flat, sheltered site in good fell walking/climbing. Very scenic. Two country pubs nearby. Open mid March-October 31.

National Trust Camp Site, Wasdale Head, Wasdale, Seascale, Cumbria CA20 IEX. *01946 726220.* National Trust. Situated athe head of Wasdale, nine miles east of Gosforth. Access from unclassified road on the west shore of Wast Water. Base for fell walking and rock climbing. Fees on application. No bookings. Head warden: A Gibson.

Sedbergh

Conder Farm Camp Site, Deepdale Road, Dent, Sedbergh, Cumbria LA10 5QT. *01539 625277.* conderfarm@aol.com. Mr & Mrs Hodgkinson. 5 miles SE of Sedburgh in the heart of the North Yorkshire Dales. Turn right at George & Dragon (Dent) if coming from Sedburgh or left if coming from Hawes. 17 miles to Kendal. March 1-October 31.

Cross Hall, Cautley, Sedbergh, Cumbria LA10 5LY. *015396 20668.* crosshall@btopenworld.com. www.dalescaravanpark.

co.uk. Mr & Mrs T R Harper. 2.5m N of Sedbergh via A683 to Kirkby Stephen. Walking country within easy reach of Howgill Fells and Cautley Spout. Featured in Wainwrights Walks. Takeaway meals nearby. Open April-October.

Ewegales Farm, Dent, Sedbergh, Cumbria. *01539 625440.* Mr J W Akrigg. Leave M6 at junc. 37 on to A684 to Sedbergh and site. 4m E of Dent. Flat, well-drained site near river. Fees on application.

High Laning Farm Caravan & Camping Park, Dent, Sedbergh, Cumbria LA10 5QJ. *01539 625239.* info@high laning.co.uk. www.highlaning.co.uk. Mr M E Taylor. Five miles SE of Sedbergh in Dent village. Leave M6, exit 37. A684 to Dent. Turn right, to Dent (5m). Site entrance edge of Dent village. Small site in pleasant scenery. Fees on application.

Pinfold Caravan Park, Garsdale Road, Sedbergh, Cumbria LA10 5JL. *01539 620576.* Mr A A & V Knowles. J37, M6 turn off follow A694 Hawes road through Sedbergh, turn right after Police station over Dales Bridge. Park on left hand side. Open March-January 4.

Yore House Farm Caravan & Camping Park, Yore House, Lunds, Sedbergh, Cumbria LA10 5PX. *01969 667358.* Jim & Liz Pedley. Six miles Hawes, 10 miles Sedbergh (A684) road. Near Moorcock pub on the North Yorkshire border. Quiet, farm site beside the River Ure. Open April-October.

Silloth

Hylton Caravan Park, Eden Street, Silloth, Cumbria CA7 4AY. *01697 331707.* enquiries@stanwix.com www.stanwix.com. E & R H Stanwix. Enter Silloth on B5302, turn left at sea front for 0.5m. Left on to Eden Street. Level site, well-positioned for touring Lake District. Quiet site, spotlessly clean. Windsurfing nearby. Sister park to Stanwix Park Holiday Centre 1 mile away. Free use of facilities. Open March 1-October 31.

Rowanbank Caravan Park, Beckfoot, Silloth, Cumbria CA7 4LA. *01697 331653.* Terry & Kay Watson. On B5300 coast road between Maryport and Silloth. Site is well signposted within the village of Beckfoot. In an area of 'Outstanding Natural Beauty'. Friendly, family run site. Static caravans for hire. Send for free brochure or simply arrive! Open March 1-November 15.

Solway Holiday Village, Skinburness Drive, Silloth, Cumbria CA7 4QQ. *01697 331236.* www.hagansleisure.co.uk. Sam Hagan. From south, leave M6 at junction 41 towards Wigton on B5305. From north, leave A74 at Carlisle, junction 44 towards Wigton on A595/596. From Wigton take B3505 to Silloth turning right at seafront towards Skinburness. Park about 1 mile on right. Open March-October.

CUMBRIA/DERBYSHIRE

Tanglewood Caravan Park, Causeway Head, Silloth, Cumbria CA7 4PE. 01697 331253. michael-tanglewood@ hotmail.com. tanglewoodcaravanpark.co.uk. M C Bowman. On B5302 Wigton to Silloth road. 1m before reaching, Silloth, 4m after Abbeytown. Friendly country site. Club. 1.5m from beach. Pets free of charge. Colour brochure and tariff available. Open Easter-October.

St Bees

Seacote Park, St Bees, Cumbria CA27 0ES. 01946 822777. reception@seacote.com. Mr T Milburn. From M6 Junction 40 (Penrith). A66 then A595 to Whitehaven then B5345 to St Bees. Just off lovely mile-long beach. Restaurant and bar. Clifftop paths, golf course close by. Open all year.

Ulverston

Bardsea Leisure Park, Priory Road, Ulverston, Cumbria LA12 9QE. 01229 584712. Terry Varley. From M6 Junction 36, take A591 Kendal, A590 Barrow and A5087 coast road. Sheltered, select site in disused quarry. Extensively landscaped. Free hot showers. Dog exercise area. Open March-November for statics.

Birch Bank Farm, Blawith, Ulverston, Cumbria LA12 8EW. 01229 885277. birchbank@btinternet.com Mrs L Nicholson. 3m SW of Coniston Water. On A5092, half mile W of Gawthwaite turn for Woodland, site 2 miles on right. Small farm site alongside stream and next to open fell. Ideal for walking. Open Mid May-October.

Whicham

Silecroft Caravan & Camping Park, Silecroft, Whicham, Cumbria LA18 4NX. 01229 772659. Mr & Mrs A Vaughan. A590 to Greenodd, take A5092 to coast and follow signs. 100yds from beach. 1m from mountains. Indoor swimming pool. New toilets/showers.

Wigton

Clea Hall Holiday Park, Westward, Wigton, Cumbria CA7 8NQ. 01697 342880. Mr & Mrs G Kennedy. From M6 S leave motorway at junction 41, B5305 Wigton. Through Hutton in the Forest, Unthank, past left turning for Hesket Newmarket and through Sebergham. Left turning B5299, Caldbeck, second crossroads turn right for 1.5 mile signposted Westward Wigton. Dogs allowed. Open all year.

Larches Caravan Park, Mealsgate, Wigton, Cumbria CA7 1LQ. 01697 371379. Mr Michael & Mrs Ethel Elliott. Located on the A595, 15 miles SW of Carlisle, nine miles north east of Cockermouth, and 12 miles north of Keswick. Quiet, rural park with full facilities. Adults only. Open March-October.

Windermere

Limefitt Park, Windermere, Cumbria LA23 1PA. 01539 432300 ext 48. www.limefitt.co.uk. South Lakeland Caravans Ltd. Spectacular Lakeland valley location. Ten minutes' drive Lake Windermere. Tourers and family campers welcome. Friendly Lakeland pub with bar meals, 'Do-it-yourself' Campers kitchen. Park shop plus full range of award winning facilities. Graded: 5 stars. Open March-October.

Park Cliffe Camping & Caravan Estate, Birks Road, Tower Wood, Windermere, Cumbria LA23 3PG. 01539 531344. info@parkcliffe.co.uk. www.parkcliffe.co.uk. J D Tattersall. M6, J36. A590 to Barrow by Newby Bridge turn right on to A592. 4 miles turn right into Birks Road. Park 1/3m on right. Fees on application. Large SAE please. Graded: 5 stars. Open March-November.

DERBYSHIRE

Ambergate

The Firs Farm Caravan & Camping Park, Crich Lane, Nether Heage, Ambergate, Derbyshire DE56 2JH. 01773 852913. thefirsfarmcaravanpark@btinternet.com. Stella Ragsdale. Quarter mile north of Belper, turn right off the A6 and follow signs. Quiet, well-maintained, friendly adults only park with panoramic views. Quality heated facilities. Good local pubs and restaurants. Sauna. Graded: 4 stars.

Ashbourne

Bank Top Farm, Fenny Bently, Ashbourne, Derbyshire DE6 1LF. 01335 350250. Mr & Mrs G M Cotterell. 2m N of Ashbourne, jct A515 and B5056. Opposite Bently Brook Hotel Inn. Peak District, 2m from Dovedale. Working farm. Dogs on leads allowed. Fees on application. Open Easter-September.

Callow Top Holiday Park, Buxton Road, Ashbourne, Derbyshire DE6 2AQ. 01335 344020. enquiries@ callowtop.freeserve.co.uk. www.callowtop.co.uk. Mr & Mrs Palmer. Half mile from Ashbourne on A515 Buxton Road. Full facilities including heated pool, games room, restaurant and pub etc. Flat pitches. Adjacent to Tissington Trail cycle path. Family site in beautiful countryside. Alton Towers 20 mins. Fishing on site. Open week before Easter-November.

Gateway Park, Osmaston, Ashbourne, Derbyshire DE6 1NA. 01335 344643. admin@gatewaycaravanpark.co.uk. www.gate waycaravanpark.co.uk. P Cranstone, K Peach, A Peach. 1m S of Ashbourne off A52. Flat site. Licensed bar open weekends, March-November, daily during school holidays. Entertainment Saturday nights during school holidays. Games room. Close to Alton Towers.

Redhurst Farm, Wetton, Ashbourne, Derbyshire. 01335 27227. Mr B Thompson. Close to Dovedale and Manifold Valley. 5 miles north of Ashbourne. Off A515.

Sandybrook Country Park, Buxton Road, Ashbourne, Derbyshire DE6 2AQ. 01335 300000. admin@sandybrook. co.uk. www.sandybrook.co.uk. Pinelodge Holidays Ltd. 1m N of Ashbourne. On A515 E side of the road nearly opposite Dovedale turn. Family campers welcome. No unaccompanied teenagers. Ideally situated for Alton Towers. Bar meals available. Cycle trails across road, cycles for hire. Indoor heated swimming pool for August 2002. Open March-October.

The Closes Farm, Atlow, Ashbourne, Derbyshire DE6 1PW. *01335 370763.* Mr Ian & Mary Webster. Four miles east of Ashbourne, at Hulland on the A517, turn north on road for Hognaston, over crossroads, site 0.5m on left. Own sanitation essential.

Bakewell

Camping & Caravanning Club Site - Bakewell, Hopping Farm, Youlgreave, Bakewell, Derbyshire DE45 1NA. *01629 636555.* www.campingandcaravanningclub.co.uk. The Camping & Caravanning Club Ltd. In the heart of the Peak National Park. One mile from Youlgreave on the A524. 100 pitches in 14 acres. Own sanitation essential. Non-members welcome. Caravans, motor caravans and tents accepted. Difficult approach for large units/vehicles. Open March-September.

> **Greenhills Caravan & Camping Park, Crow Hill Lane, Bakewell, Derbyshire DE45 1PX.** *01629 813052.* MrJ A Green. Located on the A6 trunk road, one mile north-west of Bakewell. Licensed club in main season. Advisable to telephone in advance. Peak District National Park. Shop in summer months. Closed in winter. SAE for brochure and price list. Open March 1-October 31.

Haddon Grove, Bakewell, Derbyshire DE45 1JF. *01629 812343.* Mr W J D Finney. B5055 road south about two miles from Monyash. Four miles south-west of Bakewell. Fees on application. Open March-October.

Buxton

Cold Springs Farm, Manchester Road, Buxton, Derbyshire SK17 6SS *01298 22762.* Mr J Booth-Millward. On the A5004 Buxton to Stockport road, one mile north west of Buxton. Peak District. Route London to Scotland. Open March-November.

Cottage Farm Caravan Park, Blackwell in the Peak, Buxton, Derbyshire SK17 9TQ. *01298 85330.* mail@cottage farmsite.co.uk. www.cottagefarmsite.co.uk. Mrs M Gregory. Off A6 midway between Buxton and Bakewell in the Hamlet of Blackwell in the Peak. Follow site signs. Open March-October 31.

Lime Tree Park, Dukes Drive, Buxton, Derbyshire SK17 9RP. *01298 22988.* limetreebuxton@dukes50.fsnet.co.uk. www. ukparks.co.uk/limetree. Andrew & Robert Hidderley. Situated 1m from Buxton town centre. Proceed south on A515 Ashbourne road. First left after Buxton Hospital. Situated in a sheltered valley. Ideal for walking and cycling in the peaks. Graded: 4 stars. Open March 1-October 31.

Longnor Wood Caravan & Camping Park, Just for Adults, Longnor, Buxton, Derbyshire SK17 0NG. *01298 83648.* enquiries@longnorwood.co.uk. www.longnorwood.co.uk. Paul & Lindsey Hedges. From Longnor crossroads, follow caravan and camping site sign 1.25 miles. We welcome mature visitors to our peaceful, secluded, well run adults only park. Central for many Peak District attractions including Chatsworth, Haddon Hall, Bakewell, Buxton and the beautiful Derbyshire Dales. Putting green, boules and croquet. Open March 1-October 31.

Newhaven Holiday Camping & Caravan Park, Newhaven, Buxton, Derbyshire SK17 0DT. *01298 84300.* Bob & Kay Macara. On the A515 midway between Buxton and Ashbourne at the junction with the A5012. Ten miles south of Buxton. Large holiday site, extensively equipped. Peak National Park. AA 3 pennant. Graded 3 stars. Open March-October.

Pomeroy Caravan & Camping Park, Street House Farm, Pomeroy, Nr Flagg, Buxton, Derbyshire SK17 9QG. *01298 83259.* Mr & Mrs J Melland. On A515. 5 miles S of Buxton. 16 miles N of Ashbourne. site signposted over double cattle grid. Peaceful 30 pitch, level site with good access. Tarmac road to all pitches. Separate site for campers. Adjoins High Peak Trail. Central for Peak District National Park. Open Easter-October 31.

Derby

Cavendish Caravan & Camping Site, Derby Road, Doveridge, Derby, Derbyshire DE6 5JR. *01889 562092.* Mr G Wood. On A50 in Doveridge midway between Derby and Stoke-on-Trent. 1.5 miles east of Uttoxeter. Pub and food 100 yards. Entrance to site is through double open gates across a closed garage forecourt. dogs allowed on leads.

Elvaston Castle Country Park, Borrowash Road, Elvaston, Derby, Derbyshire DE72 3EP. *01332 573735.* The Caravan Club. Derbyshire County Council site managed by the Caravan Club. On B5010 N of A6, 4m SE of Derby, or S off A52 at Ockbrook, signposted. In country park. 21 nights maximum stay. Fees on application. Non-members and tent campers welcome. Good family site. Open Easter-October.

Edale

Waterside Farm, Barber Booth Road, Edale, Derbyshire S30 2ZL. *01433 670215.* jenncooper@talk21.com . Mrs J M Cooper. Off A625. Near Sheffield. Dogs allowed on leads. Open Easter-September 30.

Eyam

Brosterfield Farm, Foolow, Eyam, Derbyshire S30 1QA.. *01433 630958.* 3m W of Calver, on A623 turn N on road at Housley. Site 0.5m on left. From Buxton A6 E for 6m then N on B6049 to A623. Turn E on A623 for 3m, and N on minor road to site. Local caves, good walks. Route Chesterfield to Manchester.
♥ ❷ ▨ ✕ ☉ ♨ ☾ ⚓ ❀ ♨ *L*

Hartington

Endon Cottage, Hulme End Sheen, Buxton, Hartington, Derbyshire SK17 0HG. *01298 84617.* Mrs J Naylor. Site is in Hulme End near Hulme End Hotel. 1.5m SW of Hartington and 10m SW of Buxton. Within reach of Dovedale and Manifold Valley. Dogs on lead. Gas supplies available nearby. Open Easter-October.
♥ ▨ ❧ ⚓ *L* ❋ ✈ ✈

High Peak

Camping & Caravanning Club Site - Hayfield, Kinder Road, Hayfield, High Peak, Derbyshire SK22 2LE. *01663 745394.* www.campingandcaravanningclub.co.uk. The Camping & Caravanning Club Ltd. A624 Glossop to Chapel On Le Frith is Hayfield by pass. Well signed to village. Follow wooden carved signs to site. Site on banks of river Sett and ideal for fell walkers. Non-members welcome. No towed caravans. 90 pitches, set in 6 acres. Motor caravans and tents accepted. Open March-October.
♥ ▨ ❧ ⚓ ☉ ☾ ♨ ▤ ☾ ❒ *L* ❸ U

Ringstones Caravan Park, Yeardsley Lane, Furness Vale, High Peak, Derbyshire SK23 7EB. *01663 747042/07790 428773.* mo@ringstones.freeserve.co.uk. Mrs M Hallworth. From Whaley Bridge A6 to Furness Vale. Turn of A6 at Cantonese restaurant by pelican crossing, then three quarters mile up Yeardsley Lane. Working farm. Beautifully situated quiet site with lovely views of the Peak District. Open March 1-October 31.
♥ ▨ ❧ ⚓ ☾ ❒ ☾ ≋ ❧ *L* ❋ ✈ ✈ ⟲ ❹ ⚘

Hope

Laneside Caravan Park, Hope, Derbyshire S33 6RR. *01433 620215.* laneside@lineone.net Mrs D Neary. On A625 E of Hope village,15m W of Sheffield. High peak touring centre. Level, riverside, sheltered valley site, bordering village with late shopping, pubs and all amenities. Open Easter-October.
♥ ❷ ▨ ❧ ☉ ☾ ⚓ ❒ ☾ ≋ ❋ ✈ ✈ ⟲ ❹ ⚘

Hope Valley

Eden Tree House Caravan Park, Eccles Lane, Bradwell, Hope Valley, Derbyshire S33 9JT. *01433 623444.* Owner: Michael Allcroft. From B6049, turn at Bath Hotel on outskirts of Bradwell. Sheltered, small, friendly site. 20 pitches. Close to all amenitites and central for Peak district National Park. Open March-October.
♥ ❷ ▨ ❧ ☉ ☾ ⚓ ❒ ☾ ≋ *L* ❋ ✈ ✈ ❹ ⚘

Fieldhead Camp Site, Edale, Hope Valley, Derbyshire S33 7ZA. *01433 670386.* bookings@campsite.co.uk. www.field head-campsite.co.uk. Peak Planning Board. 5m from A625 at Hope. Midway between village and Edale railway station. Signposted Peak National Park Information Centre. Heart of Peak District. Fees on application. Cafe/restaurant within 400 metres.
▨ ❧ ❧ ⚓ ❒ ☾ ❀ ❋ ✈ ✈ ❹ ⟲ ⚘

Highfield Farm, Nr Upper Booth, Edale, Hope Valley, Derbyshire S33 7ZJ. *01433 670245.* Mr C R Cooper. Turn off A625 at Hope Church. Take minor road to Edale, past turn for Edale Village. At bottom of hill turn right under viaduct and past picnic area. Convenient site for hill walking. Dogs must be kept on leads. Fees on application. Open Easter-October.
♥ ▨ ❧ ✕ ❧ ≋ ❧ ✈ U

Rowter Farm, CastletonHope Valley, Derbyshire S33 8WA. *01433 620271.* Mrs B Hall. 0.5m just off B6061 left at Winnats Pass. Remote, rural site near hills. Good walking, touring and mountain bike area. Easy reach of all local places of interest. Open Easter to end-October.
♥ ▨ ☾ ⚓ ❒ ☾ ❧ ✈ U ✈

Swallow Holme Caravan Park, Station Road, Bamford, Hope Valley, Derbyshire S33 0BN. *01433 650981.* John Froggatt. On A6013, 0.5m south of Bamford village. Open April 1-October 31.
❷ ▨ ❧ ☉ ☾ ⚓ ❒ ✕ ❒ ≋ *L* ❋ ✈ ✈ ❹ ⚘

Upper Booth Farm, Edale, Hope Valley, Derbyshire S33 7ZJ. *01433 670250.* The National Trust. Leave A625 at Hope, up valley to Edale, turn left by public car park-follow road W to Barber Booth, right turn to Upper Booth and Jacob's Ladder. Telephone at bottom of farm yard, up yard to farmhouse. Heart of Peak District, on Pennine Way. Dogs to be kept on leads at all times. Booking advisable. Open February 1-October 31.
▨ ❧ ⚓ ❒ ☾ ≋ ❧ *L* ✈ U

Matlock

Haytop Country Park, Whatstandwell, Matlock, Derbyshire DE4 5HP. *01773 852063.* Mrs E George. 65 acre park with river frontage for fishing and boating. Most dogs allowed.
♥ ❷ ▨ ❧ ✕ ☉ ☾ ⚓ ❒ ☾ ≋ ❧ *L* ❋ ❋ ✈ ⟲ U ⚘

Pinegroves Caravan Park, High Lane, Tansley, Matlock, Derbyshire DE4 5BG. *01629 534815.* Mr C & Mr J C Thorpe. M1 junction 28 A38 and 615 towards Matlock, through Wessington 2m—2nd left at crossroads or via A6 to Matlock-A615 Alfreton through Tansley 1m second right at crossroads. Easy access, level ground. Woodland walks. AA award-winning site. Open April-October.
♥ ❷ ▨ ❧ ☾ ☉ ⚓ ❒ ☾ *L* ❋ ✈ ✈ ✈ ❹ U ⚘ ⚘

Sycamore Caravan & Camping Park, Lant Lane, Matlock Moor, Matlock, Derbyshire DE4 5LF. *01629 55760.* Charles Boffey. 2.5m from Matlock off A632 off Lant Lane, 1.25m from Tansley off A615. Open March 15-October 31.
♥ ❷ ▨ ❧ ☉ ☾ ⚓ ❒ ☾ ≋ *L* ❋ ✈ ✈ ✈ ❹ U ⚘ ⚘

Whatstandwell

Merebrook Caravan Park, Derby Road, Merebrook, Whatstandwell, Derbyshire DE4 5HH. *01773 857010/852154.* Mr A Daley. 5m south of Matlock on A6. Site is signposted on west side of road. 15m north of Derby. Riverside site in Peak District. Dogs allowed. Tents allowed March to October. Open all year for tourers only. Fees on application. Open Easter-October 31.
♥ ❷ ▨ ❧ ☉ ☾ ⚓ ❒ ☾ ≋ *L* ❒ ❋ ✈ ✈ ❹ ⚘

DEVON

Ashburton

Ashburton Caravan Park, Waterleat, Ashburton, Devon TQ13 7HU. *01364 652552.* info@ashburtoncaravanpark.co.uk. www.ashburtonvcaravanpark.co.uk. Mr R and Mrs P Pummell. A38 Ashburton town centre, North Street, bear right before bridge following Waterleat sign. 1.25 mile. Riverside location inside Dartmoor National Park. AA 4 pennant. Graded: 4 stars. Open Easter-September.
♥ ❷ ▨ ❧ ❧ ☉ ☾ ⚓ ❒ ☾ ✈ U ⚘ ⚘

Parkers Farm Holiday Park, Higher Mead Farm, Ashburton, Devon TQ13 7LJ. *01364 652598.* parkersfarm@btconnect.com. www.parkersfarm.co.uk. Rhona Parker. A38 to Plymouth to sign reading 26m Plymouth, second left at Alston Cross marked

Woodland and Denbury. 370-acre farm ideal for touring Devon or Cornwall on edge of Dartmoor National Park. 12m sea. Children and pets welcome. Level terrace camping. Courtyard barn cottage, camping barn and holiday caravans to let. Open Easter-October.

📞🅿️♿️📺♨️⚓🍽️✕☉🐕🔥🍺🚿🎣🏪⊟🛏️↲⤴️∪💲❤️

Axminster

Andrewshayes Caravan Park, Axminster, Devon EX13 7DY. *01404 831225.* enquiries@andrewshayes.co.uk. www.andrewshayes.co.uk. H K & S D Lawrence. 3m Axminster and 6m Honiton, 100yd off A35 at Taunton Cross. Peaceful, clean caravan and camping park on a farm. Ideal for coast and countryside. AA 4 pennants. RAC appointed. Rose Award. Open March 1-November 30.

📞🅿️♿️📺♨️⚓🍽️✕☉🐕🔥🍺🚿🎣🏪⊟🛏️⇌↲⤴️∪💲❤️↙

Hunters Moon Country Estate, Hawkchurch, Axminster, Devon EX13 5UL. *01297 678402.* www.ukparks.co.uk/huntersmoon. Totemplant Ltd. Turn off A35 onto B3165 signposted Crewkerne follow signs 2.5m turn left. Touring and camping holidays available. Open March 15-November 15.

📞🅿️♿️♨️⚓🍺↲⤴️↙

Barnstaple

Brightlycott Barton Caravan & Camping Site, Barnstaple, Devon EX31 4JJ. *01271 850330.* friend.brightlycott@virgin.net. Charles & Julia Friend. 2m NE of Barnstaple, off A39. Road to farm site is signposted Brightlycott and Roborough. Central touring site with panoramic views of moor and estuary. Leisure centre in Barnstaple. Open mid-March-mid November.

📞🅿️📺♨️☉🔥🍺🏪⊟🛏️↲💲↙∪💲

Chivenor Caravan Park, Chivenor Cross, Barnstaple, Devon EX31 4BN. *07071 228478.* chivenorcp@lineone.net. Lesley & Michael Stansmore. Small family-run site with easy access off the A361 Barnstaple to Ilfracombe road. 100yd from Tarka Trail. All amenities either on site or within close proximity. Centrally located for touring. Open March 15-November 15.

📞🅿️📺♨️⚓☉🐕🔥🍺🏪⊟🚿↲❤️⤴️↙∪💲❤️↯

Lorna Doone Farm, Parracombe, Barnstaple, Devon EX31 4RJ. *01598 763262.* Miss L Hunt. Site entrance adjoins A39. Exmoor National Park. Graded: 4 stars. Open March 15-October 31.

📞📺♨️🔥🏪⊟🍺∪💲

Midland Caravan Park, Braunton Road, Barnstaple, Devon EX31 4AU. *01271 343691.* info@midlandpark.co.uk. www.vmidlandpark.co.uk Mr & Mrs D Fry. Two miles from centre of Barnstaple on right side on the A361 to Ilfracombe. Sheltered grass parkland site1. Buses stop at door. Quality graded by the West Country Tourist Board. Open Easter-October .

📞🅿️📺♨️☉🐕🔥🏪⊟🍺↲↙💲

Berrynarbor

Napps Camping Site, Old Coast Road, Berrynarbor, Devon EX34 9SW. *01271 882557.* Mr Richards. From Combe Martin towards Ilfracombe on the A399. After one mile (at bottom of hill) turn north on Old Coast Road. Site 400 yards. Touring centre for north Devon coast and Exmoor. Tennis court. Heated swimming pool. Paddling pool. Quiet bar and restaurant. Glorious sea views. Footpath to beach. Open Easter-October.

📞🅿️♿️📺♨️⚓✕☉🐕🔥🍺≋🏪⊟⇌↲❤️🔺↲⤴️∪💲❤️↙

Bideford

Dyke Green Farm Camp Site, Clovelly, Bideford, Devon EX39 5RU. *01237 431279.* Mrs J Johns. About 1.5 miles S of Clovelly at junction of B3237 & A39. Flat, sheltered site in good walking country. Close to many secluded coves and beaches. Fees on application. Dogs under control welcome. Open March-October.

📞🅿️♨️⚓✕☉🐕🔥🏪⊟🛏️↲❤️🔳🔺↲↙∪💲❤️↙

Hartland Caravan and Camping Site, Southlane, Hartland, Bideford, Devon EX39 6DG. *01237 441242/441876.* L Allin. Quiet family run site 3 mins walk from Hartland village with sea views. Fishing on site. BBQ area. 3 acres level/gentle slope, mostly sheltered. Some hardstanding. Local woodland, coastal walks. 2.5m from beaches. Map reading: 190/263243. Open all year.

📞🅿️♨️⚓🔥☉🐕🔥✳️↲❤️🔺↲↙∪💲

Steart Farm Touring Park, Horns Cross, Bideford, Devon EX39 5DW. *01237 431836.* steart@tiscali.co.uk. Robin & Lesley Croslegh. From Bideford, follow A39 west (signed Bude). Two miles after Horns Cross, site entrance on right. Set in 17 acres overlooking Bideford Bay, 1 mile from sea. Dog exercise field, children's play area, daytime dog kennelling facility. Open Easter-September 30.

📞🅿️♨️⚓✕☉🐕🔥🏪⊟🍺❤️🔺↲↙∪💲

Braunton

Lobb Fields Caravan and Camping Park, Saunton Road, Braunton, Devon EX33 1EB. *01271 812090.* info@lobbfields.com. www.lobbfields.com. Mrs J Bury, Mrs E Dodge, Mrs J Smith-Bingham. From Barnstaple west on A361 6m to Braunton. In Braunton take B3231 towards Croyde, park is 1m on right. Large holiday site, 1.5m from sea. Railway station 6m from site. Fees on application. Graded: 3 stars. Open March-October.

📞🅿️📺♨️☉🐕🔥🏪⊟🍺↲🔺↙∪💲❤️↯

Brixham

Centry Touring Caravan & Camping Site, Mudberry House, Centry Road, Brixham, Devon TQ5 9EY. *01803 853215.* jla centry.touring@talk21.com. www.english-riviera.co.uk. Mrs J Allen. From Paignton follow signs for Berry Head. Beaches and harbour, all within walking distance. Milk. Telephone in advance July and August. Dogs allowed on leads. Cafe/restaurant, laundry facilities available nearby. Graded: 2 stars. Open Easter-October 31.

📞🅿️📺♨️☉🐕🔥🏪⊟🔳↲❤️🔺↲↙∪💲❤️↯↯

Galmpton Touring Park, Greenaway Road, Galmpton, Brixham, Devon TQ5 0EP. *01803 842066.* galmptontouring park@hotmail.com. www.galmptontouringpark.co.uk. Chris & Pam Collins. A380 Torbay ring road then A379 towards Brixham, park signposted on the right through village. Family park with spectacular views of river Dart. Close to beaches and all Torbay attractions. Immaculate facilities. Good access. No dogs in peak season. Graded: 4 stars. Open Easter-September.

📞🅿️📺♿️♨️☉🐕🔥🏪⊟⇌↲❤️🔺↲↙∪💲❤️↯↯

DEVON

Buckfast

Churchill Farm, Buckfast, Devon TQ11 0EZ. *01364 642844.* apedrick@farmersweekly.net. A Pedrick. From the A38 exit at Dart Bridge, drive towards Buckfast Abbey. Up hill towards Holne and turn left at crossroads at top of hill. Farm entrance is opposite church. Family working farm overlooking Buckfast Abbey. Close to steam railway and butterfly farm. Shops, cafe/restaurant, takeaway meals available nearby. Open May-October.

Buckfastleigh

Beara Farm Camping Site, Colston Road, Buckfastleigh, Devon TQ11 0LW. *01364 642234.* Mr W John Thorn. From Exeter, leave A38 at Dart Bridge. Follow signs to South Devon Steam Railway and Butterfly Farm. Take first left after entrance. Signed Old Totnes Road. Ater 0.5m turn right, site one mile. Adjoining Dart Valley and Steam Railway. Fees on application.

Chudleigh

Finlake Holiday Park, Chudleigh, Devon TQ13 0EJ. *01626 853833.* info@finlake.co.uk. www.finlake.co.uk. Finlake Leisure Ltd. Off the A38 Exeter-Plymouth road at Chudleigh Knighton. Turn right at top of slip road, Finlake is on right. 130-acre park covering hills, valleys, woodlands and lakes. Sited between Dartmoor National Park and South Devon coastline.

Holmans Wood Tourist Park, Harcombe Cross, Chudleigh, Devon TQ13 0DZ. *01626 853785.* Mr & Mrs T Newton. One mile from Chudleigh at bottom of Haldon Hill. One mile past racecourse. Site 100 yards on left. Good touring base for Exmouth, Dartmoor and Torquay. Well-equipped site. Haldon Forest walks. Fees on application. Open March 15-October 31.

Colyton

Leacroft Touring Park, Colyton Hill, Colyton, Devon EX24 6HY. *01297 552823.* Anne & John Robinson. Signposted from A3052 Sidmouth to Lyme Regis at Stafford Cross. Do not go into Colyton. Peaceful site in open countryside with views of Lyme Bay. Ideal for touring. Hard standings, seasonal pitches. Storage facilities available. Open Easter-October.

Combe Martin

Newberry Farm, Touring & Caravans & Camping, Woodlands, Combe Martin, Devon EX34 0AT. *01271 882334.* enq@newberrycampsite.co.uk. www.newberrycampsite.co.uk. Mr T Greenaway. Level pitches in a beautiful countryside valley. Combe Martin shops, cafes and pubs, 5 minutes' walk. Coarse fishing lake. Ideally situated for Exmoor National Park & Coastal Footpath. Graded: 4 stars. Open Easter-end October.

Stowford Farm Meadows, Berry Down, Combe Martin, Devon EX34 0PW. *01271 882476.* enquiries@stowford.co.uk. www.stowford.co.uk. Mr Winston Rice. Off A3123 Combe Martin/Woolacombe Road. Situated on 450 acres of glorious Devon countryside and on the fringe of Exmoor National Park; award-winning, family-orientated touring park. Massive range of facilities at unbeatable prices. Open Easter-end October.

Crediton

Yeatheridge Farm Caravan Park, East Worlington, Crediton, Devon EX17 4TN. *01884 860330.* Mr G N Hosegood. 3.5m SW of Witheridge. From Tiverton B3137 (old A373) to Witheridge take B3042, just before Witheridge site is 3.5m on left. Spacious site situated midway between Exmoor and Dartmoor. Panoramic views on working farm. Open Easter-end September.

Croyde Bay

Bay View Farm Holidays, Croyde Bay, Devon EX33 1PN. *01271 890501.* www.bayviewfarm.co.uk. Mr & Mrs Hakin. Leave M5 junction 27 on to A361 Barnstaple and Ilfracombe, turn left off A361 at Braunton traffic lights, on to B3231 into Croyde, site on right entering Croyde village. Situated in old world village, minutes walk to sandy beach. Open March-October.

Ruda Holiday Park, Croyde Burrows, Croyde Bay, Devon EX33 1NY. *01271 890671.* enquiries@ruda.co.uk. www.parkdean.co.uk. Parkdean Holidays Plc. Leave the M5 at junction 27 for A361 to Barnstaple and Braunton, then B3231 to Croyde Bay. Holiday park 100 yards from beach. Club with entertainment. Heated indoor fun pool. Organised children's activities. Winner Best Park in West Country 1998 and 1999. Phone for colour brochure. Graded: 4 stars. Open March-October.

Cullompton

Forest Glade Caravan & Camping Park, Cullompton, Devon EX15 2DT. *01404 841381.* enquiries@forest-glade.co.uk. www.forest-glade.co.uk. Mr Norman Wellard. From Cullompton, take A373 towards Honiton. Turn north after three miles. Signposted to Sheldon. Follow Sheldon signs for 2.5 miles up hill into woods. Six miles north west of Honiton. Flat, secluded site in forest. Children's adventure playground. Free indoor swimming. Games room. All-weather tennis court. Tourers must phone for access route. Open March-November.

Dartmouth

Deer Park Caravan & Camping, Dortmouth Road, Stoke Fleming, Dartmouth, Devon TQ6 0RF. *01803 770253.* peter.keane@talk21.com. www.deerparkinn.co.uk. Peter Keane & Sarah Keane. 2m from Dartmouth on A379 at Stoke Fleming. 2m SW of Dartmouth. Near coast at Start Bay. Adventure playground. Freehouse and restaurant. Bed and Breakfast. Flats for hire. Families welcome.

Leonards Cove, Stoke Fleming, Dartmouth, Devon TQ6 0NR. *01803 770206.* enquiry@leonardscove.co.uk. www.leonardscovecamping.co.uk. 2m S via A379, in coastal village. Walking distance Blackpool Sands. Sea views from the camping field. Touring area. Wind surfing. Fees on application. Open Easter-October.

Little Cotton Caravan Park, Dartmouth, Devon TQ6 0LB. *01803 832558.* www.littlecottoncaravan park.co.uk. Paul & Dorothy White. Leave A38 at Buckfastleigh, A384 to Totnes, A381 to Halwell. Take A3122 Dartmouth Road. Park on right to entrance to town. Seven acres with scenic outlook. Open March 15-October 31.

DEVON

Sea View Campsite, Newlands Farm, Slapton, Dartmouth, Devon TQ7 2RB. *01548 580366.* camping@devon-camping.co.uk. www.devon-camping.co.uk. Mr Roger Bradford. From Totnes, take A381 towards Kingsbridge. After Halwell take 4th left signposted Slapton, go 4 miles to Buckland Cross. Proceed half mile. Site on left. Quiet site overlooking farmland and sea. Open Whitsun-October.

🚐🚉📷🎾⚡♨🚿🏊⚓♨🍴🅿🚰🖊

Woodland Leisure Park, Blackawton, Dartmouth, Devon TQ9 7DQ. *01803 712598.* fun@woodlandspark.com. www.woodlandspark.com. Chris Bendall. Highest standard facilities, level lawn pitches in beautiful setting. Visit leisure park free with two nights' stay—3 watercoasters, toboggan run, arctic gliders, falconry. See Dragons Empire—massive indoor venture centre. Open Easter-November.

🚐🚉📷🎾⚡♨🍴✕⊙♨🔥🚿⚓🍴✕🚰♨🖊🅿🚰

Dawlish

Cofton Country Holidays, Starcross, Dawlish, Devon EX6 8RP. *01626 890111.* Mr & Mrs W G Jeffery. On A379 Exeter to Dawlish road. Easy access from J30 M5. Heated swimming pool. Swan pub, family rooms and 2 bars. Take-away and pub snacks. Games room. Children's woodland play area. Free showers and hot water. Laundrette. Coarse fishing. Graded: 4 stars. Open Easter-October.

🚐🚉♨📷🎾⚡♨✕⊙♨🔥🚿≋♨🍴🚰♨🖊🅿

Lady's Mile Touring Caravan & Camping Park, Exeter Road, Dawlish, Devon EX7 0LX. *01626 863411.* P Jeffrey. On A379 Exeter to Dawlish road. Easy access from J30 M5. Heated indoor and outdoor swimming pools, 200ft chutes. New children's playground and fort. Short distance to Dawlish Warren beaches. Ideal base for Devon attractions. Open March 15-October 31.

🚐🚉♨📷🎾⚡♨✕⊙♨🔥🚿≋⚓♨🍴🚰≋♨🅿♨🚰🖊🅿🚰♨🖊

Leadstone Camping, Warren Road, Dawlish, Devon EX7 0NG. *01626 864411.* info@leadstonecamping.co.uk. www.leadstonecamping.co.uk. Mr A C I Bulpin. Leave M5 at junction 30. Take the A379 to Dawlish. On approaching Dawlish turn L on brow of hill signed Dawlish Warren. Site half mile on right. Rolling grassland in natural secluded bowl half mile from Dawlish Warren beach and nature reserve. Graded: 3 stars. Open June 18-September 6.

🚐🚉📷🎾⚡♨⊙♨🔥🚿⚓🍴♨≋♨🍴🚰♨🖊🅿🚰♨

Peppermint Park, Warren Road, Dawlish Warren, Dawlish, Devon EX7 0PQ. *01626 863436.* info@peppermintpark.co.uk. www.peppermintpark.co.uk. Mr G Hawkins. Leave the M5 at Exeter. Take A379 signpost to Dawlish. Dog exercise area. Children's play area. Licensed club, free entertainment. 680 metres from beach. Heated pool with water slide. Coarse fishing. Graded: 4 stars. Open Easter-October.

🚐🚉♨📷🎾⚡♨✕⊙♨🔥🚿⚓♨🍴🚰♨🅿🖊

Drewsteignton

Clifford Bridge Park, Clifford, Drewsteignton, Devon EX6 6QE. *01647 24226.* info@clifford-bridge.co.uk. www.ukparks.co.uk/cliffordbridge. Joe & Renee Scaife. Within Dartmoor National Park, 3m N of Moretonhampstead. Excellent walks start from park—upstream to Fingle Bridge and Castle Drogo (NT) or downstream through Dunsford Nature Reserve. Open end May-mid September.

🚐🚉📷🎾⚡♨⊙♨🔥🚿≋⚓♨🍴♨🚰🖊🅿

Exeter

Barley Meadow Caravan & Camping Park, Crockernwell, Exeter, Devon EX6 6NR. *01647 281629.* info@barleymeadow.co.uk. www.barleymeadow.co.uk. Angela & Terry Waldron. Turn off A30 Exeter-Okehampton road, site is 2.5m on left. Peaceful country site within Dartmoor National Park. Children's play area. Shop. Overnight stops welcome. Heated shower blocks. Open 15th March-15th November.

🚐🚉📷🎾⚡♨⊙♨🔥🚿⚓♨🍴♨🖊🚰♨🅿

Castle Brake, Castle Lane, Woodbury, Exeter, Devon EX5 1HA. *01395 232431.* reception@castlebrake.co.uk. www.castlebrake.co.uk. Tony & Dare Walker. M5 junction 30 and follow A3052 to Halfway Inn, onto B3180. Grassy, level park between Exeter and Exmouth. Small with excellent facilities. Holiday caravans for hire. Shower block for tents/tourers. Bar and restaurant for quiet evening meals. Caravan storage

DEVON

available. David Bellamy Gold Conservation Award. ETB: 4 stars. Open March-October.

🚐🚉⚡🎦⛺⛽✕☉🚻🛢️🔥🐕🛇⛺L♂♂✓🅿️

Culm Valley Camping Park, Rewe, Exeter, Devon EX5 4HB. *01392 841349.* Mr G Forrest-Jones. 6m N of Exeter via A396, take 1st right after Rewe. Camping sign at junc. M5 traffic take Sampford Peverell junc, via Tiverton 8m to site. Overnight stop Midlands to South Devon. Peaceful holiday centre.

🚐🚉⛺🛢️🐾☉🚻🛢️🔥🐕⛺🎦♂✓🅿️♂✎

Exeter Racecourse Caravan Club Site, Haldon Racecourse, Kennford, Exeter, Devon EX6 7XS. *01392 832107.* Devon & Exeter Steeplechases Ltd. Adjoins A38 about seven miles south of Exeter. Travelling south via Exeter bypass follow road for Plymouth. Access to site is on left of road up to Haldon Hill, just before summit. Overnight stop for Devon, Cornwall. Free access to racing during open season. Open April-October.

🚐🚉⛺🛢️☉⛽🔥🐕⛺L

Haldon Lodge Farm Caravan & Camping Site, Kennford, Exeter, Devon EX6 7YG. *01392 832312.* Mr D L Salter. Five miles south of Exeter off A38 Kennford Services. Turn left through Kennford village following sign for Haldon Lodge. Pass Post Office to Motor Bridge turn left Dunchideock. 1.5 miles to park. Peaceful, family site, excellent touring centre, 15 mins sea. Forest nature trails, riding and trekking. Open all year.

🚐🚉⛺🛢️☉⛽🔥🐕🛢️⛺🎦❄🔥🐾♂♂✓🅿️☉♂✎🦮⚡

Kennford International Caravan Park, Exeter, Devon EX6 7YN. *01392 833046.* Mr & Mrs P F Harper. 4m south of Exeter, 0.5 mile from end of M5 alongside A38. Opposite Kennford service area. Deluxe facility touring park with individually hedged pitches. Ideal location for an enjoyable south Devon holiday. Graded: 4 stars. Open all year.

🚐🚉⚡🎦🛢️✕☉⛽🔥🐕⛺🎦⛺🎦❄L♂♂✓🅿️☉♂🦮⚡

Springfield Holiday Park, Tedburn St Mary, Exeter, Devon EX6 6EW. *01647 24242.* springhol@aol.com . www.springfieldholiday-park.co.uk . Martin & Eileen Johnson. A30 W of Exeter. 3rd junction, turn right over bridge follow signs. Open March-November.

🚐🚉⚡🎦⛺🎦✕☉⛽🔥🐕⛺≈🔥⛺🛢️L♂🎦♂✓🅿️☉♂✎

Webbers Farm Caravan & Camping Park, Castle Lane, Woodbury, Exeter, Devon EX5 1EA. *01395 232276.* reception@webbersfarm.co.uk . www.webbersfarm.co.uk . Mr & Mrs S A Stokes. From M5 junc 30 take A376 then B3179 to Woodbury, then follow brown and white signs. Friendly, uncommercialised farm park on edge of village. Tremendous views over river Exe. Advanced booking recommended. Please call for brochure. Open Easter-end September.

🚐🚉⛺🛢️☉⛽🔥🐕⛺🎦⛺♂♂✓🅿️☉♂✎

Exmouth

Devon Cliffs Holiday Park, Sandy Bay, Exmouth, Devon EX8 5BT. *01395 226226.* www.havenholidays.com. Haven Leisure. Turn off M5, exit 30 and take A376 for Exmouth. At Exmouth follow signs to Sandy Bay. One of Haven's 37 tenting and touring parks across UK. Indoor and outdoor fun pools. Free kids' clubs. Mini golf. Go karts. Adventure playground. all weather multi sports court. Free daytime and evening entertainment for all the family. Graded: 3 stars. Open Easter-November.

🚐🚉⚡🎦🛢️🛢️✕☉⛽🔥🎦≈🔥🐕⛺≈🛢️♂♂✓🅿️☉♂⚡

Great Torrington

Greenways Valley, Great Torrington, Devon EX38 7EW. *01805 622153.* Mr & Mrs Jackman. Quiet family park. Level, well drained, sheltered pitches facing south over wooded valley. Open mid March-end October.

🚐🚉🎦🛢️☉⛽🔥⛺≈🔥🐕🎦✕⛺♂♂✓🅿️☉♂✎

Holsworthy

Hedley Wood Caravan & Camping Park, Bridgerule, Holsworthy, Devon EX22 7ED. *01288 381404.* alan@hedley wood.co.uk. www.hedleywood.co.uk. Mr & Mrs A Bryant. Off the A3072 and B3254. 16.5 acres, woodland site. Outstanding views. Sheltered and open camping areas. Clubroom, bar and all amentities. Dog walk and daily kennelling facility. Clay pigeon shoot. Holiday caravans for hire. Caravan storage.

🚐🚉⚡🎦🛢️⛺🛢️✕☉⛽🔥⛺🎦⛺🔥L♂⚡♂♂✓🅿️☉♂⚡

Newbuildings, Brandis Corner, Holsworthy, Devon EX22 7YQ. *01409 221305.* Mr & Mrs B Lynds. A3072 Holsworthy/Hatherleigh road. Four miles from Holsworthy towards Hatherleigh, turn left at Dunsland Cross (opposite right hand turn to Okehampton) site on left after 200 yards. Working family farm. Off road walking on National Trust lane. Dogs allowed if kept under control.

🚐🚉⚡🎦🛢️✕⛽🔥⛺✕🔥⛺❄🛢️♂✓🅿️⚡♂

Noteworthy, Bude Road, Holsworthy, Devon EX22 7JB. *01409 253731.* goldspink@easynet.co.uk Mrs Goldspink. Located 2.5f miles west of Holsworthy on A3072. One mile past golf course. Touring centre ideal for exploring moors and beaches. Quiet family-run site.

🚐🚉🎦🛢️☉⛽🔥⛺🛢️♂✓🅿️⚡♂

DEVON

Penhallym Farm, Week St Mary, Holsworthy, Devon EX22 6XR. *01288 341274.* Mrs A Brenton. Off the A39 at Treskinnick Cross, signposted Week St Mary. First right for Jacobstow to farm house and site on right. Midway between Bude and Boscastle. Quiet with sea views. No sanitation. Bottle gas supply within two miles. Open June 1st-October 31st.

🚐�"🕭✕🛢❀♨🚽⚊ 🍴 ⅃✓◡

Honiton

Camping & Caravanning Club Site - Honiton, Otter Valley Park, Northcote, Honiton, Devon EX14 8ST. *01404 44546.* www.campingandcaravanningclub.co.uk. The Camping & Caravanning Club Ltd. 5-acre site with 90 pitches. Leave exit to Honiton from A30 follow signs to site. In river Otter valley, a great stay for a visit to South West. Non-members welcome. Caravans, motor caravans and tents accepted. Open May-September.

🚐🚌🖾 ⅃🛢❀♨🚽🛢🏠🗐🚽≈⅃🗇⅃✓✲

Fishpond House Campsite, Dunkeswell, Honiton, Devon EX14 0SH. *01404 891287/891358.* Mr P Cattle & Mrs T Kennard. From A30 and A35 Honiton follow signs for Dunkeswell & Luppitt. 3m to Limers Cross and right to Luppitt and Smeathorpe. Bookings taken.

🚐🚌🖾 ⅃🛢🚽⚊✕⊙🛢🔥🛢≋♦🏠❀⅃♀🗇◡✲

Ilfracombe

Big Meadow Caravan & Camping Park, Watermouth, Ilfracombe, Devon EX34 9SJ. *01271 862502.* www.big-meadow.co.uk. Mr & Mrs Wassall. Family site on coastline between Combe Martin and Ilfracombe. Watermouth Harbour and beach 200yds. Children's play area. Old Sawmills inn and restaurant adjoins Big Meadow camping site. Open Easter-September 30.

🚐🚌🚷⚊🖾 ⅃🛢✕⊙🚽🛢🔥♦🏠🛢⅃♀🗐🛢♣♨🗇✓◡✲✲✲🏊

HALDON LODGE FARM CARAVAN & CAMPING SITE

KENNFORD, NR. EXETER TEL: 01392 832312

This family farm caravan/camping park set in beautiful peaceful forest scenery.

★ 15 MINUTES FROM THE SEA
★ AN ATTRACTION OF FARM ANIMALS
★ HORSE RIDING
★ WELL STOCKED COARSE FISHING LAKES CLOSE TO PARK
★ WEEKLY BARBECUES WITH SOUNDS OF THE SIXTIES AND HAYRIDE (SCHOOL HOLIDAYS)
★ EXCELLENT FACILITIES inc, Hook-ups, hot/cold showers, toilets, hair dryers, laundrette, adventure play area, picnic tables, and Farm Shop with bottled gas.
★ PETS ACCEPTED

Set in glorious rural Devon the site offers freedom and safety for all the family.

Open all year. For Brochure Tel: 01392 832312.

Camp site 4¹/₂ miles south of Exeter off A38 at Kennford Services, follow signs Haldon Lodge, turning left down through Kennford village 1¹/₄ miles to site. Attention & welcome given by David & Betty Salter.

Special family site fee for Caravans & Tents: Week's booking £53.50 (electrics, awning and all the family), without electric £42.00.

Hele Valley Holiday Park, Department CS, Hele Bay, Ilfracombe, Devon EX34 9RD. *01271 862460.* holidays@helevalley.co.uk. www.helevalley.co.uk. Mr D S Dovey. Turn right on A399 one mile east of Ilfracombe. Follow brown signs to Hele Valley. Peaceful holiday park a few minutes walk from Hele Bay beach. Free hot showers. Open April-October.

🚐🚉🖾 ⅃🛢⚊⊙🚽🛢🔥🏠⅃🛢◢⅃✓◡✲🎣✲

Hidden Valley Coast & Country Park, West Down, Ilfracombe, Devon EX34 8NU. *01271 813837.* Mr M J Tucker & Mrs S B Tucker. M5, turn off at Junction 27 marked Tiverton/Barnstaple. Follow A361. Beautiful wooded valley with sheltered, level pitches. Equipped to the highest standards. Woodland walks. TV hook ups. Children's play parks. Reduced rates for over 50's. Graded: 4 stars.

🚐🚉♨🖾 ⅃🛢🚷⚊✕⊙🚽🛢🔥🗐❀⅃♀⅃✓◡

Little Meadow, Lydford Farm, Watermouth, Ilfracombe, Devon EX34 9SJ. *01271 866862.* info@littlemeadow.co.uk. www.littlemeadow.co.uk. Mr N Barten. 3.5m E of Ilfracombe on A399 to Combe Martin. A small, tranquil, uncommercialised site with one of the most spectacular views of the Bristol Channel. Dogs allowed. Fees on application. Open Easter-late September.

🚐🚉🚷⚊⊙🚽🛢🏠🗐♀◢♨⅃✓◡✲🎣✲

Little Shelfin Farm, Ilfracombe, Devon. *01271 862449.* Mr W E Dallyn. 1.5m south of Ilfracombe via A361. Turn W along B3343 at Mullacott Cross for 500yd to site. Flat site in pleasant holiday country. Fees and dates on application. Open May-September.

🚐🚉🖾✕🏠🛢🚽⅃✓◡✲✲

Mill Park Camping Site, Berrynarbor, Ilfracombe, Devon EX34 9SH. *01271 882647.* millpark@globalnet.co.uk. www.millpark.co.uk. Brian & Mary Malin. Between Ilfracombe and Combe Martin, take turning off A399 for Berrynarbor. Sheltered, level park in unique woodland setting with waterfall and stream fed coarse fishing lake. Free hot water and showers. Shop, off licence. Bar, hot meals. Laundry. Play area. Dog walks. Phone for brochure or assistance. Open March 15-November 15.

🚐🚉🖾 ⅃🛢✕⊙🚽🛢🔥♣🏠⅃♀🗐◢♨⅃✓◡✲🎣✲

Mullacott Cross Caravan Park, Mullacott Cross, Ilfracombe, Devon EX34 8NB. *01271 862212.* info@mullacottcaravans.co.uk. www.mullacottcaravans.co.uk. R E Donovan. On main A361 road, 2 miles south of Ilfracombe. Gently sloping with views over Bristol Channel. Open Easter-end October.

🚐🚉🖾 ⅃🛢🚷⚊✕⊙🚽🛢🔥🏠×⚊⅃◢⅃✓◡✲🎣✲

Watermouth Cove Holiday Park, Ilfracombe, Devon EX34 9SJ. *01271 862504.* info@watermouthcoveholidays.co.uk. www.watermouthcoveholidays.co.uk. Mr & Mrs A Parr. Family management. Swimming pools. Club. Play park. Entertainment. Bar meals. Own private beach with caves and headland walks. Sea fishing. Open Easter-October.

🚐🚉♨🖾 ⅃🛢✕⊙🚽🛢≋♣🏠🛢≈⅃♀◢♨⅃✓◡✲🎣✲🏊

Ivybridge

Camping & Caravanning Club Site - California Cross, Modbury, Ivybridge, Devon PL2I OSG. *01548 821297.* www.campingandcaravanningclub.co.uk. The Camping & Caravanning Club Ltd. 4-acre site with 80 pitches accepting all units. From A38 leave at exit signed Modbury, Loddiswell and turn left at top of slip road. Cross B3210 and turn left on to B3207. A little way inland but ideal for the coast and beaches. Non-members welcome. Caravans, motor caravans and tents accepted. Open April-October.

🚐🚉🖾 ⅃🛢🚷⚊⊙🚽🛢🔥🏠⅃◡✲

DEVON

Kingsbridge

Camping & Caravanning Club Site - Slapton Sands, Middle Grounds, Slapton, Kingsbridge, Devon TQ7 1QW. *01548 580538.* www.campingandcaravanningclub.co.uk. The Camping & Caravanning Club Ltd. Site overlooks Start Bay, just a few minutes from the site. On A379 from Kingsbridge, site entrance is 0.25-mile from A39 and beyond brow of hill approaching Slapton village. Members-only caravans. Dogs welcome. Non-members welcome. Motor caravans and tents accepted. Open March-October.

Island Lodge Caravan & Camping Site, Stumpy Post Cross, Kingsbridge, Devon TQ7 4BL. *01548 852956/07968 222007.* Kay Parker. One mile north of Kingsbridge via the A381. Convenient for beaches, villages and moors. Quiet level site, totally uncommercialised in rural location with easy access. Suitable for couples and families. Sea glimpses. Licensed caravan and boat storage (undercover in secure yard).

Karrageen Camping & Caravan Park, Bolberry, Malborough, Kingsbridge, Devon TQ7 3EN. *01548 561230.* phil@karrageen.co.uk. www.karrageen.co.uk. Phil & Nikki Higgin. 1m from Hope Cove. Take A381 from Kingsbridge to Salcombe, turn sharp right into Malborough, in 0.6 mile then right signposted Bolberry, after 0.9 mile site on right. Small family-run site surrounded by National Trust coastline. Terraced level tree lined pitches with a view. Licensed shop at reception. Statics for hire. AA 3 pennants. Colour brochure, please book. Graded: 4 stars. See advertisement under Salcombe. Open March 15-November 15.

Mounts Farm Touring Park, The Mounts, East Allington, Kingsbridge, Devon TQ9 7QJ. *01548 521591.* mounts.farm@lineone.net. mountsfarm.co.uk. Phil & Karen Meacher & Mrs Peggy Wain. 3m N of Kingsbridge on A381. Quiet site in area of outstanding beauty, ideal base for visiting all areas of south Devon. Free showers and hot water. Fees on application. Open April-October.

Old Cotmore Touring Caravan & Camping Park, Old Cotmore Farm, Stokenham, Kingsbridge, Devon TQ7 2LR. *01548 580240.* graham.bowsher@btinternet. Lyn & Graham Bowsher. From Kingsbridge, take A379 towards Dartmouth. At Stokenham village turn at mini roundabout to Beesands. Park 1 mile on right-hand side, signposted. Picturesque park, 1 mile from sea and glorious beaches. Holiday cottages available. Dogs allowed. Open March 16-October 31.

Parkland, Sorley Green Cross, Kingsbridge, Devon TQ7 4AF. *01548 852723.* enquiries@parklandsite.co.uk. www.parkland site.co.uk. Mr James K Parker. Take A381 from Totnes to Kingsbridge. 1m N of Kingsbridge turn right on to A381 at Stumpy Post Cross, continue along this road for 1m to Sorley Green Cross. At crossroads go straight across, site is approx. 200yds on the left. High quality traditional site, set in 3 acres of level grounds. Free electric hook-ups. Modern facilities, family/disabled suites. Views Salcombe, nearest site to Bantham Beach. Storage.

Lynton

Camping & Caravanning Club Site - Lynton, Caffyn's Cross, Lynton, Devon EX35 6JS. *01598 752379.* www.campingand caravanningclub.co.uk. The Camping & Caravanning Club Ltd. Take A361 to Barnstaple—turn right S Mouton to Blackmoor Gate. Turn right at Blackmoor Gate SP. Lynton follow road for approximately 5 miles to Caffyn's Cross. Glorious views in all directions from site. 105 pitches set in 5.5 acres. Caravans, motor caravans and tents accepted. Dogs welcome. Non-members welcome. Open March-September.

Channel View Caravan and Camping Park, Manor Farm, Lynton, Devon EX35 6LD. *01598 753349.* channelview@bush-internet.com. www.channel-view.co.uk. Mr R Wren. On A39 2m from Lynton. 2m from beach and near Doone Valley. Open mid March-mid November.

Cloud Farm Camp Site, Cloud Farm, Oare, Lynton, Devon EX35 6NU. *01598 741278.* holiday@doonevalley.co.uk www.doonevalleyholidays.co.uk. H J & K N Burge. 6 m W of Porlock. Signposted from A39 near county boundary of Devon and Somerset. Follow signs for Lorna Doone Farm, then see Cloud Farm on left before river. In heart of Doone Valley by side of river. Well-behaved dogs allowed. Camp fires and barbecues allowed on site.

Hillsford Camping Site, Hillsford Bridge, Lynton, Devon. *01598 741256.* Mr & Mrs B Woollacott. 100yd off main A39. 3.5m from Lynton and Lynmouth. Level site 6m from Doone Valley. Open early March-end October.

Sunny Lyn Caravan & Camping Site, Lynbridge, Lynton, Devon EX35 6NS. *01598 753384.* Mr & Mrs Layton. 0.25m S of Lynton on B3234. Or 1m N of junction of this road with A39 at Barbrook, avoiding steep hill out of Lynton. Holiday site, easy reach of coast on edge of Exmoor. Open Easter-early October.

Modbury

Moor View Touring Park, California Cross, Modbury, Devon PL21 0SG. *01548 821485.* info@moorviewtouringpark.co.uk. www.moorviewtouringpark.co.uk. Edward & Liz Corwood. Rural, family run park backing onto moorland, with panoramic views towards Dartmoor, close to coastal walks and beaches. 68 individual level pitches all with electric hook-up. Hardstandings, fully serviced pitches. Seasonal pitches. Centrally heated luxury showers, shop, laundry and play area. TV/games and information room. Open March 15-November 15.

Pennymoor Camping & Caravan Park, Modbury, Devon PL21 0SB. *01548 830269/830542.* Mr R A & M D Blackler. From Exeter, leave A38 at Wrangaton Cross. Turn left for 1 mile to crossroads. Go straight across and continue for about 4 miles to petrol station, then take 2nd left and continue for 1m. Peaceful site with panoramic views. Dishwashing room, free hot water. Luxury caravans for hire. Open March 15-November 15.

Southleigh Caravan & Camping Park, Modbury, Devon PL21 0SB. *01548 830346.* From A38 turn left past Woodpecker Inn, signed Modbury. Straight ahead at crossroads, ignoring all Modbury signs, after 4 miles turn 2nd left past garage, site 1m on right. Licensed and snack bar. Entertainment. Open Easter-October.

Newton Abbot

Compass Caravans, Higher Brocks Plantation, Teigngrace, Newton Abbot, Devon TQ12 6QZ. *01626 832792.* Mr & Mrs A Setter. Alongside A38 westbound, signposted Teigngrace, entrance 100yd on left. Accessory shop.

Dornafield, Two Mile Oak, Newton Abbot, Devon TQ12 6DD. *01803 812732.* enquiries@dornafield.com. www.dornafield. com. Peter Dewhirst. Take A381 (Newton Abbot to Totnes). In 2m at Two Mile Oak turn right, after half a mile turn left. Site on right after 200yd. Beautiful 14th-century farmhouse location with superb facilities. 60 full service pitches. Quiet but convenient for discerning camper. Graded: 5 stars. Caravan Club appointed, Best of British. Open March 20-October 31.

Lemonford Caravan Park, Bickington, Newton Abbot, Devon TQ12 6JR. *01626 821242/821263.* mark@lemonford. co.uk . www.lemonford.co.uk . Mr & Mrs R Halstead. 3m NE of Ashburton. From Exeter along A38 towards Plymouth, take A382 turn-off, on roundabout take third exit Bickington. From Plymouth take the A383 turn-off to Bickington. Excellent facilities for tourers and tents. Graded: 4 stars. Open mid March-end October.

Lower Aish, Poundsgate, Ashburton, Newton Abbot, Devon TQ13 7NY. *01364 3631229.* Mr & Mrs M Wilkinson. 5m NW of Ashburton on B3357 Ashburton-Tavistock road. On edge of Dartmoor. In small hamlet on edge of good walking country. Good local pub. Open April-October.

Manor Farm Campsite & B&B, Daccombe, Newton Abbot, Devon TQ12 4ST. *01803 328294.* manorfarmdaccombe @ukgateway.net. D J Nicholls. A380 from Newton Abbot to Torquay to Kerswell Gardens. Over roundabout to traffic lights, turn left at lights up the hill. Follow campsite signs. Also provide year round bed and breakfast. Open Easter-October 1.

River Dart Adventures, Holne Park, Ashburton, Newton Abbot, Devon TQ13 7NP. *01364 652511.* enquiries@river -dart.co.uk. www.riverdart.co.uk. Mr Mark Simpson. From Exeter, Plymouth take A38 to Ashburton then follow signs to River Dart Adventures, entrance 1.25m on left. Open Easter-end November.

Twelve Oaks Farm Caravan Park, Twelve Oaks Farm, Teigngrace, Newton Abbot, Devon TQ12 6QT. *01626 352769.* www.twelveoaksfarm.co.uk. A W & A R Gale. A38 Expressway Exeter-Plymouth. About 1.25 miles past RV Teign Bridge into road. Signpost Teigngrace, through village, second drive on left. Sandy beach eight miles. Graded: 4 stars.

Ware Barton, Kingsteighton, Newton Abbot, Devon TQ12 3QQ. *01626 354025.* Mr W T Batting. On A381 Newton Abbot to Teignmouth road 1m E of Kingsteignton. 2.5m W of Teignmouth, 2.5m NE of Newton Abbot. Touring centre in pleasant holiday country. Security gate. Fees on application. Open Easter-October.

Newton Ferrers

Briar Hill Farm Caravan and Camping Park, Newton Ferrers, Devon PL8 1AR. *01752 872252.* Simon & Valerie Lister. From Exeter—A38—To Plymouth. Approximately 30 miles to Wranghton Cross, take A3121 (A379) to Yealmpton, fork left on B3186 to Newton Ferrers. At the green turn right into Briar Hill farm. Open March-November.

Okehampton

Bridestowe Caravan Park, Bridestowe, Okehampton, Devon EX20 4ER. *01837 861261.* Mrs W Young, Mr G Young & Mr M Young. 6m SW of Okehampton. Turn off A30 towards Bridestowe village, follow camping signs. Site on edge of Dartmoor. Ideal for walking, horseriding and fishing. Open March 1-December 31.

Bundu Camping & Caravan Park, Sourton Cross, Okehampton, Devon EX20 4HT. *01837 861611.* bundu sargent@aol.com. www.bundu.co.uk. Mr & Mrs Sargent. 4m SW of Okehampton via A30. Direct access off new sliproad at Sourton Cross. Turn left towards Tavistock A386, then left again 100 yards. Access good, level pitches. In Dartmoor National Park. Open March 14-November 14.

Camping & Caravanning Club Site, Lydford, Okehampton, Devon EX20 4BE. *01822 820275.* www.campingandcaravan ningclub.co.uk. The Camping & Caravanning Club Ltd. 7.5m south west of Okehampton via the A386 towards Tavistock off A30. After 4.25m on A386 turn right opposite Dartmoor Inn on road signposted Lydford. After 0.5m turn right, then fork right to site. Quiet sheltered site. Dogs welcome. Non-members welcome. 70 pitches set in 7.5 acres. Caravans, motor caravans and tents accepted. Open end March-October.

Dartmoor View Holiday Park, Whiddon Down, Okehampton, Devon EX20 2QL. *01647 231545.* info@dart moorview.co.uk. www.dartmoorview.co.uk. S D Cliff & J Cliff. Nearby junction of A30-A382. From M5 (junc 31), proceed along A30 for 17m to first island; turn left, 0.5m on right. Quiet park on edge of Dartmoor. Tourist information. Licensed club. AA 4 pennants. Rose Award park. Graded: 5 stars. Open from March 1-October 31.

Jays Barton, Weeks-in-the-Moor, Okehampton, Devon EX20 4NJ. *01837 87396.* Mrs Wilmott. 5m W of Okehampton on B3218, 1m after hump back bridge. 260-acre dairy farm. Views of Dartmoor. Hedges for shelter. No facilities, only running water.

Olditch Caravan & Camping Park, Sticklepath, Okehampton, Devon EX20 2NT. *01837 840734.* Ian & Helen Howard. 4m E of Okehampton. From Exeter on A30, 1st roundabout. Left exit signpost to Sticklepath, 3 miles. Within National Park, direct access to Moor. Ideal base for touring West Country. Licensed restaurant. TV and games room. Pets welcome. Open March 15-November 4.

Yertiz Caravan & Camping Park, Exeter Road, Okehampton, Devon EX20 1QF. *01837 52281.* yertiz@dial.pipex.com. www.dialspace.dial.pipex.com/yertiz. R & J Jefferies. Small friendly site for caravans, motorcaravans and tents. 0.75-mile from Okehampton town centre. Lovely views to the moors. Ideal for moor walking and touring Devon. About 30 miles to north and south coasts. Holiday home for hire.

Paignton

Barton Pines Inn, Blagdon Road, Paignton, Devon TQ3 3YG. *01803 553350.* Mr D & Mrs V Shearer. Turn right off A380 (Newton Abbot to Torquay) onto A380 (Torbay ring road). In two miles turn right at Preston Down roundabout

DEVON

signposted Berry Pomeroy and Barton Pines, two miles crossroads is signposted Barton Pines. Bar. Restaurant. Heated outdoor pool. Graded: 3 stars. Open March 1-October 31.

Beverley Park Holiday Centre, Goodrington Road, Paignton, Devon TQ4 7JE. 01803 843887. info@beverley-holidays.co.uk . www.beverley-holidays.co.uk . Beverley Parks (Goodrington) Ltd. On the A379 to Brixham, after one mile turn right at Waterside. Site is at top of hill (Goodrington Road), entrance on the left hand side. From the A3022, travelling to Brixham, turn left into Goodrington Road. Holiday site 0.75m from beach. Fees on application. Graded: 5 stars. Open February-November.

Byslades International Camping & Touring Park, Totnes Road, Paignton, Devon TQ4 7PY. 01803 555072. enquiries@bysladestouringpark.co.uk. www.bysladestouringpark.co.uk . Mr & Mrs R R Wedd. Two miles west of Paignton. Situated on A385. Set in 23 acres of beautiful Devon countryside. Level, terraced pitches, excellent amenities. No dogs allowed mid July-end August. Historic town of Totnes and Dartmoor National Park nearby. Open mid May - mid September.

Lower Yalberton Holiday Park, Long Road, Paignton, Devon TQ4 7PH. 01803 558127. P H Burrows. Follow A380 ring road towards Paignton. At traffic lights follow A3022 towards Brixham about one and half miles on see factory on right, garage on left. Turn right into Long Road. Half mile on right. AA 4 pennants. Open May-September.

Paignton Holiday Park, Totnes Road, Paignton, Devon TQ4 7PY. 01803 550504. Ideally situated for Torbay and Dartmoor National Park. Nightly entertainment (Whitsun-September) in the licensed clubhouse. Thatched pub. Dishwashing facilities. Open March-October.

Ramslade Touring Park, Stoke Road, Stoke Gabriel, Paignton, Devon TQ9 6QB. 01803 782575. ramslade@compuserve.com . www.ramslade.co.uk . Derek & Jill Allcock. 3m SW of Paignton. Turn off A385 at Parkers Arms. No dogs mid-July-end August. Children's logland play areas and paddling pool. Heated toilet block. Graded: 5 stars. Open March 23-October 27.

Widend Camping Park, Berry Pomeroy Road, Marldon, Paignton, Devon TQ3 1RT. 01803 550116. Roger & Heather Cowen & Family. Two miles west of Paignton. Three miles to the sea. Spacious site with marvellous scenery. Free hot water. Family room and licensed lounge bar. Takeaway. Large playgound. Families and couples only. No dogs mid-July and August. Graded: 4 stars. Open Easter-October.

Whitehill Holiday Park, Stoke Road, Paignton, Devon TQ4 7PF. 01803 782338. enquiries@whitehillfarm.co.uk www.whitehillfarm.co.uk Tenison & Co Ltd. Two miles west of Paignton via A385 Totnes road. Turn at 'Parkers Arms' 0.5m from Paignton Zoo, signposted to Stoke Gabriel. Site is 1m. Well-equipped site with children's playground, licensed bar, family room. Open May-September.

Plymouth

Brixton Camping Site, Venn Farm, Brixton, Plymouth, Devon PL8 2AX. 01752 880378. Mr B H Cane. 3m SE of Plymouth on A379 to Kingsbridge, W end of Brixton. Easy reach of sea and moors, convenient for Roscoff ferry. Shops and pub in village.

Pilgrim's Rest, 41 Knighton Road, Wembury, Plymouth, Devon PL9 0EA. 01752 863429. Mrs D Manley. Camping and caravanning certificated site for 5 caravans etc. and separate area for tents available at Pilgrim's Rest coastal village of Wembury in an area of outstanding beauty. Sea views. Beautiful walks. 5 mins drive from beach. On main bus route. 6m from Plymouth. Phone for more details and brochure. Open May-September.

Riverside Caravan Park, Lonbridge Road, Marsh Mills, Plympton, Plymouth, Devon PL6 8LD. 01752 344122. info@riversidecaravanpark.com. www.riversidecaravanpark.com. Mr I Gray. 3m from Plymouth. Fees on application.

Salcombe

Alston Farm Camping Ground, Salcombe, Devon TQ7 3BJ. 01548 561260. alston.campsite@ukgateway.net. www.welcome.to/alstonfarm. Mr P W Shepherd. 0.75m off Malborough to Salcombe road (A381). 2m N of Salcombe. Sheltered, flat site. Open March-October.

Bolberry House Farm Caravanning & Camping Park, Bolberry, Marlborough, Salcombe, Devon TQ7 3DY. 01548 561251/560926. bolberry.house@virgin.net. www.bolberryparks.co.uk. Dudley & Jessie Stidston. Quiet, family run park amid outstanding coastal countryside, good access to superb cliff walks and all boating facilities with safe sandy beaches 1 mile. Children's play area and barn. Dogs welcome with separate exercising paddock. Low season discounts with special rates for over-50s. AA 3 pennants, graded 3 stars. Please book early. Open Easter-October.

Higher Rew Farm, Malborough, Kingsbridge, Salcombe, Devon TQ7 3DW. 01548 842681. enquiries@higherrew.co.uk. www.higherrew.co.uk. Mr J S Squire. 2.5m W of Salcombe. At Malborough village. Turn right, follow signs for Soar then left at sign for Combe and South Sands. Rural situation, easy reach of beaches. Brochure on application. Open Easter-September.

Sun Park Caravan & Camping, Soar Mill Cove, Malborough, Salcombe, Devon TQ7 3DS. 01548 561378. bj.sweetman@talk21.com. www.sun-park.co.uk. Mrs B J Sweetman. On entering village of Malborough (on Kingsbridge to Salcombe road) turn sharp right signposted Soar. Site 1.5m down road on right hand-side. Walking distance of sandy cove. Peaceful site surrounded by National Trust land. Open Easter-September.

Seaton

Manor Farm Camping & Caravan Site, Seaton Down Hill, Seaton, Devon EX12 2JA. 01297 21524. Mr J M Salter. 4 miles west of Lyme Regis on A3052. Left at Tower Cross on Seaton Down Hill. 0.25m on left. Quiet, family-run farm site with beautiful views of Lyme Bay and Axe Valley. Only 5 minutes from beach. Modern facilities. No reservations required for tents. Open Easter-October 31.

DEVON

Sidmouth

Kingsdown Tail Caravan & Camping Park, Salcombe Regis, Sidmouth, Devon EX10 0PD. *01297 680313.* info@kingsdowntail.co.uk. www.kingsdowntail.co.uk. Mr I J McKenzie-Edwards. Two miles east of Sidford on the A3052. Off-licence on site. Quiet, level, sheltered family run park. Ideally located to explore East Devon's unspoiled coast and countryside.

🚐 🏠 🗻 🗷 ⊙ ⊙ 🛎 🛢 🔦 🚻 ∠ 🚲 ✓ ∪ ⚡ 🛇 ⛵ ⚓

Oakdown Touring & Holiday Home Park, Weston, Sidmouth, Devon EX10 0PH. *01297 680387.* oakdown @btinternet.com. www.bestcaravanpark.co.uk. Mr & Mrs R Franks. On the A3052 Sidford to Lyme Regis road, three miles east of Sidford. Signposted with international camping and caravan signs. Caravan site with space for tents. De-luxe centrally-heated amenities. Field trail to world famous Donkey Sanctuary. Near National Trust coastline. Alarmed caravan storage. Brochure with pleasure. Takeaway meals, shops, cafe/restaurant all available nearby. Open March 27-October 31.

🚐 🏠 🚽 🗻 🗷 ⚒ 🗻 ⊙ ⊙ 🛎 🛢 🔦 🚻 🅿 ∠ 🚲 ♿ 🛇 ✓ ⚡ 🛇 ⛵ ⚓

Salcombe Regis Caravan & Camping Park, Sidmouth, Devon EX10 0JH. *01395 514303.* info@salcombe-regis.co.uk. www.salcombe-regis.co.uk. Mr D J Boyce. Signposted off A3052. Exeter to Lyme Regis coast road. Situated in an area of outstanding natural beauty on the Heritage coast. Suitable base for exploring rural east Devon. Brochure available. Graded: 4 stars. Open Easter-November.

🚐 🏠 🚽 🗻 🗷 ⊙ ⊙ 🛎 🛢 🔦 🚻 🅿 ∠ 🚲 ♿ 🛇 ✓ ∪ ⚡ 🛇

South Brent

Cheston Caravan Park, Wrangaton Road, South Brent, Devon TQ10 9HF. *01364 72586.* enquiries@chestoncaravan park.co.uk. www.chestoncaravanpark.co.uk. E Gourley. A38 Exeter, leave at slip road marked Wrangaton Cross. Turn right at top of slip road. Follow signs. From Plymouth take South Brent Woodpecker slip road, go under A38, rejoin A38, follow direction from Exeter. Nice level site. Open March 15-January 15.

🚐 🏠 🚽 🗷 🅰 ⊙ ⊙ 🛎 🛢 🚻 🔦 ≋ 🅿 🛇 ✓ ∪ ⚡ 🛇

South Molton

Molland Camping & Caravan Park, Blackcock Inn, Molland, South Molton, Devon EX36 3NW *01769 550297.* Mr Allan Ball. From the north Devon link road between Barnstaple and J27 of M5, follow the camping signs towards Molland. A character stonebuilt family inn attached to a caravan site set in a glorious valley close to the village of Molland and Exmoor.

🚐 🏠 🚽 🗷 🅰 🗙 ⊙ ⊙ 🛎 🛢 ≋ 🔦 🚻 🅿 ≋ ✿ ∠ 🅿 🛇 🚲 ✓ ∪

Romansleigh Holiday Park, Odam Hill, Romansleigh, South Molton, Devon EX36 4NB. *01769 550259.* romhols@ lineone.net. John & Heather Gazeley. 4.5m S of South Molton on B3137. 14 acre rural site close to Exmoor, within easy reach of resorts. Licensed bar. Snooker, pool and skittle alley. Outdoor swimming pool, games room. Pet animals. Open March 15-October 31.

🚐 🏠 🚽 🗷 🅰 ⊙ ⊙ 🛎 🛢 ≋ 🔦 🚻 🅿 ∠ 🛇 ∪ ⚡

The Black Cock Inn & Camping Park, Molland, South Molton, Devon EX36 3NW. *01769 550297.* Mr & Mrs A W Bull. 4m east of South Molton. 2m off A361. Take B3227 in direction of Bampton. Following The Black Cock Inn signs on A361.

🚐 🏠 🚽 🗷 🗻 🗙 ⊙ 🗻 🛎 🛢 ≋ 🔦 🚻 🅿 ≋ ✿ ∠ 🅿 🛢 🚲 🛇 ✓ ∪ ⚡ 🛇 ⛵ ⚓

Tavistock

Dartmoor Country Holidays, Magpie Leisure Park, Bedford Bridge, Horrabridge, Tavistock, Devon PL20 7RY. *01822 852651.* On A386 Tavistock to Plymouth 2.5m SE of Tavistock. Beautiful wooded site (10 acres) on edge of Dartmoor National Park alongside river Walkham. 30 pitches. Manager: Mrs R Berks. Open March-November.

🚐 🏠 🗷 ⊙ ⊙ 🛎 🛢 🔦 🚻 ∠ 🅿 🛇 🚲 ✓ ∪

Harford Bridge Holiday Park, Peter Tavy, Tavistock, Devon PL19 9LS. *01822 810349.* enquiry@harfordbridge.co.uk. www.harfordbridge.co.uk. Mr & Mrs G Williamson. Two miles from Tavistock, off the A386 Okehampton, take Peter Tavy turn. Family run park in Dartmoor National Park, by river Tavy offering riverside camping. Level and sheltered. Holiday caravans for hire. Rose Award, David Bellamy Gold Conservation Award. Graded: 4 stars Open mid March-mid November.

🚐 🏠 🗻 ⊙ ⊙ 🛎 🛢 🔦 🚻 🅿 ∠ 🛇 🚲 ✓ ∪ ⚡ 🛇

Higher Longford Caravan & Camping Park, Moorshop, Tavistock, Devon PL19 9LQ. *01822 613360.* stay@higherlong ford.co.uk. www.higherlongford.co.uk. Messrs. Deane & Collins. From Tavistock take B3357 to Princetown. 2.5 miles on RHS before hill onto the moors. Friendly family run park with excellent facilities. Ideal for touring Dartmoor. Sheltered all-weather pitches. Dogs welcome.

🚐 🏠 🗷 🚽 🗻 🗙 ⊙ ⊙ 🛎 🛢 🔦 🚻 🅿 ≋ ✿ ∠ 🅿 🛇 🚲 ✓ ∪ ⚡ 🛇

Langstone Manor Caravan & Camping Site, Moortown, Tavistock, Devon PL19 9JZ. *01822 613371.* web@langstone-manor.co.uk. www.langstone-manor.co.uk. David & Jane Kellett. Take B3357 from Tavistock towards Princetown for 2m. Follow signs. Campsite is set within mature grounds of Manor House. Clean facilities, lounge bar, meals, games room. Quiet secluded site. Open March 15-November 13.

🚐 🏠 🗷 🚽 🗻 🗙 ⊙ ⊙ 🛎 🛢 🔦 🚻 🅿 ∠ 🅿 🛇 🚲 🛇 ✓ ∪ ⚡ 🛇

DEVON

Woodovis Park, Gulworthy, Tavistock, Devon PL19 8NY. *01822 832968.* info@woodovis.com. www.woodovis.com. John & Dorothy Lewis. 3.5m W of Tavistock via A390 Liskeard road. Turn right at crossroads signposted Lamerton. Park sign 1.5m on left. Quiet, rural 5-star park with lovely views. Heated indoor pool, sauna and spa pool. Excellent facilities. Bread and croissants baked daily on site. Games room, mini golf. Play area. Dogs welcome on leads. Open April-October.

Teignmouth

Coast View Holiday Park, Torquay Road, Shaldon, Teignmouth, Devon TQ14 0BG. *01626 872392.* info@coast-view.co.uk. www.coast-view.co.uk. Mr M Collett. 1m S of Teignmouth, 0.5m through Shaldon on A379. Superb views of Lyme Bay. Families and married couples only. Fees on application. Graded: 4 stars. Open March-October.

Wear Farm, Newton Road, Bishopsteignton, Teignmouth, Devon TQ14 9PT. *01626 775249/779265/775015.* E S Coaker & Co. On A381 between Teignmouth and Newton Abbot. 3m W of Teignmouth. Pleasant site beside river Teign with unequalled views over the estuary. Swimming pool nearby. Small play area. Fees and free brochure on application. Open Easter-October 31.

Tiverton

Minnows Caravan Club Site, Sampford Peverell, Tiverton, Devon EX16 7EN. *01884 821770.* www.ukparks.co.uk/minnows. Zig & Krystyna Grochala. Leave M5 at Junction 27 and take A361 Barnstaple. After 0.25 miles take slip road on left and follow brown signs. Small site surrounded by farmland. Adjacent Grand Western Canal. Fishing, birdwatching, walking and cycling. 0.5m to pub. Non-members welcome. Open March-November.

West Middlewick Farm, Nomansland, Tiverton, Devon EX16 8NP. *01884 860286.* Ms Stella Gibson. 1m E of Witheridge on old A373 (now B3137) to Tiverton. Central for touring. Good access. Secluded, level, meadow with view towards Exmoor. Genuine working farm with informal atmosphere. Operated for over 65 years under the same family management.

Zeacombe House Caravan Club Site, East Anstey, Tiverton, Devon EX16 9JU. *01398 341279.* Mr & Mrs P L Keeble. On B3227 Bampton/South Molton road. Level lawn site with panoramic views across Exmoor. Good centre for touring Exmoor and Somerset/Devon borders. Heated, modern shower block. Hairdriers. Adults only. Open March 9-October 31.

Torquay

Widdicombe Farm Tourist Park, The Ring Road (A380), Compton, Torquay, Devon TQ3 1ST. *01803 558325.* Mr & Mrs Glynn. A380, 2.5m from Torquay and Paignton. Lovely views; park landscaped to provide spacious, level pitches. Very easy access, no narrow country lanes. Luxurious facilities, free hot water. Launderette and baby bathroom. Bar & restaurant. Bargain breaks from £40 per 7 nights. Open mid March-mid November.

Torrington

Smytham Manor Leisure, Smytham Manor, Little Torrington, Torrington, Devon EX38 8PU. *01805 622110.* info@smytham.co.uk. www.smytham.co.uk. Great Leisure Ltd.

2m S of Torrington towards Okehampton on A386. 25 acres of beautiful grounds with ponds and water fowl. Level and gently sloping. Laundry facilities. Showers and shaver points. Play area. Games room. Restaurant, licensed bar. Dogs welcome. Pitch andputt. Outdoor pool. Open March-October.

Totnes

Edeswell Farm, Rattery, South Brent, Totnes, Devon TQ10 9LN. *01364 72177.* welcome@edeswellfarm.co.uk. www.edeswellfarm.co.uk. David & Christine Ashworth & Family. 1m from Marvey Head junction on A38. Small family-run site. Ideal for Dartmoor and South Hams. Dogs welcome. Large indoor heated pool, bar, bar food, animal centre.

Higher Well Farm Holiday Park, Stoke Gabriel, Totnes, Devon TQ9 6RN. *01803 782289.* Mr & Mrs John & Liz Ball. 4m W of Paignton via A385 to Totnes. Left at Parkers Arms Hotel. After 1.5m turn left again to site 200yds. 4m from Torbay beaches and 1m from river Dart. Open Easter-October.

Webland Farm Holiday Park, Avonwick, South Brent, Totnes, Devon TQ10 9EX. *01364 73273.* Mr & Mrs T Horne. Leave the A38 at Marley Head (A385) and follow Webland signs from roundabout. Small secluded park in south Devon countryside with breathtaking views of Dartmoor. Within easy reach of coast and main holiday resorts. Open April-October.

Umberleigh

Camping & Caravanning Club Site - Umberleigh, Over Weir, Umberleigh, Devon EX37 9DU. *01769 560009.* www.umberleigh-camping-caravanning-devon.co.uk. The Camping & Caravanning Club Ltd. On A377 from Barnstaple turn right at 'Umberleigh' nameplate. Play area. Central for touring N Devon coast and Exmoor. Plenty of space for ball games and tennis. Dogs welcome. 60 pitches in 3 acres. Non-members welcome. Caravans, motor caravans and tents accepted. Open April-October.

Woolacombe

Europa Park, Station Road, Woolacombe, Devon EX34 7AN. *01271 870159.* Full facilities with superb camping. Licensed clubhouse. Open April-October.

Golden Coast Holiday Village Woolacombe, Devon EX34 7HW. *01271 870343.* goodtimes@woolacombe.com. www.woolacombe.com. Woolacombe Bay Holiday Parcs. Leave the M5 at junction 27, take the A361 Barnstaple to Mullacott Cross. First exit to Woolacombe. Follow signs. Three pools, tennis, cabaret, kid club. Bus to beach. Rose Award. Conservation Award. Graded 4 stars. Open February-January.

Little Roadway Farm Camping Park, Woolacombe, Devon EX34 7HL. *01271 870313.* Steve & Vanessa Malin. Barnstaple to Ilfracombe at Mullacott Cross roundabout, turn towards Woolacombe. After two miles turn left on to the B3231 Georgeham/Croyde road at Roadway Corner. Entrance is on left after about 2.5 miles. Open March-November.

North Morte Farm Caravan & Camping Park, Mortehoe, Woolacombe, Devon EX34 7EG. *01271 870381.* info@north mortefarm.co.uk. www.northmortefarm.co.uk. Mr R C Easterbrook. From the A361 at Mullacott Cross. B3343 to Woolacombe and Mortehoe. Holiday park located near beach, and set in beautiful countryside. Colour brochure and fees available on application. Graded: 3 stars. Open Easter-October.

Twitchen Parc, Mortehoe, Woolacombe, Devon EX34 7ES. *01271 870343.* goodtimes@woolacombe.com. www.woola combe. com. Woolacombe Bay Holiday Parcs. A361 from Barnstaple, left on B3343, right to Mortehoe. Site on left in grounds of Twitchen House. Site within easy reach of sandy beach. Fees on application. Graded: 4 stars. Open April-October.

Warcombe Farm Camping Park, Station Road, Mortehoe, Woolacombe, Devon EX34 7EJ. *01271 870690.* Mr & Mrs Grafton. Turn left off A361 Barnstaple-Ilfracombe on to B3343 to Woolacombe. After 2m turn right onto unclassified road 'Mortehoe'. Site 1st on right in less than 1 mile. 19 acres landscaped land. Superb sea views. Family run. Open Easter-October.

Woolacombe Bay Holiday Village, Sandy Lane, Woolacombe, Devon EX34 7AH. *01271 870343.* www.woolacombe.co.uk. Woolacombe Bay Holiday Parcs. 0.5m NE of Woolacombe. On B3343 from Mullacott Cross on A361. Bear right to Mortehoe, 0.5m to entrance of site on left. Indoor pool. Entertainment. Health suite. Golf. Graded: 4 stars. Open May-September.

Woolacombe Sands Holiday Park, Beach Road, Woolacombe, Devon EX34 7AF. *01271 870569.* lifesabeach@woolacombe.sands.co.uk. www.woola combe.sands.co.uk. Richards Holidays. Set in beautiful countryside overlooking the sea and Woolacombe's golden sands. First-class facilities for tents and tourers. Licensed club and nightly entertainment. Children's club May to September. Graded: 3 stars. Open April 1-October 31.

DORSET

Bere Regis

Rowlands Wait Touring Park, Rye Hill, Bere Regis, Dorset BH20 7LP. *01929 472727.* camping@rowlandswait.co.uk. www.rowlandswait.co.uk. Mr Cargill. In Bere Regis take Wool-Bovington Camp road for 0.75m. At top of Rye Hill turn right, site 300yd. Situated in an area of outstanding natural beauty. Telephone for free brochure. Graded: 3 stars. Open March-October; open winter by arrangement.

Blandford

Lady Bailey Caravan Park, Winterborne, Whitechurch, Blandford, Dorset DT11 0HS. *01258 880829.* John Davis. On A354 Salisbury to Blandford road, at Winterborne Whitechurch. Open March-End of January.

'The Inside Park', Blandford Forum, Dorset DT11 9AD. *01258 453719.* inspark@aol.com. http://members.aol. com/inspark/inspark. Mr & Mrs W J Cooper. 2m south-west of Blandford Forum. Set in peaceful rural surroundings with first-class facilities. Children's play area. AA 3 pennants. RAC appointed. Open Easter-end October.

Rowlands Wait Touring Park

Rye Hill, Bere Regis, Dorset BH20 7LP
Tel/Fax: 01929 47 27 27
www.rowlandswait.co.uk   info@rowlandswait.co.uk

This is a family run park situated in an area of outstanding natural beauty, awash with primroses and bluebells in the spring and a paradise for bird and nature lovers. It is a peaceful site flanked by heathland on one side and views towards the Purbecks and the village of Bere Regis from other points. It is ideally situated for a host of attractions and places of interest while Monkey World and Bovington Tank Museum being within 10 mins. drive, scenic walks and cycles ways are all close to hand.

The park has 71 touring pitches with 48 of these having electric points.

A separate area is available for rallies. There is an on site shop with general provisions, an ice pack exchange service, color gas and camping gaz sales, a games room and a childrens play area. There is a large amenities block where showers are free. Member of Countryside Discovery, in the top 100 parks, AA 3 pennant, David Bellamy gold award.

2003 prices: Tents £7.30-£10.30. Caravans £10.30-£12.30 (inc.elec). Motorvans £10.30-£12.30 (inc.elec) Increase due 2004

DORSET

Bournemouth

St Leonards Farm Caravan & Camping Site, West Moors, Ferndown, Bournemouth, Dorset BH22 0AQ. *01202 872637.* james@love5.fsnet.co.uk. www.st-leonardsfarm.co.uk. W E Love & Son. Five miles west of Ringwood. On the A31 opposite Texaco Garage east of Tricketts Cross. Holidays or overnight stop, easy reach of Bournemouth. Restaurant and Pubs nearby. Fees on application. Graded: 3 stars. Open Easter-September.

Bridport

Binghams Farm Touring Caravan Park, Melplash, Bridport, Dorset DT6 3TT. *01308 488234.* binghamsfarm@hotmail.com. www.binghamsfarm.co.uk. Roy & Barbara Philpott. Turn off A35 in Bridport at roundabout on to A3066 (signpost Beaminster). In one and half miles turn left into Farm Road. Award-winning adult only park with excellent modern heated facilities. Views over Dorset's Hidden Valley yet only three miles from coast. Graded: 4 stars.

Coastal Caravan Park, Annings Lane, Burton Bradstock, Bridport, Dorset DT6 4QP. *01308 897361.* coastal@wdch.co.uk. www.westdorsetleisureholidays.com.uk. West Dorset Leisure Holidays. 3m SE of Bridport. Weymouth road to Burton Bradstock village turn left Anchor Hotel, 200 metres 2nd right. Flat, well-drained country site, 1m from sea. Open May-October.

Cummins Farm, Penn Cross, Charmouth, Bridport, Dorset. Mr B P Lugg. 1m W of Charmouth. W on A35 through Charmouth. Turn left on to A3052 after 0.5m (signposted Lyme Regis). At top of hill turn right in to lane. Penn Cross is next crossroad after 200yds. Sheltered site with good views. 1m from coast. Open Easter-September.

Eype House Caravan & Camping Park, Eype, Bridport, Dorset DT6 6AL. *01308 424903.* enquiries@eypehouse.co.uk. www.eypehouse.co.uk. Sue & Graham Dannan & Keith Mundy. Off A35 to Honiton, take turning to Eype, then the turning to Eype's Mouth. Follow lane down to the bottom, entrance to park on right. Open Easter-mid October.

Freshwater Beach Holiday Park, Burton Bradstock, Bridport, Dorset DT6 4PT. *01308 897317.* enquiries@fbhp.co.uk. www.fbhp.co.uk. Mr R Condliffe. On the B3157 Weymoutn to Bridport road. Private beach. Amusements. Club. Entertainment. Takeaway food. Swimming pools. Riding. Laundrette. Golf course adjoining site. Licensed restaurant, 3 bars. Play area. Open March 19-November 14.

Golden Cap Caravan & Camping Park, Seatown, Chideock, Bridport, Dorset DT6 6JX. *01308 422139.* holidays@wdlh.co.uk. www.wdlh.co.uk. West Dorset Leisure Holidays Ltd. 3.5m W of Bridport to Lyme Regis. In Chideock village turn S off A35 opposite church. Holiday park near beach. Coastline suitable for walking. Fees on application. Open March-November.

Highlands End Farm Caravan Park, Eype, Bridport, Dorset DT6 6AR. *01308 422139.* holidays@wdlh.co.uk. www.wdlh.co.uk. From Bridport on road to Lyme Regis (A35). After 1m take road S to Eype. First left, second right, first entrance on left. 1.5m W of Bridport. Quiet. Choice of 2 beaches. Fees by arrangement. Rose Award. Open April-October.

The Travellers Rest, Dorchester Road, Bridport, Dorset DT6 4PJ. *01308 459503.* www.thetravellersrest.net. Mrs E Shorney. 3m E of Bridport via A35 Dorchester road. Convenient for many places of interest. Panoramic views. Fishing, walking, bird-watching. Shops, beach 3miles. 6 van site. Caravans only. Adults only. Open March 1-October 31.

Uploders Farm, Dorchester Road, Bridport, Dorset DT6 4NZ. *01308 423380.* Mr S R Sheppard. 3m E of Bridport on A35. Holiday site. Open July and August.

West Bay Holiday Park, West Bay, Bridport, Dorset DT6 4HB. *01308 459491.* parkdeanenquiries@parkdean.com. www.parkdean.com. Parkdean Holidays Plc. 2m S of Bridport. From A35 at Bridport turn S at Town Hall. Take B3157 to site. Mini golf. Indoor pool, adventure playground and free kids' club. Family club and bar. Graded: 3 stars. Open March to end-October.

Charmouth

Camping & Caravanning Club Site - Charmouth, Monkton Wylde Farm, Charmouth, Dorset DT6 6DB. *01297 32965.* www.campingandcaravanningclub.co.uk. The Camping & Caravanning Club. On A358 from north signpost for Dorchester A35, take 1st left after Dorset boundary sign, site on left. Close to Lyme Regis. Good for walking and fossil hunting. Dogs welcome. Non-members welcome. Caravans, motor caravans and tents accepted. 80 pitches set in 12 acres. David Bellamy Gold Conservation Award. Open March-October.

Manor Farm Holiday Centre, Charmouth, Dorset DT6 6QL. *01297 560226.* rloosmore@freenet.co.uk. www.manorfarm holidaycentre.co.uk. R C Loosmore & Son. Enter Charmouth from east end of by pass. Manor Farm half mile on right at bridge. Roomy site, easy reach of beach. Bar. Caravans for hire. Fees on application.

Newlands Camping Site, Charmouth, Dorset DT6 6RB. *01297 560259.* Newlands Holiday Park. 0.25m E of Charmouth on A35 towards Bridport. Easy reach coast. Fossil-hunting area. Fees on application.

Wood Farm Caravan & Camping Park, Axminster Road, Charmouth, Dorset DT6 6BT. *01297 560697.* holidays@ woodfarm.co.uk. www.woodfarm.co.uk. Macbennet Ltd. On the A35 west of Charmouth. Beautiful views, less than one mile to the sea. Graded 'Excellent'. Open March-end October.

Christchurch

Holmsley Caravan & Camping Site, (Forestry Commission), Forest Road, Thorney Hill, Holmsley, Christchurch, Dorset BH23 7EQ. *01313 146505.* fe.holidays@forestry.gsi.gov.uk. www.forestholidays.co.uk. Forestry Commission (Forest Holidays). Off A35 Lyndhurst-Christchurch road, eight miles south west of Lyndhurst. Short drive to coast, ideal for the beach. Booking essential. Brochure line 01313 340066. Open March-November.

Mount Pleasant Touring Park, Matchams Lane, Hurn, Christchurch, Dorset BH23 6AW. *01202 475474.* enq@mount-pleasant-cc.co.uk. www.mount-pleasant-cc.co.uk. Mr P Dunn. 3.5m N of Christchurch. Take A338 Ringwood to Bournemouth. Follow signs to Hurn. At Hurn roundabout follow signs to Matchams for one mile. Small, sheltered, level site on the edge of the New Forest and four miles from the beach. Superb amenities block. Graded: 5 stars. AA 4 pennants. Open March-October.

Corfe Castle

Knitson Tourers Site, Knitson Farm, Corfe Castle, Dorset BH20 5JB. *01929 425121.* Mrs Jane Helfer. A351 to Swanage, first left opposite Royal Oak, left at T-junction, proceed for half a mile, site on left. Quiet, family site on working farm for self-contained units. Own sanitation necessary. One and half miles to Swanage beach. 3 miles Studland Beach. Excellent walking area. Open Easter-October.

Woody Hyde Camp Site, Valley Road, Corfe Castle, Dorset BH20 5HT. *01929 480274.* www.woodyhyde.co.uk. Laurence Jahn. On the A351 between Corfe and Swanage on the right hand side approx 1 mile from Corfe. In the heart of Purbeck country with Swanage Steam Railway nearby. Open Easter-End September.

Dorchester

Clay Pigeon Tourist Park, Wardon Hill, Evershot, Dorchester, Dorset DT2 9PW. *01935 83492.* Mr G Brook & Mr B Crook. Eight miles north of Dorchester on the A37 towards Yeovil. Two miles south of Holywell. Ideal touring centre or overnight stop. Dogs welcome. Listed on MacMillan Way footpath. Well-stocked shop on site. Go-karting and clay pigeon shooting nearby.

Giants Head Caravan & Camping Park, Old Sherborne Road, Cerne Abbas, Dorchester, Dorset DT2 7TR. *01300 341242.* Mr R M Paul. From Dorchester into town avoiding bypass from top of town roundabout take Sherborne road approx. 500yds fork right at Loders Garage signposted. From Cerne Abbas take Buckland Newton road. Touring centre or overnight London or Midlands to West Country. Dogs allowed. Graded: 2 stars. Open March-October.

Morn Gate Caravan Park, Bridport Road, Dorchester, Dorset DT2 9DS. *01305 889284.* morngate@ukonline.co.uk. www.morngate.co.uk. Attn: Mr Jackson A & M Properties (Dorset) Ltd. Located three miles west of Dorchester on the A35. Luxury Scandanavian style chalets, lodges and modern caravans. Small exclusive park set in the heart of Thomas Hardy countryside. Within short drive of Weymouth and other coastal resorts. Graded: 3 stars. Open March 16-January 12.

Sandyholme Holiday Park, Moreton Road, Owermoigne, Dorchester, Dorset DT2 8HZ. smeatons@sandyholme.co.uk. www.sandyholme.co.uk. Mike & Libby Smeaton. Minor road N of A352 6m SE of Dorchester. Site is 1m N of turning. Quiet family park in Hardy countryside with all amenities. Games room, play park and licensed bar with food available (open peak times). Central for Weymouth, Dorchester and Lulworth Cove. Open Easter or April 1-end October.

Warmwell Country Touring Park, Warmwell, Dorchester, Dorset DT2 8JD. *01305 852313.* cserve@warwell.touring. 20m.com. www.warmwell.touring.20m.com Mundays Caravan Parks Ltd. The park is on the B3390 between A35 & A352 within six miles of the historical town of Dorchester and Weymouth beaches. Visit the Jurassic Coast line, England only natural World Heritage site. Facilities include a resident manager, with cctv and electronic barrier access, licensed family bar, children's play area, laundrette, heated toilet blocks. South-west Tourism 4 stars.

Gillingham

Thorngrove Camping & Caravan Park, Common Mead Lane, Gillingham, Dorset SP8 4RE. *01747 821221.* P Richardson. Located one mile outside Gillingham, well signposted. Quiet, fishing, nearby shops and post office.

turn right into Watermill Lane. Site 1m on left signposted. Quiet farm site in countryside. Level sheltered pitches within easy reach of Battle, Hastings and Eastbourne. Large tent field at peak times. Graded: 4 stars. Open April-October.

🚐🏤📵☵⊙♁🔥🐄♦🏠🗓♖🚿🦽 L ♀ ↙ ∪ ⤳

> **Kloofs Caravan Park, Sandhurst Lane, Whydown, Bexhill-on-Sea, East Sussex TN39 4RG.** *01424 842839.* camping@kloofs.ndirect.co.uk. www.kloofs.ndirect.co. uk. Mr T Griggs & Mrs H Griggs. From Bexhill take A259 west to Little Common roundabout, turn right into Peartree Lane, 1m turn left to Whydown, signs to site. Quiet country site about 2m from sea. Dogs welcome. Graded 5 stars.
>
> 🚐🏤📵🛝🦽🐄⊙♁🔥🐄♦🏠🗓❀♨▲↙↙∪⤳

Crowborough

Camping & Caravanning Club Site - Crowborough, Goldsmith Recreation Ground, Crowborough, East Sussex TN6 2TN. *01892 664827.* www.campingandcaravanning club.co.uk The Camping & Caravanning Club Ltd. 90 pitches set in 13-acre site. Leave the M25 at exit 5, take A21 to Tonbridge, then A26 through Tunbridge Wells to the northern outskirts of Crowborough. Turn into leisure centre main entrance. Site is on the edge of Ashdown Forest and also adjacent to a sports centre. Caravans, motor caravans and tents accepted. Non-members welcome. Well-equipped kitchen available. Open March-December.

🚐🏤📵🛝🦽🐄⊙♁🔥🐄♖🗓♖🚿 L ↙↙∪⤳

Hailsham

Chicheley Farm, Hempstead Lane, Hailsham, East Sussex. *01323 841253.* Mr & Mrs T Harvey. 1m NW of Hailsham alongside A22 on Hempstead Lane. Flat, well-drained site. Storage facilities availble. Open Easter-November.

🚐🛝🦽🐄🗓🚿▲↙↙∪

The Old Mill Caravan Park, Chalvington Road, Golden Cross, Hailsham, East Sussex BN27 3SS. *01825 872532.* www.ukparks.co.uk/oldmill. D W & D B Bourne. 4 miles NW of Hailsham. Turn left off A22 just before Golden Cross Inn, if travelling from Hailsham or Eastbourne, or right from London direction. 150 yards off A22 on Chalvington Road. Flat, sheltered site with easy access for 8 tourers and 18 holiday caravan (privately owned). Open Easter/April 1-October 31.

🚐🏤📵🛝⊙♁🔥🐄♖🗓 L ↙↙✓

Hastings

Shearbarn Holiday Park, Barley Lane, Hastings, East Sussex TN35 5DX. *01424 423583.* shearbarn@pavilion.co.uk. www. shearbarn.co.uk. Mr M & Mrs J Patten. 1.5m E of Hastings via A259 towards Rye. Turn right onto Harold Road at Stables theatre, right after 500yd into Gurth Road left into Barley Lane, site 120yds on right. Period of opening and fees on application. Graded: 4 stars. Graded: 3 stars. Open March 1-January 15.

🚐🏤⚡📵🛝🦽🐄⊙🔥🐄♖🗓♖🚿↙↙∪⤳⤳

Stalkhurst Camping & Caravan Park, Ivyhouse Lane, Hastings, East Sussex TN35 4NN. *01424 439015.* stalkhurst@bt.internet.com. Mr & Mrs D R Young. 2.5m from centre of Hastings via A259. At lights turn left on B2093, after 0.5m Ivyhouse Lane is on right. From the A21, turn left onto the B2093. Gently sloping, well-sheltered site 2.5m from sea. Suitable touring centre for Kent and E Sussex. Riding and bowls available nearby. Free swimming on site. Static caravans for hire. Takeaway meals nearby. Graded: 3 stars. Open March 1 to mid-January.

🚐🏤📵🛝⊙♁🔥≋♦🐄♖🗓♖🚿 L ♀▲↙↙∪⤳⤳🦽⤳

Heathfield

Greenviews Caravan Park, Co-Partnership Caravan Assoc Ltd. Burwash Road, Broad Oak, Heathfield, East Sussex TN21 8RT. *01435 863531.* Situated 1.5m east of Heathfield on north side of A265. Privately-owned site, maintained to high standard. Open April 1-October 31.

🚐🏤📵🛝🦽⊙♁🔥🐄♖⤶ L

Horam

> **Horam Manor Touring Park, Horam, East Sussex TN21 0YD.** *01435 813662.* camp@horam-manor.co.uk. www.horam-manor.co.uk. M T Harmer. On the A267 south of Horam Village, 10m north of Eastbourne, Three miles south of Heathfield. Tranquil, rural site with lovely views, excellent facilities, plenty to do. Free hot water. Mother and toddler room. Cafe nearby. Graded: 4 stars. Open March-October.
>
> 🚐🏤📵🛝🦽🐄⊙♁🔥🐄♖🗓♖↙↙∪🦽

Pevensey

Bayview Caravan & Camping Park, Old Martello Road, Pevensey Bay, East Sussex BN24 6DX. *01323 768688.* holidays @bay-view.co.uk. www.bay-view.co.uk. Michael & Diana Adams. Award-winning park next to beach. 2002 David Bellamy Gold Conservation Award. On A259 Eastbourne to Pevensey Bay. Graded: 5 stars. Open end March-October.

🚐🏤📵🛝⊙♁🔥🐄♖🗓♖ L ♀▲↙↙⤳⤳

Camping & Caravanning Club Site - Normans Bay, Pevensey, East Sussex BN24 6PR. *01323 761190.* www.campingandcaravanningclub.co.uk. The Camping & Caravanning Club Ltd. 3-acre site with 200 pitches. From Eastbourne take A259 through Pevensey Bay, along beach road. Site is north of beach road near Martello Tower, next to own privately-owned beach. Non-members welcome. Caravans, motor caravans and tents accepted. Open March-November.

🚐🏤📵🛝🦽🐄⊙♁🔥🐄♦🗓♖🚿 L 🦽⤳🦽

Robertsbridge

Lordine Court Caravan Park, Staplecross, Robertsbridge, East Sussex TN32 5TS. *01580 830209/01580 831792.* enq@lordine-court.co.uk. www.lordine-court.co.uk. Miss C Horvath. 10m N of Hastings. From London take the A21 to Johns Cross. Bear left to Cripps Corner, left again on to the

B2165 through Staplecross. Signposted Lordine Court. Clubhouse with two bars and amusement room. Restaurant. Swimming pool. Fees on application. Open April-October.

🌮🕹🚹🍴🍽🖳✕⊙🌣🔥🛢≋🔦🍿🍽🛎 *L* ♀ ♂ ✓

Park Farm Caravan Site, Bodiam, Robertsbridge, East Sussex TN32 5XA. *01580 830514.* Mr Richard Bailey. Beautiful rural site near river and Bodiam Castle. Children's play area. Free fishing in river Rother. Barbecues allowed. Winter storage available. Many walks around farm. 3m south of Hawkhurst on B2244. Open April 1-October 30.

🌮🕹🚹🔒🍴⊙🔥🔦🛎 *L* ♂

Seaford

Buckle Caravan & Camping Park, Marine Parade, Seaford, East Sussex BN25 2QR. *01323 897801.* holiday@buckle-park.freeserve.co.uk. www.buckle-camping.ukti.co.uk. Mr & Mrs Perry. A259 coast road between Newhaven and Seaford, adjacent to beach. Adult only fields available, seasonal and storage pitches available. Free showers, toilets, dish washing, individual pitches. Quiet park—no groups. Takeaway meals, cafe/restaurant available nearby. Open March 1-January 2.

🌮🕹🖳🍴🔒🌣⊙🌣🔥🛢🍴🛎≋ *L* 🛆 ♂ ✓ ⚡ ♀ ✈ 🛶

Uckfield

Heaven Farm, Furners Green, Uckfield, East Sussex TN22 3RG. *01825 790226.* butlerenterprises@farmline.com. wwwheavenfarm.co.uk. Mr & Mrs J Butler. On A275 one mile south of Dane Hill and 1.5 miles north of the Bluebell Railway. Grass site sloping in a few places. Open March-November.

🌮🕹🔒🍴✕⊙🔥🍴≋ *J* ✓ ∪ ⚡

EAST YORKSHIRE

Beverley

Lakeminster Park, Hull Road, Beverley, East Yorkshire HU17 0PN. *01482 882655.* Mr.B & N Rushworth. 1m S of Beverley off A1174 Beverley to Hull road. Well-drained site close to woods, stream and lake. 30 minutes to coastal resorts. Drinks licence.

🌮🕹🚹🖳🔒🍴🍴✕⊙🌣🍴≋🔦×🛎≋ *L* ♀ ♂ ✓ ∪ ⚡ ♀

Bridlington

South Cliff Caravan Park, Wilsthorpe, Bridlington, East Yorkshire YO15 3QN. *01262 671051.* East Riding of Yorkshire Council. 1.5m S of Bridlington on the seaward side of A165. Holiday site close to excellent beaches and places of interest. Boat launch nearby. Fees on application. Caravans for hire. Special offers. Open March-November 30.

🌮🕹🚹🖳🔒🍴✕⊙🌣🔥🛎🔦×🛎≋ *L* ♀ ✓ ∪ ⚡ ♀

Driffield

Barmston Beach Holiday Park, Sands Lane, Barmston, Driffield, East Yorkshire YO25 8PJ. *01262 468202.* Take A165 from Bridlington to Kingston-upon-Hull. Road to Barmston Beach on left 6m S of Bridlington. One of Havens 37 touring parks around the UK. Free kids' club. Outdoor pool. Family clubroom. Close to places of interest. Open Easter-October.

🌮🕹🚹🖳🍴✕⊙🌣🔥🛢≋🔦🛎 *L* ♀ ♂ ✓ ✈

Dacre Lakeside Park, New Road, Brandesburton, Driffield, East Yorkshire YO25 8RT. *01964 543704.* dacresurf@aol.com. www.dacrepark.co.uk. Sandfield Gravel Co Ltd. 14-acre site with 120 pitches accepting all units. 10-acre lake (Dacre Lakeside Park) with windsurfing and 18 hole golf course. From M62 exit 38, take B1230 east to Beverley then follow signs to Bridlington. Site entrance off A165. Open March-October.

🌮🕹🚹🖳🔒🍴🌣⊙🌣🍴🔥🛢🍴🛎≋ *L* ♀ 🛆 ♂ ✓ 🛶 ∪ ⚡ ♀ ✈ 🛶

Seaside Caravan Park, Ulrome, Driffield, East Yorkshire YO25 8TT. *01262 468228.* W M Houghton. Turn off the A165 Hull to Bridlington at Lissett. B1242 to Ulrome, turn left in village. On leaving village turn left to Park. Good location for beach holiday with views of Bridlington Bay. Open March 25-October 31.

🌮🕹🚹🖳🍴✕⊙🌣🔥🛎🔦🍴♀🛎🛆 ♂ ✓ ∪ ⚡ ♀ 🛶

Thorpe Hall Caravan & Camping Site, Rudston, Driffield, East Yorkshire YO25 4JE. *01262 420393/420574.* caravansite @thorpehall.co.uk. www.thorpehall.co.uk. Sir Ian Macdonald. 4m W of Bridlington, adjacent to B1253. 4.5 acres situated in former walled garden at Thorpe Hall. Fees on application and subject to 10% discount for stays over seven days. Close to village and restaurant. Open March 1-October 31.

🌮🕹🚹🖳🔒🍴🌣⊙🌣🔥🛢≋🔦🍴♀♂ ✓ ∪ ⚡ ♀

Flamborough

Thornwick and Sea Farm Holiday Centre, North Marine Road, Flamborough East Yorkshire YO15 1AN *01262 850369* enquiries@thornwickbay.co.uk. www.thornwickbay. co.uk. Mr S H Gibbon From Bridlington, A164, follow B1255 to Flamborough, go through the village to the 'North Landing'. The park is to your left. Open March 1-October 31.

🌮🕹🚹🖳🔒🍴✕⊙🌣🔥🛢≋🔦🍴 *L* ♀ ♂ ✓

Hornsea

Springfield Caravan Park, Atwick Road, Hornsea, East Yorkshire HU18 1EJ. *01964 532253.* Mr & Mrs Hartley. 1m N of Hornsea via B1242 to Bridlington. The site is the first farm on the left at the top of the hill. Near sea and Hornsea Mere. Please ring office hours only. Open May-October.

🌮🕹🖳🍴⊙🌣🔥🛎🔦×🛎🛎 ♂ ✓ ⚡

Hull

Burton Constable Caravan Park, Old Lodges, Hull, East Yorkshire HU11 4LN. *01964 562508.* Mr J R Chichester Constable. From Humber Bridge follow A63 leading to A1033 to Saltend roundabout. Pick up Burton Constable sign. 10 miles from Humber Bridge. Open March-October.

🌮🕹🔒🍴🌣🛆🔥🛎🔦 *L* ♀ 🛆 ♂ ✓ ∪ ⚡ ♀

Skipsea

Far Grange Park, Skipsea, East Yorkshire YO25 8SY. *01262 468293/468248.* enquiries@fargrangepark.co.uk. www.far grangepark.co.uk. Messrs. McCann. On B1242 5m N of Hornsea and 10m S of Bridlington. Midway between Skipsea and Atwick. A cliff park with shelter. Bar and food. Coarse fishing. Family entertainment. Snooker and pool. Swimming pool on site. Rose Award. Open March-October and weekends out of season.

🌮🕹🚹🔒🍴✕⊙🌣🔥🛢≋🔦🍴♀🛎 *L* 🛆 ♂ ✓ ∪ ⚡ ♀ 🛶

Low Skirlington, Skipsea, East Yorkshire YO25 8SY. *01262 468213/466.* M B & J Goodwin Ltd. Three miles north of Hornsea on B1242 to Skipsea and Bridlington. Site signposted on east side of road. Holiday site 400yd from sandy beach. Fees on application. Dogs allowed on leads. Open March-October.

🌮🕹🚹🔒🍴✕⊙🌣🔥🛢≋🔦🍴 *L* ♂ ✓ ⚡

Mill Farm Country Park, Mill Lane, Skipsea, East Yorkshire YO25 8SS. *01262 468211.* Judy Willmott. B1242 into Skipsea, look for Cross Street which leads onto Mill Lane. Site on right after Mill Farm on edge of village. Level site surrounded by mature hedges. Farm walk. Free hot water. Dogs welcome. Bottle gas supply, laundry, dairy produce available nearby. Pub in village. Sea 0.5m. Rail station 8 miles. Open March 1-October 5.

🌮🕹🚹🖳🔒🍴✕⊙🔥🍴🔦🍴 *L* 🛆 ♂ ✓ ⚡ 🛶

Stamford Bridge

Weir Caravan Park, Stamford Bridge, East Yorkshire YO41 1AN. *01759 371377.* enquiries@yorkshireholidayparks.co.uk. www.yorkshireholidayparks.co.uk. Mr & Mrs D Hind. 8m E of York on A166. Site is on river Derwent. Conveniently situated for York and coast. Fees on application. Open March-October.

York

Fangfoss Old Station Caravan Park, Fangfoss, York, East Yorkshire YO41 5QB. *01759 380491.* Mr F L Arundel. 8m from York. 2m off A1079 at Wilberfoss. Small, peaceful park. At the foot of the Wolds. Easy access to coast moors and cities. Open March 1-October 31.

The Sycamores Touring Caravan Park, Feoffe Common Lane, Barmby Moor, York, East Yorkshire YO4 5HS. *01759 388838.* bookings@sycamorescaravans.co.uk. www.sycamores caravans.co.uk. Mr R A Wright. Three-acre site between the villages of Wilberfoss and Barmby Moor, at the foot of the picturesque Yorkshire Wolds, 7 miles east of the historic city of York. Open March 1-November 30.

ESSEX

Brentwood

Camping & Caravanning Club Site - Kelvedon Hatch, Warren Lane, Doddington, Kelvedon Hatch, Brentwood, Essex CM15 0JG. *01277 372773.* www.campingandcaravanning club.co.uk. The Camping & Caravanning Club Ltd. 12-acre site with 90 pitches. From Brentwood take the A128. After 3m look for Bentley Garage on left. After 500yds, turn right (just past the 'no entry' into Frog Street). Continue to junction of Frog Street and Warren Lane, turn right and the site entrance is on the left. Caravans, motor caravans and tents accepted. Non-members welcome. Open March-October.

Clacton-on-Sea

Sackett's Grove Caravan Park, Jaywick Lane, Clacton-on-Sea, Essex CO16 8AZ. *01255 427765.* TST Parks Ltd. From Colchester A133 turn right at Clacton roundabout. After 0.75m turn left at Jaywick Lane. Large level site. Tents separate from caravans. Fees on application. Open Easter-end September.

Colchester

Colchester Camping & Caravan Park, Cymbeline Way, Lexden, Colchester, Essex CO3 4AG. *01206 545551.* enquiries@colchestercamping.co.uk. www.colchestercamping. co.uk. David & Sylvia Thorp. Site is at junction of A12 and A133 follow tourist signs. 1m W of Colchester. Well-equipped site 1m from Colchester. Play area. 3 toilet and shower blocks with facilities for disabled people. Laundry. Constable country. 30-minute drive to ferry ports. Graded: 4 stars.

Mill Farm Camp Site, Harwich Road, Great Bromley, Colchester, Essex CO7 7JQ. *01206 250485.* Dean Bros. From A120 to Harwich, 6m E of Colchester. Follow signs to Mill Farm. Quiet, peaceful site on cycle route from Harwich. Open May-September.

Seaview Holiday Park, Seaview Avenue, West Mersea, Colchester, Essex CO5 8DA. *01206 382534.* Glynian (Leisure Parks) Ltd. B1025 from Colchester to Mersea Island. Well signed. Manager: Mr B J Borrman. Open March 15-October 31.

The Grange Caravan Park, East Bergholt, East End, Colchester, Essex CO7 6UX. *01206 298567/298912.* Mr B W & Mrs P J Arnold. Eight miles south west of Ipswich. On A12 Ipswich to Colchester road. Turn south on B1070 towards Manningtree, then fourth turning on the left. At crossroads signposted to Bentley and Tattingstone, continue about 0.75m to site on left. Heart of Constable Country. Open 11 months-closed January.

Waldegraves Holiday Park, Mersea Island, Colchester, Essex CO5 8SE. *01206 382898.* holidays@waldegraves. co.uk. www.waldegraves.co.uk. Mr David Lord. Ten miles south of Colchester. From Colchester take the B1025 for 10m. Fork left to East Mersea and take second road right and follow signs. Rose Award park. Graded: 3 stars. Open March 1-November 30.

East Mersea

Fen Farm, East Mersea, Essex CO5 8UA. *01206 383275.* fen farm@talk21.com. Mr & Mrs R Lord. Off the B1025 three miles from West Mersea, take left fork at causeway. First turn on right past Dog and Pheasant. Quiet, rural, family site by sea, near country park. Toilets and showers. Cafe/restaurant nearby. Open April-October.

Gosfield

Gosfield Lake Touring Park, Church Road, Gosfield, Essex CO9 1UG. *01787 475043.* turps@gosfieldlake.co.uk. www.gosfieldlake.co.uk. Mr C W Turp. 4.5 miles north of Braintree via the A131 Sudbury road. Fork left on to the A1017 to Gosfield and site. Flat, sheltered site with picnic area and adjacent to large lake.

Loughton

Debden House Camp Site, Debden Green, Loughton, Essex IG10 2PA. *020 8508 3008.* London Borough of Newham. 15m north of London in Epping Forest, 2m north of Loughton. M25 to Junction 26 then A121 (Loughton); Left on A1168 (Rectory Lane); 2nd left (Pyrles Lane); over crossroads; right on to Englands Lane then 2nd left. Epping Forest is 40 minutes from London. Open April-October.

Elm's Caravan & Camping Park, Lippitt's Hill , High Beech, Loughton, Essex IG10 4AW. *0208 5025652.* terry@elmscamp site.freeserve.co.uk. www.theelmscampsite.co.uk. Terence & Patricia Farr. Leave M25 junction 26 first left for Waltham Cross, first roundabout left for Chingford A112 proceed 1m to Plough Pub turn left signs to camp site. Open March 1-October 31.

Rochford

Riverside Village Holiday Park, Wallasea Island, Rochford, Essex SS4 2EY. *01702 258297.* K Parks. A127, Rochford or the A130 Hullbridge. Flat, well cut parkland with trees and lakes. Ideal for walking, birdwatching, windsurfing and boating. No single sex groups. Open March 1-October 31.

Roydon

Roydon Mill Leisure Park, Roydon, Essex CM19 5EJ. *01279 792777.* info@roydonpark.com. www.roydonpark.com. Global Enterprises Ltd. Three miles west of Harlow on the B181 near Roydon railway station. Near river Stort. Convenient for visiting London. Open all year restricted to 15 trailers November to February. 40 acres watersports lake. Fees on application.

Southend

East Beach Caravan Park, East Beach, Shoeburyness, Southend, Essex SS3 9SG. *01702 292466.* Leshome Ltd. A127 or A13 to Shoebury then follow camp signs. Graded: 2 stars. Open mid-March to October 31.

Southminster

Beacon Hill Holiday Village, St Lawrence Bay, Southminster, Essex CM0 7LS. *01621 779248.* Cinque Ports Leisure. 8m E of Maldon via B1018 and B1010 to Latchington. Left at T-junction and after Latchington take minor roads to Mayland, Steeple and St Lawrence. Farmland setting. Boat launching into adjoining river Blackwater. Manager: Debbie Allchin. Open April-October.

Steeple Bay Holiday Park, Steeple, Southminster, Essex CM0 7RS. *01621 773991.* info@cinqueports leisure.com. www.cinqueportsleisure.com. Cinque Ports Leisure Ltd. Turn off the A12 on to the A414, then onto B1010/1012 to Latchingdon, straight across mini roundabout. Follow signs through Mayland, then Steeple Village. Turn left into small lane. Steeple Bay is half a mile past the farm. Free kids' club. Free evening entertainment. Graded: 3 stars. Open April-October.

St Lawrence Bay

Saint Lawrence Holiday Home Park, 10 Main Road, St Lawrence Bay, Essex CM0 7LY. *01621 779434.* St Lawrence Caravans Ltd. A127 take A132 turn-off to Latchingdon, follow Bradwell road and tourism signs to 'The Stone' at St Lawrence Bay. Quiet, luxury, family, holiday park adjacent to river Blackwater. Launching facilities for sailing and water-skiing. David Bellamy Silver Conservation Award. Welcome Host. Open March 15-November 30.

St Osyth

The Orchards Holiday Village, Point Clear, St Osyth, Essex CO16 8LJ. *01255 820651.* British Holidays. Follow A12 from London, then A133 towards Clacton. Continue on to B1027 to St Osyth signposted to Point Clear. Indoor and outdoor swimming pool, bowling greens and multi sports area. Family entertainment. Open Easter-September.

Walton-on-Naze

Naze Marine Holiday Park, Hall Lane, Walton-on-Naze, Essex CO14 8HL. *0870 442 9292.* holidays@gbholidayparks.co.uk. www.gbholidayparks.co.uk. GB Holiday Parks Ltd. A12 to Colchester—follow A120 Harwich Road as far as A133. Take A133 to Weeley then B1033 all the way to Walton Seafront. Naze is on left. No tents. Open March-November.

GLOUCESTERSHIRE

Aust

Boars Head Camping Site, Aust, Gloucestershire BS12 3AX. *01454 52278.* 12m North of Bristol. Leave M4 at junction 21 (Severn Bridge). Turn left on to A403 Avonmouth road and 1st left in to village. Site is behind public house in village centre. Open March-October.

Cambridge

Riverside Caravan Park, The George, Cambridge, Gloucestershire GL2 7AL. *01453 890270.* Mr & Mrs E Hogben. A38 Bristol to Gloucester. Exit M5 junction 13 or 14. Pub/restaurant on site. Summer barbecues. Children's play area. Pets corner. Storage available. Open all year, according to ground conditions.

Cheltenham

Briarfields Touring Park, Gloucester Road, Cheltenham, Gloucestershire GL51 0SX. *01242 235324.* Mr D M Stevens. 1m off M5, J11. New site set in superb location.

Stansby Caravan Park, The Reddings, Cheltenham, Gloucestershire GL51 6RS. *01242 235324.* Mr D Stevens & Mrs J Stevens. Flat, grassy orchard site, five minutes from M5 junction 11. Within easy reach of Gloucester and Cheltenham. Dogs allowed on leads. Open February 1-December 31.

Cirencester

Cotswold Hoburne, Broadway Lane, South Cerney, Cirencester, Gloucestershire GL7 5UQ. *01285 860216.* Hoburne Ltd. From J15 M4, take A419 signposted Cirencester to 4m S of Cirencester. Follow signs to Cotswold Water Parks. 70 acre park with 2 fishing lakes, Lakeside club house, indoor leisure pool, outdoor pool etc. Open April-October.

Mayfield Touring Park, Cheltenham Road, Perrotts Brook, Cirencester, Gloucestershire GL7 7BH. *01285 831301.* www.mayfield.co.uk. Jan & Adrian, June & Peter Yates. Ideal for touring the Cotswolds, directly off A435 overlooking 'Churn Valley', designated area of outstanding natural beauty, 2m N of

Cirencester, 13 miles south of Cheltenham. 4 acres for camping, 8 acres for recreation. Graded: 4 stars.

🚐 🏕 📶 🅿 ♿ 🔌 ☉ ♨ 🔥 🛒 🏧 🚻 ☕ ✻ L ♀ ♨ ♨ ✈ ✓ ∪ 💧 ⚲

Coleford

Braceland Caravan and Camping - Forest of Dean, (Forestry Commission), Bracelands Drive, Coleford, Gloucestershire GL16 7NN. *01594 833376.* fe.holidays@forestry.gsi.gov.uk. www.forestholidays.co.uk. Forestry Commission (Forest Holidays). North of Coleford on minor road towards Symonds Yat Rock. Advance booking advisable. Brochure request line: 01313 340066. Open March-November.

🚐 🏕 📶 ♿ 🔌 ☉ ♨ 🔥 🛒 ✈ ✓ 🅱 ∪ 💧

Christchurch Caravan and Camping - Forest of Dean, (Forestry Commission), Bracelands Drive, Coleford, Gloucestershire GL16 7NN. *01594 833376.* fe.holidays@forestry.gsi.gov.uk. www.forestholidays.co.uk. Forestry Commission (Forest Holidays). North of Coleford on minor road towards Symonds Yat Rock. Advance booking advisable at all times. Brochure request line: 01313 340066. Open end March-November.

🚐 🏕 📶 ♿ 🔌 ☉ ♨ 🔥 🛒 🏧 ♨ ✻ ⚲ ♀ ⚷ ✈ 🅱 ∪ 💧

Woodland Caravan & Camping Site - Forest of Dean, Forestry Commission, Bracelands Drive, Coleford, Gloucestershire GL16 7NN. *01594 833376.* fe.holidays@forestry.gsi.gov.uk. www.forestholidays.co.uk. Forestry Commission (Forest Holidays). 1m N of Coleford, at A4136 crossroads, go N for half mile. Signposted. Brochure request line: 01313 340066. Book in at Christchurch. Open early March-November.

🚐 🏕 🛒 ☉ ✈ ✈ ✓

Dursley

Hogsdown Farm Touring Site, Lower Wick, Dursley, Gloucestershire GL11 6DS. *01453 810224.* Mrs J M Smith. Mid-way between Bristol and Gloucester J13-14 M5 on A38. Level site in rural position, ideal for Cotswolds and Severn Valley. Barbecue. Excellent walking and touring country.

🚐 🏕 📶 🅿 🔌 ☉ ♨ 🔥 🛒 🏧 ♨ ≋ ✻ ♞ L ✈ ✓

Gloucester

Gables Farm, Moreton Valance, Gloucester, Gloucestershire GL2 7ND. *01452 720331.* Mrs D M Dickenson. 6m S of Gloucester on A38. Leave M5 J13, then 2m N on A38.Or M5 J12 then 1.5 miles south on A38. Suitable as an overnight stop or a local touring site. Slimbridge Wildfowl and Wetlands is six miles away. Open March-November.

🚐 🏕 📶 ✗ ☉ ♨ 🔥 🛒 🅱 🏧 L ♀ ✈

Red Lion Caravan & Camping Park, Wainlode Hill, Norton, Gloucester, Gloucestershire GL2 9LW. *01452 730251.* www.redlioninn-caravancampingpark.co.uk. Mr G Skilton. Off A38 at Norton, sp Wainlode Hill 1.5m. On banks of river Severn. Idyllic country location. Statics hire/sale. Open all year if ground suitable.

🚐 🏕 ♿ 🍴 ♨ 🛒 ✗ ☉ ♨ 🔥 🛒 🏧 ✻ ✈ ✓ ∪ 💧

Lechlade

Bridge House, Lechlade, Gloucestershire GL7 3AG. *01367 252348.* Mr R Cooper. On A361 Lechlade to Swindon, 0.25m south of Lechlade. Near river Thames and Cotswolds. Fees on application. Cafe/restaurant nearby. Open March-October.

🚐 🏕 📶 ♿ 🔌 ☉ 🔥 🛒 🅱 🏧 L ♨ ✈

St Johns Priory Parks Ltd, Faringdon Road, Lechlade, Gloucestershire GL7 3EZ. *01367 252360.* Mr T C Worsfold. 0.5-mile outside Lechlade on A417 Faringdon. Entrance on left immediately prior to Eriba sign. Open March 1-October 31.

🚐 🏕 📶 ☉ ♨ 🔥 🛒 🅱 L ♨ ✈ ✓ ⚡

Slimbridge

> **Tudor Caravan & Camping Site, Shepherd's Patch, Slimbridge, Gloucestershire GL2 7BP.** *01453 890483.* info@tudorcaravanpark.co.uk. www.tudorcaravanpark. co.uk. Mr & Mrs K Fairall. From A38 Bristol to Gloucester road. Turn at roundabout WWT Wetlands Centre, Slimbridge sign. Site entrance is at far side of public house, 50yd from canal bridge. Small site near Wetlands centre and Berkeley Castle. Holiday or night halt travelling SW.
>
> 🚐 🏕 📶 🛒 ✗ ☉ ♨ 🔥 🏧 🅱 ≋ ✻ L ✈ ✈ ∪ 💧

Tewkesbury

Camping & Caravanning Club Site - Winchcombe, Brooklands Farm, Alderton, Tewkesbury, Gloucestershire GL20 8NX. *01242 620259.* www.campingandcaravanning club.co.uk. The Camping & Caravanning Club. M5, junc 9 take A46 Evesham road. At Teddington roundabout take B4077 Stow road. Site 3m on right. Coarse fishing on site. Ideal base for exploring Cotswolds. 80 pitches set in 20 acres. Non-members welcome. Caravans, motor caravans and tents accepted. David Bellamy Gold Conservation Award. Open March-January.

🚐 🏕 📶 ♿ 🔌 🛒 ☉ ♨ 🔥 🛒 🏧 ♞ L ✈

Dawleys Caravan Park, Owls' Lane, Shuthonger, Tewkesbury, Gloucestershire GL20 6EQ. *01684 292622.* From M50 junction 1, take A38 south to Tewkesbury. Turn right after 1 mile opposite car sale ground. Quiet site in rural surroundings. Good walking and fishing nearby. Ideal for touring the Cotswolds, Malverns and Vale of Evesham. Manager: Richard Harrison. Open May-September.

🚐 🏕 📶 🅿 🔌 ☉ 🔥 🛒 🏧 🅱 ♨ ✈ ✓ ∪ 💧 ⚲

Sunset View Touring Tent & Caravan Park, Church End Lane, Twyning, Tewkesbury, Gloucestershire GL20 6EH. *01684 292145.* cheryl@goldensprings.freeserve.co.uk. A B & C D Goulstone. 2 miles north of Tewkesbury on A38, almost opposite Crown Inn. Turn right. Site 200 yards on right. 2-acre level site. Ostrich farm on site.

🚐 🏕 📶 ♿ 🔌 🛒 ☉ 🔥 🏧 🅱 ✻ L ♨ ✈ ✓ ∪ 💧

GREATER MANCHESTER

Wigan

Gathurst Hall Farm Camp Site, Gathurst Lane, Shevington, Wigan, Greater Manchester WN6 8JA. *01257 253464.* Mrs Helen Smith. 5m NW of Wigan halfway between M6 junctions 26 and 27. Off B5206 at Shevington. Alongside Leeds andLiverpool Canal. Near to the Navigation public house. About4.5m from Wigan Pier. Advance booking advisable. Open March-October.

🚐 🏕 📶 🛒 ☉ ♨ 🔥 🅱 ≋ ✈ ✓ ∪ 💧

HAMPSHIRE

Andover

Wyke Down Touring Caravan & Camping Park, Picket Piece, Andover, Hampshire SP11 6LX. *01264 352048.* wyke down@wykedown.co.uk. www.wykedown.co.uk. Mr William Read. International Camping Park signs from A303 truck road, follow signs to Wyke Down. Touring centre. Country pub. Restaurant. TV and recreation room. Swimming pool. Golf driving range. Fees on application. Supermarket nearby. Graded: 3 stars.

🚐 🏕 📶 ✗ ☉ ♨ 🔥 🏧 ≋ 🅱 ≋ ✻ ✈

HAMPSHIRE

Ashurst

Ashurst Caravan & Camping Site, (Forestry Commission), Lyndhurst Road, Ashurst, Hampshire SO40 7AR. *01313 146505.* fe.holidays@forestry.gsi.gov.uk. www.forestholidays. co.uk. Forestry Commission (Forest Holidays). 5m SW of Southampton on A35 signposted. Part wooded site. Booking recommended. Brochure request line: 0131 3340066. Graded: 4 stars. Open March-September.

♥ ⊠ ♿ ⊙ ♨ ⊟ ⋔ ⅹ ⊟ ⇌ L

Brockenhurst

Aldridge Hill Caravan & Camping Site, (Forestry Commission), Brockenhurst, Hampshire SO42 7QD. *01313 146505.* fe.holidays@forestry.gsi.gov.uk. www.forestholidays. co.uk. Forestry Commission (Forest Holidays). Off A337, 1m NW of Brockenhurst village. Open grassland site near stream. Note: site has no toilet facilities. Brochure request line: 01313 340066. Open June-September.

♥ L

Decoy Pond Farm, Beaulieu Road, Beaulieu, Brockenhurst, Hampshire SO42 7YQ. *023 8029 2652.* Mr D N Horton. Lyndhurst to Beaulieu B3056; over railway bridge, immediately left opposite Beaulieu Hotel. Small site in heart of New Forest, 3m from Beaulieu and 3m from Lyndhurst. Open Easter-October.

♥ ⊠ ♨ ⋔ ⇌ ⅃ ↖

Hollands Wood Caravan & Camping Site, (Forestry Commission), Lyndhurst Road, Brockenhurst, Hampshire SO42 7QH. *01313 146505.* fe.holidays@forestry.gsi.gov.uk. www.forestholidays.co.uk. Forestry Commission (Forest Holidays). 0.5m N of Brockenhurst on A337, signposted. Woodland setting. Booking recommended. Brochure request line: 01313 340066. Graded: 4 stars. Open March-September.

♥ ⊠ ♿ ⚲ ⊙ ♨ ⊟ ⅀ ⊟ ⇌ L ♀ ♡

Roundhill Caravan & Camping Site, (Forestry Commission), Beaulieu Road, Brockenhurst, Hampshire SO40 7QL. *01313 146505.* fe.holidays@forestry.gsi.gov.uk. www.forestholidays. co.uk. Forestry Commission (Forest Holidays). On B3055 2m SE of Brockenhurst off A337 signposted. Heathland and forest site within easy reach of coast and Lymington. Brochure request line: 01313 340066. Open March-September.

♥ ⊠ ♿ ⊙ ♨ L

Fordingbridge

Sandy Balls Holiday Centre, Sandy Balls Estate, Godshill, Fordingbridge, Hampshire SP6 2JZ. *01425 653042.* post@sandy-balls.co.uk. www.sandy-balls.co.uk. Sandy Balls Estate Ltd. From Salisbury A338 to Fordingbridge, take B3078 signed Godshill. Set in 120 acres of woods and parkland on edge of New Forest.

♥ ♙ ♿ ⊠ ♿ ♨ ⅹ ⊙ ♨ ⊟ ⅀ ≋ ♦ ⋔ ⊟ ✿ L ♀ ♨ ⅃ ♡ ⇌ ↗

Gosport

Kingfisher Caravan Park, Browndown Road, Stokes Bay, Gosport, Hampshire PO13 9BE. *023 9250 2611.* info@king fisher-caravan-park.co.uk. www.kingfisher-caravan-park.co.uk. Mr S D Sargeant. Exit 11 on M27. Take A32 to Gosport for approx 3 miles. At Fort Brockhurst, follow the caravan signs at

Stokes Bay. Well situated near historic Portsmouth with its many places of interest and ferries to the Continent and Isle of Wight. Graded: 4 stars. Open all year for touring.

♥ ♙ ♨ ⊠ ♿ ♨ ⅀ ⅹ ⊙ ♨ ♨ ⅀ ♦ ⋔ ⊟ ⇌ ✿ L ♀ ♨ ⅃ ↗ ⇌ ↖ ↗

Hayling Island

> **Fishery Creek Caravan & Camping Park, Fishery Lane, Hayling Island, Hampshire PO9 11NR.** *023 9246 2164.* camping@fisherycreek.fsnet.co.uk. D Emersic. From A27, go over bridge to Hayling Island; followbrown tourist signs—Fishery Creek, pass town, turn left, signs to site. Quiet, clean and peaceful site surrounded by water on beautiful tidal creek. Footpath to beach, own slipway and fishing. Graded: 3 stars. Open March-October 31.
>
> ♥ ♙ ⊠ ♨ ⅀ ♨ ⊙ ♨ ♨ ⅀ ♦ ⋔ ⊟ ♨ ⅃ ♡ ↗ ⇌ ↖

Fleet Farm Caravan & Camping Park, Yew Tree Road, Hayling Island, Hampshire PO11 0QE. *023 9246 3684.* www.haylingcampsites.co.uk. Zita Good & Colin Good. Exit M27 or A3M motorways at Havant and follow A3023. After crossing bridge on to Island, site approx 1.5m on left. Family site, excellent touring area. Storage and rallies. Dogs allowed. Open March-November 1.

♥ ♙ ⊠ ♨ ⅀ ♨ ⊙ ♨ ♨ ⅀ ⊟ ⇌ L ⊟ ♨ ⅃ ♡ ↗ ⇌ ↖

Lower Tye Camp Site, Copse Lane, Hayling Island, Hampshire PO11 0QB. *023 9246 2479.* Mrs Z Good. A3023 across Langstone Bridge, turn left into Northney Road. Follow road approx 2m. Site on left. Close to sea , blue flag award, and several holiday resorts, Portsmouth, Isle of Wight etc. Boardsailing. Play area. Caravan storage and long term caravan parking. Rallies welcome. Dogs allowed. Open March-November.

♥ ♙ ⊠ ♨ ⊙ ♨ ⅀ ♨ ⋔ ⇌ ♀ ♨ ⅃ ♡ ↗ ⇌ ↖

The Oven Camping Site, Manor Road, Hayling Island, Hampshire PO11 0QB. *023 9246 4695.* lowertye@euphony.net. www.haylingcampsites.co.uk. Mrs Z Good. On A3023 from Havant entrance, then B2149 on Hayling. After approx 2.5m on island fork right at roundabout. Entrance just before St Patrick's RC Church on left. Near beaches. Rallies catered for. Caravan storage. Dogs allowed. Manager: Mr J Macallum. Open March-January 1.

♥ ♙ ♨ ⊠ ♨ ⅀ ♨ ⅹ ⊙ ♨ ♨ ⅀ ≋ ♦ ⋔ ⊟ ⇌ L ♀ ♨ ⅃ ♡ ↗ ⇌ ↖ ↗

Lymington

Lytton Lawn Touring Park, Lymore Lane, Milford-on-Sea, Lymington, Hampshire SO41 0TX. *01590 648331.* holidays @shorefield.co.uk. www.shorefield.co.uk. Shorefield Holidays Ltd. 3m S of Lymington via A337 to Everton, then B3058 to site. 2nd turn on left. Flat, well-drained site, 1m from beach and close to New Forest. Shop. Graded: 4 stars. Open February-January 5.

♥ ♙ ⊠ ♨ ♿ ⊙ ♨ ♨ ⅀ ⊟ ⇌ L ♨ ⅃ ♡ ↗ ⇌ ↖

Lyndhurst

Denny Wood Caravan & Camping Site, (Forestry Commission), Beaulieu Road, Lyndhurst, Hampshire SO32 7FZ. *01313 146505.* fe.holidays@forestry.gsi.gov.uk. www. forestholidays.co.uk. Forestry Commission (Forest Holidays). On B3056, 3m SE of Lyndhurst. Grassland site among

---

SOUTH COAST on the SOLENT
KINGFISHER PARK

STOKES BAY, GOSPORT PO13 9BE. TEL: (02392) 502611 FAX: (02392) 583583

We are in an ideal central position for seeing the South Coast. On site we have a bar, restaurant, laundrette, children's playground and games room. Electric hook-ups for tourers. Static caravans for sale and for hire.

scattered oak trees. Site has no toilet facilities. No dogs. Brochure request line: 01313 340066. Open March-September.
🏕 ✕ *L*

Matley Wood Caravan & Camping Site, (Forestry Commission), Beaulieu Road, Lyndhurst, Hampshire SO32 7FZ. *01313 146505.* fe.holidays@forestry.gsi.gov.uk. www. forestholidays.co.uk. Forestry Commission (Forest Holidays). On B3056, 2m SE Lyndhurst. Small secluded site in open forest woodland. No toilet facilities. Advance booking recommended. Brochure request line: 01313 340066. Reception at Denny Wood. Open March-September.
🏕 *L*

Ocknell/Longbeech Caravan & Camping Site, (Forestry Commission), Fritham, Lyndhurst, Hampshire SO43 7HH. *01313 146505.* fe.holidays@forestry.gsi.gov.uk. www.forest holidays.co.uk. Forestry Commission (Forest Holidays). B3079 off A31 at Cadnam, then B3078 via Brook and Fritham. Ocknell is an open heathland campsite. Longbeech is a woodland site. Toilet facilities Ocknell only. Brochure request line: 01313 340066. Open March-September.
🏕 ▨ ⊙ ♨ *L*

New Milton

Setthorns Caravan & Camping Site, (Forestry Commission), Wootton, New Milton, Hampshire BH25 5WA. *01313 146505.* fe.holidays@forestry.gsi.gov.uk. www.forestholidays. co.uk. Forestry Commission (Forest Holidays). Signposted from A35. Secluded forest site with marked pitches. Site has no toilet facilities. Booking recommended. Brochure request line: 01313 340066.
🏕 ☕ ✿ *L*

Ringwood

Camping International, Athol Lodge, 229 Ringwood Road, St Leonards, Ringwood, Hampshire BH24 2SD. *01202 872817/872742.* Pegville Ltd. On southern side of A31, 3 miles west of Ringwood. Popular family touring park for Bournemouth, New Forest, country and sea. AA 4 Pennant. Graded: 4 stars. Open March-October.
🏕 ☕ ⚡ ▨ 🍴 ♨ ✕ ⊙ ☕ ♨ ≋ ♠ ☏ 🚿 *L* ♀ ♩ ✓ ♒ ❀ ❊

Oakdene Forest Park, St Leonards, Ringwood, Hampshire BH24 2RZ. *01590 648331.* holidays@shorefield.co.uk. www.shorefield.co.uk. Shorefield Holidays Ltd. Off main A31 3 miles west from Ringwood. 9m from beach at Bournemouth. Bordering Avon Forest. Adventure playground. Indoor and outdoor pools. Leisure club. Graded: 3 stars. Open February-January 3.
🏕 ☕ ⚡ ▨ 🍴 ♨ ✕ ⊙ ☕ ♨ ≋ ♠ ☏ *L* ♀ ♩ ♒ ✓

Red Shoot Camping Park, Linwood, Ringwood, Hampshire BH24 3QT. *01425 473789.* Mrs S J Foulds. In New Forest. Minor road off A338-2m N of Ringwood. From E of Ringwood turn off M27 at junction 1 on to B3078 Fordingbridge/Cadnam. Follow signs to Linwood. Fees on application SAE. Owner supervised to a high standard. Mountain bike hire. Graded: 4 stars. Open March-October.
🏕 ☕ ▨ 🍴 ♨ ✕ ⊙ ☕ ♨ ♠ *L* ♀ ♩ ✓ ♒ ❊

Shamba Holiday Park, 230 Ringwood Road, St Leonards, Ringwood, Hampshire BH24 2SB. *01202 873302.* holidays@shamba.co.uk. www.shamba.co.uk. T E & J K Gray. 2m W of ringwood on the A31 (sign on roadside). Family run park which is always friendly and always clean. Bar, takeaway, play area, free showers. Winter storage. Graded: 3 stars. Open March 1-October 31.
🏕 ☕ ⚡ ▨ 🍴 ♨ ✕ ⊙ ☕ ♨ ≋ ♠ ☏ *L* ♀ ♩ ✓ ♒ ❀ ❊

The Back of Beyond, 234 A Ringwood Road, St Leonards, Ringwood, Hampshire BH24 2SB. *01202 876968.* Mr Pike. 3.5 miles south west of Ringwood off the A31 opposite Boundary Lane at St Leonards. New site opens in 2004. 28 acres of unspoilt countryside, well off the beaten track. Easy access coast and New Forest. Open Easter-October.
🏕 ☕ ▨ 🍴 ♨ ✕ ⊙ ☕ ♨ ♠ ☏ *L* ♀ ♩ ☾

Romsey

Green Pastures Farm, Ower, Romsey, Hampshire SO51 6AJ. *023 8081 4444/07796 188641.* enquiries@greenpastures farm.com. www.greenpasturesfarm.com. Mrs J Pitt & Mr A Pitt. Signposted from junction 2 of the M27 (Salisbury direction) and from A36 and A3090 at Ower. Family run site on working farm near New Forest. Convenient for ferries to Europe and Isle of Wight. Space for children to play safely. Takeaway and cafe/restaurant nearby. Graded: 3 stars. Open March 15-October 31.
🏕 ☕ ▨ 🍴 ♨ ⊙ ☕ ♨ ♠ ☏ 🍴 🔊 *L* ♩ ✓ ♒

Hill Farm Caravan Park, Branches Lane, Sherfield English, Romsey, Hampshire SO51 6FH. *01794 340402.* gjb@hill-farmpark.com. www.hillfarmpark.com. Geoff & Suzy Billett. Located four miles west of Romsey on the A27 towards Salisbury. Turn at crossroads marked 'Branches Lane'. Site is 0.5m on right. Set in the heart of glorious countryside. Eleven acre park for tourers and campers surrounded by fields and woodland. Close to historic cities of Salisbury, Winchester and Southampton. South Coast, New Forest and ferry terminals all within easy reach. Graded: 4 stars. Open March 1-October 31.
🏕 ☕ ▨ 🍴 ♨ ⊙ ☕ ♨ ♠ ☏ ≋ ♀ ♩ ✓ ♒ ❊ ❀

Southampton

Dibles Park, Dibles Road, Warsash, Southampton, Hampshire SO31 9SA. *01489 575232.* Mr L Baker. M27, junc 9, to Park Gate. Left at traffiuc lights, right at bottom of road. 1st left Fleet End road, 2nd right Dibles Road. Pleasant site located half way between Portsmouth and Southampton, ideal for ferry stopovers. Graded: 4 stars.

Riverside Park, Satchell Lane, Hamble, Southampton, Hampshire SO31 4HR. *023 8045 3220.* enquiries@riverside holidays.co.uk. www.riversideholidays.co.uk. Davidson Country Park Homes. Exit 8 off M27 signposted Southampton East then B3397 to Hamble, left turn into Satchell Lane. Site overlooks marina and Hamble river. Picturesque village nearby, set among green fields. Graded: 4 stars. Open March 1-October 31.

Southbourne

Camping & Caravanning Club Site, Chichester Club Site, Main Road, Southbourne, Hampshire PO10 8JH. *01243 373202.* www.campingandcaravanningclub.co.uk. The Camping & Caravanning Club Site. 6m W of Chichester, 3m E of Havant, site is well marked on N side of old A259. Follow signs for Bosham and Southbourne. Well placed for visiting the Sussex Downs and south coast resorts. 60 pitches set in 3 acres. Non-members welcome. Caravans, motor caravans and tents accepted. Open February-November.

Southsea

Southsea Leisure Park, Melville Road, Southsea, Hampshire PO4 9TB. *023 9273 5070.* Southsea Caravans Ltd. From M27-A27-A3M take A2030 Southsea exit and follow signs. 12-acre site at end of Southsea seafront, with direct access to beach. Children's playground and play room, restaurant, bar and shop. Site handy for ferries to the Continent and the Isle of Wight. Dogs allowed. Graded: 3 stars.

Winchester

Morn Hill Caravan Club Site, Morn Hill, Winchester, Hampshire SO21 1HL. *01962 869877.* www.caravanclub. co.uk. The Caravan Club. Leave M3 exit 9 on to A33, then on to A31. Dogs on leads. Convenient for ferries to France, Spain and Isle of Wight. Many local attractions for tourers. Graded: 4 stars. Non-members and tent campers welcome. Open April-October.

HARTLEPOOL

Hartlepool

Ash Vale Holiday Park, Easington Road, Hartlepool, Hartlepool TS24 9RF. *01429 862111/01429 862900.* Tony & Joy Pinto. Take A179 (off A19) to Hartlepool at 3rd roundabout turn left on to A1086 coast road. Over next roundabout, 400yds on left. A picturesque, quiet, rural park, 1m from long, sandy beach. Dogs allowed.

Seaton Carew

Seaton Carew Caravan Park, Queen Street, Seaton Carew, Hartlepool. *01429 274776.* Lookers Burtree Caravans Ltd. Near the coast. Dogs allowed on leads.

HEREFORDSHIRE

Craswall

Old Mill Camp Site, Craswall, Herefordshire HR2 OPN. *01981 510226.* Mr J Watkins. Eight miles off the A465 at Pandy. A quiet camping site near to river and the Offa's Dyke path. Situated at the foot of the Black Mountains. Open Easter-October 31.

Hay-on-Wye

Penlan Caravan Park, Brilley, Hay-on-Wye, Herefordshire HR3 6JW. *01497 831485.* p.joyce@btinternet.com. Peter & Margaret Joyce. Park is located mid way between Kington to Whitney on Wye by road. A small, secluded site, offering peace and space with magnificent views. Situated on a small National Trust farm. Advanced booking is essential. Brochure available on request. Graded: 4 stars. Open Easter-October 31.

Hereford

Cuckoos Corner, Moreton-on-Lugg, Hereford, Herefordshire HR4 8AH. *01432 760234.* cuckoos.corner @ic24.net. www.geocities.com/cuckooscorner. Mrs J M James. Easy access off the A49 opposite Moreton-on-Lugg, turning four miles north of Hereford. Flat grass site with excellent views. Ideal family site with games room, toilet block and shower. Archery and croquet also available.

Lower Ruxton Farm, King's Caple, Hereford, Herefordshire HR1 4TX. *01432 840223.* Mr H D Jenkins. Off A49 Ross/Hereford signs to King's Caple. Turn right at sign to Ruxton. Second farm on right. Level, riverside site, easily accessible. Disposal pit for chemical toilets. Mains water taps only. Open mid July-end August.

Mordiford

Lucks-All Caravanning & Camping Park, Mordiford, Herefordshire HR1 4LP. *01432 870213.* www.lucksallpark. co.uk. Mr & Mrs G Powell. Take B4224 out of Hereford for 5m. From end of M50 take A449; after 1m fork left on to B4224 for Fownhope. Site 1m on Hereford side of Fownhope. On bank of river Wye. Popular canoeist's stop. Open March 1-end November.

Peterchurch

Poston Mill Park, Golden Valley, Peterchurch, Herefordshire HR2 0SF. *01981 550225.* enquiries@poston-mill.co.uk. www.ukparks.co.uk/postonmill. Glenn & Wayne Jones. On the B4348 one mile on Hereford side of Peterchurch. Between the Wye Valley and the Black Mountains. Near the Brecon Beacons. Licensed restaurant adjoining park. Highly recommended, well kept, quality park.

Vowchurch

Upper Gilvach Farm, St Margarets, Vowchurch, Herefordshire. *01981 510618.* Mr A Watkins. South off the B4348 Hay to Hereford road at Vowchurch. Quiet country site near Black Mountains, only the birds and rabbits. Many churches and castles. Route to Midlands and mid Wales. Fees on application. Open May-October.

HERTFORDSHIRE

Baldock

Radwell Lake Caravan Site, Radwell Mill, Radwell, Baldock, Hertfordshire SG7 5ET. *01462 730253.* Michael F Meredith-Hardy. A507 from Baldock and A507 from Shefford. Turning marked Radwell only on A507. Small site with lake and bird reserve. Exit 10 A1 (M). Open Easter-October 31.

Hertford

Camping & Caravanning Club Site - Hertford, Hertford Club Site, Mangrove Road, Hertford, Hertfordshire SG13 8QF. *01992 586696.* www.campingandcaravanningclub.co.uk. The Camping & Caravanning Club Ltd. From the A1 of A602 avoid town centre signs at Hertford and follow A414. From A10, take A414 to Hertford, cross first roundabout, then first left into Mangrove Road. Site on left 32 acres with 250 pitches. Sports field. Play area. Just 20 miles from London. Caravans, motor caravans and tents accepted. Non-members welcome.David Bellamy Gold Conservation Award.

Hoddesdon

Lee Valley Caravan Park, Dobbs Weir, Essex Road, Hoddesdon, Hertfordshire EN11 0AS. *01992 462090.* Lee Valley Regional Park. 1.75m E of A10. Take Hoddesdon exit from A10. Follow Dinant link road and Essex road. Attractive riverside setting. Part of Lee Valley Park. Dogs on leads allowed. Restaurant/takeaway nearby. Open March 1-November 30.

Waltham Cross

Camping & Caravanning Club Site - Theobalds Park, Bulls Cross Ride, Bullsmore Lane, Waltham Cross, Hertfordshire EN7 5HS. *01992 620604.* www.campingandcaravanning club.co.uk. The Camping & Caravanning Club Ltd. 14-acre site with 90 pitches. Leave the M25 exit 25 (A10). Bulls Cross Ride crosses the motorway by a bridge. Play area. There is plenty of space for games on this site. 13 miles from London. Non-members welcome. Caravans, motor caravans and tents accepted. Open March-October.

ISLE OF MAN

Douglas

Glen Dhoo Farm Camp Site, Hillberry, Onchan, Douglas, Isle of Man IM4 5BJ. *01624 621254.* glendhoo@m.c.b.net. www.caravanningcampingsites.co.uk. Mr H R C Cain. On A18 near Hillberry Corner on TT course. Car ferry 3m. Holiday site in sheltered valley. Fees on application. Open Easter-October.

Glenlough Farm, Union Mills, Douglas, Isle of Man. *01624 851326.* glenloughcampsite@manx.net. Mr Quayle. On A1 from Douglas to Peel via Union Mills. Douglas 3m. Peel 7m. Sheltered site. Open May-October.

Kirk Michael

Glen Wyllin Campsite, Kirk Michael, Isle of Man. *01624 878231(Apr-Sept).* Michael Commissioners. Site in National Glen, about 100yd S of Kirk Michael on A3. Adjoins beach. Close to TT course. Brochure and fees on application. Furnished tents for hire. 5 minutes walk to village. Open May-September.

Peel

Peel Campsite, Derby Road, Peel, Isle of Man. *01624 842341.* Peel Town Commissioners. 0.25miles from Peel. Near Peel Castle and 0.5m from beach. Level, rural site, edge of town, close to all amenities. TT course 3 miles. Takeaway, cafe/restaurant available nearby. Fees on application. Open mid April-end September.

ISLE OF WIGHT

Atherfield Bay

Chine Farm Camping Site, Military Road, Atherfield Bay, Isle of Wight PO38 2JH. *01983 740228.* Mrs H M Goody. Site is on A3055 coast road. Midway between Brighstone and Chale. Flat site with access to beach. Fossil area. Three and half miles from Blackgang Chine. Fossil hunting. Graded: 2 stars. Open May-September.

Bembridge

Whitecliff Bay Holiday Park, Hillway, Bembridge, Isle of Wight PO35 5PL. *01983 872671.* holiday@whitecliff-bay.com. www.whitecliff-bay.com. Whitecliff Bay Holiday Park. 2.5 miles north-west of Sandown. On unclassified road off the B3395. Family site only. Fees on application. Licensed clubs, entertainment, heated pools, snack bar, restaurant, shop, Humphray's play zone. Graded: 4 stars. Open Easter-October.

Brighstone

Grange Farm Caravan & Camping Site, Brighstone Bay, Military Road, Brighstone, Isle of Wight PO30 4DA. *01983 740296.* James & Chris Dungey. Located on the A3055 coast road, midway between Freshwater Bay and Chale. 2-acre level site on small, family-run working farm, many animals. One minute walk to our sandy beach. Safe swimming. Graded: 3 stars. Dogs under control welcome. Open March-end October.

Cowes

Comforts Farm Camping Park, Pallance Road, Northwood, Cowes, Isle of Wight PO31 8LS. *01983 293888.* Mrs A E Annett. One mile SW of Cowes off the A3020. Open May-end September.

Gurnard Pines Holiday Village, Cockleton Lane, Cowes, Isle of Wight PO31 8QE. *01983 292395.* Maritime Leisure Investment Ltd. Follow signs from Newport to Cowes. At Nortwood garage take the left fork to next junction then straight on down Cockleton Lane. In 55 acres of grass and woodland, the village is an ideal base for your holiday. Graded: 4 stars. Open March-September.

Thorness Bay Holiday Park, Thorness, Cowes, Isle of Wight PO31 8NJ. *01983 523109.* Park Resorts. Four miles west of Cowes at Thorness Bay. One of Park Resorts six tenting and touring parks around the UK. Free kids' club. Free entertainment. Indoor and outdoor pools. Graded: 3 stars. Open Easter-October.

ISLE OF WIGHT

East Cowes

Waverley Park Holiday Centre, Old Road, East Cowes, Isle of Wight PO32 6AW. *01983 293452.* sue@waverly-park.co.uk. www.waverleypark.co.uk. Peter & Susan Adams. Signposted from Red Funnel Terminal, East Cowes. Friendly family-run site, open air heated pool, entertainment, bar and evening meals in high season (Spring bank holiday-early September). Graded: 3 stars. Open March 23-November 2.

Freshwater

Heathfield Farm Camping Site, Heathfield Road, Freshwater, Isle of Wight PO40 9SH. *01983 756756.* web@heathfieldcamping.co.uk. www.heathfieldcamping.co.uk. Mr & Mrs Osman. Two miles from Yarmouth ferry port off A3054 road at Freshwater. Family camping on level field with sea and downland views. Excellent modern shower facilities. Ideal walking area. Open May 1-September 30.

Ryde

Beaper Farm, Ryde, Isle of Wight PO33 1QJ. *01983 615210/875184.* beaper@btinternet.com. 3m S of Ryde on A3055 towards Sandown. Family site with play area in 13 acres of countryside. New toilet facilities. Holiday caravans for hire. Phone for brochure. Graded: 3 stars. Open May-October.

Carpenters Farm, St Helens, Ryde, Isle of Wight PO33 1JL. *01983 872450.* Mrs M Lovegrove. 1m W of St Helens. From Ryde on A3055, turn E on B3330. 1m to site. Graded: 2 stars. Open June 1-September 30.

Nodes Point Holiday Park, St Helen, Ryde, Isle of Wight PO33 1YA. *01983 872401.* Park Resorts. From Fishbourne on A3054 E towards Ryde. At junction with A3055, then left on to B3330 to St Helens. Nodes Point is on the left. From Cowes on A3021, then as above. One of Park Resorts 6 tenting and touring parks across the UK. Indoor pool. Free kids' clubs. Free family entertainment. Graded: 3 stars. Open May-October.

Pondwell Holidays, Ryde, Isle of Wight PO34 5AQ. *01983 612330.* Self Catering Ltd. 2m E of Ryde via Esplanade to Appley Road and B3330. Site is beside Wishing Well before village of Nettlestone. Holiday site near village and short distance from beach. Graded: 3 stars. Open May-September.

Sandown

Camping & Caravanning Park - Adgestone, Lower Road, Adgestone, Sandown, Isle of Wight PO36 0HL. *01983 403432.* www.campingandcaravanningclub.co.uk. The Camping & Caravanning Club. Turn off A3055 at the Fairway by Manor House pub in Lake, which is between Sandown and Shanklin, past golf course on left, turn right at T-junction. Park is 200yd on right. 250 pitches set in 17 acres. Non-members welcome. Caravans, motor caravans and tents accepted. Open March-October.

Cheverton Copse Caravan & Camping Park, Sandown, Isle of Wight PO36 0JP. *01983 403161.* holidays@cheverton-copse.co.uk. www.cheverton-copse.co.uk. M & D Berry. 2m E of Sandown. Take A3055 S for 0.75m. Turn right at traffic lights at Lake on to A3056. Site is 0.75m on right. Pleasant, rural site 1.5m from beach. Licensed club adjoining caravan park. Graded: 3 stars. Open April-September.

Fairway Holiday Park, The Fairway, Sandown, Isle of Wight PO36 9PS. *01983 403462.* Off Sandown to Shanklin road. Into Fairway at Manor House Hotel. Facilities for child. Dogs welcome. Clubhouse with entertainment. Graded: 2 stars. Open April-October.

Old Barn Touring Park, Cherverton Farm, Newport Road, Apse Heath, Sandown, Isle of Wight PO36 9PJ. *01983 866414.* oldbarn@weltinet.com. www.oldbarntouring.co.uk. Mr & Mrs A F Welti. 500yd south of Apse Heath on A3056 Newport to Sandown. Serviced super pitches. 1.5m to sandy beaches at Sandown and Shanklin. Open April-September.

Southland Camping Park, Newchurch, Sandown, Isle of Wight PO36 0LZ. *01983 865385.* info@southland.co.uk. www.southland.co.uk. Viv & Vanessa McGuinness. Take A3056 towards Sandown, turn left down 2nd road on left after Fighting Cocks pub towards Newchurch. Site one mile on left. Quiet, rural camping park. Open Easter to end-September.

Village Way, Newport Road, Apse Heath, Sandown, Isle of Wight PO36 9PJ. *01983 863279.* Norma - Dennis. On main road (A3056) between Sandown and Shanklin. Holiday site 1.5m from beach. Level pitches. Downland views. Dogs allowed. free on-site fishing. Graded: 3 stars.

Shanklin

Landguard Camping Park, Landguard Manor Road, Shanklin, Isle of Wight PO37 7PH. *01983 867028.* landguard@fsbdial.co.uk. landguard-camping.co.uk. Mr & Mrs A F Welti. From Newport to Sandown on A3056. Turn right 0.5m after Lake town sign. Site is 400yd on right. Swimming pools. 10 minutes walk from town centre. Graded: 4 stars. Open Easter-September.

Lower Hyde Holiday Village, Landguard Road, Shanklin, Isle of Wight PO37 7LL. *01983 866131.* Haven Leisure. Approach Shanklin on A3020. Turn L at traffic lights, through High Street L at Boots, 2nd left, R into Languard Road. Park on left. One of Haven's 37 tenting and touring parks around the UK. Free kids club. Free daytime and evening entertainment. Graded: 5 stars. Open Easter-October.

Ninham Country Holidays, Ninham, Shanklin, Isle of Wight PO37 7PL. *01983 864243.* info@ninham.fsnet.co.uk. www.ninham-holidays.co.uk. Mr D H & Mrs V J Harvey. Turn off A3056 near Safeway superstore 1m W of Lake. Site signposted

from there. 1m NW of Shanklin. Wooded valley with small lakes. Family campers only. Caravan storage. Barbecues. Baby care cubicles. Hair care. Dish-washing area. Graded: 4 stars. Open May 1-September 15.

Ninham Farm, Shanklin, Isle of Wight PO37 7HZ. *01983 866 040.* meadow@ninham.fsnet.co.uk. www.ninham-holidays.co.uk. Mr D H & Mrs V J Harvey. Signposted off A3056 Newport-Sandown Road. Four stars. Full-facility site in wooded country park setting. Pets accepted. Open Easter-End September.

Ventnor

Appuldurcombe Caravan & Camping Park, Appuldurcombe Road, Wroxall, Ventnor, Isle of Wight PO38 3EP. *01983 852597.* appuldurcombe@freeuk.com. www.appuldurcombe.freeuk.com. Mr A & Mrs S Hicks. 2.5m from Ventnor. 3m from Shanklin. Very pretty family site, surrounded by open countryside. 100 marked camping pitches, some with electric. Suitable base for walkers and cyclists. Graded: 4 stars. Open April 1-October 31.

Yarmouth

Orchards Holiday Caravan Park, Newbridge, Yarmouth, Isle of Wight PO41 0TS. *01983 531331.* info@orchards-holiday-park.co.uk. www.orchards-holiday-park.co.uk. Mr & Mrs T Gray. In village of Newbridge opposite post office on B3401. Good domestic arrangements. Package holidays inc return ferry fares for cars & trailers. Indoor and outdoor heated swimming pools. Fees on application. David Bellamy Gold Conservation Award 2000, 2001 & 2002. Graded: 5 stars.

ISLES OF SCILLY

Bryher

Jenford, Bryher, Isles of Scilly. *01720 422886.* Mrs K Stedeford. On island reached by boat from Hugh Town. Open April-October.

St Agnes

Troytown Farm, St Agnes, Isles of Scilly TR22 0PL. *01720 422360.* troytown@talk21.com. www.scillonia.org.uk/st-agnes. Mrs S J Hicks. Quiet, family-run grassy tent only site. At western end of island with views of other islands and Bishop Rock Lighthouse. No cars on site. Travel by ship or helicopter from Penzance. Transport for luggage available from quay to site. Dogs by arrangement. Graded: 3 stars. Open March-October.

St Martin's

St Martin's Campsite, Middle Town, St Martin's, Isles of Scilly TR25 0QN. *01720 422888.* info@stmartinscampsite.co.uk. www.stmartinscampsite.co.uk. Mr & Mrs C Savill. Ferry, helicopter or plane from Penzance/Lands End. Launch from St Mary's to St Martin's. Level, grassy, sheltered site with 50 touring pitches on quiet, unspoilt island. Booking essential. Graded: 4 stars. Open Easter-end-October.

St Mary's

Garrison Holidays, St Mary's, Isles of Scilly TR21 0LS. *01720 422670.* tedmoulson@cs.com. www.isles-of-scilly.co.uk. Mr & Mrs E W Moulson. Friendly family-run site. Reasonable shelter, small, level fields). Near to beach and places of historical

interest. Lovely walking area. Transport and towing of trailers available. Beautiful sub-tropical islands. AA 3 pennants. Open end March-October.

KENT

Ashford

Broadhembury Holiday Park, Steeds Lane, Kingsnorth, Ashford, Kent TN26 1NQ. *01233 620859.* enquiries@broadhembury.co.uk. www.broadhembury.co.uk. Keith & Jenny Taylor. From exit 10, M20, take A2070 and continue to second roundabout following signs for Kingsnorth. Left at second crossroads in village. Rail station 3 miles. Country Park convenient to many places of interest. 20 minutes to channel crossings and tunnel. Graded: 5 stars.

Dunn Street Farm, Westwell, Ashford, Kent TN25 4NJ. *01233 712537.* www.caravancampingsites.co.uk. Joe Stuart-Smith. On North Downs Way, 4 miles NW of M20 Junc 9, 2 miles N of A20 at Hothfield. Quiet farm site within easy reach of Canterbury, Chilham, Sissinghurst etc. Dish-washing facilities. Open March 1-October 31.

Spill Land Farm Holiday Park, Benenden Road, Biddenden, Ashford, Kent TN27 8BX. *01580 291379.* www.ukparks.co.uk/spilland. Mr A K Waite & Mr D S Waite. From A262 Biddenden to Tenterden road after 0.25 mile turn right on to road marked 'Vineyard' and Hospital, site 0.25 mile on right behind white farmhouse. Dogs allowed on leads. Latest arrival 6pm. Quiet countryside park, ideal for touring the Kent Weald. No motor caravans. Holiday caravans for sale. Open March-October (ground conditions permitting).

Biddenden

Woodlands Park, Tenterden Road, Biddenden, Kent TN27 8BT. *01580 291216.* Mr R E Jessop. Located on the A262 three miles north of Tenterden. Quiet, sheltered site. Excellent location for visiting tourist attractions. Site shop, gas and camping accessories. New toilet/shower block. Open March-October.

Birchington

Two Chimneys Caravan Park, Shottendane Road, Birchington, Kent CT7 0HD. *01843 841068/843157.* info@twochimneys.co.uk. www.twochimneys.co.uk. Mrs L Sullivan. A28 to Birchington turn right into Park Lane opposite church, bear left into Manston road. Turn left at crossroad B2049 to Margate. Site on right. Ferry terminal and central for all resorts. Snacks available. Licensed club. Graded: 4 stars. Open March-October.

Canterbury

Ashfield Farm Caravan & Camping Site, Waddenhall, Petham, Canterbury, Kent CT4 5PX. *01227 700624* mpatterson@ashfieldfarm.freeserve.co.uk. M C Patterson. From Canterbury take B2068. Ashfield Farm is approx 6 miles on right. From M20 Junction 11 take B2068 towards Canterbury. Level, screened site situated in an area of outstanding natural beauty. Modern toilet block with washroom and showers. 20 pitches. Open April 1-October 31.

Camping & Caravanning Club Site - Canterbury, Bekesbourne Lane, Canterbury, Kent CT3 4AB. *01227 463216.* www.campingandcaravanningclub.co.uk. The Camping & Caravanning Club Ltd. A257 towards Sandwich. Site is signposted from city. 1m E of Canterbury opposite golf course. Canterbury within easy reach. A popular stop-over for holiday makers heading for Dover and the Continent. 200 pitches set in 20 acres. Play area. Non members welcome. Caravans, motor caravans and tents accepted. Gold David Bellamy Gold Conservation Award.

'Rose and Crown', Stelling Minnis, Canterbury, Kent CT4 6AS. *01227 709265.* Stewart Jackson & Jackie Pinkney. 6.5m S of Canterbury E off B2068 Canterbury to Hythe road or Junction 11 off M20 take Canterbury road. Sheltered rural site, easy reach many places of interest. Fees on application. Open March-October.

Royal Oak, 114 Sweechgate, Broad Oak, Canterbury, Kent. *01227 710448.* K Hollingsbee. Two and a half miles north east of Canterbury via the A28 to Sturry. Then take the A291 towards Herne Bay and first turn left to Broad Oak. Site is behind inn. Small orchard site. Fees on application. Open April-October.

South View, Maypole Lane, Hoath, Canterbury, Kent CT3 4LL. *01227 860280.* Keith & Vivienne Underdown. Off the A28 and A299. Rural situation. Dogs allowed by arrangement but not bank holidays. Good food and drink 100yd country pub. Open April 1-October 31.

Yew Tree Park, Stone Street, Petham, Canterbury, Kent CT4 5PL. *01227 700306.* info@yewtreepark.com. www.yewtreepark. com. Mr & Mrs Zanders. On B2068 4 miles south of Canterbury and 9 miles north M20, J11. Small picturesque country park overlooking beautiful Chartham Downs. Ideally situated for exploring local heritage and Kent. Both level and sloping ground. Graded: 4 stars. Open March-October.

Chatham

Woolmans Wood Tourist Caravan Park, Bridgewood, Chatham, Kent ME5 9SB. *01634 867685.* John Weston. Leave motorway M2 at exit 3 then take the A229 and B2097. Secluded site ideal for touring Kent. Graded: 3 stars.

Dover

Hawthorn Farm Holiday Park, Station Road, Martin Mill, Dover, Kent CT15 5LA. *01304 852658.* www.keatfarm.co.uk. Keat Farm (Caravans) Ltd. 3m north-east of Dover. 0.5m off A258 Dover to Deal road. Site is signposted. Closest park to Dover ferries. Large, family site in landscaped grounds. Dover Castle 3m, beach 2.5m. Graded: 5 stars. Open March 1-November 30.

Dymchurch

New Beach Holiday Village & Touring Park, Hythe Road, Dymchurch, Kent TN29 0JX. *01303 872233.* info@cinqueportsleisure.com. www.cinqueports leisure.com. Cinque Ports Leisure. On main coast road between Hythe and Dymchurch. A259. Open March 1-January 11.

Folkestone

Black Horse Farm, 385 Canterbury Road, Densole, Folkestone, Kent CT18 7BG. *01303 892665.* www.caravan club.co.uk. The Caravan Club. Four miles north of Folkestone A260 towards Canterbury. Two miles from Junction A20, 80yd from Black Horse Inn. Holiday centre or overnight stop on Channel Tunnel/ferry route. Fees on application. Non-members and tent campers welcome. Ideal family site. Graded: 5 stars.

Camping & Caravanning Club Site - Folkestone, The Warren, Folkestone, Kent CT19 6PT. *01303 255093.* www.campingandcaravanningclub.co.uk. The Camping & Caravanning Club Ltd. Leave the A20 at roundabout and follow signs to Folkestone Harbour. 85 pitches. Site is adjacent to a fine sandy beach, ideal for all the family. Short walk to the beach. Non-members welcome. Tents and motor caravans accepted; no caravans. Open March-October.

Folkestone Racecourse Caravan Club Site, Folkestone Racecourse, Westenhanger, Folkestone, Kent CT21 4HX. *01303 261761.* www.caravanclub.co.uk. The Caravan Club. Leave M20 at exit 11, turn right at roundabout on to A20. Follow signs to racecourse. Night halt for cross-Channel travellers. Non members and tent campers welcome. Free racing (except Arab fixture in August). Open March-Setpember.

KENT

Little Satmar Holiday Park, Winehouse Lane, Capel-le-Ferne, Folkestone, Kent CT18 7JF. *01303 251188*. www.keat farm.co.uk . Mr S French. Inland off B2011 Folkestone to Dover. Rose Award. Open March-October 31.

🛞🐕📶🔥⊙🚿🍴🎣🛗🚻⇌🛒⚡*L*♪⚓↝⚓

Little Switzerland Caravan & Camping Park, Wear Bay Road, Folkestone, Kent CT19 6PS. *01303 252168*. little switzer land@lineone.net. caravancampingsites.co.uk/littleswitzerland. D Gasson. Breathtaking views across English Channel, Weir Bay Road and Harbour. Fees on application. Small family-run site, booking adviseable. Open March 1-October 30.

🛞🐕♨📶🔥🛒×⊙🚿🔥🛗🍴🚻⇌*L*♿🚮♨♪♪↝∪↝⚓⇙🛶

Isle of Sheppey

Priory Hill, Wing Road, Leysdown, Isle of Sheppey, Kent ME12 4QT. *01795 510267*. philip@prioryhill.co.uk. www.priory hill.co.uk. P S & M Butcher. M2/M20, A249, B2231 to Leysdown, Wing Road 2nd on left. All-inclusive price for stay. Swimming pool, clubhouse, showers. Graded: 4 stars. Adjacent 45 acre coastal park and seaside. Open March-October.

🛞🐕📶🛒×⊙🚿🔥🚿🎱🍴🎣🏊⇙

Maidstone

Coldblow Farm, Coldblow Lane, Thurnham, Maidstone, Kent ME14 3LR. *01622 735038*. Jeffrey Pilkington. From J7 M20 take A249 towards Detling. Turn to Detling village, right into Pilgrims Way, 2nd crossroads turn left towards Hucking. Site 0.5m on right. Camping barn 200yd from North Downs Way.

🛞🐕📶⊙🚿🍴⇌❄🛗∪

Pine Lodge Touring Park, Ashford Road, Hollingbourne, Maidstone, Kent ME17 1XH. *01622 730018*. booking@ pinelodgetouringpark.co.uk. www.pinelodgetouringpark.co.uk. Jan & Stan Hollingsworth. From J8, M20 (Leeds Castle exit), park 1m towards Bearsted and Maidstone. sheltered site with rural views. Ideal for Continental ports and touring Kent. Graded: 5 stars.

🛞🐕📶🔥🛗🛒🚿🔥🛗×🚻❄⚙⇙∪↝⚓

Riverside Caravan Park, Farleigh Bridge, East Farkeigh, Maidstone, Kent ME16 9ND. *01622 726647*. Mr D J Sunnucks. From M20 J5 turn right, at traffic lights turn left (Hermatage Lane) Straight across two sets of traffic lights and down hill, over level crossing immediately right into entrance. Open March 1-October 31.

🛞🐕📶⊙🚿🍴🚻⇌*L*🛗♿♪♪⇙∪↝⚓

New Romney

Marlie Farm Caravan & Camping Site, Dymchurch Road, New Romney, Kent TN28 8UE. *01797 363060*. info@cinqueportsleisure.com. www.cinqueportsleisure. com. Cinque Ports Leisure. On main A259 0.25m E of New Romney. Suitabnle base for touring Kent, Sussex also Channel ports. Well-drained, mown grass for tents. Children's playground. Fees, brochure on application SAE. Manager: Mr P Kinch. Open March-October.

🛞🐕♨📶🔥🛒⊙🚿🔥🎱🍴🎣⚓🚻⇌🏊*L*♿🛗♿♪♪⇙∪↝⚓🛶

Paddock Wood

The Hop Farm Country Park, Beltring, Paddock Wood, Kent TN12 6PY. *01622 872068*. The Hop Farm Ltd. M25 junction 5. M20 Junction 4. On the A228 between Tonbridge and Maidstone. The beautiful surroundings of the county's top tourist attractions offers visitors a wonderful opportunity to stay in this unique setting. Open Easter-October.

🛞🐕📶🔥♿🛒×⊙🚿🔥🛗🍴🚻⇌🏊*L*⇙↝⚓

Ramsgate

Manston Caravan & Camping Park, Manston Court Road, Manston, Ramsgate, Kent CT12 5AU. *01843 823442*. enquiries@manston-park.co.uk. www.manston-park.co.uk. Messrs Neale & Austen. 2.5m W of Ramsgate. From A253 eastturn left at Minster roundabout. Take B2048 for 400yd. Turn right on to B2190 which leads to B2050. Through airfield to 'Manston Court' garage, left to Manston Court Road. From Ramsgate, join B2050 from A253. Graded: 4 stars. Open April-October.

🛞🐕📶🔥♿🛒×⊙🚿🔥🛗🍴🚻⇌♪♪⇙∪↝⚓🛶

Nethercourt Park Camp Site, Nethercourt Hill, Ramsgate, Kent CT11 0RZ. *01843 595485*. P Barrowcliffe. Follow the A253 into Ramsgate. At Nethercourt Circus roundabout. Bear left to site entrance 150 yards on left. Half a mile from beach and one mile to yacht marina and ferry. TV room. Limited facilites for the disabled. Fees on application. Open Easter-October.

🛞🐕♨📶🔥♿🛒⊙🚿🔥🛗🍴🚻⇌*L*♿🚮♪♪⇙∪↝⚓🛶

Sandwich

Sandwich Leisure Park, Woodnesborough Road, Sandwich, Kent CT13 0AA. *01304 612681*. info@coastand countryleisure.com. www.coastandcountryleisure.com. Coast & Country Caravans. Half a mile outside town centre. Follow touring caravan signs from A257 and A258. Quiet, secluded, park just outside the medieval Cinque Port at Sandwich. Highly recommended. Graded: 4 stars. Open March-October.

🛞🐕📶🔥♿🛒⊙🚿🔥🛗🍴🚻⇌*L*🛗♿♪⇙

Sevenoaks

Camping & Caravanning Club Site - Oldbury Hill, Styants Bottom, Seal, Sevenoaks, Kent TN15 0ET. *01732 762728*. www.campingandcaravanningclub.co.uk. The Camping & Caravanning Club Ltd. 6-acre site with 60 pitches. Caravans, motor caravans and tents accepted. Levelling ramps are required. 0.5-mile off the A25 between Sevenoaks and Borough Green. Non-members welcome. Open April-October.

🛞🐕📶🔥♿🛒⊙🚿🔥🛗🍴🚻⇌*L*∪

'To the Woods', Botsom Lane, West Kingsdown, Sevenoaks, Kent TN15 6BN. *01322 863751*. Mrs E Helsdon. Four miles north west of Wrotham. Turn left at Botsom Lane off A20. Site (800 yards). Site is high on North Downs, but sheltered by trees and well-drained. Near Brands Hatch circuit. Site Manager: Mr M J Firman.

🐕📶🛒⊙🚿🚻❄⇙

WOOLMANS WOOD
TOURIST CARAVAN AND CAMPING PARK
Tel: 01634 867685
Rochester Road (B2097), Rochester, Kent ME5 9SB
Web site: **woolmans-wood.co.uk**
email: **woolmans.wood@currantbun.com**

Open all year · Easy access to M2/M2o and Channel ports
Local attractions include Rochester Castle and Cathedral
Charles Dickens Centre · Chatham Historic Dockyard and
Royal Engineers Museum · Leeds Castle nearby
Trains to London 40 mins

Toilet and shower (Free) facilities . Laundry . Hardstanding . Electric hook-up
Major supermarket within walking distance . Dogs welcome • Unsuitable for children

Sheerness

Sheerness Holiday Park, Halfway Road, Minster on Sea, Sheerness Kent ME12 3AA. *01795 662638*. info@cinqueportsleisure.com. www.cinqueportsleisure. com. Cinque Ports Leisure. Off the M25 to the M2 and take A249 towards Sheerness and then A250 to the town, 0.5m from centre. March-October.

Warden Springs Caravan Park Ltd, Warden Point, Eastchurch, Sheerness, Kent ME12 4HF. *01795 880216.* jackie@wscp.freeserve.co.uk. www.wardensprings.co.uk. Mr Clive Spurrier. From M20 junction 7 or M2 junction 5 onto the A249. A family site overlooking the sea and surrounded by open country. Facilities include nine-hole Pitch and Putt, licensed bar and children's play area. Graded: 3 stars. Open March-October.

Tonbridge

Tanner Farm Park, Goudhurst Road, Marden, Tonbridge, Kent TN12 9ND. *01622 832399.* enquiries@tannerfarm park.co.uk. www.tannerfarmpark.co.uk. J W Mannington & Mrs L R Mannington. From A229 or A262 on to the B2079 mid-way between Marden and Goudhurst. 15-acre park set in the centre of a 150-acre farm. In peaceful surroundings. Shower block with free showers. Graded: 5 stars.

Whitstable

Primrose Cottage Caravan Park, Golden Hill, Whitstable, Kent CT5 3AR. *01227 273694.* Mr Brian Campbell. A2990 1m east of Whitstable roundabout. 0.5m south of Whitstable. Next to Tesco's on the Thanet Way—A2990. Open March-October.

Seaview Holiday Village, St Johns Road, Swalecliff, Whitstable, Kent CT5 2RY. *01227 792246.* info@cinque portsleisure.com. www.cinqueportsleisure.com. Cinque Ports Leisure. From M2 go to A299 turn off to A2990 towards Whitstable.

Wrotham

Thriftwood Caravan & Camping Park, Plaxdale Green Road, Stansted, Wrotham, Kent TN15 7PB. *01732 822261.*

Mr & Mrs G Bass. Turn north off the A20 into Plaxdale Green Road half a mile east of radio mast visible from all over Kent. Near Horse and Groom. About one and a half miles from Wrotham. Touring centre or overnight stop from London to Dover. Dogs are allowed. Graded: 5 stars. Open March 1-January 31.

LANCASHIRE

Blackburn

Harwood Bar Holiday Park, Mill Lane, Great Harwood, Blackburn, Lancashire BB6 7UQ. *01254 884853.* South Lakeland Caravans. From A59, join A680, proceed towards Great Harwood for 2.5m 1st left after Nightingales garage. Park is on right. Quiet, on edge of Ribble Valley. Open 11 months.

Blackpool

Gillett Farm Caravan & Camping Park, Peel Road, Peel, Blackpool, Lancashire FY4 5JU. *01253 761676.* Mr S J Routledge. From exit 4 on M55, left on to A583. Straight on at roundabout to traffic lights, turn right and immediately left into Peel Road. Second site on right. Open March-October.

Kneps Farm Holiday Park, River Road, Thornton Cleveleys, Blackpool, Lancashire FY5 5LR. *01253 823632.* enquiries @knepsfarm.co.uk. www.knepsfarm.co.uk. Mr Jonathan Porter. Leave A585 at roundabout (B5412) Little Thornton. Right at mini roundabout after school on to Stanah Road, straight over 2nd mini roundabout to River Road. Quiet, family-run park close to Blackpool and Wyre countryside. Open March 1-November 15.

Mariclough Hampsfield Camping, Preston New Road, Peel Corner, Blackpool, Lancashire FY4 5JR. *01253 761034.* tony@mariclough.fsnet.co.uk. www.maricloughhampsfield camping.com. Mr Tony & Jeanne Cookson. Off M55 at junc 4 left on A583. Straight through lights, 300yd on left. Dogs welcome. Brochure available. AA and RAC listed. Adults only. Mid-week offer available. Open Easter-November.

Marton Mere Holiday Village, Mythop Road, Blackpool, Lancashire FY4 4XN. *01253 767544.* Bourne Leisure. Leave the M55 at Junction 4, turn right at roundabout, take A583 towards Blackpool, pass the windmill then turn right at the Clifton Arms traffic light, on to Mythop Road. Open Easter-September.

Pipers Height Caravan & Camping Park, Peel, Blackpool, Lancashire FY4 5JT. *01253 763767.* Mr Rawcliffe. 3m S of Blackpool from M55 junction 4. 40yd to Peel Corner turn into Peel Road, site is 50yds on right. Families only. Dogs welcome. Fees by arrangement. Licensed clubhouse with entertainment high season, restaurant. Open March-November.

Stanah House Caravan Park, River Road, Thornton, Blackpool, Lancashire FY5 5LW. *01253 824000.* stanah house@talk21.com. S E Adams. Leave M55 at Junction 3 on to A585 Black & White roundabout, turn right into B5415. Follow signs to Stanah picnic area. Small, select site near river. Views of fells and Lake District. Open March 1-October 31.

Under Hill Caravan & Camping Site, Penny Farm, Peel, Blackpool, Lancashire FY4 5JS. *01253 763107.* ILPH Ltd. From M55 junction 4 take first left on to A583. Site first on right after traffic lights. Family site 3.5m from Blackpool. Peaceful location. Wardens: Brian & Jacqui Buddle. Open Easter-end October.
🚐🏪📶🗑🛉⚡✕⊙🔥🛢️🏪🦯♿➡🥾 L ♀🛶 ♒ ◡ ↺ ⚓

Windy Harbour Holiday Park, Little Singleton, Blackpool, Lancashire FY6 8NB. *01253 883064.* info@windyharbour.net. www.windyharbour.net. Partington's Holiday Centre Ltd.From M55, exit J3. Take 3rd exit, signed A585, Fleetwood and follow road for approx. 3m to set of traffic lights, go straight on, park is 300m straight ahead, by river. Open March 1-November 15.
🚐🏪🦯🗑🛉♿⚡✕⊙🔥🛢️≋🏪♿➡ L ♀🛶 ♒ ◡ ↺ ⚓

Carnforth

Bolton Holmes Farm, off Mill Lane, Bolton-le-Sands, Carnforth, Lancashire LA5 8ES. *01524 732854.* Mr G Mason. On the W side of A6 at Bolton-le-Sands. 3m N Morecambe. 2m S of Carnforth. Easy reach of beach. Extensive views over Morecambe Bay. Open April-September.
🚐🏪📶🦯⚡⊙🔥🏪🦯➡🥾 L 🛶 ♒

Detron Gate Farm, Bolton-le-Sands, Carnforth, Lancashire LA5 9TN. *01524 732842.* Mr E Makinson. Off A6, 4m N of Lancaster, 3m to Morecambe. 1.5m S of Carnforth. Exit 35 from M6. Near canal. Fees on application. Open April-September.
🚐🏪📶🦯⚡⊙♿🔥🛢️🏪🦯➡🥾 L ♀🛶 ♒ ↺ ⚓

Gibraltar Farm, Silverdale, Carnforth, Lancashire. *01524 701706.* Mr Frank W Burrow. 4.5 miles north of Carnforth on unclassified roads. Signposted Silverdale north out of Carnforth. At Silverdale turn west on road signposted to hospital and Gibraltar, to T-junction in Lindeth Road; farm entrance opposite. Peaceful situation near beach and woodland. Open Easter-November.
🚐📶🦯⚡⊙♿🏪🦯➡🥾 L 🛶 ♒ ◡ ↺ ⚓

Hollins Farm, Far Arnside, Silverdale, Carnforth, Lancashire LA5 0SL. *01524 701767.* V & C Ribbons. 4.5m NW of Carnforth. Leave M6 at junction 35. Into Carnforth follow minor road Warton & Silverdale sign, next sharp left, right after level crossing. Fork left past phone box, right into Cove Road and 2nd left after children's home into farmyard. Open Easter-end October.
🚐📶🦯✕⊙🔥🏪➡🥾 🛶 ♒ ◡ ⚓

Red Bank Farm, Bolton-le-Sands, Carnforth, Lancashire LA5 8JR. *01524 823196.* Matthew Archer & Son. 3m N of Lancaster on A6 turn left on to A5105. After 300yd turn right, then right again over railway bridge then left on the shore to the farm. Close to shore and within easy reach of resorts and Lake District. Open April-October.
🚐📶⊙♿🔥🏪

Sandside Caravan & Camping Park, St Michaels Lane, Bolton-le-Sands, Carnforth, Lancashire LA5 8JS. *01524 822311.* Mr R Sedgwick. From J35, M6 follow signs for Morecambe. Turn right after the Pavillion restaurant in Bolton-le-Sands 0.5m past level crossing. Only 5 minutes from seashore with sea views. Open March-November.
🚐🏪📶🦯⊙♿🔥🛢️🏪➡ L ♀🛶 ♒ ◡

Woodclose Caravan Park, Kirkby Lonsdale, Carnforth, Lancashire LA6 2SE. *01524 271597.* michaelhodgkins@woodclosecaravanpark.fsnet.co.uk. www.woodclosepark.com. Mr F Hodgkins. Half mile SE of Kirkby Lonsdale on the A65. Quiet, family park. Lake District, Yorkshire Dales and seaside all within easy driving distance. Open March 1-October 31.
🚐🏪📶🦯⚡⊙♿🔥🛢️🏪🦯➡ L ♀🛶 ♒ ↺ ⚓

Clitheroe

Camping & Caravanning Club Site, Edisford Bridge, Edisford Road, Clitheroe, Lancashire BB7 3LA. *01200 425294.* www.campingandcaravanningclub.co.uk. The Camping & Caravanning Club Ltd. 5.8-acre site with 80 pitches. On banks of river Ribble in Ribble Valley. M6 exit 31 and follow A59. Site 1m west of Clitheroe on B6243. Adjacent to the site are a play area and pitch and putt course. Caravans, motor caravans and tents accepted. Non-members welcome. Open March-October.
🚐🏪📶🦯⚡⊙♿🔥🛢️🏪🦯➡ L 🛶 ♒ ↺ ⚓

Three Rivers Park, Eaves Hall Lane, West Bradford, Clitheroe, Lancashire BB7 3JG. *01200 423523.* Ribble Motels Ltd. Leave M6 Junction 31, take A59 to Clitheroe North, B6478 turn-off. Follow signs to West Bradford. At T-junction in West Bradford go left, take next right which is Eaves Hall Lane (300 yards). Open March 1-October 31.
🚐🏪📶🦯⚡⊙♿🔥🛢️🏪🦯➡ L ♀⚓

Todber Caravan Park, Gisburn, Clitheroe, Lancashire BB7 4JJ. *01200 445322.* T.D. & B A Varley. Off A682 1.5m S of A59 at Gisburn or M65 junction 13, 6m on A682 towards Kendal and Gisburn. Licensed club house. Children's play areas. Holiday caravans only. Open March-October.
⊙🦯🏪 L

Garstang

Claylands Caravan Park, Cabus, Garstang, Lancashire PR3 1AJ. *01524 791242.* alan@claylands-caravan-park.co.uk. www.claylands-caravan-park.co.uk. Mr F Robinson. On A6 2m N of Garstang. End of tarmac track road 40yd S of petrol station. Site by river. Excellent coarse fishing on site. Graded: 4 stars. Open March-January 4.
🚐🏪📶🦯⚡🛢️✕⊙♿🔥🛢️🏪🦯 L ♀🛶 ♒ ◡ ↺ ⚓

Smithy Caravan Park, Cabus Nook Lane, Winmarleigh, Garstang, Lancashire PR3 1AA. *01995 606200.* Mr J Wilding. 2m N of Garstang along A6. Turn left on B5272 to Smithy Garage, turn right over canal bridge, park on right-hand side. Open March 1-January 4.
🚐🏪📶⊙♿🔥🏪🦯 L ♀🛶 ♒ ◡ ↺

Lancaster

Moss Wood Caravan Park, Crimbles Lane, Cockerham, Lancaster, Lancashire LA2 0ES. *01524 791041.* info@mosswood.co.uk. www.mosswood.co.uk. S & H Wild. 1 mile west of Cockerham along the A588. Level, tree-lined park in unspoilt countryside. Convenient for Blackpool, Morecambe and Forest of Bowland. Holiday caravans for sale. Graded: 5 stars. Open March 1-October 31.
🚐🏪📶🦯⚡⊙♿🔥🏪🦯 L ♀🛶 ♒ ◡ ↺

Riverside Caravan Park, Bentham, Lancaster, Lancashire LA2 7HS. *01524 261272.* info@riversidecaravanpark.co.uk. www.riversidecaravanpark.co.uk. John Marshall & Son. This is a secluded park on the banks of the river Wenning, set in an unspoilt and delightful part of the countryside, yet within walking distance of the town. Open March 1-October 31.
🚐🏪📶🦯⚡⊙♿🔥🛢️🏪🦯➡ L ♀🎾🛶 ♒ ◡ ↺ ⚽ ⚓

Morecambe

Hawthorn Camping Site, Carr Lane, Middleton Sands, Morecambe, Lancashire LA3 3LL. *01524 852074.* Mr Humphries. A5105 from Morecambe through Heysham. Turn W at Pontin's Holiday Camp to Middleton Sands. Holiday site is 150yd from safe beach and within easy reach of Lake District. Licensed bar. Open Easter-October.
🚐🏪📶🦯⊙♿🔥🏪🦯 L ♒ ↺

Melbreak Camp, Carr Lane, Middleton, Morecambe, Lancashire LA3 3LH. 01524 852430. A E & G Syson. From Morecambe on road to Middleton and Overton. A589 at Middleton turn right by church towards beach. 3m SSW of Morecambe. Easy drive of beach and seaside attractions. Open March-October.

Venture Caravan Park, Langridge Way, Westgate, Morecambe, Lancashire LA4 4TQ. 01524 412986. mark@ venturecaravanpark.co.uk. www.venturecaravanpark.co.uk. D & S & M R Needham. 1m from sea front off A589, 6m from M6 junction 34. Bar/bar meals. Shop. Off licence. Play areas. Dogs on leads allowed.

Ormskirk

Abbey Farm, Dark Lane, Ormskirk, Lancashire L40 5TX. 01695 572686. abbeyfarm@yahoo.com. www.abbeyfarmcaravan park.co.uk. Joan & Alan Bridge. M6, junc 27, A5209 Parbold/Newburgh. Left B5240 immediate right Hobcross Lane. Site 1.5m on right. Halfway between London and Scotland. Level grass. Mature trees. Open April 1-October 31 for tents. Fees on application.

Shaw Hall Caravan Park, Smithy Lane, Scarisbrick, Ormskirk, Lancashire L40 8HJ. 01704 840298. shawhall @btconnect. www.shallhall.co.uk. Barley Mow Ltd. 4m E of Southport off A570 400yd past Little Chef. Canal-side site with licensed social club. Graded: 3 stars. Open March-January.

Preston

Beacon Fell View Holiday Park, 110 Higher Road, Longridge, Preston, Lancashire PR3 2TF. 01772 785434/783233. Hagans Leisure Group.Leave M6 at junction 32 to Garstang A6. Follow sign to Longridge (not Beacon Fell). At Longridge, straight across roundabout then left at White Bull. Park one mile ahead on right. One of Haven's 37 tenting and touring parks around the UK. Indoor fun pool. Free kids' club. Family clubroom. Open Easter-October.

High Moor Farm Caravan Park, Singleton Road, Weeton, Preston, Lancashire PR4 3JJ. 01253 836451. John & Joan Colligan. 1.5m S of Singleton on B5260, and 6m E of Blackpool. Leave M55 towards Fleetwood on A585, then B5260 is 3rd turn on left. Easy reach of Blackpool. Fees on application. Open March-October.

Royal Umpire Caravan Park, Southport Road, Croston, Preston, Lancashire PR5 7JB. 01772 600257. F Rowe & Sons. On A581 midway between A59 and A49. Britain's favourite tourist attractions within an hour's drive of this renowned touring park. 10m east of Southport, 5m west of Chorley, 1m east of Croston. Some facilities restricted November and December.

Rochdale

Gelder Wood Park, Ashworth Road, Heywood, Rochdale, Lancashire OL11 5UP. 01706 364858. gelderwood@aol.com. www.adultstouring.co.uk/gelderwood. Mr P Chadwick. M62 exit 18 to M66 to Bury A58 to Heywood on right, turn left into Bamford Road to T-junction B6222. Turn left 100 yds at Ashworth Rd, top of hill, right side opposite Scout Camp. Adults only park. BH&HPA. Graded 5 stars. Open March-November.

Hollingworth Lake Caravan Park, Rakewood, Littleborough, Rochdale, Lancashire OL15 0AT. 01706 378661. Mr D & Mr F Mills. M62, exit 21. Follow Hollingworth Lake Country Park signs. 4m NE of Rochdale via A58 and B6225 to Hollingworth Lake. Turn at signpost for Rakewood by Fishermans Inn. Small site by lake.

LEICESTERSHIRE
Hinckley

Villa Farm Caravan & Camping, Wolvey, Hinckley, Leicestershire LE10 3HF. 01455 220493/220630. Mr H Rusted. From Coventry A46 to M6, then take B4065 (old A46) for four miles. From Leicester B4114 or M69 juntion 1. Grassy, flat site. Central for day trips. Fees on application.

LINCOLNSHIRE
Alford

Woodthorpe Hall Leisure Park, Woodthorpe, Alford, Lincolnshire LN13 0DD. 01507 450294. Mr Stubbs. On B1373 between Alford & Withern. In heart of Lincolnshire countryside. Huge range of activities including all-weather bowling. Golf course on site. Open March 1-January 2.

Barton-on-Humber

Silver Birches Tourist Park, Waterside Road, Barton-on-Humber, Lincolnshire DN18 5BA. 01652 632509. Mr Richard & Carol Shelton. On A15 or 1077 follow viewing area signs to Waterside road. Next to Humber Bridge. Dogs allowed on leads. Open April 1-November.

Boston

Midville Caravan Park, Midville, Stickney, Boston, Lincolnshire PE22 8HW. 01205 270316. Jan & Ray Maley. A16 Boston to Grimsby road. At Stickney turn east to Midville and follow tourist brown signs to park. Adjacent to Duke of Wellington pub. Level, family-run, country park. Weekend entertainment at adjacent pub. Open March 1-November 30.

Pilgrim's Way C& C, Church Green Road, Fishtoft, Boston, Lincolnshire PE21 0QY. 01205 366646. maria@pilgrims-way.co.uk. www.pilgrims-way.co.uk. Maria & Tony Potts. Take the A52 out of Boston towards Skegness at Bargate bridge, first road sign, second sign on Wain Fleet Road or take any road to Fishtoft. AA 4 pennant. First class park (not suitable for small children). Open Easter-end September.

The Plough, Swineshead Bridge, Boston, Lincolnshire PE20 3PT. 01205 820300. Mr Wilson. On main A17 Newark-King's Lynn. 1.5m from junction A52 Nottingham-Boston road which joins A17 at Swineshead. Dogs allowed. Open March-September.

White Cat Caravan & Camping Park, Shaw Lane, Old Leake, Boston, Lincolnshire PE22 9LQ. 01205 870121. kevin@klannen.freeserve.co.uk. www.whitecatpark.com. Mr & Mrs Lannen. On main A52 Boston to Skegness. 8m from Boston, turn right opposite B1184 Sibsey road. Free showers.

Swings. Post office, restaurant and pub nearby. Suitable base for Skegness and touring the Fens. Open April-October.

🚐 🏪 📶 ⛽ 🛒 ✗ ⊙ 🅖 ♨ 📷 🎣 💡 🏊 ↙

Cleethorpes

> **Thorpe Park Holiday Centre, Humberston, Cleethorpes, Lincolnshire DN35 0PW.** *01472 813395.* Bourne Leisure. 2m S of Cleethorpes. Holiday site near sea. Fees on application. Open March-October.
> 🚐 🏪 ⛺ 📶 ⛽ 🚿 🛒 ✗ ⊙ 🅖 ♨ 🏍 📻 ≋ 🎣 ≈ 💡 🏊 ⚓ ↙ 🎿 ∪ ⟳ ☇ 🛶

Grantham

Woodland Waters, Willoughby Road, Ancaster, Grantham, Lincolnshire NE32 3RT. *01400 230888.* info@woodlandwaters.co.uk. www.woodlandwaters.co.uk. Mr & Mrs M Corradine. Easy accessible from A1 north, leave at Newark A17 then B6403. South A1 leave at Colsterworth to B6403. Woodland Waters on A153 Grantham-Sleaford road opposite petrol station. Holiday lodges.

🚐 🏪 ⛺ 📶 ⛽ 🚿 🛒 ✗ ⊙ 🅖 ♨ 🏍 📻 ≋ 🎣 ☼ 💡 🎣 🎿 ∪ ⟳ ☇

Horncastle

> **Ashby Park, West Ashby, Horncastle, Lincolnshire LN9 5PP.** *01507 527966.* ashbyparklands|@aol.com. www. ukparks.co.uk/ashby. M & R Francis. Between A153 and A158, 1.5m N of Horncastle. Six fishing lakes, set in 69 acres of Lincolnshire Wolds in river Bain valley. 4 star park in unspoilt countryside. David Bellamy Gold Conservation Award. Open March 1-November 30.
> 🚐 🏪 📶 ⛽ 🚿 🛒 ⊙ 🅖 ♨ 🏍 📻 🎣 💡 🎣 🎿 ∪ ☇

Lincoln

Hartsholme Country Park Camp Site, Skellingthorpe Road, Lincoln, Lincolnshire LN6 0EY. *01522 873578.* Lincoln City Council. Signposted from A46, three miles south of Lincoln. Sheltered, level site, beautifully situated in country park with woods, meadows and lakes. Perfect location for exploring the historic city of Lincoln. Graded: 2 stars. Open March 1-October 31 and Christmas market period.

🚐 🏪 🚿 📶 ⛽ 🛒 ✗ ⊙ 🅖 ♨ 🏍 📻 ≋ 💡 🎣 ⟳ ☇ ⚓

Willow Holt Caravan & Camping Park, Lodge Road, Tattershall, Lincoln, Lincolnshire LN4 4JS. *01526 343111.* enquiries@willowholt.co.uk. www.willowholt.co.uk. B & R Stevenson. Leave A153 road at Tattershall market place signposted Woodhall Spa. Site on left in 1.5m. Well-drained parkland wirh woods, lakes and abundant wildlife. New toilet block with laundry and washing up rooms. Fishing on site. Family run. Dogs on leads allowed. Open March 15-October 31.

🚐 🏪 📶 ⛽ 🛒 ⊙ 🅖 ♨ 🏍 📻 ≋ 💡 🎣 🎿 ∪ ⟳ ☇ ⚓ 🛶

Louth

Saltfleetby Fisheries, Louth, Lincolnshire LN11 7SS. *01507 338272.* Mr & Mrs C J Musgrave. B1200, 6 miles east of Louth. Quiet, peaceful, adult only site. Fishing lakes, well stocked. Shop on entrance to site. Close to Mablethorpe and Skegness. Open March 1-October 31.

🚐 🏪 📶 ⛽ 🚿 🛒 ♨ 🏍 📻 🎣 💡 🎣 ☇

Mablethorpe

Camping & Caravanning Club Site - Mablethorpe, Highfield, 120 Church Lane, Mablethorpe, Lincolnshire LN12 2NU. *01507 472374.* www.campingandcaravanclub.co.uk. The Camping & Caravanning Club Ltd. 6-acre site with 105 pitches accepting all units. On entering Mablethorpe on A1104, just after 'Welcome to

Mablethorpe' sign, turn right to Church Lane. Site is on right. 1m to beach. Play area. Non-members welcome. Caravans, motor caravans and tents accepted. Open March-October.
🚐🚉📺🛅🦽⚓☺🅿🛒🏧🍴🚿🅇🍴♿️🚭🔍⛽

Denehurst Camp Site, Alford Road, Mablethorpe, Lincolnshire LN12 1PX. *01507 472951*. Chris Lewin. East into Mablethorpe on A1104. Less than a mile to shops and beach. sheltered site. Open all year, dependent on field condition.
🚐🚉🚽📺🛅🆇☺⚓🛒🏧♿️🍴🍴🚿

> **Golden Sands Holiday Park, Quebec Road, Mablethorpe, Lincolnshire LN12 1QJ.** *01507 477871*. Bourne Leisure Ltd. From Mablethorpe town centre follow the sea front road to the north end for Golden Sands. One of Haven's 37 tenting and touring parks around the UK. Indoor and outdoor pools. Free kids' club. Free evening entertainment. Mini-golf. All-weather multi sports court. Graded: 3 stars. Open Easter-October.
> 🚐🚉🚽📺🛅🦽🆇☺🛒🏧🍽🏧🍴🍴🍴🍴🚿🅇🔍

Market Deeping
Deepings Caravan Park, Outgang Road, Towngate Market Deeping, Lincolnshire PE6 8LQ. *01778 344535*. info@thedeepings.com. www.thedeepings.com. Mr DM & Mrs BJ Young. From Market Deeping take the B1525 towards Spalding and after 2.5m turn left on to an unclassified road, the park is 0.25m on the right. Fees on application. Open February 1-December 31.
🚐🚉📺🛅🦽🛒☺⚓🏧🍴🍴🍴🅇🔍⛽

Market Rasen
The Rother Camp Site, Gainsborough Road, Middle Rasen, Market Rasen, Lincolnshire LN8 3JU. *01673 842433*. Mr & Mrs K A Steed. 1.5m west of Market Rasen and 200yd east of junction A46 and A631. Within easy access of Lincoln city and coastal resorts.Suitable touring base. Open March-October.
🚐🚉🛒☺⚓🏧🍴🍽🍴🍴🍴🍴🅇☺

Viking Way Walesby, Mill House Farm, Walesby, Market Rasen, Lincolnshire LN8 3UR. *01673 838333*. Mr A J & Mrs K Burton. On Viking Way footpath or at cross roads. A46 and A1103. One and a half miles NW Market Rasen. Follow sign Walesby. A quiet, secluded site at the foot of the Lincolnshire Wolds. Excellent yet non-demanding circular walks. Open March 1-December 31.
🚉📺🛅🛒☺⚓🏧🍽🍴🍴🍴🅇☺

Walesby Woodlands Caravan Park, Walesby Road, Market Rasen, Lincolnshire LN8 3UN. *01673 843285*. R H & B Papworth. Take the B1203 from Market Rasen. In 0.75 mile turn left to Walesby. Site is located 0.25 mile on the left (signposted). High-quality site on edge of the Lincolnshire Wolds, bordered by forest. Offering woodland walks, peace and fresh air. AA 3-pennant. RAC appointed. Open March 1-November 1.
🚐🚉📺🦽🛒☺⚓🏧🍴🍽🍴🍴🅇🍴🍴🍴🅇🔍⛽

Metheringham
The White Horse Inn Caravan & Camping Park, Dunston Fen, Metheringham, Lincolnshire LN4 3AP. *01526 398341*. Jackie & Barrie Darling. From B1188 Lincoln/Sleaford road, turn into Dunston village. Follow signs in village to Dunston Fen and River Witham. Five miles down Fen Road to river. Small, family run site adjacent to the river Witham. Located 12 miles from Lincoln. Booking advisable. Open February 1-December 31.
🚐🚉🚽📺🛅🆇☺⚓🏧🍴🍴

Peterborough
Lakeside Caravan Park, Station Road, Deeping St James, Peterborough, Lincolnshire PE6 8RQ. *01778 343785*. R J Charlesworth. B1166 from Market Deeping, signposted from level crossing. Open February 1-December 31.
🚐🚉🚽📺🛅☺🏧🍴🅇🔍⛽

Skegness
Conifer Park Touring Site, Walls Lane, Ingoldmells, Skegness, Lincolnshire PE25 1JH. *01754 762494*. Chris & Marian Brookes. Walls Lane is opposite Butlins Holiday camp A52. Park is half a mile down on right. Site best appreciated by more mature campers who like a clean peaceful site with a country environment. 0.75m from seafront. Cafe/restaurant, bottled gas supply, laundry facilities all available nearby. Open March 1-October 31.
🚐🚉🦽🛒☺⚓🏧🍽🍴🍴🍴🔍⛽

Countrymeadows Holiday Park, Anchor Lane, Ingoldmells, Skegness, Lincolnshire PE25 1LZ. *01754 874455*. info@countrymeadows.co.uk. www.countrymeadows.co.uk. J G & G D Hardy. N from Skegness on A52, 4m to Ingoldmells, through village 0.5m turn right (sea front) into Anchor Lane, site is 0.5m on left. Level site with good access and close to beach etc. Open March 25-end October.
🚐🚉📺🛅🦽🛒☺⚓🏧🍴🍽🍴🍴🅇🦽🍴🍴🅇🔍⛽

Retreat Farm, Croft, Skegness, Lincolnshire PE24 4RE. *01754 762092*. Mr D Smith. 1m S of Skegness on Boston A52 road. Open April-October.
🚐🚉📺☺⚓🆇🍴🅇🍽🍴🍴🍴🔍

Riverside Caravan Park, Wainfleet Bank , Wainfleet, Skegness, Lincolnshire PE24 4ND. *01754 880205*. Mrs & Mrs Bingham. 6m SW of Skegness on A52 towards Boston. Leave bypass onto B1195. In Wainfleet turn right to site before bridge over river. Secluded caravan site with limited space for tents. Fees on application. Open March 15-October 31.
🚐🚉📺🛅☺⚓🏧🍴🆇🍽🍴🍴🍴

Skegness Water Leisure Park, Walls Lane, Skegness, Lincolnshire PE25 1JF. *01754 769019/769905*. enquiries@skegnesswaterleisurepark.co.uk. www.skegnesswaterleisurepark.co.uk. Conveniently situated 3m N of Skegness, just off A52 - Down Walls Lane. 400yd from Butlins and just 1m from existing new complex at Fantasy Island. Open first Saturday March-last Saturday October.
🚐🚉🚽📺🛅🦽🆇☺⚓🏧🍽🍴🍴🅇🍴🍴🍴🅇🔍⛽

Sleaford
Low Farm Touring Park, Spring Lane, Folkingham, Sleaford, Lincolnshire NG34 0SJ. *01529 497322*. Mr & Mrs N Stevens. Situated just off A15 midway between Bourne & Sleaford. Quiet, secluded park with 36 pitches. Converted farm buildings have licensed bar and indoor barbecue facility at peak periods. Open Easter-mid October.
🚐🚉🚽🛅☺⚓🍴🏧🍴🍴

Low Farm Touring Park, Spring Lane, Folkingham, Sleaford, Lincolnshire NG34 0SJ. *01529 497322*. Mr & Mrs N R Stevens. Just off A15 midway between market towns of Bourne and Sleaford. Quiet secluded park within walking distance of conservation village with all facilities. Open Easter-end October.
🚐🚉🛒☺⚓🍴🏧🍴🍴

Spalding
Delph Bank Just For Adults Touring Caravan & Camping Park, Oldmain Road, Fleet Hargate, Holbeach, Spalding, Lincolnshire PE12 8LL. *01406 422910*. enquiries@delphbank.co.uk. www.delphbank.co.uk. Mr M Watts & Miss J Lawton. Located 150 yards off the A17 between Kings Lynn

and Sleaford. Quiet site in centre of village; adults only. Pubs, shops and eating places all within easy walking distance. Graded 4 stars. Open March-November.

Foremans Bridge Caravan Park, Sutton St James, Spalding, Lincolnshire PE12 0HU. *01945 440346.* Mrs A Strahan. From A17, follow signs for Sutton St James on B1390. From B1165 follow signs for Long Sutton B1390. Rural location adjacent to tranquil Fen waterway. Graded: 4 stars. Open March-November.

Lake Ross Caravan Park, Dozens Bank, West Pinchbeck, Spalding, Lincolnshire PE11 3NA. *01775 761690.* Mr Martyn Frey. Take the A151 Spalding to Bourne. Quiet countryside location with own fishing lake. Within easy reach of local interests. Dogs allowed on leads. SAE for brochure. Open February-December.

Orchard View Caravan and Camping Park, Broadgate, Sutton St Edmund, Spalding, Lincolnshire PE12 0LT. *01945 700482.* Mr R A Oddy. A47 Peterborough to Wisbech. At Guyhirn take B1187 to Murrow, pass through Parson Drove and follow signs (about five miles from A47 to park) over double bridge, 2nd right, on right. Level, grassy, rural site convenient for north Norfolk and Lincolnshire resorts and Hull to Harwich cycle route, licensed bar. Rally field. Open March 31-October 31.

Stamford

Tallington Lakes, Barholm Road, Tallington, Stamford, Lincolnshire PE9 4RJ. *01778 347000.* Tallington Lakes Ltd. On A16 between Stamford and Market Deeping. Turn N at petrol station. Water sports park with over 160 acres of water; water-skiing, jet ski, windsurfing and fishing, plus dry ski slope. Open March-January.

Sutton-on-Sea

Cherry Tree Site, Huttoft Road, Sutton-on-Sea, Lincolnshire LN12 2RU. *01507 441626.* murray.cherry tree@virgin.net. www.caravancampingsites.co.uk. Geoff & Margaret Murray. 1.5 miles south of Sutton on Sea on left hand side (A52). Entrance is via layby. Family run site close to safe, sandy beaches. Perfect for touring Lincolnshire. Children's playground. Cafe/restaurant nearby. Open March-end October.

Swinderby

Oakhill Leisure, Butt Lane, Thurlby Moor, Swinderby, Lincolnshire LN6 9QG. *01522 868771/07773 814057.* Mr Ronald De Raad. From the A46 between Lincoln /Newark, take junction to Bassingham/Thurlby. Turn right at junction. Round S-bend, and right into Oakhill Leisure. Site is flat and grassed.

Tattershall

Tattershall Park Country Club, Sleaford Road, Tattershall, Lincolnshire LN4 4LR. *01526 343193.* Located on a A153 Sleaford to Skegness road. Set in 365 acres of woodland, parkland and lakes. Restaurant, bars, canoeing. jet skiing, squash, waterskiing school. Coarse fishing. Pony trekking. Nature trails.

Woodhall Spa

Bainland Country Park, Horncastle Road, Woodhall Spa, Lincolnshire LN10 6UX. *01526 352903.* bookings@bainland.com. www.bainland.com. Mr W Craddock. On the B1191 1.5 miles from Woodhall Spa towards Horncastle just before WCF petrol station.

Camping & Caravanning Club Site - Woodhall Spa, Wellsyke Lane, Kirkby on Bain, Woodhall Spa, Lincolnshire LN10 6YU. *01526 352911.* www.campingandcaravanning club.co.uk. The Camping & Caravanning Club Ltd. 6.4-acre site with 90 pitches. At main crossroads in Woodhall Spa take B1191 for Horncastle. Take first right 1.5m turn left into Wellsyke Lane. Non-members welcome. Wildlife including woodpeckers, kestrels and kingfishers often seen from site. Caravans, motor caravans and tents accepted. Open March-October.

Jubilee Park, Stixwould Road, Woodhall Spa, Lincolnshire LN10 6QH. *01526 352448.* Near centre of town junction B1191 and B1192. Park overlooking woods, with all amenities close by. Fees on application to Park Manager. Graded: 3 stars. Open Easter or April 1-October 31.

LONDON

Abbey Wood

Abbey Wood Caravan & Camping Site, Federation Road, Abbey Wood, London SE2 0LS. *020 83117708.* www.caravanclub.co.uk. The Caravan Club. Signposted from the A2. Dogs on lead, exercise off site. Non-members and tent campers welcome.

Chingford

Lee Valley Campsite, Sewardstone Road, Chingford, London E4 7RA. *020 8529 5689.* scs@leevalleypark.org.uk. www.leevalleypark.org.uk. Lee Valley Regional Park. Leave M25 at Junction 26 and follow signs. On the A112, two miles north of Chingford. Overlooking King George V reservoir. Touring base for London. Part of Lee Valley Park. Open April-October.

Crystal Palace

Crystal Palace Caravan Club Site, Crystal Palace Parade, Crystal Palace, London SE19 1UF. *020 8778 7155.* www.caravanclub.co.uk. The Caravan Club. On the A212 near Crystal Palace bus terminal. Near National Sports Centre. Non-members welcome. Perfect site for all of London's attractions.

Edmonton

Lee Valley, Caravan & Camping Park, Meridian Way, Edmonton, London N9 0AS. *020 8803 6900.* leisurecentre @leevalleypark.org.uk. www.leevalleypark.org.uk. Lee Valley Regional Park. Park is situated in the grounds of a large complex. Facilities include 12 screen cinema, tex mex bar, pizza restaurant, barbecues, TV, 18-hole golf course. Convenient for London. Part of the Lee Valley Park. Dogs are allowed, on leads. Closed Christmas/Boxing Day and New Year's Day.

Leyton

Lee Valley Cycle Circuit & Campsite, Quartermile Lane, Leyton, London E10 5PD. *020 8534 6085.* www.leevalley park.org.uk. Lee Valley Regional Park. Off A102M East Way Route. Four miles from central London. Open April-October.

🚐📶🛢️♿🐕‍🦺🅿️✕☉🛢️🛗🏪🍴♨️∠🔌🔍

MERSEYSIDE

Southport

Riverside Touring & Camping Leisure Centre, Southport New Road, Banks, Southport, Merseyside PR9 8DF. *01704 228886.* Riverside Leisure Centre Ltd. 2.5m W of Tarleton Cross Roads on S of A565 4m East Southport. Flat pasture land. Car parking by tents. On main Southport to Preston trunk road. Near Rufford Old Hall National Trust. Open March-January.

🚐📶🚿📶🛢️♿🐕‍🦺🅿️✕☉🛢️🛗🏪♨️🏹🍴∠🔌🔍🍴🏊🔍

NORFOLK

Attleborough

Oak Tree Caravan Park, Norwich Road, Attleborough, Norfolk NR17 2JX. *01953 455565.* oaktree.cp@virgin.net. www.oaktree-caravan-park.co.uk. Mr & Mrs D A M Birkinshaw. Turn R off A11 (Thetford-Norwich) at SP Attleborough, in 2m continue through Attleborough passing Sainsbury's, fork left, immediately past church at T junction, site on right in 0.5m.

🚐📶☉🛗🏹🍴♨️❄️🔌

Banham

Applewood Caravan & Camping Park, Banham Zoo, The Grove, Banham, Norfolk NR16 2HB. *01953 888370.* Mr M Goymour. Located next door to Banham Zoo off A11 and A140, Norfolk. 13 acre countryside site. Electric hook-ups, full disabled facilities. Caravan accessories shop. Freezer service.

🚐📶🚿📶🛢️♿🐕‍🦺🅿️✕☉🛢️🛗🏪🍴∠🔌

Clippesby

Clippesby Hall, Clippesby, Norfolk NR29 3BL. *01493 367800.* holidays@clippesby.com. www.clippesby.com. The Lindsay Family. Located 400yd along lane opposite village sign on the B1152 Acle to Martham/Potter Heigham road. In the Norfolk Broads National Park close to nature reserves and coastal resorts. Perimeter parking in a woodland and parkland setting. Sheltered, grassy, family-owned. David Bellamy Gold Conservation Award. Colour brochure available. Open Easter to September.

🚐📶🛢️♿🐕‍🦺🅿️✕☉🛗🏪📶🏹🍴♨️∠🔌🏊🍴⛳🔍🔌🔍

Cromer

Beeston Regis Caravan & Camping Park, Cromer Road, West Runton, Cromer, Norfolk NR27 9NG. *01263 823614.* beestonregis@btinternet.com. www.beestoneregis.co.uk. BRCP Ltd. A149 Sheringham to Cromer road 1m from Sheringham. Cliff top with panoramic views, overlooking the sea. 440 touring and tent units. Open mid March-end October.

🚐📶📶🛢️♿🐕‍🦺🛗☉🛗🏪📶🏹🍴♨️∠🔌🏊🍴∠🔌🔍🏊⛳↗️🔍

Camping & Caravanning Club Site - West Runton, Holgate Lane, West Runton, Cromer, Norfolk NR27 9NW. *01263 837544.* www.campingandcaravanningclub.co.uk. The Camping & Caravanning Club Ltd. 15-acre site with 200 pitches. About 1m from the sea in secluded surroundings. From Kings Lynn on the A148 turn left at Roman Camp Inn. Play area. Non members welcome. Caravans, motor caravans and tents accepted. Open March-November.

🚐📶📶🛢️♿🐕‍🦺🛗☉🛗🏪📶🏹🍴♨️∠🔌∠🔌🏊🔍

Forest Park Caravan Site, Northrepps Road, Cromer, Norfolk NR27 0JR. *01263 513290.* forest-park@netcom.co.uk. www.forest-park.co.uk. Off the B1159. Adjacent to Cromer golf course. Open March 15-January 15.

🚐📶🚿📶🛢️♿🐕‍🦺🅿️✕☉🛗🏪📶🏹∠🔌🏊🔍

NORFOLK

Manor Farm Camp Site, East Runton, Cromer, Norfolk NR27 9PR. *01263 512858.* caravansite@manor-farm.sage-host.co.uk. www.manor-farm.sageweb.co.uk. Mr S T Holliday. One mile west of Cromer. Turn off the A148 at brown/white Manor Farm sign. Manor Farm .75m. Secluded, family run farm site with sea and woodland views. Well-drained. Separate field for campers with dogs. No motorcycles on site. Takeway, cafe/restaurant available nearby. Fees on application. Open Easter-September.

Seacroft Camping Park, Runton Road, Cromer, Norfolk NR27 9NH. *01263 511722.* www.ukparks.co.uk/seacroft. Epton Leisure Ltd. 0.5m W of Cromer on A149 to Sheringham. Holiday site near sandy beach. Fees on application. Open March 20-October 31.

Woodhill Caravan & Camping Park, East Runton, Cromer, Norfolk NR27 9PX. *01263 512242.* info@woodhill-park.com. www.woodhill-park.com. Blue Sky Leisure, Timewell Properties Ltd. On A149, between Cromer and Sheringham. High quality, cliff top park at affordable prices offering peace and tranquillity. Rose Award. N.N.D.C.'s Best Touring Park 1995. Open March 20-October 31.

Diss

Willows Caravan & Camping Park, Diss Road, Scole, Diss, Norfolk IP21 4DH. *01379 740271.* Mr & Mrs R Wedd. 1.50 miles east of Diss on A1066, 250 yards from Scole A140 round-about. On Norfolk/Suffolk boundary. Level, peaceful site on the banks of river Waveney, surrounded by conservation area. Open May-October.

Fakenham

Fakenham Racecourse Caravan & Camping Site, The Racecourse, Fakenham, Norfolk NR21 7NJ. *01328 862388.* Manager: David Hunter. Set in beautiful countryside. Ideally located for visiting Norfolk's coastal resorts, stately homes, wildlife and many other attractions.

The Old Brick Kilns, Little Barney Lane, Barney, Fakenham, Norfolk NR21 0NL. *01328 878305.* enquire@old-brick-kilns.co.uk. Alan & Pam Greenhalgh. Off A148 at B1354 to Aylsham. follow brown Tourist Board signs to Barney. Quiet, family park with clean, modern facilities. Licensed restaurant. Small fishing pond. David Bellamy Gold'Conservation Award. AA 4 pennants. Open March 1-January 6.

Great Yarmouth

Burgh Castle Marina, Butt Lane, Burgh Castle, Great Yarmouth, Norfolk NR31 9PZ. *01493 780331.* burghcastle marina@aol.com Mr R D Wright. Off A143 Yarmouth to Beccles 3 miles west of Gorleston on Sea. Pontoon moorings. Slipway. Generous space, quiet, rural setting. Full service pitches with water and drainage. Spectacular views and walks to Roman ruins; visiting exhibitions by heritage and wildlife conservation trusts. Close to bird reserve. Riverside pub and restaurant. Swimming pool. Free hot showers. Wash-up facility. Open March 1-October 31.

Liffens Holiday Park, Burgh Castle, Great Yarmouth, Norfolk NR31 9QB. *01493 780357.* www.liffens.co.uk. Mr P Liffen. 4m SW of Gt Yarmouth. Take A12 from Gt Yarmouth. From bypass follow signs to Burgh Castle until T-junction. Turn

right to Queen's Head Public house, then left to site on the right. Well-equipped, flat site, 10 minutes from sea. Play area, bars, entertainment. Graded: 4 stars. Open Easter-October.

🚐 🔌 ♨ 📺 ♿ 🛁 ✕ ☺ ⏱ 🔥 🔯 ≈ 🛒 🏠 🚻 🛒 L 💧 ♨ ♪ ✓ ⚓ ⚓

Liffens Welcome Holiday Centre, Butt Lane, Burgh Castle, Great Yarmouth, Norfolk NR31 9PU. *01493 780481.* www. liffens.co.uk. Mr P Liffen. 4m S of Gt Yarmouth, W off A143. Turn right to Burgh Castle, 0.5 mile turn right we are 0.5 mile on right. Family run holiday centre close to Great Yarmouth and Broads. Great facilities: bars, entertainment, gym, solarium. Graded 4 stars.

🚐 🔌 ♨ 📺 ♿ 🛁 ✕ ☺ ⏱ 🔥 🔯 ≈ 🛒 🏠 ✿ L 💧 ♨ ♪ ✓ ⚓ ⚓ ↗ ⚡

Long Beach Caravan Park, Hemsby, Great Yarmouth, Norfolk NR29 4JD. *01493 730023.* Off B1159 at Beach Road, Hemsby. 30 acres. Own private sandy beach. Licensed club. Supermarket, laundrette. Open March-October.

🚐 🔌 📺 🔥 ☺ ⏱ 🔥 🏠 🛒 L 🛒 ⚓

Rose Farm Touring & Camping Park, Stepshort, Belton, Great Yarmouth, Norfolk NR31 9JS. *01493 780896.* S & T Myhra. Off 143 into new road at signpost to Belton and Burgh Castle. First right. First site on right. Clean, quiet site in peaceful surroundings. 4m from Great Yarmouth and 2m from Gorleston. Shops & pubs close by. Local transport.

🚐 🔌 📺 ♿ 🔥 ☺ ⏱ 🔥 🔯 🏠 🚻 ✿ 🛒 🛒 ⚓

Scratby Hall Caravan Park, Scratby, Great Yarmouth, Norfolk NR29 3PH. *01493 730283.* Mrs B Rawnsley. 2m N of Caister via A149 and B1159. About 1m from junction. Holiday site near Broads and sea. Signposted. Graded: 4 stars. Open Easter-October.

🚐 🔌 📺 ♿ 🔥 ☺ ⏱ 🔥 🔯 🏠 🚻 L 💧 🛒 ✓ ☺ ⚓

**LONG BEACH
CARAVAN PARK
HEMSBY
GREAT YARMOUTH
NR29 4JD
Tel: 01493 730023
Fax: 01493 730188
E-mail: info@longbeach.fsnet.co.uk**

Acres of private sandy beach.
Self Service shop.
Licensed bar with children's room.
Laundry. Electric Hook-ups.
First-class toilet blocks.

A FAMILY-RUN SITE FOR ALL THE FAMILY

The Grange Touring Park, Yarmouth Road, Ormesby St Margaret, Great Yarmouth, Norfolk NR29 3QG. *01493 730306/730023.* Located three miles north of centre of Great Yarmouth. On the B1159. One mile to beach. Close to the Norfolk Broads. Restaurant adjoining park. Open Easter-September.

🚐 🔌 📺 🔥 ✕ ☺ ⚙ 🔥 🔯 🏠 🚻 L 🛒 🛒 ✓ ☺ ⚓

Vauxhall Holiday Park Ltd, Acle New Road, Great Yarmouth, Norfolk NR30 1TB. *01493 857231.* vauxhall. holidays@virgin.net. www.vauxhall-holiday-park.co.uk. Mr S G Biss. In town on A47 Norwich to Great Yarmouth road. Children's playgrounds. Free entertainment. Indoor swimming complex. David Bellamy Silver Conservation Award. Top 100 Touring Parks in UK. Graded: 4 stars. Open Easter and mid-May-September.

🚐 🔌 ♨ 📺 🔥 🔥 🔥 ✕ ☺ ⏱ 🔥 🔯 ≈ 🛒 🏠 ✕ 🚻 ⚖ L 💧 🛒 ♪ ✓ ☺ ⚓ ⚓

Waxham Sands Holiday Park, Warren Farm, Horsey, Great Yarmouth, Norfolk NR29 4EJ. *01692 598325.* C L Associates (Inc). 12m N of Great Yarmouth. Secluded site with own sandy beach. Adventure playground. Shop. Dogs welcome. Open May 26-September 30.

🚐 🔌 ♨ 📺 🔥 🔥 🔥 ☺ ⏱ 🔥 🔯 🏠 🛒 ⚖ L 💧 🛒 ♪ ✓ ☺ ⚓ ⚓ ↗ ⚡

White House Farm, Main Road, Repps With Bastwick, Great Yarmouth, Norfolk NR29 5JH. *01692 670403.* Mrs P J Hunn. 10m north of Great Yarmouth on the A149. A flat, sheltered site. 5m from beach and close to Norfolk Broads. Open March-October.

🚐 🔌 📺 ✕ ☺ 🔥 🏠 🚻 ⚖ L 🛒 🛒 ☺

Willowcroft Caravan Park, Staithe Road, Repps with Bastwick, Great Yarmouth, Norfolk NR29 5JU. *01692 670380.* www.willowcroft4.freeserve.co.uk. Mr & Mrs Trigg-Dudley. On A419 10m north-west of Great Yarmouth. In Repps village. Take local roads towards Thurne at village playing field. After 0.5m turn right into Staithe Road for site. Secluded Broadland site, launching ramp nearby. Fees on application (SAE).

🚐 🔌 📺 🔥 🔥 ☺ ⏱ 🔥 🔯 🏠 🚻 ✿ L 💧 🛒 ⚖ ☺

NORFOLK

Harleston

Little Lakeland Caravan Park, Wortwell, Harleston, Norfolk IP20 0EL. *01986 788646.* information@littlelakeland.co.uk. www.littlelakeland.co.uk. Jean & Peter Leatherbarrow. Off A143 (Diss to Bungay) at roundabout signed Wortwell. In village turn right 350yds past Bell pub. Quiet, family touring park with fishing lake and library. Modern toilet block. Graded: 4 stars. Open March 15-October 31.

🚐🅿️⚡📶♿🛁☉🕐🔥🌸☕♨️🔌 *L* 🅿️♨️🚲↗️ ⚓

Holt

Kelling Heath Holiday Park, Weybourne, Holt, Norfolk NR25 7HW. *01263 588181.* info@kellingheath.co.uk. www.kelling heath.co.uk. Blue Sky Leisure (Timewell Properties). From A148 turn north at sign near Bodham. From A149 turn south at Weybourne Church. 250-acre estate of heath and woodland. Supermarket. Launderette. Restaurant and bars. Nature trails. Fees on application. Open March 1-December 15.

🚐🅿️⚡📶♿🛁✖️☉🕐🔥🌸♨️♿🔌 *L* 🅿️♨️↗️ ∪ ⚓

Hunstanton

Searles Holiday Centre, South Beach, Hunstanton, Norfolk PE36 5BB. *01485 534211.* bookings@searles.co.uk. www. searles.co.uk. On the B1161 off the A149. 14m north of King's Lynn, near seafront. Advance booking advisable. Individual pitches. Brochure on request. Open March-November.

🚐🅿️⚡📶♿🛁✖️☉🕐🔥🌸♨️♿🔌🏪 *L* 🅿️♨️🚲↗️↗️ ∪ ⚓🏊⚓

King's Lynn

Diglea Caravan & Camping Park, Beach Road, Snettisham, King's Lynn, Norfolk PE31 7RA. *01485 541367.* Mrs M Carter. 10.5m N of King's Lynn on A149 Hunstanton Road. Turn left at sign marked 'Snettisham Beach'. Park 1.5m on left. 0.25 mile from beach and RSPB Reserve. Friendly family run park in rural setting. Children's playground. Cafe/restaurant and takeaway available a few yards away. Rally field available. Dogs on leads welcome. Fees on application. Graded: 3 stars. Open April-October.

🚐🅿️⚡🛁☉🕐🔥🏪🔌🏊 *L* ♨️ ∪ ⚓🏊⚓

Heacham Beach Holiday Park, South Beach Road, Heacham, King's Lynn, Norfolk PE31 7BD. *01485 570270.* Haven Leisure. Off the A149 from Kings Lynn to Hunstanton road. Heacham first village after Snettisham. turn left at sign for Heacham beach and fork left about one mile. One of Haven's 37 tenting and touring parks across the UK. Indoor pool. Free kids' club. Family entertainment. Club and lounge bar. Open Easter-October.

🚐🅿️⚡📶♿🛁☉🕐🔥🌸♨️♿🔌 *L* 🅿️♨️↗️ ∪ ⚓⚓

Pentney Park Caravan & Camping Site, Narborough, King's Lynn, Norfolk PE32 1HU. *01760 337479.* holidays@pentney.demon.co.uk. www. pentney-park.co.uk. B & H Webster. Nine miles south-east of King's Lynn on the A47. Just before Narborough village. Pleasant woodland setting with children's playground. Two heated pools (indoor/outdoor). Fees on application.

🚐🅿️⚡📶♿🛁✖️☉🕐🔥🌸♨️♿🔌🏪❄️🔌 *J* ∪

'The Rickels', Caravan & Camping Site, Bircham Road, Stanhoe, King's Lynn, Norfolk PE31 8PU. *01485 518671.* Heather Crown. From Kings Lynn, take the A148 to Hillinton. Left onto B1153, fork right on to B1155. Site on left 100 yards after crossroads. Quiet, friendly, high quality family site offering a peaceful and relaxed atmosphere. Open March-October.

🚐🅿️⚡📶🛁🔌☉🕐🔥🏪 *L* 🅿️

King's Lynn Caravan & Camping Park, New Road, North Runcton, King's Lynn, Norfolk PE33 0RA. *01553 840004.* klynn_campsite@hotmail.com Paul & Claire Yallop. 1.5m from A17, A10, A47, A149 main King's Lynn Hardwick roundabout, on right of A47 towards Swaffham. Well sited for King's Lynn, inland market towns and north Norfolk coast. Set in 3.5 acres of pleasant parkland. Dogs allowed. Laundry facilities and dairy produce available nearby.

🚐🅿️⚡📶♿🛁✖️☉🕐🔥🏪🔌❄️♻️🏕️ *L* 🅿️♨️↗️ ∪ ⚓🏊⚓

Woodlakes, Holme Road, Stowbridge, King's Lynn, Norfolk PE34 3PX. *01553 810414.* robin@woodlakes.com. www.wood lakes.com. Woodlakes Leisure Ltd. Three miles north of

---

Downham Market via the A10. Turn left for one mile to Stowbridge. Well-equipped, level site. 5 fishing lakes. Fees on application. 30 pitches for tents. Open April 1-October 31.

North Walsham

Two Mills Touring Park, Yarmouth Road, North Walsham, Norfolk NR28 9NA. *01692 405829.* enquiries@twomills.co.uk. www.twomills.co.uk. Hilary Scales & Graham Hoyland. 1m S from North Walsham town centre on old A149 past police station and hospital. Sheltered park. Country inn and restaurant within 150yd. Clean facilities. Adults only. Open March 1-January 3.

Norwich

Camping & Caravanning Club Site - Norwich, Martineau Lane, Lakenham, Norwich, Norfolk NR1 2HX. *01603 620060.* www.campingandcaravanningclub.co.uk. The Camping & Caravanning Club Ltd. Off A47 Norwich ring road between A140 and A146. 2.5-acre site with 50 pitches. Within easy reach of the Norfolk Broads. Non-members welcome. Caravans, motor caravans and tents accepted. Open March-October.

Golden Beach Holiday Centre, Beach Road, Sea Palling, Norwich, Norfolk NR12 0AL. *01692 598269.* Mr D Waller. From Norwich A1151 to Stalham, then B1159 to Sea Palling. Site is in Beach Road, near sea. Holiday site near extensive sands. Jet skis nearby. Fees on application. Open March-October.

Haveringland Hall Caravan Park, Cawston, Norwich, Norfolk NRI0 4PN. *01603 871302.* haveringland@claranet.com. www.haveringlandhall.co.uk. Mr M Ward. 2m W off B1149. 2m S of Cawston. Part of 120 acre wooded estate with private 12 acre coarse fishing lake. Quiet, non-commercialised. Pitches level & well drained. Modern amenity block. Dogs allowed. Open March-October.

Pampas Lodge, Haddiscoe, Norwich, Norfolk NR14 6AA. *01502 677265.* pampas@globalnet.co.uk . CJC & VJ Shirley. 5m N of Beccles and 10m SW of Great Yarmouth on A143. Broads holiday centre. Site behind Pampas Lodge pub.

Reedham Ferry Touring Park, Reedham, Norwich, Norfolk NY13 3HA. *01493 700429.* Mr David N Archer. A47 to Acle. Follow signs to Reedham, 7m S. 4 acre, flat, landscaped site. adjacent to 17th century pub serving fine food. Modern toilet facilities, tumble dryer and standpipes. Barbecue. Slipway. Well-behaved dogs allowed. Graded: 3 stars. Open Easter-end October.

Swans Harbour Caravan & Camping Site, Barford Road, Marlingford, Norwich, Norfolk NR9 4BE. *01603 759658.* Mr & Mrs Morter. B1108 signposted Norwich/Watton, turn off Norwich southern bypass. In 3m, turn right signposted Marlingford. Follow brown tourist signs to site. 4 acre grassy, level site beside river. Designated unspoilt area of river valley.

The Dower House Touring Park, East Harling, Norwich, Norfolk NR16 2SE. *01953 717314.* info@dowerhouse.co.uk. www.dowerhouse.co.uk. Mr David Bushell. Off A11 Thetford to Norwich or A1066 Thetford to Diss signed from East Harling. 20 acres level grassland set in Thetford forest. Shower room for disabled. Baby wash room. David Bellamy Gold Conservation Award. Open March 16-October 7.

Sandringham

Camping & Caravanning Club Site - Sandringham, The Sandringham Estate, Double Lodges, Sandringham, Norfolk PE35 6EA. *01485 542555.* www.campingandcaravanningclub.co.uk. The Camping & Caravanning Club Ltd. A149 from King's Lynn towards Sandringham, turn right onto A148 and take B1440 to site. In grounds of Royal Estate a few miles from beach. Non-members welcome. 275 pitches set in 28 acres. Caravans, motor caravans and tents accepted. Open end February-end November.

Swaffham

Breckland Meadows Touring Park, Lynn Road, Swaffham, Norfolk PE37 7PT. *01760 721246.* info@brecklandmeadows. co.uk. www.brecklandmeadows.co.uk .Arthur & Hilary Farrar. Take Swaffham turn off from A47 between King's Lynn and Norwich. 3 acre site approx. 1m W of Swaffham. Central for touring Norfolk. Heated amenity block with free showers. Hard standing available. Strictly bookings only. Open November 1-March 1.

Thetford

Puddledock Farm, Gt Hockham, Thetford Norfolk IP24 1PA. *01953 498455.* Wendy A Rands. On A1075 5m from Thetford roundabout 100yds past picnic site on left, turn at fire route, sign 83 and bear right to farm gate. Open March-November.

Thorpe Woodland Caravan & Camping Site, (Forestry Commission), Shadwell, Thetford, Norfolk IP24 2RX. *01842 751042.* fe.holidays@forestry.gsi.gov.uk. www.forestholidays. co.uk. Forestry Commission (Forest Holidays). Take A1066 from Thetford. After 5m bear left to East Harling. Site .25m on left. Secluded site in Thetford Forest Park, on banks of river Thet. No toilet facilities. Brochure request line: 01313 340066. Open March-November.

Wells-next-the-Sea

Pinewoods Holiday Park, Beach Road, Wells-next-the-Sea, Norfolk NR23 1DR. *01328 710439.* holiday@pinewoods.co.uk. www.pinewoods.co.uk. Pinewoods Partnership. N from B1105 at Wells Quay. Off A149. On north Norfolk coast beside national nature reserve. Good facilities for camping. Open March 15-October 31.

NORTH LINCOLNSHIRE
East Halton

Killingholme Caravan Site, Church End, East Halton, North Lincolnshire DN40 3NX. *01469 540594.* Mrs T J Chapman. From A180 take the A160 towards Killingholme, turn left at roundabout. After about 1.5 miles. go past sign to North Killingholme Wharf. Site is one right opposite church.

NORTH YORKSHIRE
Boroughbridge

Blue Bell Caravan Site, Kirby Hill, Boroughbridge, North Yorkshire YO51 9DN. *01423 322380.* Mrs J Townend. 1m N of town on A1 (not the bypass). Open April 1-October 31.

Camping & Caravanning Club Site - Boroughbridge, Bar Lane, Roecliffe, Boroughbridge, North Yorkshire YO51 9LS. *01423 322683.* www.campingandcaravanningclub.co.uk. The Camping & Caravanning Club Ltd. From A1(M) Junction 48 follow North/Southbound slip roads, follow A168 and signs for Bar Lane Industrial Estate and Roecliffe Village. Park is 0.75m on right. Grassy and level. All units accepted. All-weather/all-service pitches. Play area. Non-members welcome. 85 pitches, set in 5 acres. Caravans, motor caravans and tents accepted.

Filey

> **Blue Dolphin Holiday Park, Gristhorpe Bay, Filey, North Yorkshire YO14 9PU.** *01723 515155.* www.havenholidays.com. Haven Leisure. Two miles north of Filey off the A165 to Scarborough road. One of Haven's tenting and touring parks around the UK. Free kids' club. Free entertainment. Indoor and outdoor pools. Mini ten-pin bowling. Adventure playground. All-weather sports court. Open Easter-November.

Crows Nest Caravan Park, Gristhorpe, Filey, North Yorkshire YO14 9PS. *01723 582206.* enquiries@crowsnest caravanpark.com. www.crowsnestcaravanpark.com. Mr Ian Palmer. Two miles north of Filey, 5m south of Scarborough off A165. Friendly, privately owned Rose Award park with full facilities. Fees on application. Open March-October.

Orchard Farm Holiday Village, Stonegate, Hunmanby, Filey, North Yorkshire YO14 0PU. *01723 891582.* Mr David & Mrs Sharon Dugdale. Off A165 signposted Hunmanby. Quarter mile on right is entrance, follow signs. Privately-owned park with secluded, level, well protected pitchers. Ideal for tenting with land drained pitches. Dogs allowed. Open 1 March-31 October.

Primrose Valley Holiday Centre, Primrose Valley, Filey, North Yorkshire YO14 9RF. *01723 513771.* www.havenholidays.com. Haven Leisure. Take the main A165 Scarborough to Bridlington road. Signposted about a mile from Filey turnoff. One of Haven's 29 touring parks around coast. Open Easter-October.

> **Reighton Sands Holiday Park, Reighton Gap, Filey, North Yorkshire YO14 9SJ.** *01723 890476.* www.havenholidays.com. Haven Leisure. Follow A165 between Filey and Bridlington. Site 1m overlooking the sea. Central for touring Yorkshire countryside. Sports and play area. Licensed club. Free kids' club. Free entertainment. Open Easter-October 30.

Harrogate

Bilton Park, Village Farm, Bilton Lane, Harrogate, North Yorkshire HG1 4DH. *01423 863121.* biltonpark@tcsmail.net. north east of centre of Harrogate on outskirts of town. Leave A59 east at Dragon Hotel, into Bilton Lane and site is one mile. Touring site for central Yorkshire. Some resident and static areas. Riverside walks. Fees on application. Open April-October.

High Moor Farm Park, Skipton Road, Harrogate, North Yorkshire HG3 2LT. *01423 563637/564955.* Mr & Mrs P M Kershaw. 4m W of Harrogate off A59 Harrogate to Skipton road. Holiday site surrounded by trees. On the edge of Yorkshire Dales, ideal touring base. Licensed bar on site. Open April or Easter if earlier-October.

Manor House Farm Caravan Park, Manor House Farm, Summerbridge, Harrogate, North Yorkshire HG3 3JS. *01423 780322.* T J Houseman & M J Liddle. Take the A61 from Harrogate to Ripon, leave at 2nd Ripley roundabout for Pateley Bridge. Small, quiet site near river. Near Brinhan Rocks and Fountain Abbey. Hard standings, on different levels. Open March 1-October 3.

Ripley Caravan Park, Ripley, Harrogate, North Yorkshire HG3 3AU. *01423 770050.* Mr Peter & Valerie House. Three miles north of Harrogate. Access is 300 yards down the B6165 Knaresborough road from roundabout junction with A61. Indoor heated pool, sauna, nursery playroom, games room, playroom, children's adventure playground. Colour TV. Football pitch. Close to many places of interest. Open Easter-October 31.

Riverside Caravan Park, Low Wath Road, Pateley Bridge, Harrogate, North Yorkshire HG3 5HL. *01423 711383.* river side-cp@lineone.net. D H & C A Weatherhead. B6265 or B6165 into Pateley Bridge. Park situated approx. 0.25m along Low Wath Road on right. Fees on application. Open April-October.

Rudding Holiday Park, Follifoot, Harrogate, North Yorkshire HG3 1JH. *01423 870439.* holiday-park@ruddingpark.com. www.ruddingpark.com. Mr Simon Mackaness. 3m SE of Harrogate via A661 Wetherby road. AA Best Campsite in Britain 2001. Graded 5 stars. Open March-November.

Shaws Trailer Park, Knaresborough Road, Harrogate, North Yorkshire HG2 7NE. *01423 884432.* www.residentialpark.co.uk. Mr J Shaw. 1m E of Harrogate on A59. Well-lit site. 1m to floral resort and spa town of Harrogate. 3m to Knaresborough. Graded: 3 stars.

Studfold Farm, Lofthouse, Harrogate, North Yorkshire HG3 5SG. *01423 755210.* S & F Walker. 7m N of Pateley Bridge. B6265 to Lofthouse. Follow Middlesmoor sign and first left signposted 'Stean'. Flat, well-drained site in good walking country. Fees on application. Graded: 2 stars. Open April-October.

Westfield Caravan Site, Heathfield, Pateley Bridge, Harrogate, North Yorkshire HG3 5BX. *01423 711880.* Mrs E Simpson. 2m NW of Pateley Bridge. 1m N towards Ramsgill. Left at sign for Heathfield, then left again after 100yd and 0.5m to site. Dales touring centre. Fees on application. Open April-October.

Yorkshire Hussar Inn Holiday Caravan Park, Markington, Harrogate, North Yorkshire HG3 3NR. *01765 677327.* yorkshirehussar@yahoo. www.ukparks.co.uk/yorkshirehussar. J S Brayshaw (Caravans) Ltd. Midway between Harrogate and Ripon. W off A61 at Wormold Green, over rail crossing. 5m S of Ripon. Caravans for hire with all services. Fees on application. Brochure. Touring caravans and tents. Holiday caravans for hire. Open March-October.

NORTH YORKSHIRE

Hawes

Bainbridge Ings Camping Site, Hawes, North Yorkshire DL8 3NU. *01969 667354.* janet@bainbridge-ings.co.uk. www.bainbridge-ings.co.uk. Mr & Mrs M Facer. On A684 from Bainbridge, before entering Hawes turn left. (Follow signpost for Gayle). 0.5m E of Hawes. Good centre for places of interest. Quiet family-run site. Beautiful views. Graded: 2 stars. SAE for terms. Open April-October.

Brown Moor, Brunt Acres Road, Hawes, North Yorkshire DL8 3PS. *01969 667338.* www.caravanclub.co.uk. The Caravan Club. On A684 through Wensleydale. Turn north on Muker road at roundabout in Hawes to site, sign on farm gate. NE from Hawes. Centre of the National Park and near halfway point on Pennine Way. Caravan Club members only. Open Easter-January.

Shaw Ghyll Caravan & Camping Site, High Shaw, Simonstone, Hawes, North Yorkshire DL8 3LY. *01969 667 359.* rogerstott@aol.com. Mr Roger Stott. A flat, secluded, quiet site beside Fossdale Beck. Ideal for young families and walkers who appreciate a peaceful and relaxing holiday. Two miles from Hawes: shops, pubs, restaurants etc. Very central position for exploring the Yorkshire Dales. Open March-end October.

Helmsley

Foxholme Touring Caravan Park, Harome, Helmsley, North Yorkshire YO62 5JG. *01439 770416/771696.* Ken Binks & Family. Leave Helmsley on A170 in direction of Scarborough. After quarter-mile turn right for Harome, turn left at church, through village then follows signs. Attractive site, well sheltered by trees. Use of indoor swimming pool 2miles away. Open March-October 31.

Golden Square Caravan Park, Oswaldkirk, Helmsley, North Yorkshire YO6 25YQ. *01439 788269.* barbara@goldensquarecaravanpark.com. www.goldensquarecaravanpark.com. Mr & Mrs D Armstrong. Quiet site, surrounded by open country and woodland with magnificent views. In North Yorkshire Moors National Park, 2m south from Helmsley off B1257 to Malton. Turn R to Ampleforth, from where site is 0.5m. From A19 follow 'Caravan Route' signs to Ampleforth. Play areas. Sports centre nearby. Open March 1-October 31.

Wren's of Ryedale Caravan Site, Nawton, Hemsley, North Yorkshire YO62 7SD. *01439 771260.* dave@wrensofryedale.fsnet.co.uk. wrensofryedale.fsnet.co.uk. G D & L J Smith. 600 yards north of the A170. 2.5 miles east of Hemsley. Delightful, small family run site in the heart of Ryedale countryside. Ideal for exploring the North Yorkshire moors, coast, dales and city of York. The facilities of a larger park with the personal touch of a small site. Open April-October.

Kirkbymoorside

Wombleton Caravan Park, Moorfield Lane, Kirkbymoorside, North Yorkshire YO6 5RY. *01751 431684.* www.europage.co.uk/wombletonpark. Mr C Procter. Head east on A170 from Helmsley for four miles. Turn right for Wombleton. Through village, site on left. Quiet, level park situated among open countryside. Seasonal pitches available. Graded: 5 stars. Open March 1-October 31.

Knaresborough

Allerton Park Caravan Park, Allerton, Mauleverer, Knaresborough, North Yorkshire HG5 0SE. *01423 330569.* www.yorkshireholidayparks.co.uk. Mr & Mrs D Hind. From A1 take A59 for 1m towards York. Turn left from A59. Peaceful site ideally placed for exploring the Yorkshire Dales, Herriot country and the north Yorkshire Moors. Open February 1-January 3.

Kingfisher Caravan Park, Low Moor Lane, Farnham, Knaresborough, North Yorkshire HG5 9DQ. *01423 869411.* Mr Richardson. Knaresborough via A6055 travel out of Knaresborough then left at Farnham, turn left, park about 1m on left.15 acres, flat, country site with tourers in tree-sheltered paddock. Open March 1-October 31.

Leyburn

Akebar Park, Wensleydale, Leyburn, North Yorkshire DL8 5LY. *01677 450201/450591.* www.akebarpark.co.uk. Mr J C P Ellwood. On A684 7m W of A1. Excellent facilities, set in James Herriot country. Bowling green. 9 and 18-hole golf, covered driving range, pro shop and PGA golf professional on park. Regret no unaccompanied young persons. The Friar's Head country pub and restaurant adjacent. Dogs on leads. Open March-January 2.

Little Cote Farm, West Burton, Leyburn, North Yorkshire DL8 4JY. *01969 663450.* Mrs B Spence. 1m SE of Aysgarth. Take A684 from Leyburn. A6160 to West Burton to site 0.5m beyond on no through road. Signposted Walden. Quiet, remote Dale site. No sanitation, but emptying point provided. Open March-October.

Street Head Caravan Park, Newbiggin, Bishopdale, Leyburn, North Yorkshire DL8 3TE. *01969 663472/663571.* Mr D J Cooper. Seven miles West Leyburn. Turn left off the A680 on B6160 Kettlewell to Skipton road. Site 2.5 miles on right. Adjacent to Street Head Inn. Open March 1-October 31.

Westholme Caravan & Camping Park, Aysgarth, Leyburn, North Yorkshire DL8 3SP. *01969 663268.* A & I Woodhouse Ltd. 1 mile east of Aysgarth, off the A684. Delightful park in beautiful Wensleydale, within Yorkshire Dales National Park. Secluded with striking views, set in splendid walking country. Licensed club. Restaurant. Graded: 4 stars (AA). Open March 1-October 31.

Low Bentham

Goodenbergh Country Holiday Park, Low Bentham, North Yorkshire LA2 7EU. *01524 262022.* office@goodenbergh.freeserve.co.uk. Howard Luscombe. Off A65 to Low Bentham, right at Sundial Inn. Left at crossroads, one mile on left. M6 J34 follow A683, right onto B6480, at Wennington take second left, park signed one mile on right. Open March 1-January 4.

Malton

Flamingoland Theme Park, Zoo & Holiday Village, Kirby Misperton, Malton, North Yorkshire YO17 6UX. *01653 668585.* Mrs M Gibb. 4m S of Pickering. Signposted off A169 Pickering to Malton road. Flat, well drained site with made-up roads. Within Flamingo Theme park and zoo where for one price entry, all rides, slides and shows are free. Over 100 attractions spread over 375 acres of country park. Open April-October.

NORTH YORKSHIRE

The Snooty Fox, East Heslerton, Malton, North Yorkshire YO17 8EN. *01944 710 554.* vassb@tinyworld.co.uk. Close to Ganton golf course. 10 miles to coast. Near to moors.

Masham

Fearby Caravan & Camping Site, Rear Black Swan Hotel, Fearby, Masham, North Yorkshire HG4 4NF. *01765 689477.* info@blackswanholiday.co.uk. www.blackswanholiday.co.uk. Mr J McCourt. 2m W of Masham. Turn left off A6108 NW of Masham. Site is 2m on left at rear of Black Swan Inn in Fearby. Close to many places of interest including Jervaulx Abbey and Druid's Temple. Open March 1-October 31.

Northallerton

Cote Ghyll Caravan & Camping Park, Osmotherley, Northallerton, North Yorkshire DL6 3AH. *01609 883425.* hills@coteghyll.com. www.coteghyll.com. J & H Hill.Exit A19 dual carriageway at A684 Northallerton in Osmotherley centre, turn left 0.5m to site. Beautiful secluded valley location in N Y Moors National Park with stream. Pubs and walking nearby. Open March 1-October 31.

Hutton Bonville Caravan Park, Church Lane, Hutton Bonville, Northallerton, North Yorkshire DL7 0NR. *01609 881416.* hutton_b@hotmail.com. J R & S Peel. 4m N of Northallerton off A167. National Park areas and Yorkshire Dales within easy reach. Open March-October.

Pembroke Caravan & Camping Site, 19 Low Street, Leeming Bar, Northallerton, North Yorkshire DL7 9BW. *01677 422652.* G & S Liddell. Turn off A1 at Leeming Services on to A684 to Northallerton. In Leeming Bar, keep left at crossroads into Leases Road. Site on right in 0.25miles. Ideal for touring North Yorkshire Dales and North Yorkshire Moors National Park. Dogs and pets allowed. Graded: 4 stars. Open March-October.

Pickering

Overbrook Caravan Site, Maltongate, Thornton-le-Dale, Pickering, North Yorkshire YO18 7SE. *01751 474417.* Mr & Mrs K J Bennett. Turn right off A169 to Thornton-le-Dale site old railway station. Level, family run site level, well sheltered by trees with lovely views over countryside. Unsuitable for children. Open March 1-October 31.

Rosedale Caravan & Camping Parks, Rosedale Abbey, Pickering, North Yorkshire YO18 8SA. *01751 41 7272.* Flower of May Holiday Parks Ltd. 9m N of Pickering via A170. At Wrelton turn N towards Rosedale on to unclassified road to Rosedale Abbey. Site on left in village. Site is situated in North Yorkshire Moors National Park. In the village on the banks of shallow river Seven. Open Easter to mid-October.

Spiers House Campsite, Cropton, Pickering, North Yorkshire YO18 8ES. *01751 417591.* fc.holidays@forestry.gsi.gov.uk. www.forestholidays.co.uk. Forestry Commission (Forest Holidays). A170 west from Pickering 2.5m to Wrelton north to Cropton. 1m north of Cropton turn right to site. Woodland setting. North Yorkshire Moors National Park. Graded: 3 stars. Open end March-end September.

The Black Bull Camp & Caravan Park, Malton Road, Pickering, North Yorkshire YO18 8EA. *01751 472528.* Louise Wright. 1m S of Pickering on A169. Situated behind the Black Bull public house. Quiet family site. Dog walk, playfield, children's playground, games room. Holiday caravans for hire on separate field. Open March 1-October 31.

Upper Carr Touring Park, Upper Carr Lane, Malton Road, Pickering, North Yorkshire YO18 7JP. *01751 473115.* harker @uppercarr.demon.co.uk. www.uppercarr.demon.co.uk. Martin & Josette Harker. On A169 Malton Road. 1.5m south of Pickering. Opposite Black Bull pub. Level, family park, licensed shop, laundry and pot wash. Pets corner, play area and cycle hire. Pub. Walking and fishing nearby. 30 minutes to York, Scarborough, Whitby and North Moors National Park. Brochure available. Open March-October.

Vale of Pickering Caravan Park, Carr House Farm, Allerston, Pickering, North Yorkshire YO18 7PQ. *01723 859280.* tony@valeofpickering.co.uk. www.valeofpickering.co.uk. W Stockdale & Sons. Fully-lit site. The most luxurious site in the north of England. RAC Excellent. AA 4 pennant. Consistently top rated park in Yorkshire by YTB. White Rose Runner-up. Cafe/restaurant available nearby. Open March-January 10th.

Wayside Caravan Park, Wrelton, Pickering, North Yorkshire YO18 8PG. *01751 472608.* waysideparks@freenet.co.uk. www.waysideparks.co.uk. V R Goodson. Off A170, follow signs. 2.5m W of Pickering at Wrelton. Touring centre for moors. South facing park with country views. Inn with food within 250 yards. Historic steam railway nearby. Fees on application. Graded: 4 stars. Open Easter-October 2.

Richmond

Brompton-on-Swale Caravan & Camping Park, Brompton-on-Swale, Richmond, North Yorkshire DL10 7EZ. *01748 824629.* brompton.caravanpark@btinternet.com. www.bromptoncaravanpark.co.uk. www.ukparks.com. Marshall & Gregson Family partnership. Leave A1 at Catterick A6136 exit, take B6271 to Brompton-on-Swale. Park 1m on left after Brompton-on-Swale on Richmond road. Friendly site set on bank of river Swale. Gateway to Yorkshire Dales. Fishing. Fully-serviced pitches. David Bellamy Gold Conservation Award. Graded: 5 ticks. Open March 21-October 31.

Park Lodge Farm, Keld, Richmond, North Yorkshire DL11 6LJ. *01748 886274.* babrarukin@ukonline.co.uk. www.rukins-keld.co.uk. Mrs B Rukin. In Keld village on B6270 3m NW of Muker, 9m from Hawes. 23m from Richmond and 11m from Kirkby Stephen. Good base for touring the Dales. Hour's drive to Lakes. Fees on application. Open April-October inclusive.

Scotch Corner Caravan Park, Richmond Road, Scotch Corner, Richmond, North Yorkshire DL10 6NS. *01748 822530.* W & E Marshall. Entrance off A6108 Richmond road 200yd from Scotch Corner junction with A1. Charges include free showers and dish-washing facilities. Open Easter-end October.

Swaleview Caravan Site, Reeth Road, Richmond, North Yorkshire DLL10 4SF. *01748 823106.* Mr M A Carter. 3m W of Richmond via A6108 towards Leyburn and Reeth. Level site set in Yorkshire Dales natural park on banks of river Swale. Open March 1-October 31.

Tavern House Caravan Park, Newsham, Richmond, North Yorkshire DL11 7RA. *01833 621223.* Stephen Thompson. 8 miles from Scotch Corner on A66. 6 miles to Barnard Castle. 8 miles from Richmond. Suitable for walking. A quiet site with various birds. Adults only. Open March 1-October 31.

Usha Gap, Muker, Richmond, North Yorkshire DL11 4DW. *01748 886214.* ushagap@aol.com. www.ushagap.btinternet. co.uk. Mrs A Metcalfe. On B6270 Richmond to Hawes and Kirkby Stephen Road. Pleasant site by stream. Clothes dryer. Fees on application. Clothes drier. Dogs allowed. SAE.

Ripon

Gold Coin Farm, Galphay, Ripon, North Yorkshire HG4 3NJ. *01765 658508.* Mrs C Weatherhead. 5m W of Ripon via B6265 Pateley Bridge road. After 1m turn right to Galphay and site. Centre for touring Dales. Flat and sloping well-drained and quiet site in unspoilt countryside. 6m from Fountains Abbey. Campers must have their own toilets. Open April 1-September 30.

Sleningford Watermill Caravan & Camping Park, North Stainley, Ripon, North Yorkshire HG4 3HQ. *01765 635201.* Sleningford Watermill Co Ltd. This beautiful, quiet, riverside park can be reached by following signs for the Lightwater Valley, taking A6108 out of Ripon, site is signposted. Alternatively, leave A1 at the B6267 Masham to Thirsk road and follow Lightwater Valley signs. Open Easter or April 1-October 31.

Woodhouse Farm Caravan & Camping Park, Winksley, Ripon, North Yorkshire HG4 3PG. *01765 658309.* woodhouse.farm@talk21.com. www.woodhousewinksley.com. Alison Hitchen. W of Ripon on B6265 turn N 3.5m from Ripon. Signpost to Grantley. Then follow caravan and camping signs to site. Site is 1m. Touring centre for dales and moors. SAE for details. Graded: 4 stars. Open April 1-end October.

Scarborough

Arosa Camp Site, Ratten Row, Seamer, Scarborough, North Yorkshire YO12 4QB. *01723 862166.* suebird@arosa131. fsnet.co.uk. Messrs D G & N R Cherry. 4m from Scarborough on A64 York to Scarborough road. From York, first left in Seamer. Night stop London to Scotland route via A64. A quiet, family site close to National Parks, moors & beaches. Flat, close-mown and well-drained. Ideal touring site. Graded: 4 stars. Open March-January 4.

Cayton Village Caravan Park, Dept 11, Mill Lane, Cayton Bay, Scarborough, North Yorkshire YO11 3NN. *01723 583171.* info@caytontouring.co.uk. www.caytontouring.co.uk. Ms Carol Croft. A165 south of Scarborough, turn inland at Cayton Bay. Site on right-hand side in 0.5m. Sheltered 0.5 m to beach, playground, free showers, dish-washing, 3-acre dog walk. Adjoining church. 2 pubs, fish shop, bus service. Seasonal pitches. Special super saver and OAP weeks. Graded: 4 stars. Open Easter-October.

Camping & Caravanning Park - Scarborough, Field Lane, Burniston Road, Scarborough, North Yorkshire YO13 0DA. *01723 366441.* www.campingandcaravanningclub.co.uk. The Camping & Caravanning Club. On West side of A165, 1m north of Scarborough. 20 acres, 375 pitches. All units welcome. Footpath to nearby beach. Open March-October.

Flower of May Caravan & Camping Site, Lebberston Cliff, Scarborough, North Yorkshire YOll 3NU. *01723 584311.* info@flowerofmay.com. www.flowerofmay.com Situated on the A165 4.5 miles south of Scarborough and 2.5 miles north of Filey. Tent and touring caravan park for families only. Leisure centre-indoor swimming pool, etc. Fees and brochure on application. Open Easter-October.

Jacobs Mount Caravan & Camping Park, Stepney Road, Scarborough, North Yorkshire YO12 5NL. *01723 361178.* jacobsmount@yahoo.co.uk. www.jacobsmount.co.uk. Mr George Dale. Park is sited two miles west of Scarborough on the A170 towards Thirsk. Manager: Mr Paul Benjamin. Licensed clubhouse. Fees on application. Rose Award. Graded: 5 stars. AA. 4 flag. CC recommended. Open March-November.

Jasmine Caravan Park, Cross Lane, Snainton, Scarborough, North Yorkshire YO13 9BE. *01723 859240.* info@jasminepark.co.uk. www.jasminepark.co.uk. Mr & Mrs D Hinchliffe. Signposted in Snainton off A170. Flat, attractive park. Ideally located for exploring North Yorkshire Moors and heritage coast. David Bellamy Gold Conservation Award. Open March-January.

Scalby Close Park, Burniston Road, Scarborough, North Yorkshire YO13 0DA. *01723 365908.* P F & M Bayes. Two miles north of Scarborough's North Bay, signposted 400yd. Family-run, sheltered, level site. Close to Scarborough yet suitable for touring the moors and coast. Open March-October.

NORTH YORKSHIRE

Spring Willows Touring Caravan & Camping Park, Main Road, Staxton, Scarborough, North Yorkshire YO14 9RS. 01723 891505. A64 turn off A1039 (Filey). Sauna. Solarium. Free entertainment. Dogs allowed. AA 4 pennants. Open March-December.

🐾 📺 ♨ 🅿 ⚓ ⚡ 🆑 ✗ ⊙ 🚿 🔥 🗑 ≋ 🔌 🏠 ☎ ≠ L 🥄 ♿ ✈ ↙ ✓ ∪ ⚓ ⚡ 🏄 ⚡

St Helens Caravan & Camping Park, Wykeham, Scarborough, North Yorkshire YO13 9QD. 01723 862771. St Helens in the Park Ltd. On A170 Scarborough to Pickering. In North Yorkshire Moors National Park. Playgrounds. Fees on application. Manager: C Tedman. Open February 15-January 15.

🐾 🅿 ♨ 🆑 ⚡ ✗ ⊙ 🚿 🔥 🗑 ≋ 🔌 🏠 ☎ ❄ ♿ 🏴 ♿ ✈ ↙ ∪ ⚡

Selby

Cawood Holiday Park, Ryther Road, Cawood, Selby, North Yorkshire YO8 3TT. 01757 268450. william.archer13@btopenworld.com. www.cawoodholidaypark.co.uk. Amanda & Gerry Archer. From A1 or York, take B1222 to Cawood lights, turn on B1223, signed Tadcaster for 1m. Park on your left. Overnight stop. Touring centre for York. Launderette. Pool room. Amusements. Weekend entertainment. Indoor swimming pool. Fishing. AA 4 Pennants & RAC listed. Graded 5 stars. Adults only; no under-18s. Seasonal pitch/holiday caravans excluded subject to proprietor's discretion.

🐾 🅿 ♨ 🆑 ⚡ 🆒 ⚡ ✗ ⊙ 🚿 🔥 🗑 ≋ 🔌 🏠 ☎ ❄ ☀ L 🥄 ♿ ✈ ↙ ∪ ⚡ 🏄 ⚡

Settle

Knight Stainforth Hall, Settle, North Yorkshire BD24 0DP. 01729 822200. info@knightstainforth.co.uk. www.knightstainforth.co.uk. Mrs S Maudsley. 2.5m N of Settle. Leave A65 at Stackhouse Lane. (Opposite Settle High School) between Settle and Giggleswick and continue north for about 2.5m. Beside river in Dales National Park. Booking advised. Fees on application. Graded: 3 stars. Open March-October.

🐾 🅿 📺 ⚡ ⊙ 🆒 🔥 🗑 🏠 🏴 ❄ L 🥄 ♿ ✈ ∪ ⚡ ✓

Langcliffe Caravan Park, Settle, North Yorkshire BD24 9LX. 01729 822387. info@langcliffe.com. www.langcliffe.com. Miss K Brooks & Mr A Brooks. From Settle town take B6479 for 0.5m. Turn left after Watershed Mill at Langcliffe Lodge. Site is mostly level. Modern amenity block. Picturesque setting. Open March-October.

🐾 🅿 📺 ⚡ 🆑 🆒 🅿 ⊙ 🔥 🗑 🏠 🏴 ☎ ❄ ♿ 🥄 ♿ ✈ ↙ ✓ ∪ ⚡

Sheriff Hutton

Camping & Caravanning Club Site - Sheriff Hutton, Bracken Hill, Sheriff Hutton, North Yorkshire YO60 6QG. 01347 878660. www.campingandcaravanningclub.co.uk. The Camping & Caravanning Club Ltd. 6-acre site with 90 pitches. Laundry. Accepts all units. 1m S of Sheriff Hutton on road to York. Close to York and a suitable base for exploring North Yorkshire moors. Play area. Non-members welcome. Caravans, motor caravans and tents accepted. Open March-October.

🐾 🅿 📺 ⚡ 🆒 ⊙ 🆒 🔥 🗑 🏠 🏴 L 🔲 ♿ ✓

Skipton

Eshton Road Caravan Site, Gargrave, Skipton, North Yorkshire BD23 3PN. 01756 749229. Fred Green & Son. 500yd off A65, near Leeds and Liverpool Canal. Signposted Malham and Grassington. 4.5 miles north west of Skipton. Useful site on edge of Yorkshire Dales. Fees on application.

🐾 🅿 📺 ⚡ 🆒 ⊙ 🆒 🔥 🗑 🏠 ✗ 🏠 ❄ ≠ L 🥄 ♿ ✈ ↙ ∪ ⚡

Fold Farm, Kettlewell, Skipton, North Yorkshire BD23 5RH. 01756 760886. Mr C W Lambert. 14m N of Skipton via B6160, close to village. From King's Head Inn in village centre, upstream for 100yd, farm, upstream for further 300yds, camp site. Quiet scenic amid moors. Fees on application.

🐾 📺 ⚡ 🆒 ⊙ 🆒 🔥 🏠 🗑 🏴 ♿ 🏄 ∪

Gordale Scar Camping Site, Malham, Skipton, North Yorkshire BD23 4DL. 01729 830333. Mr A Wilson. 12m NW of Skipton. From Skipton take A65 to Gargrave. Go N (right) for 1m then left to Airton and Kirkby Malham to Malham. In Malham turn right over bridge and keep right for site, 1m along no through road. Pleasant picturesque site in good walking country. Restaurants, hotels nearby. Telephone afternoons and evenings only. Open March 1-October 31.

🐾 🅿 📺 ⊙ 🆒 🔥 🏠 🏴 L 🏄 ∪

Hawkswick Cote Caravan Park, Arncliffe, Skipton, North Yorkshire BD23 5PX. 01756 770226. Lakeland Leisure Estates Ltd. 5m NW of Grassington. Via B6265 and B6160 and road to Littondale. B6265 from Skipton. At Threshfield take B6160. Quarter mile past Kinsey bear left to Arncliffe. Park one and half miles. Manager: Edward Carter. Open March 7-November 16.

🐾 🅿 📺 ⚡ 🆒 ⊙ 🆒 🔥 🏠 L 🥄 🏄 ♿ 🏴 ∪ ⚡

Howgill Lodge, Barden, Bolton Bridge, Skipton, North Yorkshire BD23 6DJ. 01756 720655. info@howgill-lodge.co.uk. www.howgill-lodge.co.uk. Bernard & Ann Foster. About five miles N of Bolton Bridge and eight miles NE of Skipton. From Bolton Bridge N on B6160 to Barden Tower, turn E on the Appletreewick road for about 1m then along lane on right, opposite phone box, to site. Fine Wharfedale views. Graded: 5 stars. Open April-October.

🐾 🅿 📺 ⚡ ✗ ⊙ 🆒 🔥 🏠 🗑 🏠 L 🥄 🏄 ♿ 🏴

Threaplands House Farm, Cracoe, Skipton, North Yorkshire BD23 6LD. 01756 730248. Mr J C Wade. From Skipton to Grassington on B6265 to Cracoe. Past Cracoe continue on narrow lane marked 'Unsuitable for motors' when main road turns L. After 200yd, it is 2nd farm on left. Amid Yorkshire Dales. Dogs on lead only. Open March-October.

🐾 🅿 📺 ⚡ 🆑 ✗ ⊙ 🆒 🏠 🏴 🏠 L 🥄 ♿ ∪ ⚡

Wood Nook Camping Park, Skirethorns, Threshfield, Skipton, North Yorkshire BD23 5NU. 01756 752412. caravans@woodnook.net. www.woodnook.net. G F & E Thompson. From Skipton take B6265 to Threshfield then B6160 for 100 yards. Turn left after garage into Skirethorns Lane. Entrance clearly signposted at 300 yards and 600 yards. Welcome coffee on arrival. Graded: 4 stars. Open March 1-October 31.

🐾 🅿 📺 ⚡ 🆒 ⊙ 🆒 🔥 🏠 🗑 🏠 🏴 L 🥄 🏄 ♿ ∪ ⚡

Slingsby

Camping & Caravanning Club Site - Slingsby, Railway Street, Slingsby, North Yorkshire YO62 4AA. 01653 628335. www.campingandcaravanningclub.co.uk. The Camping & Caravanning Club Ltd. 3-acre site with 60 pitches. Site is mainly grass with some hard standings. Some all-weather pitches

available on site. At Slingsby on B1257 turn downhill to site on right at end of village. Dogs welcome. Non-members welcome. Caravans, motor caravans and tents accepted. Open March-October.

🚐🔌♨🛆🔋🏧🛒♨🔋🛍🏧🍴↺ L ✐✓

Robin Hood Caravan & Camping Park, Slingsby, North Yorkshire YO62 7AP. *01653 628391.* Peter & Alma Richardson. 2m E of Hovingham on B1257. A64 from York then left for Castle Howard, 7m to Slingsby from A64. Attractive, sheltered touring site. 10% discount on pre-booked 7 night stays. New luxury toilet block. Laundry. Children's play area. Open March-October.

🚐🔌♨🛆🔋✗☉⌀♨🛍🏧🍴 L ♀♂✐↺⇄♋

Stokesley

Toft Hill Farm, Kirby in Cleveland, Great Broughton, Stokesley, North Yorkshire TS9 7HJ. *01642 712469.* D G & A Scott. In Stokesley near junction of A172-173, take road S to Kirby. At Kirkby crossroads leave Black Swan Inn on right and take road to hills. Near National Trust Land and Cleveland Hills. Open April 1-October 31.

🚐♨🔋⌀🏧🍴🔋 L ✐↺⇄♋

Tadcaster

Whitecote Caravan Park, Ryther Road, Ulleskelf, Tadcaster, North Yorkshire LS24 9DY. *01937 835231.* Ms J A Hunter. Off A162 2m S of Tadcaster on to B1223 road easterly direction for 3m. Site 0.5m E of village opposite greenhouses and nurseries on Selby road. Dogs allowed. Open March-January.

🚐🔌♨🛆🔋✗☉🔋♣🏧🍴⇄ L ✐✐✓⇄

Thirsk

Quernhow Cafe and Caravan Site, Great North Road, Nr Sinderby, Thirsk, North Yorkshire YO7 4LG. *01845 567221.* On northbound carriageway of A1. 9m N of Boroughbridge and 3m N of junction of A1 and A61 (Baldersby flyover). Route from south to north. Games room. Washing-up room. Fees on application. Graded: 3 stars.

🚐🔌♨♨🔋✗☉🔋♣❀ L ♀♋

Thirsk Racecourse Caravan Club Site, Station Road, Thirsk, North Yorkshire YO7 1QL. *01845 525266.* www.caravan club.co.uk. The Caravan Club. Off A61 on outskirts of town. On racecourse. Close to Dales, Moors and York City centre, best of both worlds. Non-members welcome. Open April-October.

🚐🔌♨♨☉♨🔋🛍🏧✓

York House Caravan Park, Balk, Thirsk, North Yorkshire YO7 2AQ. *01845 597495.* phil-brierley@which.net. www.yhc parks.info. York House Caravans. Three miles south of Thirsk heading towards York on the A19. Turn left signed Bagby,

Balk and Kilburn. Through Bagby, turn right at end. Site is 300 yards on the left. Fees on application. Open April 1-end October.

🚐🔌♨♨☉♨🔋🛍🏧🍴 ✐✓↺⇄

Tollerton

Tollerton Holiday Park, Station Road, Tollerton, North Yorkshire YO611RD. *01845 501360.* www.greenwood parks.co.uk. Owners: Pratt Family. A19 from York turn left for Tollerton at Cross Lanes village. Behind station, hotel chinese restaurant by railway bridge. March November 30.

🚐🔌♨🔋♣✗☉🔋🛍🏧 L 🔲✐✓⇄

Whitby

'Serenity' Touring Caravan & Camping Park, High Street, Hinderwell, Whitby, North Yorkshire TS13 5JH. *01947 841122.* Dave & Sue Newton. 8 miles north of Whitby on A174. Cleveland Way 1 mile. Village pubs and shops all nearby. Adult only. Fees on application, telephone or SAE. Dogs allowed. Open March-October.

🚐🔌♨🔋♨☉🔋🏧🍴 L 🔲🛆✐✓↺⇄♋

Abbots House Farm, Goathland, Whitby, North Yorkshire YO22 5NH. *01947 896270/896026.* goathland@enterprise.net. www.homepages.enterprise.net/goathland. Mr & Mrs Cox & Mr & Mrs Jenkinson. 9m SW of Whitby. From Whitby S on A169, take Goathland sign. Site 0.5m along lane beside Goathland Hotel. Moorland scenery and North Yorkshire Moors Steam Railway. 'Heartbeat' country. Fees on application. Open Easter-October.

🚐♨🔋☉🔋🏧🍴⇄🔋♀

Brow House Farm, Goathland, Whitby, North Yorkshire YO22 5NP. *01947 896274.* Mr J T Jackson. 9m SW of Whitby. S on A169 towards Pickering. Then W on road signposted to Goathland. Large site on edge of moors. Open March 1-November 1.

🚐🔌♨🛆🔋✗☉♨🔋🏧🍴⇄🔋 L ♀🛆✐✓↺⇄♋

Burnt House Holiday Park, Ugthorpe, Whitby, North Yorkshire YO21 2BG. *01947 840448.* www.caravancamp ingsites.co.uk A & S Booth. A171 Whitby to Guisborough road signed to Ugthorpe village, site 275yd on right. Well lit. Hard standings or grass. Children's play area. Pubs nearby. Holiday cottage for hire. Open March-October.

🚐🔌♨🔋✗☉♨🔋🏧🍴 L 🛆✐✓

Northcliffe Holiday Park, Bottoms Lane, High Hawsker, Whitby, North Yorkshire YO22 4LL. *01947 880477.* enquiries@northcliffe-seaview.com. www.northcliffe-seaview. com. Steve & Sue Martin. Whitby's top award-winning park. Fabulous seaviews. Touring park with super pitches. Luxury caravans for sale. 3m South Whitby (A171), left on to B1447, 0.5m left on to private lane. Open mid March-End October.

🚐🔌♨♨🛆🔋✗☉♨🔋♣🏧×🔋⇄♀🛆✐✓↺⇄♋🔋

Hollins Farm, Glaisdale, Whitby, North Yorkshire YO21 2PZ. *01947 897516.* Mr & Mrs A Mortimer. From A171, 4m to Glaisdale village. Take Glaisdale Dale only sign for 1.5m. Small farm on edge of Moors, handy for coast, steam railway and many lovely village. Tents only. Farmhouse breakfast if needed. Takeaway meals in village pub. Dogs by arrangement. Open all year.

Rigg Farm Caravan Park, Stainsacre, Whitby, North Yorkshire YO22 4LP. *01947 880430.* J W & L Elders. Approaching Whitby on A171 take B1416. 1.5 miles south of Ruswarp, turn onto unclassified road signposted Sneatonthorpe. Hawkser, Stainsacre (and Rigg Farm). Park about two miles. Small, quiet site in National Park with scenic views, separate site for tents (July/August only). Open March-October.

Ugthorpe Lodge Caravan Park, Ugthorpe, Whitby, North Yorkshire. *01947 840518.* Sited nine miles north west of Whitby via the A171. Between moors and coast. Dogs allowed on lead. Quiet family site. Separate field for rallies. Caravan sales. Pub and restaurant on site. Open April-October.

Whitby Holiday Park, Saltwick Bay, Whitby, North Yorkshire YO22 4JX. *01947 602664.* Normanhurst Enterprises Ltd. From Scarborough fork right after Hawkser. Sign about two miles further on, 2nd turn on right. 1.5 miles south east of Whitby. Family campers only. Licensed club. Extra fee for dogs. Fees on application. One of Haven's 29 tenting and touring parks. Open Easter-October.

York

Castle Howard Caravan & Camp Site, Coneysthorpe, York, North Yorkshire YO60 7DD. *01653 648316.* Castle Howard Estate Ltd. Six miles south west of Malton. Follow Castle Howard signs. Good touring centre, adjoining 70-acre lake. Well-drained site, good position for woodland and country walks. Dogs allowed under strict control. Fees on application. Open March-October.

Easingwold Caravan & Camping Park, White House Farm, Thirsk Road, Easingwold, York, North Yorkshire YO6 3NF. *01347 821479.* Mr & Mrs G Hood. 9m south of Thirsk. One mile north of Easingwold. On old A19 just off northern end of

bypass. Quiet stop over site, easy for York and North Yorkshire moors. Open March-October.

Goose Wood Caravan Park, Sutton-on-the-Forest, York, North Yorkshire YO61 1ET. *01347 810829.* www. ukparks.co.uk/goosewood. Sue & Eddie Prince. From A1237 (York outer ring road) take the B1363 north, pass Haxby-Wigginton junction. Take next right, and follow signs. Or when coming from north, take first left after second Easingwold roundabout (A19) into Huby then Sutton-on-the-Forest.

Holly Brook Caravan Park, Penny Carr Lane, Easingwold, York, North Yorkshire YO6 3EU. *01347 821906.* enquiries@hollybrookpark.co.uk. www.hollybrookpark.co.uk. Chris & Alice Cameron. Turn right off the A19 into Stillington Road. In half a mile, turn right into Penny Carr Lane—all signposted. Quiet, level, grassy site. No children. Dogs allowed. Open March 1-December 31.

York Touring Caravan Park, Greystones Farm, Towthorpe Moor Lane, York, North Yorkshire YO32 9ST *01904 499275.* info@yorkcaravansite.co.uk. www.yorkcaravansite.co.uk. 1 mile off A64 signposted Strensall. Secluded, spacious site. Own golf driving range and putting course. All new facilities. Children's play area. Dogs allowed. Graded 4 stars.

NORTHAMPTONSHIRE

Brackley

Bungalow Farm, Greatworth, Banbury, Brackley, Northamptonshire OX17 2DJ. *01295 760303.* Baylis & Sons. Four miles north of Brackley. Quiet rural site. Fees on application. Open Easter-October.

Kettering

Mill Marina, Midland Road, Thrapston, Kettering, Northamptonshire NN14 4JR. *01832 732850.* www.mill-marina. co.uk. Messrs. L & A Phillips. Eight miles east of Kettering via the A14. Take Thrapston exit from A14 (exit 13) or from A605. Site is signposted. Flat, well-drained, family-run site of some 5 acres by the river Nene. Fishing on site. Open April 1-October 31.

Northampton

Billing Aquadrome, Crow Lane, Great Billing, Northampton, Northamptonshire NN3 9DD. *01604 408181.* Billing Aquadrome Ltd. Off the A45 three miles from Northampton. Seven miles from M1 exit 15. Directional signs on M1 and thereafter. Open March-November.

NORTHUMBERLAND

Alnwick

Camping & Caravanning Club Site - Dunstan Hill, Craster, Alnwick, Northumberland NE66 3TQ. *01665 576310.* www.campingandcaravanningclub.co.uk. The Camping & Caravanning Club Ltd. Leave A1 at Seahouses, follow Embleton signs to Craster. 150 pitches accepting caravans, tents, motorhomes. WC. Washbasins. Showers. Shaver points. Shop. Secluded site ideal for exploring Northumberland coast. Play area. Dogs welcome. Non-members welcome. Open March-October.

Ashington

Wansbeck Riverside Park, Wellhead Dene Road, Ashington, Northumberland NE63 8TX. *01670 812323.* Wansbeck District Council. Touring site in picturesque Wansbeck Riverside Park. On banks of river Wansbeck. Ideal touring base. 75 pitches, tents and caravans. Warden lives on site and runs well-stocked shop. Children's play area and paddling pool. Graded: 3 stars.

Bamburgh

Waren Caravan Park, Waren Mill, Bamburgh, Northumberland NE70 7EE. *01668 214366.* waren@meadow-head.co.uk. www.meadowhead.co.uk. Meadowhead Ltd. Follow B1342 from A1 to Waren Mill towards Bamburgh. By Budle Bay turn right, follow signs to caravan park. Heated outdoor swimming pool. David Bellamy Silver Consevation Award. Graded: 4 stars. Open March-January.

Beadnell

Camping & Caravanning Club Site - Beadnell Bay, Anstead, Chathill, Beadnell, Northumberland NE67 5BX. *01665 720586.* www.campingandcaravanningclub.co.uk. The Camping & Caravanning Club Ltd. 6.3-acre site with 150 pitches—motor caravans, trailer tents and tents accepted—no towed caravans. Lovely beach 50yd, great for children. Dogs welcome. Non-members welcome. Superb site for walkers and cyclists. Open May-September.

Berwick-upon-Tweed

Beachcomber House Campsite, Goswick, Berwick-upon-Tweed, Northumberland TD15 2RW. *01289 381217.* john gregson@microplus.web.net. & Sheila Gregson. 4m south of Berwick on A1. 4m past Holy Island turn off. From south signposted Goswick, follow road to end through golf club, approx 4m from A1. Small site in remote spot on sandunes overlooking Goswick Sands. Excellent facilities with glorious views over Cheviot Hills. Horse riding on site. Open March-End September.

Berwick Holiday Centre, Magdalene Fields, Berwick-upon-Tweed, Northumberland TD15 1NE. *01289 307113.* Bourne Leisure Group. Berwick is signposted on the A1 from both the north and south and you will find signs directing you to Berwick Holiday Centre. Open April-September.

Haggerston Castle Holiday Park, Beal, Berwick-upon-Tweed, Northumberland TD15 2PA. *01289 381333.* British Holidays. Park signposted from the A1, 7 miles south of Berwick-on-Tweed. Open April-October.

Marshall Meadows Farm, Berwick-upon-Tweed, Northumberland TD15 1UT. *01289 307375.* Mr J Fairbairn. 2.5m N of Berwick on A1 turn right, 500yd to site. Overnight stop or holiday centre on cliff top, beach access limited. Fees on application. Graded: 3 stars. Open April-October.

Ord House Country Park, East Ord, Berwick-upon-Tweed, Northumberland TD15 2NS. *01289 305288.* enquiries@ord house.co.uk. www.ordhouse.co.uk. Howard Marshall. Leave A1 at roundabout follow signpost for East Ord. Park is opposite Post Office. 6 hole practice golf course. mini golf and children's play area.

Haltwhistle

Camping & Caravanning Club Site - Haltwhistle, Burnfoot, Park Village, Haltwhistle, Northumberland NE49 0JP. *01434 320106.* www.campingandcaravanningclub.co.uk. The Camping & Caravanning Club Ltd. 2m W of Haltwhistle on road to Featherstone. On 1200-acre Bellister Castle Estate on S bank of South Tyne river. 4m from Hadrian's Wall, 3m from Pennine Way. Dogs welcome. Non-members welcome. 50 pitches—caravans, motor caravans and tents accepted. Open March-October.

Seldom Seen Caravan Park, Haltwhistle, Northumberland NE49 0NE. *01434 320571.* Mr W Dale. Off A69, signposted Haltwhistle. Quiet, riverside park. David Bellamy Gold Conservation Award. Birdwatching, peaceful walks. 2m from Hadrian's wall world heritage site. Near Northumberland National Park, Historical Borders, High Pennines. Open March-January.

Yont the Cleugh Caravan Park, Coanwood, Haltwhistle, Northumberland NE49 0QN. *01434 320274.* larlwhit@aol.com. www.yonthecleugh.co.uk. Mr & Mrs I L Whitaker. 4.5m S from A69 at Haltwhistle on roads to Coanwood. 3.5m E from A689 at Lambley. River valley amid moors. Country pub on site. Near major Roman Wall sites. Open March-January.

Hexham

Barrasford Park, 1 Front Drive, Hexham, Northumberland NE48 4BE. *01434 681210.* barrasfordpark@hotmail.com. T & M Smith. Off A68, 8m N of Corbridge signposted, park is 0.75m. 60 acres of woodland, licensed clubhouse. Salmon fishing within 2 miles. Open April 1-October 31.

Causey Hill Caravan Park, Causey Hill, Hexham, Northumberland NE46 2JN. *01434 602834.* causeyhillcp@aol.com. 1.5m SW Hexham. Follow B6306 Blanchland Road to Hoxham Racecourse. Turn right by our signpost. Quiet site, sheltered by mature tree belt. Scenic views, near Roman Wall. Graded: 3 stars. Open March 1-October 31.

Fallowfield Dene, Nr Acomb, Hexham, Northumberland NE46 4RP. *01434 603553.* den@fallowfielddene.co.uk. www.fallowfielddene.co.uk. Philip Straker. 2m N of Hexham via A69 bypass (N of river Tyne) for 0.5m W. Turn N on to A6079.

Site 1m beyond village of Acomb. Roman wall nearby. Manager: Dennis Burnell. Graded: 4 stars. Open March-January 2.
🅿🚐📷♿⚡☉♨🔥🏠☕🅗🍴♪ 🏊🚻🎣

Hexham Racecourse, High Yarridge, Hexham, Northumberland NE46 3NN. *01434 606847.* hexrace@aol.com. www.hexham-racecourse.co.uk. Hexham Steeplechase Co Ltd. B6306 from centre of Hexham; take first right. Continue up hill to crossroads signposted to right Hexham Racecourse. Close to Hadrian's Wall, Derwent Reservoir (10m). Open end-April to end-September.
🅿🚐📷☉♨🔥🏠♦☕≈🅛♪♫🛁🚻🎣

Kielder Caravan & Camping Site, (Forestry Commission), Kieder Village, Hexham, Northumberland NE48 1AX. *01434 250291.* fe.holidays@forestry.gsi.gov.uk. www.forestholidays. co.uk. Forestry Commission (Forest Holidays). 500yds N of Kielder village, just 3 miles from the Scottish border. Kielder is in the heart of Britain's largest forest. Brochure request line: 01313 340066. Open early March-end September.
🅿🚐📷♿☉♨🔥🏠🅛♪🛁🚻

Poplars Riverside Park, East Land Ends, Haydon Bridge, Hexham, Northumberland NE47 6BY. *01434 684427.* Mrs N Pattison. Secluded riverside site at Haydon Bridge near A69 Carlisle to Newcastle-upon-Tyne. Near village and convenient for Hadrian's Wall. Free fishing. Graded: 4 stars. Open March 1-end October.
🅿🚐📷♿⚡☉♨🔥🏠☕≈🅛♪♫🛁🚻🎣

Riverside Leisure, Tyne Green, Hexham, Northumberland NE46 3RY. *01434 604705.* B Pickering, B Pickering & A Davidson. Take A69 to Hexham, cross river & railway bridge. Park signposted. Proceed past Safeway on left and keep to road. Shell petrol station on right. Then crossroads. Turn right, signposted. An ETB graded park in country garden theme. Open March 1-November 30.
🅿🚐📷♿⚡☉♨🔥🏠♦☕≈🅛♫🛁🚻🎣

Springhouse Caravan Park, Slaley, Hexham, Northumberland NE47 0AW. *01434 673241.* enquire@spring housecaravanpark.co.uk. www.springhousecaravanpark.co.uk. Mr C Phillips. From the A68 turn for Slaley at Kiln Pit Hill. Follow signposts for park (about four miles). Quiet park surrounded by forest. Site sloping. Magnificent views. Open March 1-October 31.
🅿🚐📷⚡☉♨🔥🏠♦♫🛁🚻

Morpeth

Clennell Hall, Alwinton, Morpeth, Northumberland NE65 7BG. *01669 650341.* David Pulman. At foot of Cheviot Hills in the grounds of a 16th Century, Grade 2 listed building. Quiet, family run site in rural setting. Fully licensed.
🅿🚐📷♨♿⚡☕✕☉♨🔥🏠♦🅛♪🛁🚻🎣🛁🚻

Percy Wood Caravan Park, Swarland, Morpeth, Northumberland NE65 9JW. *01670 787649.* Mrs L Bates. A1 6m S of Alnwick, west 2m to Swarland. Woodland setting close to National Park, Cheviot Hills, Heritage coast. Static caravans for sale and hire. Graded: 4 stars. Open all year except February.
🅿🚐📷⚡☕☉♨🔥🏠♦☕🅛♪♫🛁🚻🎣

Otterburn

Border Forest Caravan Park, Cottonshopeburnfoot, Otterburn, Northumberland NE19 1TF. *01830 520259.* www.borderforestcaravanpark.co.uk. Mrs M E Bell & Mr S A Bell. Family run park in beautiful unspoilt Northumberland border country. Next to A68. 6m S of Scottish border. (Carter Bar.) Timber lodge & caravan hire. B&B en-suite rooms. Bunkhouse. Restaurant nearby. Graded: 4 stars. Open March-October 31.
🅿🚐📷⚡🅛✕☉♨🔥🏠♪🛁🚻

Rothbury

Coquetdale Caravan Park, Whitton, Rothbury, Northumberland NE65 7RU. *01669 620549.* enquiries @coquetdalecaravanpark.co.uk. www.coquetdalecaravanpark. co.uk. Coquetdale Holidays Ltd. 0.5m SW of Rothbury on road to Newtown. Near hill walking area of Simonside Hills. Public telephone. Calor Gas and Camping Gaz sales. Playground. Shops, pubs and restaurants locally. Familes and couples only. AA 3 pennant. Graded: 3 stars. Open Easter-October.
🅿🚐📷⚡☉♨🔥🏠🅗🅛♪♫🛁🚻🎣↦

Wooler

Highburn House Caravan & Camping Park, Burnhouse Road, Wooler, Northumberland NE71 6EE. *01668 281344.* relax@highburn-house.co.uk. Mr R D Tait. 400 yds west of town centre via Burnhouse Road. Flat, well sheltered site with good views. Easy reach of Cheviot Hills, castles, ancient monuments. Good walking area. Games field. Takeaway meals, cafe/restaurant, diary produce available nearby. Open March-December.
🅿🚐📷♨🅛⚡✕☉♨🔥🏠♦♨🅛🅛🅣♪🛁🚻🎣☕🚻🎣

Riverside Holiday Park, Wooler, Northumberland NE71 6AG. *01668 281447.* Haven Leisure. From Newcastle follow signs for Morpeth, then Coldstream, thus joining A697 to Wooler. From Scotland, take A697 from Coldstream to Wooler. On SE outskirts of town. One of Haven's 37 tenting and touring parks across the UK. Indoor fun pool. Free kids' club. Lounge bar and family clubroom. Graded: 4 stars. Open Easter-November.
🅿🚐📷♨🅛✕☉♨🔥🏠≈♦🅛♪♫🛁🚻🎣

NOTTINGHAMSHIRE

Mansfield

Sherwood Forest Caravan Park, Old Clipstone, Nr Edwinstowe, Mansfield, Nottinghamshire NG21 9HW. *01623 823132.* torksey caravans Ltd. 4m NE of Mansfield via B6030 and N to Warsop. Overnight stop London to Scotland and local touring.
🅿🚐📷♨🔥♿🏠♦🅛♪🛁🚻🎣

Newark

Carlton Manor Caravan Park, Ossington Road, Carlton on Trent, Newark, Nottinghamshire NG23 6NU. *01530 835662.* S A Goodman. On A1, 7m N of Newark, site is signposted. Caravan park but space for overnight tents. Village with all shops, good pubs and food. Route London to Scotland. Dogs allowed. Fees on application to the Manager. 3 fishing lakes 0.5 m. Hotel opposite site gate. Children's play area. Open Easter-November.
🅿🚐📷⚡🏠♦🅛♪♫

Greenacres Caravan & Touring Park, Lincoln Road, Tuxford, Newark, Nottinghamshire NG22 0JN. *01777 870264.* bailey-security@freezone.co.uk. www.freezone.co.uk/bailey-security. S & M Bailey. On A6075 about 1m E of crossing with A1 in town. Well signposted. Ideal for night halts and touring Robin Hood country. Open March-October.
🅿🚐📷♿⚡☕✕☉♨🔥🏠🅛♪♫

Milestone Caravan Park, North Road, Cromwell, Newark, Nottinghamshire NG23 6JE. *01636 821244.* Mr Stephen Price. On old A1, at north end of village. 4.5m north of Newark. Level, grass site with hard standings, overlooking course lake. Fishing on site. Full amenities. Graded: 4 stars.
🅿🚐📷♨🅛⚡☉♨🔥🏠♦❉🅛♪🛁🚻🎣

Orchard Park Caravan & Camping Park, Marnham Road, Tuxford, Newark, Nottinghamshire NG22 0PY. *01777 870228.* info@orchardcaravanpark.co.uk. www.caravanparks nottinghamshire.com. Pam & Brian Clark. 1.25m SE of A1. Off A6075 Lincoln road. Turn right in 0.75m on to Marnham Road.

NOTTINGHAMSHIRE/OXFORDSHIRE

Site on right in 0.75m. Quiet sheltered level site with excellent facilities. Ideal for Sherwood Forest and many attractions. Open mid-March to end-October.

The Hawthorns, Dunham-on-Trent, Newark, Nottinghamshire NG22 0VA. *01327 358161.* Billy & Sally-Anna Buckland. A1 Tuxford, turn towards Lincoln.

The Shannon Caravan & Camping Park, Wellow Road, Ollerton, Newark, Nottinghamshire NG22 9AP. *01623 869002.* www.caravan-sitefinder.co.uk. Mrs Buxton. Turn left off A1 (Newark-Worksop) onto A614 signposted Nottingham. In 6.5 miles at roundabout take 616 signposted Ollerton. In 0.25 mile at roundabout turn right towards Newark. Park in one mile on left. Cafe/restaurant, bottled gas supply nearby.

Nottingham

Holme Pierrepont Caravan & Camping Park, National Water Sports Centre, Adbolton Lane, Nottingham, Nottinghamshire NG12 2LU. *01159 824721.* The Sports Council. 3.5m SE of Nottingham via A52 Grantham road. Country park site, good picnic areas, quiet walks nature reserve. Water sports. Fees on application. Open April-October.

Thorntons Holt Camping Park, Stragglethorpe, Radcliffe-on-Trent, Nottingham, Nottinghamshire NG12 2JZ. *01159 332125.* camping@thorntons-holt.co.uk. Mr P G Taylor. Signposted from A46 and A52. Toilets. Showers. Hot and cold water to basins. Washing-up rooms. Laundry room. Indoor heated swimming pool. Play area. Information room. Limited facilities November to April. 100 yards to pub and restaurant. Half mile to golf driving range and golf course.

Worksop

Camping & Caravanning Club Site - Clumber Park, The Walled Garden, Clumber Park, Worksop, Nottinghamshire S80 3BD. *01909 482303.* www.campingandcaravanningclub.co.uk. The Camping & Caravanning Club Ltd. 2.5-acre site within an old walled garden. 55 pitches. Tents, trailers and motor caravans. Site owned by the National Trust on the estate formerly owned by the Dukes of Newcastle. 5 miles south-east of Worksop 4.5m south-west of East Retford. Members only caravans July & August. Dogs welcome. Graded: 3 stars. Open March-October.

Riverside Caravan Park, Central Avenue, Worksop, Nottinghamshire S80 1ER. *01909 474118.* Mr S Price. At

roundabout at junction of A57/A60 Mansfield, follow international-al site signs to town centre. Level, grassy site with waterside walks. Secluded yet adjacent to town centre. Graded: 4 stars.

OXFORDSHIRE

Abingdon

Bridge House Caravan Site, Clifton Hampden, Abingdon, Oxfordshire OX14 3EH. *01865 407725.* Elizabeth Gower. A 415 from Abingdon to Clifton Hampden, turn right at lights over bridge. Site situated on river. Open April 1-October 31.

Banbury

Anita's Touring Caravan Park, Formerly 'Mollington', The Yews, Mollington, Banbury, Oxfordshire OX17 1AZ. *01295 750731.* anitagail@btopenworld.com. Darrel & Anita Gail Jeffries. Leave M40 Junction 11 (Banbury). Take A423 Southam road. After 4 miles site entrance 200yds past Mollington turn on left as signed. Situated on outskirts of lovely village well situated for Stratford-on-Avon, Banbury, Blenheim and Stoneleigh. Graded: 4 stars.

Bo-Peep Caravan Park, Aynho Road, Adderbury, Banbury, Oxfordshire OX17 5NP. *01295 810605.* Mrs M A Hodge. Situated on the B4100 half mile E of Adderbury and three miles south of Banbury. Tranquil 13-acre touring site set in 85 acres of farmland. Mostly level views. river frontage and three and half miles of woodland/river walks. dogs welcome. Central for Oxford, Blenheim, Stratford-on-Avon and Warwick Castle. Caravan storage available. RV point, caravan wash bay etc. Graded: 4 stars. Open April-October.

Benson

Benson Waterfront, Benson Cruiser Station, Benson, Oxfordshire 0X10 6SJ. *01491 838304.* B North & Sons (WW) Ltd. Beside river Thames in Benson. 1.5 miles north of Wallingford A423. Fees on application. Open April-October.

Bicester

Godwin's (Oxford) Ice Cream Farm, Manor Farm, Northampton Road, Weston-on-the-Green, Bicester, Oxfordshire OX25 3QL. *01869 350354.* neil@westononthe-greeen.freeserve.co.uk. Neil & Lorna Godwin. Leave at J9 M40 going towards Oxford, after 2 miles, take left turn to Weston-on-the-Green, at mini roundabout turn right, our farm is the first entrance on the right (clearly sighposted). Open March-October.

Leys Farm Caravan Site, Upper Heyford, Bicester, Oxfordshire OX6 3LU. *01869 232048/232665.* D J & B J Buxey & Son. Off B4030 Chipping Norton to Bicester. 2 miles from M40. Children's play area.

Burford

The New Inn, Nether Westcote, Burford, Oxfordshire OX7 6SD. *01993 830827.* Mr Steve Rix. 4m S of Stow on the Wold via A424. Secluded site forming centre for touring Cotswolds. Pub food. Dogs allowed on leads.

Chadlington

Camping & Caravanning Club Site, Chipping Norton Road, Chadlington, Oxfordshire OX7 3PE. *01608 641993.* The

Camping & Caravannning Club Ltd. 4.5-acre site with 104 pitches accepting all units. A rural setting mostly level with some trees and shelter. Take Oxford ring road then A3400 to Stratford upon Avon. Then A44. In Chipping Norton take A361 for Burford. Play area. Dogs welcome. Non-members welcome. Graded: 4 stars. Open March-November.

Charlbury

Cotswold View Caravan & Camping Site, Enstone Road, Charlbury, Oxfordshire OX7 3JH. 0800 0853474/01608 810314. Mr & Mrs G F Widdows. On B4022, 1m N of Charlbury on road to Enstone. High standard. Children's recreation area. On a working farm. Graded: 4 stars. Open Easter-October 31.

Chipping Norton

Camping & Caravanning Club Site - Chipping Norton, Chipping Norton Road, Chadlington,Chipping Norton, Oxfordshire OX7 3PE. 01608 641993. www.campingandcaravanningclub.co.uk. Camping & Caravanning Club. A44 to Chipping Norton on A361. Pick up A361 Burford Road, turn left at crossroads. Site in 150 yd. Non-members welcome. Perfect for exploring Cotswolds. 150 pitches available. Open March-October.

Churchill Heath Caravan & Camping Site, Kingham, Chipping Norton, Oxfordshire OX7 6UJ. 01608 658317. Ms R A Edwards. Four miles south west of Chipping Norton on the B4450. Between Churchill and Bledington. Centre for the Cotswolds. Separate area for tents. Children's play areas, serving food lunchtime and evenings between April and September.

Henley-on-Thames

Swiss Farm International Caravan Park, Marlow Road, Henley-on-Thames, Oxfordshire RG9 2HY. 01491 573419. Mr J W Borlase. 400 yds north of Henley on west side of A4155 towards Marlow. Roomy site in the Thames valley. Excellent position for visiting London, Windsor and Oxford. Swimming pool, fishing lake and licensed site. Open March-October.

Kidlington

Lince Copse Caravan & Camping Park, Enslow, Kidlington, Oxfordshire OX5 3AY. 01869 351321. R Haynes. A4095, one and half miles from the junction with the A4260. Seven miles north of Oxford. Quiet, family site in heart of Cherwell Valley, close to the Cotswolds and Blenheim Palace. Ideal touring area for Oxford and Banbury. Open March 21-October 31.

Oxford

Camping & Caravanning Club Site - Oxford, 426 Abingdon Road, Oxford, Oxfordshire OX1 4XN. 01865 244088. www.campingandcaravanningclub.co.uk. The Camping & Caravanning club. From south of Oxford take A4144 to the city centre from the ring road. Site 400yd on left at rear of Touchwoods Outdoor Life Centre, 1.5 miles south of city centre signposted from the A34. A level, grassy site. Suitable centre for sightseeing in Oxford area. Non-members welcome. Accept caravans, motor caravans and tents—84 pitches. Cafe and takeaway available nearby.

Diamond Farm Caravan & Camping Park, Bletchingdon, Oxford, Oxfordshire OX5 3DR. 01869 350909. Mr Roger Hodge. 7m N of Oxford via A34 for 6m then left on to B4207 for 1m. Site on left. Snooker and games room. Licensed bar. Convenient for

Oxford, Cotswold and Blenheim Palace. Fees on application.

Wallingford

Bridge Villa Caravan & Camping Park, Crowmarsh Gifford, Wallingford, Oxfordshire OX10 8HB. 01491 836860. Messrs E L Townsend and Son. Touring site off A4130 in village of Crowmarsh Gifford near Wallingford Bridge. Dogs on leads only. Fees and information on application. Open 11 months-closed January.

Riverside Park, The Street, Wallingford, Oxfordshire OX11 8EB. 01491 835232. South Oxfordshire District Council. On east bank of river Thames 120yd north of Wallingford bridge. Off A4130. Flat, riverside site within reach of Chilterns, Oxford and Berkshire Downs. Fees on application. Open May-September.

Witney

Hardwick Parks Ltd, Downs Road, Standlake, Witney, Oxfordshire OX8 7PZ. 01865 300501. info@hardwick parks. co.uk. www.hardwickparks.co.uk. 4m S of Witney via A415 to Hardwick Parks signpost. Spacious site with 40-acre lake (fishing, windsurfing, water-skiing, jet-ski available on site). Holiday homes for hire. Oxford and Cotswolds within 12m. Near Blenheim Palace, safari parks and museums. Graded: 3 stars. Open April-October.

Lincoln Farm Park, Standlake, Witney, Oxfordshire OX29 7RH. 01865 300239. Mr K Fletcher. 5.5m SE of Witney using A415. In Standlake High Street. Flat, grassy, sheltered site, convenient for Oxford, Cotswolds, Blenheim Palace. Children's play area. Indoor leisure centre. Graded: 5 stars. Open February-November.

RUTLAND

Oakham

Ranksborough Hall, Langham, Oakham, Rutland LE15 7SR. 01572 722984. Mr & Mrs Barney. Two miles NW of Oakham on the A606 at west end of Langham Village. Touring centre. Squash courts. Solarium. Mini golf. Indoor pool.

Rutland Caravan & Camping, Greetham,Oakham, Rutland LE15 7NX. 01572 813520. info@rutlandcaravanandcamping. co.uk. www.rutlandcaravanandcamping.co.uk. Mr Hinch. From A1 turn north or southbound on to B668 towards Greetham village. Turn right at crossroads before village and 2nd left to site. Rutland Water 4m.

Wing Caravan & Camping Park, Wing Hall, Wing Village, Oakham, Rutland LE15 8RY. 01572 737283. winghall@post mark.net Wing Estates. From A1 Wansford, A47 to Leicester, 8 miles to Morcott, turn right then first left to Wing two and half miles outside village by 400yd. Parkland setting. Fishing on site. Pubs with meals. Shop in village. Rutland Water 2m. Eyebrook 8 miles. Dogs allowed.

SHROPSHIRE

Bishop's Castle

Cwnd House Farm, Wentnor, Bishop's Castle, Shropshire. 01588 650237. Mr R E B Jones. A489 at Craven Arms. Right off A489 at Lydham Heath signed Wentror. Past Inn on the Green. Site on right after 1m. Peaceful farm site. Open May-October.

SHROPSHIRE

Poplar Farm Caravan/Camping Ltd, Prolley Moor, Wentnor, Bishop's Castle, Shropshire SY9 5EJ. *01588 650383/381.* poplarfarm99@aol.com. www.poplarfarm99.com. Mr & Mrs Christian. 7 miles NE of Bishop's Castle. From Ludlow A49 N to Ch Stretton. 1.5m past Craven Arms fork left on to A489 for about 4 miles, turn right to Asterton then straight through to Prolley Moor, near the Long Mynd. Paragliding, hang-gliding, walking, trekking, cycling (hire on site), bird watching available all nearby. Park adjacent to National Trust Property. Open: March-October 31.

The Green Caravan & Camping Park, Wentnor, Bishop's Castle, Shropshire SY9 5EF. *01588 650605.* info@greencaravanpark.co.uk. www.greencaravanpark.co.uk. Mr & Mrs J H Turley & Family. Follow brown tourist signs from A488/A489. Peaceful riverside park set in the Shropshire hills, an area of outstanding natural beauty. Birdlife. Pub at site entrance. David Bellamy Gold Conservation Award. Open Easter-October.

Bridgnorth

Stanmore Hall Touring Park, Stourbridge Road, Bridgnorth, Shropshire WV15 6DT. *01746 761761.* stanmore@morris-leisure.co.uk. Morris Leisure. 2m from Bridgnorth on A458 to Stourbridge. Heart of England park of the year (2000 & 2001). Silver award England for Excellence 2000.

Three Horse Shoes, Brown Clee View Wheathill, Burwarton, Bridgnorth, Shropshire WV16 6QT. *01584 823206.* Mr C J Pritchard. 7m NE of Ludlow on B4364 to Bridgnorth. Overnight stop Midlands to Wales. Open Easter-October.

Church Stretton

Small Batch, Ashes Valley, Little Stretton, Church Stretton, Shropshire SY6 6PW. *01694 723358.* Mrs P R Prince. Leave A49 at turn for Little Stretton. Site is at foot of Ashes Valley, 2m S of Church Stretton. Near Long Mynd Hills. Fees on application. Open April-September.

Craven Arms

Bush Farm, Clunton, Craven Arms, Shropshire SY7 0HU. *01588 660330.* Mr & Mrs M Adams. From A49 at Craven Arms, 7 miles west on B4368. Signposted from Crown Inn at Clunton. River fishing on site. Forest walks. Stables for hire. Self-contained cottage. Children welcome only if booked in advance. Takeaway, shops, cafe and bottled gas supply all available nearby. Open April-October inclusive.

Kevindale Camping Site, Kevindale Broome, Craven Arms, Shropshire SY7 0NT. *01588 660199.* Mr Keith Rudd. From Craven Arms on A49. Take B4368 Clun/Bishops Castle. 2m left on B4367 to Knighton. 1.5m to Broome village on right. Close to village inn. Good food. Scenic views in Clun Valley. Close to mid-Wales border. Good walking. Open 1st April-1st October.

Pontesbury

Middle Darnford, Ratlinghope, Pontesbury, Shropshire SY5 0SR. *01694 751320.* Mr R H Hamer. 4m NW of Church Stretton. Opposite Long Mynd hills. On A49 turn W at Leebotwood 3m N of Church Stretton through Woolstaston. Quiet, country site, attractive to children. Open later than October if weather permits. Pets welcome. Washbasins.

Shrewsbury

Beaconsfield Farm, Battlefield, Shrewsbury, Shropshire SY4 4AA. *01939 210370.* www.beaconsfield-farm.co.uk. P W & J Poole. Adults only 1.5m N of Shrewsbury on A49. Best of British Park, Loo of the Year 1998, 99, 2000 and 2001. AA 5 pennants.

Cartref, Ford Heath, Shrewsbury, Shropshire SY5 9GD. *01743 821688.* Mr T Edwards. From A5 Shrewsbury by-pass take A458 to Welshpool for two miles (Now signposted from A5 Shrewsbury by-pass on Montgomery Junction B4386). Signposted from Ford village or take B4386 Montgomery road for two miles to Cruckton crossroads. Signposted from Cruckton crossroads. 5m Shrewsbury, 14m Welshpool. Dogs on leads allowed. SAE for terms. Open April-October.

Mill Farm Holiday Park, Hughley, Shrewsbury, Shropshire SY5 6NT. *01746 785208/255.* mail@millfarmcaravanpark.co.uk. www.millfarmcaravanpark.co.uk. Mr M D & P Bosworth & M Roberts. A458 Much Wenlock to Shrewsbury road. 3.5m from Harley. Turn left, after 2m at signpost for Harley, signposted. Attractive, sheltered site skirted by a trout stream. Pony-trekking. Bus service 2 days a week. Open all year except February.

Oxon Hall Touring Park, Welshpool Road,Shrewsbury, Shropshire SY3 5FB. *01743 340860.* oxon@morris-leisure.co.uk. www.morris-leisure.co.uk. Located on town centre side of Shrewsbury by-pass. Leave at A458 roundabout. site on left after 500yds. Level site near to town centre with park and ride bus stop adjacent to park. Graded: 5 stars.

Telford

Camping & Caravanning Club Site, Ring Bank, Ebury Hill, Haughton, Telford, Shropshire TF6 6BU. *01743 709334.* simann@weeks42.fsnet.co.uk. www.campingandcaravanning club.co.uk. The Camping & Caravanning Club Ltd. 18-acre site with 100 pitches accepting all units. Campers must provide own chemical toilets. East of Shrewsbury near B5062. Turn left at signpost 'Haughton and Upton Magna'. No sanitation. Non-members welcome. David Bellamy Gold Conseration Award. Open March-October.

Severn Gorge Park, Bridgnorth Road, Tweedale, Telford, Shropshire TF7 4JB. *01952 684789.* info@sevengorgepark.co.uk. www.sevengorgepark.co.uk. Webb Park Home Estates Ltd. From M54 J4, take A442 for one mile, then A442 signposted Kidderminster for 1.6 miles. Follow signpost for Madeley then Tweedale. Level, sheltered site set amongst woodland. All modern facilities. Ideal for exploring Ironbridge and the rest of Shropshire.

Wem

Lower Lacon Caravan Park, Wem, Shropshire SY4 5RP. *01939 232376.* info@llcp.co.uk www.llcp.co.uk. Mr C H Shingler. One mile NE of Wem via B5065 off B5476 or two miles on B5065 from A49 jct. Quiet, rural site. Lounge bar. Fees on application.

Whitchurch

Green Lane Farm Camping Site, Green Lane, Prees, Whitchurch, Shropshire SY13 2AH. *01948 840460.* www.greenlanefarm.northshropshire.biz. Mrs J Bower. On the

SOMERSET

A41 Whitchurch/Newport road. Turn on to the A442 Telford. In 150yd, turn right. Site entrance on right, white farm house. level site with 20 pitches and 20 hook-ups. Games green. Ideal site for tents. Open April-October.

SOMERSET

Bridgwater

Fairways International Touring Caravan & Camping Park, Bath Road, Bawdrip, Bridgwater, Somerset TA7 8PP. *01278 685569.* fairwaysint@btinternet.com. www.fairwaysint.btinternet.co.uk. Mr W Walker. 1.5m off M5 junction 23 in Glastonbury direction. Situated at junction of A39 and B3141. Purpose built park. Winner of the 'Loo of the Year' award every year since 1994. Open March 1-November 16.

> **Mill Farm Caravan & Camping Park, Fiddington, Bridgwater, Somerset TA5 1JQ.** *01278 732286.* www.mill-farm-uk.com. Mr M J Evans. M5 Junctions 23 or 24 to Bridgwater, take A39 (Minehead direction) for 6 miles. Turn right to Fiddington, follow camping/caravans signs. Beautiful sheltered site. Three heated swimming pools, riding centre, canoes and boating on shallow lake. Phone for brochure.

Burnham-on-Sea

> **Burnham-on-Sea Holiday Village, Marine Drive, Burnham-on-Sea, Somerset TA8 1LA.** *01278 783391.* British Holidays. Situated on the Esplanade facing the sea and adjoining town centre. 3 mile site 22 off M5. 95 acres of level parkland with indoor and outdoor swimming pools. Club with live entertainment and a wide range of family activities. Open Easter-September.

Burnham on Sea Touring Park, Stoddens Road, Burnham-on-Sea, Somerset TA8 2NZ. *01278 788355.* Association of Sports Clubs. M5, J22 exit Burnham on Sea. At next roundabout straight over, signposted to Burnham-on-Sea. 1.5 miles to next roundabout turn right into Stoddens Road, 0.25 miles sharp left hard bent. Entrance 100 yards on right over Cattle grid. Clubhouse, bars, skittle alley, pool, darts.

Diamond Farm Caravan & Touring Park, Weston Road, Brean, Burnham-on-Sea, Somerset TA8 2RL. *01278 751263/01278 751041.* trevor@diamondfarm42.freeserve.co.uk. www.diamond farm.co. uk. Mr T Hicks. From J21 of M5. Follow directions to Brean. Travel through Brean on coast road towards Weston-super-Mare. Quiet, family run site by river Axe. Free fishing and horseriding on site. Graded: 3 stars. Open April-October 31.

Holiday Resort Unity, Coast Road, Brean Sands, Burnham-on-Sea, Somerset TA8 2RB. *01278 751235.* claire@hru.co.uk. www.hru.co.uk. The House family. On coast road to Brean N of Burnham-on-Sea. From M5 J22, follow signs to Brean. Nightly entertainment from end-May to end-September. Ten-pin bowling. Pool complex. Indoor & outdoor pools with giant waterslides. Funfair with 30 rides and attractions. Open February 8-November 17.

Home Farm Park & Country Club, Edithmead, Burnham-on-Sea, Somerset TA9 4HD. *01278 788888.* homefarm holidaypark@compuserve.com T S Martin Ltd. Off M5 at exit 22 take road to Burnham-on-Sea, Edithmead. Level site. Heated showers and bathrooms. Launderette. Gift shop. Adventure playground. Fishing. Licensed bars. Live entertainment. Go-karts. Caravan service and sales. Holiday homes. Graded: 4 stars.

Northam Farm Caravan & Touring Park, Brean, Burnham-on-Sea, Somerset TA8 2SE. *01278 751244.* M M Scott. Easy access from M5 Junction 22, Burnham-on-Sea. Follow signs to Brean. 0.5 mile past Leisure Park on right. Open April 1-October 31.

Southfield Farm Caravan Park, Brean, Burnham-on-Sea, Somerset TA8 2RL. *01278 751233.* A G Hicks Ltd. Centre of Brean village 4m N of Burnham-on-Sea, M5 junction 22. Open May-September.

Warren Farm Holiday Park, Brean Sands, Burnham-on-Sea, Somerset TA8 2RP. *01278 751227.* H G & J H Harris & Son. Flat, grassy park. 100yd from five miles of sandy beach. Family park with excellent facilities. Open April 1-mid October.

Chard

Alpine Grove Touring Park, Alpine Grove, Forton, Chard, Somerset TA20 4HD. *01460 63479.* ask@alpinegrovetouring park.co.uk. www.alpinegrovetouringpark.co.uk. Julian Giddings. Follow signs to Forton from A438 onto B3162 and A30 on to B3167. 7.5 acre park of oaks and rhododendrons. Hard-standing area. Free showers, laundry, swings, heated pool, trampoline, walking and cycling. 2m from Cricket St Thomas, 10m from coast. Graded: 3 stars. Open Easter-September 30.

Snowdon Hill Farm, Barleymow's Farm Shop, Chard, Somerset TA20 3PS. *01460 66828/63213.* Mrs J & Mrs R Burrough. One mile from Chard on main A30 Chard/Honiton road. Turn right into lane opposite farm entrance, farm shop car park. Lovely views, very peaceful. Children and dogs welcome. Country walks.

South Somerset Holiday Park, Turnpike, A30 Exeter Road, Howley, Chard, Somerset TA20 3EA. *01460 66036.* R M Weeks. 3 miles west of Chard on the A30. Set in 20 acres, overlooking the Blackdown Hills. Close to many tourist attractions.

Cheddar

> **Broadway House Caravan & Camping Park, Albridge Road, Cheddar, Somerset BS27 3DB.** *01934 742610.* enquiries@broadwayhouse.uk.com. Mr & Mrs D R Moore. Exit 22 (M5) follow brown signs for Cheddar Gorge. On A371 midway between Cheddar and Axbridge. Heated pool. Licensed bar with family room. TV. Playgrounds. Nature trails, canoeing, abseiling, caving and archery. Crazy golf and skate board ramps. David Bellamy Gold Conservation Award. Graded: 4 stars. Open March-November.

SOMERSET

Bucklegrove Caravan & Camping Park, Rodney Stoke, Cheddar, Somerset BS27 3UZ. *01749 870261.* info@bucklegrove.co.uk. www.bucklegrove.co.uk. Mr & Mrs D Clarke. On A371 midway between Wells and Cheddar. Free indoor heated swimming pool. Shop, playground, bar, laundry, centrally heated immaculate toilet block. Friendly family-run park with level secluded pitches. Open March-January.

Cheddar Bridge Touring Park, Draycott Road, Cheddar, Somerset BS27 3RJ. *01934 743048.* melandsuepike217 @aol.com. M & S Pike. From M5 (J22) take A38 north on to A371, following Cheddar signs. Through Cheddar, pass market cross and church. Entrance right after "Froglands Farm". New adults-only, level sheltered riverside site, views of Mendip Hills. Superb facilities. Open Easter-October.

Froglands Caravan & Camping Site, Cheddar, Somerset BS27 3RH. *01934 742058.* jfroglands@aol.com. www.froglandsfarm.co.uk. Mr J Moore. In Cheddar, on A371 Wells to Weston road, near Cheddar Church. Close to village and Gorge. In good walking country. Fees on application. Open Easter-October.

Netherdale Caravan & Camping Site, Bridgwater Road, Sidcot, Winscombe, Cheddar, Somerset BS25 1NH. *01934 843007.* camping@netherdale.net. www.netherdale.net. Mr V J Mortimer. 3m north of Cheddar, 8m SE of Weston-super-Mare, 15m south-west of Bristol. On A38 2m south west of Churchill at Sidcot, near junction with A371 from Weston. Holiday centre on edge of Mendip Hills, or overnight stops (30 approx). Excellent walking area, footpath from site to Halecoombe. Dogs on leads allowed. Childrens play area. Dry ski, tobogganing slopes, sports complex nearby. Takeaway meals, cafe/restaurant, dairy produce all available nearby. Open March-October.

Rodney Stoke Camp Site, Rodney Stoke, Cheddar, Somerset BS27 3XB. *01749 870209.* Neil Sinclair. From Wells, take the A371 towards Cheddar. Site abut 5m. Rodney Stoke Inn is a large Victorian building at the foot of the Mendips and an ideal place to stop. Lots to do and see.

Clevedon

Warren's Holiday Village, Lake Farm, Colehouse Lane, Clevedon, Somerset BS21 6TQ. *01275 871666.* www. warrensholidayvillage.co.uk. Richard Warren. Sited 1.5 miles south of Clevedon via the B3133 Yatton Road. Turn right after river bridge. 1 mile from the sea. Open March-January.

Emborough

Old Down Touring Park, Emborough, Somerset BA3 4SA. *01761 232355.* olddown@talk21.com. www.ukparks.co.uk/old down. Mr & Mrs L Bleasdale. Six miles north east of Wells via the B3139. Or from Shepton Mallet. Take the A37 towards Bristol for six miles, right on the B3139. Site is at the A37 and B3139 junction, 0.75m east of Emborough opposite the Old Down Inn. Touring centre convenient for many places of interest. Booking advisable. Open March 15-November 15.

Glastonbury

Isle of Avalon Touring Caravan Park, Godney Road, Glastonbury, Somerset BA6 9AF. *01458 833618.* Mr & Mrs M Webb. A39 west of Glastonbury. B3151 signed Godney. 500 yards on right. flat, level park located in quiet location within easy walking distance of Glastonbury. Excellent facilities. Free family sized showers. Restaurant nearby. Cycle hire.

Rose Farm, Westhay, Glastonbury, Somerset BA6 9TR. *01458 860 256.* Mrs P Willcox. 5m W of Glastonbury on B3151 to Westhay village. 4m S of Wedmore. Flat moors. Overnight stop London or Midlands to Devon and Cornwall. Open May-October.

The Old Oaks Touring Park, Wick Farm, Wick, Glastonbury, Somerset BA6 8JS. *01458 831437.* info@theoldoaks.co.uk. www.theoldoaks.co.uk. Mr & Mrs White. Take A361 Shepton Mallet road from Glastonbury, in about 2m turn left at signpost Wick. Site in 1m. A tranquil adult only park, offering excellent facilities in an outstanding environment. Graded: 5 stars. Open March 1-October 31.

Ilchester

Halfway Way Caravan Park, Trees Cottage, Chilthorne Domer, Ilchester, Somerset BA22 8RE. *01935 840350.* halfway@paulspub.freeserve.co.uk. Mrs T Barow. A37 between Ilchester and Yeovil.

Langport

Bowdens Crest Caravan & Camping Park, Bowdens, Langport, Somerset TA10 0DD. *01458 250553.* bowcrest@aol.com. www.bowdenscrest.co.uk. Mrs May. Off A372 Langport to Bridgwater. Licensed bar. Free hot showers. Dogs allowed. Play area. Tranquil, level site. Graded: 2 stars. Meals available. Static caravan available for hire. Open February 14-January 14.

Martock

Southfork Caravan Park, Parrett Works, Martock, Somerset TA12 6AE. *01935 825661.* southfork.caravans@virgin.net. www.ukparks.co.uk/southfork. Mr & Mrs S Metcalfe. 8m NW Yeovil, two miles off the A303. Small peaceful park in open countryside near river Parrett. Clean, modern, heated toilet block with free hot showers. Play area. Numerous places of interest nearby for all age groups. AA 4-pennant. Graded: 5 stars.

SOMERSET

Minehead

Blue Anchor Park, Blue Anchor Bay, Minehead, Somerset TA24 6JT. *01643 821360.* Hoburne Ltd. A39 at Willinton towards Minehead. After about 4m turn right onto B3191 at Carhampton Park. 1.5 miles on right. Level pitches, close to sea. Views of local hills. Close to Exmoor and Quantocks. Perfect touring base. No tents allowed, caravans and motor caravans only. Rose Award. Graded: 4 stars. Open March-October.

Burrowhayes Farm Caravan & Camping Site, and Riding Stables, West Luccombe, Porlock, Minehead, Somerset TA24 8HT. *01643 862463.* info@burrowhayes.co.uk. www.burrowhayes.co.uk. Mr & Mrs J C Dascombe. Five miles west of Minehead on A39. Left hand turning to West Luccombe. Site 0.25 miles on right. In glorious National Trust scenery. Numerous walks from site through woodland and open moorland. Open March-October.

Camping & Caravanning Club Site - Minehead, Hill Road, North Hill, Minehead, Somerset TA24 5LB. *01643 704138.* www.campingandcaravanningclub.com. The Camping & Caravanning Club Ltd. 3.75-acre site with 60 pitches. From town centre move towards seafront, turn left into Blenheim Road, then left into Martlett Road, left around War Memorial into St Michael's Road. Past church into Moor Road, site on right. Non-members welcome. No caravans. Tents and motor caravans accepted. Open May-September.

Downscombe Farm Camp Site, Downscombe Farm, Exford, Minehead, Somerset TA24 7NP. *01643 831239.* J Howard. From A39 turn S on to A396. To Wheddon Cross then W on B3224. Site 1m from Exford. Turn north on Porlock road. Fork left and continue for 0.5m. Site on left. Quiet, level site beside river Exe, in beautiful countryside. Near to coast. Dogs allowed. Open March-October.

Halse Farm Caravan & Camping Park, Winsford, Minehead, Somerset TA4 7JL. *01643 851259.* enquiries@halsefarm.co.uk. www.halsefarm.co.uk. Mrs Julia Brown. Signposted from A396 (Tiverton/Minehead road). In Winsford turn left in front of Royal Oak and up lane 1m. Entrance immediately on the left after cattle grid. In the Exmoor National Park, adjacent to the moor. Graded: 4 stars. Open March 21-October 31.

Minehead & Exmoor Caravan Park, Porlock Road, Minehead, Somerset TA24 8SW. *01643 703074.* Mr & Mrs R B Jones. Official sign from A39, one mile west of Minehead centre. Small family park in open country. All level sites with first class facilities. Dogs on leads allowed. Open March 1-third week October.

Porlock Caravan Park, Porlock, Minehead, Somerset TA24 8ND. *01643 862269.* info@porlockcaravanpark.co.uk. www.porlockcaravanpark.co.uk. Tony & Denise Hardwick. A39 Minehead to Porlock. In Porlock turn right B3225 Weir, park signposted. Quiet, family run park in Vale of Porlock. Excellent touring and walking centre for Exmoor, 2 mins to village. Beach close by. Phone or write for brochure. Graded: 3 stars. Open March 15-October 31.

Westermill Farm, Exford, Minehead, Somerset TA24 7NJ. *01643 831238.* holidays@westermill-exmoor.co.uk. www.exmoor-camping.co.uk. The Edwards Family. Leave Exford on Porlock road. After 0.25m fork left. Go past another camp site before seeing 'Westermill' on tree fork left. This is a beautiful, secluded site beside river Exe in heart of Exmoor. 4 waymarked walks over 500 acres. Log cabins for hire.

Shepton Mallet

Greenacres Camping, Barrow Lane, North Wootton, Shepton Mallet, Somerset BA4 4HL. *01749 890497.* harvie.greenacres@talk21.com. Mr & Mrs D V Harvie. Quiet 4.5 acre site near Glastonbury, Bath & West Showground. A39 follow campsite sign at Brown's Garden Centre, Wells. A361 follow campsite sign at Steanbow. Facility block. Free use of fridges and freezers. 30 pitches on level site. Open March-October.

Manleaze Caravan Park, Cannards Grave, Shepton Mallet, Somerset BA4 4LY. *01749 342404.* A A Manley. One mile south of Shepton Mallet between the A37 and A371. Entrance is on the A371. Overnight stop London to South West.

Phippens Farm, Stoke St Michael, Oakhill, Shepton Mallet, Somerset BA3 5JH. *01749 840395.* Mr & Mrs S A Francis. 4m NE of Shepton Mallet via A37 and A367 to Oakhill. Turn E to Stoke St Michael and site. Central for touring. Open Easter-September.

Street

Bramble Hill Caravan & Camping Park, Bramble Hill, Walton, Street, Somerset BA16 9RQ. *01458 442548.* www.caravancampingsites.co.uk. Mrs M Rogers. M5, approx. 12m. One mile W of Street on A361-A39 towards Taunton. Site signs on roadside. Situated in centre of Polden Hills. Ideal touring site close to Clark's Village. Winter storage for caravans. Dogs on leads welcome. Graded: 2 stars. Open April-October.

Taunton

Ashe Farm Caravan & Camp Site, Thornfalcon, Taunton, Somerset TA3 5NW. *01823 442567.* camping@ashe-farm.fsnet.co.uk. Ms S M Small. Off the A358 at Nag's Head inn 400 yards along West Hatch road. Four miles south east of Taunton. Quiet, informal farm site central for touring. Open April-October.

SOMERSET

Holly Bush Park, Culmhead, Taunton, Somerset TA3 7EA. *01823 421515.* hollybush.park@virgin.net. hollybushpark.co.uk. Gary & Rachel Todd. From M5, J25, head towards Taunton. Follow signs for Corfe and the racecourse on B3170. 3.5 miles after Corfe, turn right at crossroads towards Wellington. Turn right at next T-junction. Site 150yd on left. Peaceful, family site in an area of outstanding natural beauty.

Quantock Orchard Caravan Park, Crowcombe, Taunton, Somerset TA4 4AW. *01984 618618.* Mr & Mrs E C Biggs. Ten miles from Taunton on the A358 Minehead road just outside village of Crowcombe. Small, clean, friendly, family run site at foot of beautiful Quantock Hills. Close to Exmoor and coast. Ideal touring base with many delightful rural attractions. Graded: 4 stars.

Watchet

Doniford Bay Holiday Park, Watchet, Somerset TA23 0TJ. *01984 632423.* www.havenholidays.com. Haven Leisure. Leave M5 at J24. Take A39 for West Quantoxhead. Turn right for Doniford Holiday Park. On edge of Exmoor National Park, by the sea and less than four miles from Blue Anchor. Sports and play area. Licensed club. Graded: 3 stars. Open Easter to end-October.

Warren Bay Caravan & Camping Park, Watchet, Somerset TA23 0JR. *01984 631460.* Mr A P Pring. 1m W of Watchet on the B3191 Blue Anchor coast road. Open Easter-October.

Wedmore

Splott Farm, Blackford, Wedmore, Somerset BS28 4PD. *01278 641522.* Mrs B G Duckett. Four miles east of Highbridge on the B3139 Highbridge to Wells road. A quiet site, set off the road. An ideal centre for touring Wells, Cheddar and Weston-super-Mare. Excellent views. Open March-November.

Wells

Ebborlands Camping Grounds, Wookey Hole, Wells, Somerset BA5 1AY. *01749 672550.* Mrs E A Gibbs. Located 2.5 miles north-west of Wells. Pass the car park at Wookey Hole Caves. Site is located 400yd on the left Priddy to Cheddar road. A small, friendly, non-commercial site with views of the Mendip Hills. Wells Cathedral two and half miles away. Wookey Hole Caves and Ebbor Gorge nearby. Open May-October.

Homestead Caravan & Camping Park, Wookey Hole, Wells, Somerset BA5 1BW. *01749 673022.* homesteadpark@onetel. net.uk. Ingledene Ltd. One mile north of the A371 in Wookey Hole. Flat, sheltered, well-drained site near Wookey Hole Caves and Ebbor Gorge Nature Reserve. Adults only, no children under 14. Fees on application. Open Easter-October.

Mendip Heights Caravan & Camping Park, Townsend, Priddy, Wells, Somerset BA5 3BP. *01749 870241.* enquiries@mendipheights.co.uk. www.mendipheights. co.uk. Mr & Mrs J Dickson. From A39 take B3135 (Cheddar) 4.5 miles signposted. From A38, take A368 (Bath) for two miles, turn right on to B3134 seven miles then right again on B3135. Quiet family park in heart of the Mendip Hills. Suitable for touring and walking. David Bellamy Gold Conservation Award. Graded: 4 stars. Open March 1-November 15.

Weston-super-Mare

Ardnave Holiday Park, Kewstoke, Weston-super-Mare, Somerset BS22 9XJ. *01934 622319.* Mr & Mrs C G Thomas. From Junction 21, follow signs to Kewstoke. A flat, grassy site. Restaurant nearby. Dogs are allowed. Open March 1-October 31.

Camping & Caravanning Club Site - Weston-super-Mare, West End Farm, Locking, Weston-super-Mare, Somerset BS24 8RH. *01934 822548.* www.campingandcaravanning club.co.uk. The Camping & Caravanning Club. Leave M5 at Junction 21. Follow signs for Helicopter Museum, first right after museum and follow signs to site. Close to Cheddar Gorge. Members only. Non-members are welcome to join. Ideal for a traditional seaside holiday. Caravans, motor caravans and tents accepted—90 pitches. Open March-September.

Country View Caravan Park, Sand Road, Sand Bay, Weston-super-Mare, Somerset BS22 9UJ. *01934 627595.* Giles & Vicki Moroney. Kewstoke toll road to Sand Bay. From

Weston-super-Mare, or exit Junction 21 M5 follow sign for 'Sand Bay' along the Queensway and Norton Lane. You see Country View on your right 200yd before the beach. Open March-October.

Dulhorn Farm Holiday Park, Weston Road, Lympsham, Weston-super-Mare, Somerset BS24 0JQ. *01934 750298.* John & Gladys Bowden. M5, J22, A38 to Bristol, then A370 signposted Weston-super-Mare. through traffic lights on A370, approx 0.75mile on left. Working farm ideal for touring. Country surroundings. Graded: 2 stars. Open March 1-October 30.

Purn Holiday Park, Bridgwater Road, Bleadon, Weston-super-Mare, Somerset BS24 0AN. *01934 812342.* G J & B J Duffy. From north, leave M5 Junction 21. Take signs for Weston and hospital. Turn left at hospital roundabout onto A370. Park 1 mile on right. Licensed club with live entertainment, dining and dancing. Children allowed in both. Outdoor heated pool (May-September). Open March 1-November 7.

Rugby Football Club W-S-M, The Recreation Ground, Sunnyside Road, Weston-super-Mare, Somerset BS23 3PA. *01934 625643/623118.* W-W-M R-F-C. Off A370. Situated directly behind railway station, within easy walking distance from shops, beach and town centre. Open end March-end October.

Weston Gateway Tourist Park, West Wick, Weston-super-Mare, Somerset BS24 7TF. *01934 510344.* W J & E G Davies. From M5 J21 take A370 towards Weston. Turn left to West Wick and site is on right. Clubhouse. Open end March-end October.

Wheddon Cross

Blagdon Farm, Blagdon Cross, Wheddon Cross, Somerset TA24 7ED. *01643 841280.* Mr C H Melhuish. 0.75 mile west of Wheddon Cross on B3224 towards Exford. Seven miles from A39 at Dunster on the A396. Edge of Exmoor. Toilet at farm, also chemical toilet disposal point. Open May-October.

Wincanton

Wincanton Caravan Club Site, Wincanton Racecourse, Wincanton, Somerset BA9 8BJ. *01963 34276.* www.caravanclub.co.uk. The Caravan Club. 0.5m N of Wincanton on B3081 towards Bruton, off A303. Amid well wooded farmland. Route London to West Country. Non-members welcome. Open April-September.

Winscombe

Longbottom Farm, Shipham, Winscombe, Somerset BS25 1RW. *01934 743166.* langbottombandb@hotmail.com. Mr & Mrs R A Craggs. 1m N of Cheddar and 1m E of Shipham. On unclassified road towards Charterhouse. Quiet situation on Mendip Hills. Outstanding views. Bring your horse and camping/B&B acres of Downland woodland. Open all year by arrangement.

Wiveliscombe

Waterrow Touring Park, Waterrow, Wiveliscombe, Somerset TA4 2A2. *01984 623464.* taylor@waterrowpark.co.uk. www.waterrowpark.co.uk. Mr A G Taylor. 3m SW of Wiveliscombe via B3227. 300yd past Rock pub at Waterrow. Gently sloping site in attractive river valley. Adults only. Cafe/restaurant nearby.

Yeovil

Long Hazel International Caravan & Camping Park, High Street, Sparkford, Yeovil, Somerset BA22 7JH. *01963 440002.* longhazelpark@hotmail.com. www.sparkford.f9.co.uk/lhi.htm. Mr & Mrs A R Walton. 400 yds from new roundabout and Sparkford by-pass, A303, on old road into village. 8 miles north of Yeovil. Sheltered, level, grassy site. Inn & MacDonalds close by. Disabled showers/WC room. Dogs allowed. Public transport available. Graded: 4 stars. Open February 16-January 16.

SOUTH YORKSHIRE

Barnsley

Cinderhills Farm, Cawthorne, Barnsley, South Yorkshire S75 4JA. *01226 790318.* Mr R Barr. Located off the A635. Four miles west of Barnsley. Near Cannon Hill museum. One flush toilet.

Greensprings Touring Park, Rockley Abbey Farm, Rockley Lane, Worsborough, Barnsley, South Yorkshire S75 3DS. *01226 288298.* Mr J B & M Hodgson. 2m S of Barnsley. From junction 36 on M1 go towards Barnsley. Turn left in Birdwell 400 yds along road signposted for Pilley. Carry on to bottom of hill, site entrance is on left by lake, 1m from Birdwell village. Cycle hire. Open April-October.

Doncaster

Hatfield Waterpark, Old Thorne Road, Hatfield, Doncaster, South Yorkshire DN7 6EQ. *01302 841572.* Doncaster Metropolitan Borough Council. Close to Hatfield village with its excellent facilities. Motorway travellers leave M18 at junction 5. Take A18 and follow signs to Hatfield. Graded: 3 stars.

Hope Valley

Stocking Farm, Calver, Hope Valley, South Yorkshire S32 3XA. *01433 630516.* Mrs O Harvey & Mrs M Newton. 4m N of Bakewell. Take the A622 to Calver then E of A623. Take first turning left before bridge. On A619 through Baslow over bridge at Calver and turn right. In climbing, walking country. Open April-October.

Sheffield

Fox Hagg Farm, Lodge Lane, Rivelin, Sheffield, South Yorkshire S6 5SN. *01142 305589.* M Dyson & Son. 4m W of Sheffield on A57. Between Sheffield and Peak District. Near Rivelin post office. Dogs on leads allowed. Fees on application. Open April-October.

STAFFORDSHIRE

Cheadle

Hales Hall Camping & Caravan Park, Oakamoor Road, Cheadle, Staffordshire ST10 4BQ. *01538 753305.* Mr R M & C L T Clare. On the B5417 half a mile from Cheadle. Games room and playground. Licensed bar with bar meals. 10-acre rally field available. Sheltered camping. Open March-November.

STAFFORDSHIRE/SUFFOLK

Leek

Camping & Caravanning Club Site - Leek, Blackshaw Grange, Blackshaw Moor, Leek, Staffordshire ST13 8TL. *01538 300285.* www.campingandcaravanningclub.co.uk. The Camping & Caravanning Club. Two miles from Leek on the A53 to Buxton. Site is 200yd past sign 'B.Moor' on left side of road. On the edge of the Peak district, ideal for visiting Alton Towers. Caravans, motor caravans, tents accepted. Non-members welcome. 75 pitches. Dogs welcome.

Glencote Caravan Park , Churnet Valley, Station Road, Leek, Staffordshire ST13 7EE. *01538 360745.* Syd & Hilda Birch. 3.5m S of Leek on A520 Leek to Stone road. Small, family-run park which is flat, firm and well lit. Accommodates up to 40 touring caravans. David Bellamy Gold Conservation Award. Rose Award. Graded: 4 stars. Open April-October.

The Gallery Restaurant & Rooms & Campsite, The Old School, Butterton, Leek, Staffordshire ST13 7SY. *01538 304320.* Mr & Mrs J Swain. 4m SE of Leek, on A523, turn left to Longnor on B5053, then right to Butterton village. Flat, sheltered site ideal for families. Fees on application. Open March-October.

Rugeley

Camping & Caravanning Club Site - Cannock Chase, Old Youth Hostel, Wandon, Cannock Chase, Rugeley, Staffordshire WS15 1QW. *01889 582166.* www.campingandcaravanningclub.co.uk. The Camping & Caravanning Club Ltd. 5-acre site with 60 pitches accepting caravans, motorcaravans and tents. Surrounded by Forestry Commission land. From Cannock follow A460 and signs to Hednesford. At traffic lights at end of town turn right, after 1m turn left at sign 'Hazelslade 0.5m'. Site on left. Non-members welcome. Open end March-end October.

Stafford

Park View Farm Caravan & Camping Club Site, Park View Farm, Little Haywood, Stafford, Staffordshire ST18 0TR. *01889 808194.* christine-hill3@ntlworld.com. Mrs Christine Hill. Turn off A51 for villages of Great Haywood, Little Haywood and Colwich. Farm is at top of hill between Great and Little Haywood. Within walking distance of Shugborough Hall. Restaurant and pub food nearby. Friendly working farm atmosphere. Open all year weather permitting.

Stoke-on-Trent

The Cross Inn Caravan Park, Cauldon Low, Stoke-on-Trent, Staffordshire ST10 3EX. *01538 308338.* adrian_weaver@hotmail.com. www.crossinn.co.uk. A B Weaver & P Wilkinson. On A52 Stoke to Ashbourne Road. Alton Towers 3 miles. Peak Park 5 minutes. Pub/restaurant on site. Carvery all day Sunday. Families welcome. Open March 1-October 31.

The Star Caravan & Camping Park, Cotton, Nr Alton Towers, Stoke-on-Trent, Staffordshire ST10 3BW. *01538 702219.* www.starcaravanpark.co.uk. Mark & Margaret Mellor. Situated 0.75m from Alton Towers. Within easy reach of Peak District. 15m from Stoke on Trent. Large rallies can be catered for. Tents, caravans and motor caravans. Static caravans for hire. Dogs on leads allowed. Open end March-beginning November.

Tamworth

Drayton Manor Park Ltd, Fazeley, Tamworth, Staffordshire B78 3TW. *01827 287979.* www.draytonmanor.co.uk. M42 junction 9 or 10. On A4091. No bookings taken. Telephone for rates. Open Easter-October.

Tameview Caravan Site, Cliff, Kingsbury, Tamworth, Staffordshire B78 2DR. *01827 873853.* Mr & Mrs P Hollis. Near pub, Kingsbury Water Park and Drayton Manor Park, Tamworth Castle and National Exhibition Centre. Twycross zoo.

Uttoxeter

Uttoxeter Racecourse Caravan Club Site, Wood Lane, Uttoxeter, Staffordshire ST14 8BD. *01889 564172.* www.caravanclub.co.uk. The Caravan Club. Off B5017 at Wood Lane on outskirts of town. On racecourse, follow racecourse signs, enter at 2nd gate. Games area. Close to Alton Towers. Non-members and tent campers welcome. Fees on application. Open March-November.

SUFFOLK

Beccles

Ilketshall Camp Site, The Garage, Ilketshall, St Lawrence, Beccles, Suffolk NR34 8LB. *01986 781241.* W J, K J & V J Gowing. On A144, 4m N of Hawesworth, 5m S of Bungay. 7.5 miles W of Beccles. Level grass, surrounded by trees. Ideal touring area, 20 miles south of Norwich. Open Easter-October.

Waveney Lodge Caravan Site, Waveney Lodge, Elms Road, Aldeby, Beccles, Suffolk NR34 0EJ. *01502 677445.* waveneylodge25@hotmail.com. Mrs M J Goodwin. From A146 onto A143 Great Yarmouth road. Turn first right after one mile. First left into Elms Road, site on right in 0.25 miles. Secluded rural site with easy access. Ideal for exploring Norfolk and Suffolk, close to good beaches. Graded: 3 stars. Open April-October.

Waveney River Centre, Burgh Staithe Peter, Burgh St Peter, Beccles, Suffolk NR34 0BT. *01502 677343.* Mr A I Martin. Off A143. Indoor leisure centre, restaurant and public house. Adjacent to river Waveney. Day boat hire and coarse fishing. Play area. Open March-October.

Bungay

Outney Meadow Caravan Park, Bungay, Bungay, Suffolk NR35 1HG. *01986 892338.* Mr C R Hancy. Signposted from the junction of the A144 and the A143. Situated in Waveney Valley at Bungay. Between river Waveney and golf course. Riverside campsite, canoe trail, bike hire and fishing. Open March-October.

Bury St Edmunds

The Dell Touring Park, Beyton Road, Thurston, Bury St Edmunds, Suffolk IP31 3RB. *01359 270121.* thedellcaravanpark@btinternet.com. Mr & Mrs Derek Webber. Follow A14 E from Bury St Edmunds to Thurston (signposted). Midway between Cambridge and Ipswich, one hour from coast. Family run site with excellent facilities for disabled persons and children. Under new ownership. Dogs allowed. Ideal for touring East Anglia.

SUFFOLK

Eye

Honeypot Camp and Caravan Park, Wortham, Eye, Suffolk IP22 1PW. *01379 783312.* honeypotcamping@talk21.com. www.honeypotcamping.co.uk. Mr N Smith. Four miles south west of Diss on the A143 to Bury St Edmunds, in Wortham. On S side of road. Ideal inland touring centre for Norfolk to Suffolk. Quiet, family run, well organised site in 6.5 acres of landscaped parkland with lake facing due south. Open May 1-September 22.

🚐🏠⚡🖵⚓🗙⊙☕♨🛢🏠🔌≈ L ♪

Felixstowe

Suffolk Sands Holiday Park, Carr Road, Felixstowe, Suffolk IP11 2TS. *01394 273434.* info@cinqueports leisure.com. www.cinqueportsleisure.com. Cinque Ports Leisure. A14 Ipswich to Felixstowe right at first roundabout. Across next roundabout along Walton Avenue, to traffic lights, turn right. Site 200 yards on left. One of Havens 37 tenting and touring parks around the UK. Situated by the seafront. Free kids' club. Graded: 3 stars. Open April-October.

🚐🏠⚡🖵⚓🛢🗙⊙☕♨🛢🔶🏠🔌≈ L ♀🛆♪⤴ ⤵ 🐟

Hadleigh

Polstead Caravan & Camping Park, Holt Road, Polstead Heath, Hadleigh, Suffolk CO6 5BZ. *01787 211969.* C & J Walker. Situated between Boxford and Hadleigh on the A1071, opposite 'Brewers Arms Inn'. 3.5 acres, level landscaped grounds. Hard standings, dog walk area. Ideal for touring Constable country.

🚐🏠⚓🛢🗙⊙🛢🏠🔌✿ L ♪⤵ ⤴

Ipswich

Low House Touring Caravan Centre, Bucklesham Road, Foxhall, Ipswich, Suffolk IP10 0AU. *01473 659437.* john.e. booth@talk21.co.uk. www.tourbritain.com. Mr John Booth. Small tranquil touring park set in 3.5 acres. Small children's play area, set on grass with a pets corner. Felixstowe eight miles, Ipswich five miles.

🚐🏠🖵⚓⚡⊙☕🛢🏠≈ L 🛆♪⤵ ∪

Orwell Meadows Leisure Park, Priory Lane, Ipswich, Suffolk IP10 0JS. *01473 726666.* recpt@orwellmeadows.co.uk. Mr & Mrs D Miles. One mile from the A14 bypass; follow signs for Orwell meadows. Family run. Grassy, level well-drained pitches. Open March 1-January 16.

🚐🏠⚡🖵⚓🗙⊙☕♨≈🔶🏠🔌 L ♀🛆♪⤴ ⤵

Priory Park, Ipswich, Suffolk IP10 0JT. *01473 727393.* jwl@priory-park.com. www.priory-park.com. Priory Park Ltd. Two miles east of Ipswich via the A14 to A12 new Ipswich south bypass. Take Nacton Road Industrial Estate exit, follow caravan & camping signs.Superbly situated park adjoining the river Orwell estuary. Licensed club. 9-hole golf course. Tennis courts. Adventure play area. Heated outdoor swimming pool open from May-September. Open April 1-October 31.

🚐🏠🖵🗙⊙☕🛢🔶🏠 L 🛆♪⤵ 🐟

The Oaks Caravan Park, Chapel Road, Bucklesham, Ipswich, Suffolk IP10 0BJ. *01394 448837.* P Brown. Take A14 east towards Felixstowe, exit left signposted Bucklesham/Brightwell and continue for about one mile turn right signposted Kirton site on right-hand side. Open April-October.

🚐🏠🖵⚓🗙⊙☕🛢🏠🔌 L 🛆♪⤵ ∪

Kessingland

Heathland Beach Caravan Park, London Road, Kessingland, Suffolk NR33 7PJ. *01502 740337.* heathlandbeach@btinter net.com. www.heathlandbeach.co.uk. Reader Family. 3 miles south of Lowestoft off A12, one mile north of Kessingland village on B1437. 11.5-acre camping and touring meadow. Children's play area. Private beach access. Bar and restaurant. Open April 1-October 31.

🚐🏠⚡🖵⚓🛢🗙⊙☕♨🛢≈🔶🏠🔌≈ L ♀🛆♪⤴ ∪ 🐟 🐟

Lowestoft

Beach Farm Residential & Holiday Park, Arbor Lane, Pakefield, Lowestoft, Suffolk NR33 7BD. *01502 572794/519398.* beachfarmpark@aol.com. www.beachfarm-park.co.uk. Mr G Westgate. On the A12 Kessingland to Yarmouth road. Few minutes walk from sea. TV room. Laundry. Ample showers. Heated pool. Licensed bar. children's play area. Five minutes from supermarket. Open March 1-December 31.

🚐🏠⚡🖵⚓🛢🗙⊙☕🛢≈🔶🏠🔌 L 🛆♪⤴ ∪ 🐟 🐟

Camping & Caravanning Club Site - Kessingland, Suffolk Wildlife Park, Whites Lane, Kessingland, Lowestoft, Suffolk NR33 7SL. *01502 742040.* www.campingandcaravanning club.co.uk. The Camping & Caravanning Club Ltd. Follow signs to wildlife park off A12 from Lowestoft towards London. Site within easy reach of east coast resorts and next to the Suffolk Wildlife Park. Play area. Motor caravans, caravans and tents welcome - 90 pitches. Cafe and take away meals available nearby. Non-members welcome. Open end March-end October.

🚐🏠🖵⚓🛢⊙☕🛢🏠🔌 L 🚽

SUFFOLK

Chestnut Farm, Giseleham, Lowestoft, Suffolk NR33 8EE. *01502 740227.* Mrs J Collen. Turn west off the A12 at southern roundabout on Kessingland bypass, opposite Wildlife Park. Signposted Rushmere to Mutford to Gisleham. Then second on left and first drive on left. 3 acres, 20 pitches, level, grassy site. Private fishing. AA 2 pennant. Open Easter-October.

Kessingland Beach Holiday Park, Beach Road, Kessingland, Lowestoft, Suffolk NR33 7RN. *01502 740636.* Haven Leisure. Four miles from Lowestoft on the A12. Indoor and outdoor pools. Free kids' clubs. Free evening and daytime entertainment for all the family. Graded: 3 stars. Open April-October.

White House Farm, Giseleham, Lowestoft, Suffolk NR33 8DX. *01502 740248.* Mr B Collen. A12 from Ipswich, left at roundabout at Kessingland, signposted Gisleham. Site on right in 1 mile. From Lowestoft south take Gisleham turning at Safeway roundabout, left at church, site 300 yards on left. Large, level, well-maintained open meadow. Open April 1-October 31.

Nayland

Rushbanks Farm, Winston, Nayland, Suffolk CO6 4NA. *01206 262350/01787 375691.* G F Bates. Two miles off the A134 of Nayland and seven miles from Colchester. A beautiful unspoilt riverside campsite on north bank of the river Stour, suitable for fishing and boating (no engines). Open April-October.

Saxmundham

Carlton Park Camping Site, Saxmundham, Suffolk IP17 1AT. *01728 603638.* Saxmundham Sports Club. Left side of B1121, N from Saxmundham. Quiet site for camping, attatched to sports ground. Overnight London to east coast, also suitable for longer stay. Open Easter-October.

Haw-Wood Caravan Park , Haw-Wood Farm, Darsham, Saxmundham, Suffolk IP17 3QT. *01986 784248.* Mr A Bloise. Off A12. Turn right off A12, 1.5m N of Darsham level crossing at Little Chef. Park 0.5m on right. The perfect site for discovering the Suffolk coast and countryside. Quiet site with showers and play area. Managers: Tony & Mavis Wiggins. Open April 1-October 31.

HAW-WOOD CARAVAN & CAMPING PARK

Haw-Wood Farm, Darsham, Saxmundham,
Suffolk, IP17 3QT

Tel: (01986) 784248

Quiet secluded site surrounded by fields with lovely walks and beaches nearby. Ideal for touring, cycling and birdwatching, close to pretty villages and small country towns with plenty of places to eat. Midway between Ipswich and Norwich, approx 10 mls from Lowestoft. Toilets, showers, chemical disposal point and electric hook-ups. Dogs welcome on leads. Open April 1st to Oct 31st, this is a good level site with room to park next to unit. Directions from Ipswich: 25 mls north on A12, 1 mile after Darsham level crossing turn right at Little Chef, site is ½ mile on right. Call at Farm House.

Lakeside Leisure Park, Saxmundham, Suffolk IP17 2QP. *01728 603344.* enquiries@carlton-meres.co.uk. M A & J A Walker. 1.5m W of Saxmundham, off A12 via B1119 Framlingham road, follow camp signs to site. Country park with two coarse fishing lakes. Clubhouse and entertainment. Two shower blocks. Heated swimming pool open Spring Bank Holiday to 1st week September. Open May 1-September 30.

Whitearch Touring Caravan Park, Main Road, Benhall, Saxmundham, Suffolk IP17 1NA. *01728 604646.* Mr M & Mrs V Rowe. Junc. of A12 and B1121. Park offers 40 pitches with hook-ups. One acre coarse fishing lake. Play area. Tended dogs welcome. Tennis Court, TV points. Open April 1-October 31.

Stowmarket

Orchard View Caravan Park, Stowupland Service Station, Thorney Green, Stowmarket, Suffolk IP14 4BJ. *01449 612326/677774.* I D & B G Leeks. 1m off A14 on A1120, situated at rear of service station. Quiet, level, grassy site, close to orchard. Good touring centre. Dogs allowed under control. Open April-October inclusive.

Sudbury

Willowmere Caravan Park, Bures Road, Little Cornard, Sudbury, Suffolk CO10 0NN. *01787 375559.* Mrs A Wilson. 1.5m S of Sudbury on B1508 Bures Road. Flat site. Tarmac roads. Swimming pool nearby. Open Easter-September 30.

Theberton

Cakes & Ale, Abbey Lane, Theberton, Suffolk IP16 4TE. *01728 831655.* Peter Little. Leave A12 onto B1121 to Saxmundham, E on B1119 towards Leiston. After 3m turn on to Theberton and follow camping park signs. 1m N of Leiston. Touring centre, 2m from sea. AA 3 pennant. Lounge bar. Recreation area, golf driving range and practice nets. Open Easter-October.

Woodbridge

Forest Camping, Butley, Woodbridge, Suffolk IP12 3NF. *01394 450707.* admin@forestcamping.co.uk. www.forestcamping.co.uk. Mrs C M Lummis. Off B1084 Woodbridge to Orford. Follow Rendlesham Forest Centre brown trourist signs. 7-acre site in centre of pine forest. A beautiful spacious unspoilt site. Ideal for cycling and walking. Dogs allowed on leads. Limited facilities November-January. Open April 1-January 10.

Forest Camping, in Rendlesham Forest Centre, Tangham Campsite, Butley, Woodbridge, Suffolk IP12 3NF. *01394 450707.* admin@forestcamping.co.uk. www.forestcamping.co.uk. Mrs C M Lummis. Off B1084 between Woodbridge and Orford. Follow Rendlesham Forest Centre Tourist brown signs. Spacious site in centre of Forestry Commission forest. Miles of walks and cycle trails, space for children to play. Limited facilities in December/January. Open April 1- January 10.

Moon & Sixpence, Waldringfield, Woodbridge, Suffolk IP12 4PP. *01473 736650.* moonsix@dircon.co.uk. www.moonsix.dircon.co.uk. Turn off A12 Ipswich eastern bypass and follow road signposted towards Waldringfield. Park is signposted. 2m S of Woodbridge. All facilities of a holiday park. Lake and private beach. Fishing September and October. Near river Deben. AA 5 pennant. Open Easter-October.

Queens Head Inn, Brandeston, Woodbridge, Suffolk IP13 7AD. *01728 685307.* M D & A P Smith. 8m N of Woodbridge, 8m W of Saxmundham. N from A12. Signs for Wickham Market, Easton, Kettleburgh on local road to Brandeston. From A1120 about 14m from Stowmarket, turn S at Earl Soham, 3m to Brandeston. Site in old world village. Family room.

St Margaret's Caravan & Camping Park, Shottisham, Woodbridge, Suffolk IP12 3HD. *01394 411247.* ken.norton@virgin.net. Mr K Norton. On the B1083, from A12 signposted Bawdsey, left at Shottisham T-junction. Site on left past Sorrel Horse Inn. Within five miles of the sea. Bird sanctuary six miles. Open April (Easter if earlier)-October.

The Sandlings Centre (formerly Maple Leaf), Lodge Road, Hollesley, Woodbridge, Suffolk IP12 3RR. *01394 411202.* Mr M J & W A Adams. 6.5m NE of Woodbridge via B1083 and local roads. Quiet, rural site. Fees on application. Open Easter-October.

SURREY

Chertsey

Camping & Caravanning Club Site - Chertsey, Chertsey Site, Bridge Road, Chertsey, Surrey KT16 8JX. *01932 562405.* www.campingandcaravanningclub.co.uk. The Camping & Caravanning Club Ltd. Leave M25 exit 11. Follow signs to Chertsey to Shepperton. Site is 200 yards from Chertsey Bridge on B375. 8-acre site with 200 pitches. Caravans, motor caravans and tents accepted. Boat launching available. Children's play area. On the banks of river Thames, close to London. Non-members and international visitors welcome.

East Horsley

Camping & Caravanning Club Site - Horsley, Ockham Road North, East Horsley, Surrey KT24 6PE. *01483 283273.* www.campingandcaravanningclub.co.uk. The Camping & Caravanning Club. 9.5 acre site with 130 pitches accepting motor caravans, caravans and tents. Car park for visitors. Recreation hall and children's playground. Take B2039 from the A3. Exit marked 'Ockham, East Horsley'. Look for post box on right at Green Lane, access road to site signposted on the right shortly after. Play area. Next to Horsley lake, ideal for fishing. Non-members welcome. Open March-October.

Godalming

The Merry Harriers, Hambledon, Godalming, Surrey GU8 4DR. *01428 682883.* merry.harriers@virgin.net. Mr Colin Beasley. 4m S of Godalming via B2130. Follow Hambledon signposts. Flat site in very pretty countryside; 16th-century pub opposite.

Lingfield

Long Acres Caravan & Camping Park, Newchapel Road, Lingfield, Surrey RH7 6LE. *01342 833205.* Mr Jeffrey Pilkington. From M25 take Junction 6 on to A22 south towards East Grinstead for 6 miles. Turn left onto B2028 Lingfield. 700 yards on right. Superb, clean, family run site. All facilities including tourist information. AA 3-pennant. Graded: 4 stars.

Mytchett

Canal Visitor Centre, Mytchett Place Road, Mytchett, Surrey GU16 6DD. *01252 370073.* info@basingstoke-canal.co.uk. Basingstoke Canal Authority. Near Junction 4 of M3. Open all year.

Staines

Laleham Park Camping Site, Thameside, Laleham, Staines, Surrey TW18 1SH. *01932 564149.* Spelthorne Borough Council. From Staines or Shepperton (B376 and B377). Take turning opposite Three Horseshoes Inn to riverside. Site is 500yds down river along tow path road. From Chertsey, cross Chertsey Bridge (B375), on to tow path road. Riverside site. Open April-September.

Walton-on-Thames

Camping & Caravanning Club Site - Walton-on-Thames, Fieldcommon Lane, Hersham, Walton-on-Thames, Surrey KT12 3QG. *01932 220392.* www.campingandcaravanningclub.co.uk. The Camping & Caravanning Club Ltd. 9-acre site with 115 pitches accepting motor caravans, caravans and tents. Large pavilion for indoor recreation. On banks of river Mole. Turn off Molesey/Hersham road east at Fieldcommon Lane. Minimum facilities, own sanitation essential. Only 15m from London. Members only. Non-members welcome to join. Open March-October.

TYNE & WEAR

Rowlands Gill

Derwent Park Camping & Caravan Site, Rowlands Gill, Tyne & Wear NE39 1LG. *01207 543383.* Gateshead Metropolitan Borough Council. At junction of A694 and B6314 in Rowlands Gill. Seven miles south west of Newcastle-on-Tyne. Flat, sheltered site, beside river Derwent. Ideal touring base for Northumbria. Near Beamish Open Air Museum and Gateshead Metro Centre. Fees on application. Graded: 4 stars. Open April 1-September 30.

South Shields

Lizard Lane Camping & Caravan Park, Marsden, South Shields, Tyne & Wear NE34 7AB. *01914 544982.* Borough of South Tyneside. Two miles south east of South Shields town centre via A183. 9 hole put on site. Children's play area up to 8 years. Close to museums, leisure centre and Roman remains. Fees on request (advance bookings only for weekly stays). Sea 100 yards. Graded: 3 stars. Open March 1-October 31.

WARWICKSHIRE

Aston Cantlow

Island Meadow Caravan Park, The Mill House, Aston Cantlow, Warwickshire B95 6JP. *01789 488273.* holiday@islandmeadowcaravanpark.co.uk. www.islandmeadowcaravanpark.co.uk. MD & KE Hudson. Off A3400 and A46 north west of Stratford (6 miles) in village of Aston Cantlow. Quiet, rural park on the river Alne in historic and picturesque village. Booking essential at peak periods. Fishing free to guests. Cafe/restaurant nearby. Open March 1-October 31.

Bidford-on-Avon

Cottage of Content, Welford Road, Barton, Bidford-on-Avon, Warwickshire B50 4NP. *01789 772279.* Mr John F Gash. Open March 1-October 31.

Meriden

Somers Wood Caravan & Camping Park, Somers Road, Meriden, Warwickshire CV7 7PL. *01676 522978.* enquiries@somerswood.co.uk. www.somerswood.co.uk. Mr & Mrs Fowler. From the A45 take the 452, signposted Meriden/Leamington. One mile at next roundabout turn left on to the B4102 (Hampton Lane) site is half mile on the left. Park is open exclusively to adults only. Overlooking golf course and adjacent to coarse fishery. Three miles from the National Exhibition Centre. Open February 1-December 20 inclusive.

Rugby

Sherwood Farm, Stretton-on-Dunsmore, Rugby, Warwickshire. *01788 810325.* Mr B S Chandler. Five miles west of Rugby on A45. Appeals more to short-stay campers. Convenient for visits to Coventry Cathedral and Warwick Castle.

Shipston-on-Stour

Mill Farm, Long Compton Mill, Shipston-on-Stour, Warwickshire CV36 5NZ. *01608 684663.* J H Salmon. Turn west off the A3400 in Long Compton and head towards Barton for half a mile. Site is on right. Open Easter-October.

Parkhill Farm, Halford, Shipston-on-Stour, Warwickshire CV36 5DQ. *01608 662492.* 2.5m N Shipston on A34 turn right on A429, turn E in Idlicote road 0.5m to site. Children welcome. Good fishing and canoeing. Booking advised. Open April-end October.

Southam

Holt Farm, Southam, Warwickshire CV47 1NJ. *01926 812225/07790 959638.* N G & A C Adkins. From Southam bypass follow the camping and caravan signs. Three miles from Southam off the Priors Marston Road. Near Oxford Canal. Overnight stop or local touring. Open March 1-October 31.

Stratford-upon-Avon

Avon Estates, Riverside Caravan Park, Tiddington Road, Stratford-upon-Avon, Warwickshire CV37 7AB. *01789 292312.* From Stratford-on-Avon on B4086 (1 mile). Riverside moorings. TV hook-ups available. Open April-October.

Dodwell Park, Evesham Road, B439 Stratford-upon-Avon, Warwickshire CV37 9ST. *01789 204957.* enquiries@dodwell park.co.uk. www.dodwellpark.co.uk. M J R & S B Bennett. Take B439 from Stratford towards Bidford. Continue over large hill. Dodwell Park is on left. Country walks to Luddington Village and river Avon. Ideal for visiting Cotswolds and Warwick Castle.

Warwick

Newlands Caravan Park, Loxley Lane, Wellesbourne, Warwick Warwickshire CV35 9EN. *01789 841096/0776 1747282.* Mr Chris Warr. From M40/A46 Juntion take A429 through Barford. Turn right go through Charlecote to crossroads. Straight over past all flying schools. Newlands is second bungalow on right, opposite helicopter school.

WEST MIDLANDS

Halesowen

Camping & Caravanning Club Site - Clent Hills, Fieldhouse Lane, Romsley, Halesowen, West Midlands B62 0NH. *01562 710015.* www.campingandcaravanningclub.co.uk. The Camping & Caravanning Club Ltd. 6.5-acre site in the heart of the country with 105 pitches. Caravans, motor caravans and tents accepted. Car park for visitors and children's playground. From M5 leave at exit 3 and follow A456 to Kidderminster. Turn on to B4551 and turn off at Sun Inn. Dogs welcome. Non-members welcome. Open March-October.

Sutton Coldfield

Camping & Caravanning Club Site - Kingsbury Water, Bodymoor Heath, Sutton Coldfield, West Midlands B76 0DY. *01827 874101.* www.campingandcaravanningclub.co.uk. The Camping & Caravanning Club Ltd. 18-acre site with 150 pitches. Caravans, motor caravans and tents accepted. Site is in 500 acres of disused gravel workings reclaimed and landscaped forming lakes and woodland. Leave the M6 at exit on to the A446. Turn right on to the A4097 to Kingsbury. Dogs welcome. Non-members welcome.

WEST SUSSEX

WEST SUSSEX

Arundel

Camping & Caravanning Club Site - Slindon, Slindon Park, Slindon, Arundel, West Sussex BN18 0RG. *01243 814387.* www.campingandcaravanningclub.co.uk. The Camping & Caravanning Club Ltd. 2-acre site with 40 pitches. Campers must provide their own chemical toilets. From Petworth follow A285 for 7.5m then fork left for Bognor. Bear left in Eartham then first left to Slindon. Site on right. Limited number of towed caravans. Dogs welcome. Non-members welcome. Caravans, motorcaravans and tents accepted. Open March-end September.

Maynards Caravan & Camping Park, Crossbush, Arundel, West Sussex BN18 9PQ. *01903 882075.* Mr R Hewitt. A27 Arundel to Worthing. Turn into car park Beefeater pub. Showers. Beefeater restaurant, hotel and petrol station adjacent to site. Convenient for Arundel Castle, bird sanctuary and large Sunday market. Dogs allowed.

Ship & Anchor Marina, Ford, Arundel, West Sussex BN18 0BJ. *01243 551262.* 2.5m N of Littlehampton and 2.5m S of Arundel. On road W of river Arun, S off A27 in Arundel or N off A259 at Climping. Touring centre, beside river. Pub on site. Dogs allowed. Fees on application. Graded: 3 stars. Open March 1-October 31.

Billingshurst

Bat and Ball Inn, New Pound, Wisborough Green, Billingshurst, West Sussex RH14 0EH. *01403 700313.* Mr K W Turril. Follow tourist signs from A272 junction with B2133. Site on left. 3m N of Billingshurst. Quiet, uncrowded site. Dogs on leads. Pub and restaurant. Open April 1-March 31.

The Limeburners Camping Ltd, Newbridge, Billingshurst, West Sussex RH14 9JA. *01403 782311.* limeburnerscampingltd@tinyworld.co.uk. Mr R C Sawyer. From A29 in town, take A272 towards Petworth. Left on to B2133, site about 150yds. 1.5m W of Billingshurst. Quiet, clean country site attached to 16th-century public house. Fees on application. Open April-October.

Chichester

Ellscott Park, Sidlesham Lane, Birdham, Chichester, West Sussex PO20 7QL. *01243 512003.* www.idms.co.uk/ellscott park. Angela & Michael Parks. On B286 Bracklesham Bay to Wittering, 4m S of Chichester, turn left into Sidlesham Lane, signposted Butterflies and Gardens, down Sidlesham Lane on right. Lovely, quiet country site. Own produce available. Open March 1-October 31.

Goodwood Racecourse, Chichester, West Sussex PO18 0PS. *01243 755033.* www.goodwood.co.uk. Goodwood Racecourse Ltd. A286 at Singleton, follow signs. Via Petworth on A285. 1.25m E of Singleton. 6m S of Midhurst, 7m N of Chichester. Not open race days. Graded: 3 stars. Open April-September.

> **Lakeside Holiday Village, Vinnetrow Road, Chichester, Sussex PO20 6LB.** *01243 787715.* info@cinqueports leisure.com. www.cinqueportsleisure.com. Cinque Ports Leisure. Take A27 to Chichester until Bognor road roundabout, take Pagham exit.

Red House Farm Camping Site, Bookers Lane , Earnley, Chichester, West Sussex PO20 7JG. *01243 512959.* clayred house@hotmail.com. Clay & Son. Wittering road S from Chichester. Turn left at Total Garage, then after 0.5m left into Bookers Lane. On bend site 500yds on left 7m S of Chichester. 1m from sea. Flat, level site. Car recommended. Children's adventure playground. Booking advised at peak holiday periods. Open Easter-October.

The Gees Camp, 127 Stocks Lane, East Wittering, Chichester, West Sussex PO20 8NY. *01243 670223.* Mrs L Grigg. A286 S from Chichester and B2198 to Brackelsham Bay. Site is in lane opposite British Legion headquarters. 7m S of Chichester. Close to sea. Open March-October.

Wicks Farm Camping Park, Redlands Lane, West Wittering, Chichester, West Sussex PO20 8QD. *01243 513116.* www.wicksfarm.co.uk . Mr R C Shrubb. On A286 from Chichester then B2179 from Birdham (turn right into Redlands Lane at West Wittering name board) Close to sea and Chichester Harbour. David Bellamy Gold Conservation Award. Fees on application. Graded: 5 stars. Open March-October.

Haywards Heath

Brighton Sun Club, Hamshaw Sloop Lane, Scaynes Hill, Haywards Heath, West Sussex RH17 7NP. *01444 831675.* www.endormat.co.uk/bsc/ Hugh Bentley. All bookings by phone, letter or e-mail only. Site not suitable October-April.

Henfield

Downsview Caravan Park, Bramlands Lane, Woodmancote, Henfield, West Sussex BN5 9TG. *01273 492801.* phr.peter@lineone.co.uk. Mr & Mrs P & J Harries-Rees. Signed on the A281 in village of Woodmancote. 2.5 miles east of Henfield. 9m north of Brighton Seafront. A small peaceful site in a beautiful rural area. Ideal for walking and cycling, yet within easy access of Brighton. Seasonal pitches available. No facilities for children. Graded 4 stars. Open April 1 or Easter-October 31.

Farmhouse Caravan & Camping Site, Tottington Drive, Small Dole, Henfield, West Sussex BN5 9XZ. *01273 493157.* Mrs R Griffiths. 2m S of Henfield on A2037 turn E in Small Dole. Site at end of Tottington Drive. Small farm site on South Downs. 5m from sea. Peaceful setting, wide countryside views. Ideal for families and walkers. Fees on application. Open March-November.

Harwoods Farm, West End Lane, Henfield, West Sussex BN5 9RF. *01273 492820.* Mr P D Spear. This site is on A281, 12m from Horsham, 10m from Brighton. Nine miles from Steyning. Road opposite White Hart PH continue for two miles to end of lane, then over junction, farm is 50 yards along on right. Signposted in Henfield High Street. No youth groups except Duke of Edinburgh Award. Fees on application. Open Easter-October.

Horsham

Honeybridge Park, Honeybridge Lane, Dial Post, Horsham, West Sussex RH13 8NX. *01403 710923.* enquiries@honey bridgepark.co.uk. www.honeybridgepark.co.uk. Jeff & Val Burrows. Ten miles south of Horsham on A24. Turn at the 'Old Barn Nurseries'. Park is 300yd on the right. Spacious park nestling within peace and quiet of an area of outstanding natural beauty, centralised for south coast resorts one hour from London theme parks and ferry ports. Seasonal pitches and storage facilities also available. Graded: 4 stars.

Raylands Caravan Park, Jackrells Lane, Southwater, Horsham, West Sussex RH13 7DH. *01403 730218/731822.* www.roundstonecaravans.com. Mr R Morris. Off the A24 about two miles through to park out of Southwater Village. AA Award for Excellence for sanitation facilities and attractive environment. Graded: 4 stars. Open March 1-October 31.

Littlehampton

Rutherford's Touring Park, Cornfield Close, Worthing Road, Littlehampton, West Sussex BN17 6LD. *01903 714240.* rutherford@zoom.co.uk. www.camping-caravaning.co.uk. L Rutherford. From Worthing/Brighton A259. From Arundel A284. Level, well drained site. Takeaway meals, laundry facilities available nearby.

White Rose Touring Park, Mill Lane, Littlehampton, West Sussex BN17 7PH. *01903 716176.* snowdondavid@ hotmail.com. www.whiterosetouringpark.co.uk. Mr & Mrs D Snowdon. Between Arundel and Littlehampton on A284. Award-winning quiet family site close to sandy beaches and South Downs. Mixture of hedged and open pitches, heated shower block, play area, dog area, seasonal pitches. Open March 15-January 15.

Petworth

Camping & Caravanning Club Site - Graffham, Great Bury, Graffham, Petworth, West Sussex GU28 0QJ. *01798 867476.* www.campingandcaravanningclub.co.uk. The Camping & Caravanning Club Ltd. 2m from Petworth off A285. 20 acres of sandy peat including a hill and tumulus with 90 pitches dispersed in trees and rhododendrons. Caravans, motorcaravans and tents accepted. Dogs welcome. Non-members welcome. Open March-October.

Selsey

Warner Farm Touring Park, Warner Lane, Selsey, West Sussex PO20 9EL. *01243 604499.* White Horse Caravan Co Ltd. From Chichester, B2145, park signposted. New park opened in July 1992 with all modern facilities. Graded: 5 stars. Open March 1-October 31.

West Wittering

Nunnington Farm Camping Site, Rookwood Road, West Wittering, West Sussex PO20 8LZ. *01243 514013.* camping site@nunningtonfarm.fsnet.co.uk. www.camp-sites.co.uk. Mr G M J A Jacobs. On A286 half a mile from village, about 7m south of Chichester. Holiday site is 1m from the beach. Fees on application. Open Easter-October.

Washington

Washington Caravan & Camping Park, London Road, Washington, West Sussex RH20 4AT. *01903 892869.* Mr M F Edlin. North of Washington on A283 east of roundabout with A24 signposted. Half way stop on South Downs Way below Chanctonbury Ring. Walking. Cycling. Close to many places of great interest. Graded: 4 stars.

WEST YORKSHIRE

Bingley

Harden & Bingley Caravan Park, Goit Stock Estate, Harden, Bingley, West Yorkshire BD16 1DF. *01535 273810.* D & A Sharples. 2.5 miles SE of Keighley. B6429 from A650 at Bingley to Harden. In Harden turn to Wilsden, then just before bridge turn into Goit Stock Lane to site. Holiday caravan site with space for tents. Fees on application. Open April-October.

Hebden Bridge

Pennine Camp & Caravan Site, High Greenwood House, Heptonstall, Hebden Bridge, West Yorkshire HX7 7AZ. 01422 842287. Mr Geoffrey Sunderland. From Hebden Bridge take Heptonstall road then follow tent and caravan signs. Small site overlooks Hardcastle Crags. Centre for Bronte, Emmerdale and Compo country, Pennine Way and Worth Valley railway. Open April-October.

Holmfirth

Holme Valley Camping & Caravan Park, Thongsbridge, Holmfirth, West Yorkshire HD9 7TD. 01484 665819. peaker @mytholmbridgeccpfreeserve. www.holmevalleycamping. com. Mr P M & Mrs H M Peaker. Midway between Holmfirth and Honley off A6024. In beautiful ' Summer Wine' country, bordering Peak District. Solarium. Kiddies' play area. Well-stocked shop with off-licence. David Bellamy Gold Conservation Award. Autogas sales. 16-amp hook-ups. Angling on site. Graded: 4 stars.

Keighley

Bronte Caravan Park & Storage, Off Halifax Road, Keighley, West Yorkshire BD25 5QF. 01535 694146/667951. Marshall & Gregson Ltd. From Keighley follow Halifax and Haworth signs to pick up Halifax Road (A629). Park 1.5m on right. Peaceful, quiet site, excellent fishing facilities. Own deer park and lake with black swans and other wildlife. Security barriers with access/exit key.

Brown Bank Caravan Park, Brown Bank Lane, Silsden, Keighley, West Yorkshire BD20 0NN. 01535 653241. Tim Laycock. Good walking area on edge of Ilkley Moor and close to Yorkshire Dales. Signposted from A6034 from Silsden or Addingham. Open April 1-October 31.

Dales Bank Holiday Park, off Bradley Road, Low Lane, Silsden, Keighley, West Yorkshire BD20 9JH. 01535 653321/656523. R M Preston. Fees on application. Graded: 2 stars. Open April-October 31.

Lower Heights Farm, Silsden, Keighley, West Yorkshire. 01535 653035. mmrowling@aol.com. Mr F & Mrs K Rowling. 4m south east of Skipton on road north off the A6034 at Cringles. Haworth, Bronte country, Bolton Abbey, Ilkley Moor and Skipton Castle within 5m. Fees on application. Open Easter-November.

Leeds

Moor Lodge, Blackmoor Lane, Bardsey, Leeds, West Yorkshire LS17 9DZ. 01937 572424. Mr R Brown. From Leeds, seven miles on A58 follow sign, left hand turn signposted Shadwall, Wike, Harewood. Graded: 4 stars.

Roundhay Park, Elmete Lane, Wetherby Road, Leeds, West Yorkshire LS8 2LG. 01132 652354. City of Leeds Promotion & Tourism. Ideal base for exploring the city of Leeds and surrounding countryside from historic York to Tropical World, Harewood House, Bronte and Herriot country. The Yorkshire Dales are 20 minutes away. Visit the Leeds Royal Armouries. Open March-early November.

Otley

Stubbings Farm, Leeds Road, Otley, West Yorkshire LS24 1DN. 01943 464168. Mr M Rimmer. On A660,1m E of Otley to Leeds. Farm site within easy reach of Dales. Quiet, rural, old fashioned camping site with beautiful views over Wharfe valley.

Shipley

Dobrudden Caravan Park, Baildon Moors, Baildon, Shipley, West Yorkshire. 01274 581016. elawrii@aol.com. www.dobrudden.co.uk. Mr & Mrs P A Lawrence. 2m N of Baildon. Close to Ilkley Moor and Haworth. Bronte country. Open March-December.

Wakefield

Nostell Priory Holiday Park, Nostell, Wakefield, West Yorkshire WF4 1QD. 01924 863938. Nostell Priory Holiday Homes Ltd. From Wakefield take A638 (Doncaster road) for 5m, entrance on left in Foulby. Level, sheltered, woodland site in grounds of stately home. Joint managers: Stephen & Patricia Fuller. Graded: 4 stars. Open April 1-September 30.

Wetherby

Maustin Caravan Park Ltd, Kearby cum Netherby, Wetherby, West Yorkshire LS22 4DA. 01132 886234. info@maustin.co.uk. www.maustin.co.uk. The Webb Family. 7m south of Harrogate and five miles west of Wetherby. At Harewood on A61 cross river then right to Kirkby Overblow, then sign to Kearby. Touring centre for Dales and stately homes. Flat green bowling on the park. Suit adults as no facilities for children. Brochure on request. Graded: 5 stars. Open March-November.

WILTSHIRE

Calne

Blackland Lakes Holiday & Leisure Centre, Stockley Lane, Calne, Wiltshire SN11 0NQ. 01249 813672. bookings@blacklandlakes.co.uk. www.blacklandlakes.co.uk. Mr & Mrs John Walden - Blackland Leisure Ltd. Signposted from A4 on E side of Calne. Rural, scenic, sheltered and quiet. Wildfowl/nature reserve. Coarse fishing. Excellent holiday and touring centre. Dogs welcome. Fees on application. AA 4 Pennants. Open March 1-October 31.

BLACKLAND
LEISURE LTD
STOCKLEY LANE
CALNE
WILTS, SN11 0NQ
TEL 01249 813672
FAX 01249 811346
Email:
info@blacklandlakes.co.uk

A natural well equipped family run site at the foot of the Marlborough Downs. Ideal for young children, couples, supervised groups, walking, riding, cycling. Good coarse fishing. 17 acres 180 pitches (130 with electric) 1mile visitor trail. Concessions for students. Sign posted from A4 East of Calne. 15 "Superpitches". Colour Brochure, site plan, tarrif and booking form on request. Visit our website www.blacklandlakes.co.uk

FULLY OPENED MARCH TO END OCT

Chippenham

Piccadilly Caravan Park, Folly Lane West, Lacock, Chippenham, Wiltshire SN15 2LP. *01249 730260.* piccadillylacock@aol.com. Peter & Frances Williams. Turn right off A350 Chippenham to Melksham road, signposted to Gastard and caravan symbol. Park is in open countryside 0.5m from the historic National Trust village of Lacock. Ideal touring centre. Graded: 5 stars. Open April 1-October 31.

Devizes

Camping & Caravanning Club Site - Devizes, Spout Lane, Nr Seend, Melksham, Devizes, Wiltshire SN12 6RN. *01380 828839.* www.campingandcaravanning.co.uk. The Camping & Caravanning Club. On A361 from Devizes turn right on to A365. Over canal and next left down lane beside 'Three Magpies' public house. Site on right. Site borders Kennet and Avon canal, 5m from Devizes. 90 pitches. Caravans, motor caravans and tents accepted. Non-members welcome.

Malmesbury

Burton Hill Caravan & Camping Park, Burton Hill, Malmesbury, Wiltshire SN16 0EJ. *01666 826880.* Burton Hill, off A429/Chippenham road, opposite Malmesbury Hospital, Arches Lane. Quiet country site. Riverside walk. Easy walking distance to the historic town of Malmesbury. Ideal for touring the Cotswolds, Bath and Westonbirt Arboretum. Graded: 2 stars. Open April 1-October 31.

Marlborough

Hillview Park, Oare, Marlborough, Wiltshire SN8 4JE *01672 563151.* Mr R Harriman. On A345 Marlborough to Pewsey road. Junction with Sunnyhill Lane. Booking advisable. SAE for brochure. Graded: 3 stars. Open April-end September.

Postern Hill - Savernake Forest, Postern Hill, Malborough, Wiltshire SN8 4ND. *01672 515 195.* fe.holidays@forestry.gsi.gov.uk. www.forestholidays.co.uk. Forestry Commission (Forest Holidays) One mile south of Marlborough on the A346 towards Tidworth. Set in a woodland park. Brochure request line: 0131 3340066. Open March - October.

Marston Meysey

Second Chance Touring Park, Marston Meysey, Wiltshire SN6 6SZ. *01285 810675/810939.* B Stroud. Midway between Cirencester and Swindon along A419. Turn off at Fairford and Latton signpost. Proceed 3 miles, turn right at Castle Eaton signpost. Park 150yd on right. On the edge of the Cotswolds, ideal for touring. Upper Thames riverside location, fishing and canoeing on site. AA 3 Pennant. Open March 1-November 30.

Salisbury

Alderbury Caravan & Camping Park, Old Southampton Road, Whaddon, Salisbury, Wiltshire SP5 3HB. *01722 710125.* Mrs S Harrison. From Salisbury take A36 to Southampton. Follow signs for Alderbury and Whaddon. 3m from Salisbury centre in pretty village opposite 3 Crowns inn, excellent food. Good location for Stonehenge, New Forest and Bournemouth.

Brades Acres Camp Site, Tilshead, Salisbury, Wiltshire SP3 4RX. *01980 620402.* G R Beades. At Tilshead off A360 Salisbury-Devizes road. Flat, well-drained site within reach of Stonehenge, Beaulieu, Salisbury Cathedral, Longleat. Open April-October.

Camping & Caravanning Club Site - Salisbury, Hudson's Field, Castle Road, Salisbury, Wiltshire SPI 3RR. *01722 320713.* www.campingandcaravanning.co.uk. The Camping & Caravanning Club Ltd. 4.5-acre site with 150 pitches. Caravans, motor caravans and tents accepted. From Salisbury follow the A345 for 2m towards Old Sarum. Hudson's Field lies on left below Old Sarum. Dogs welcome. Non-members welcome. Open March-October.

Coombe Touring Caravan Park, Coombe Nurseries, Race Plain, Netherhampton, Salisbury, Wiltshire SP2 8PN. *01722 328451.* Mr & Mrs B Hayter. 4m from Salisbury. Take A30/A36 Salisbury to Wilton Road, turn on to A3094 Netherhampton, in 1m straight onto Stratford Tony Road 0.5m, 2nd left behind racecourse. Well signposted. Rallies welcome. Children's play area. Flat racing adjacent to park.

Stonehenge Touring Park, Orcheston, Salisbury, Wiltshire SP3 4SH. *01980 620304.* stonehengetouringpark@supanet.com. www.stonehengetouringpark.supanet.com. Mrs J Young. Off A360 Salisbury to Devizes road 0.5m from Shrewton. Small, pretty site in centre of villages. Level with some hardstandings. Always a warm welcome. Graded: 3 stars. Open January-December.

Westbury

Brokerswood Country Park, Brokerswood, Westbury, Wiltshire BA13 4EH. *01373 822238.* woodland.park@virgin.net. brokerswoodcountrypark.co.uk. Mrs S H Capon. 3.5m N of Westbury and 5m from Trowbridge. From A361 on outskirts of Southwick village, 1.5m along lane on right. Site adjoins forest park and Heritage Centre. Adventure playgrounds and undercoat play centre. Narrow gauge railway (seasonal).

WORCESTERSHIRE

Hanley Swan

Camping & Caravanning Club Site - Blackmore, Camp No 2, Hanley Swan, Worcestershire WR8 0EE. *01684 310280.* www.campingandcaravanning.co.uk. The Camping & Caravanning Club Ltd. 16-acre site with 200 pitches accepting all units. A38 to Upton on Severn. Turn North over bridge. Take 2nd left then 1st left signed Hanley Swan site is on right. Located in the Malvern Hills close to river Severn. Non-members welcome. Caravans, motor caravans and tents accepted.

Hartlebury

Shorthill Caravan & Camping Centre, Worcester Road, Crossway Green, Hartlebury, Worcestershire DY13 9SH. *01299 250571.* Mr P R George. Mid-way between Kidderminster & Worcester on A449, next to Little Chef. Small family site in heart of beautiful Worcestershire countryside. Ideal base for sightseeing. Dogs allowed. New rally site available. Fees on application.

Hawford

Mill House Caravan & Camping Site, Hawford, Worcestershire WR3 7SE. *01905 451283.* millhousecaravan site@yahoo.co.uk. www.caravancampingsites.co.uk. Mrs J G M Ellaway. Three miles north of centre of Worcester on east side of A449. International camping signs at site entrance. Quiet, level, grassy site in riverside setting. Central for touring Stratford and Cotswolds. Fees on application. Open Easter-October.

Kidderminster

Camping & Caravanning Club Site - Wolverley, Brown Westhead Park, Wolverley, Kidderminster, Worcestershire DY10 3PX. *01562 850909.* www.camping andcaravanningclub.co.uk. The Camping & Caravanning Club Ltd. 12-acre site with 120 pitches accepting all units. Turn right from the A449 onto the B4189, site is on the right. Children's play area. Close to Severn Valley Railway. Non-members welcome. Caravans, motor caravans and tents accepted. Open March-November.

The Old Vicarage Activity Centre (Camp-Easy), Stottesdon, Cleobury Mortimer, Kidderminster, Worcestershire DY14 8UH. *01746 718436.* Mr B G & A B Eddies-Davies. Off Bridgnorth/Cleobury Mortimer road. B4363, follow signs for Stottesdon. Our equipment on site if required. Set in 27 acres of nature reserve. Group activities through Activity Centre by arrangement. Hill boarding, archery, bike hire. Dogs on leads. Open March-October.

Malvern

Riverside Caravan Park, Little Clevelode, Malvern, Worcestershire WR13 6PE. *01684 310475.* Mr & Mrs Nock. 3.5 miles east of Great Malvern on the B4424. Midway between Worcester and Upton on Severn. Flat, well-drained site with splendid views. Site borders the river Severn. Malvern's premier riverside site. Open April-October for touring.

Three Counties Park, Sledge Green, Berrow, Malvern, Worcestershire WR13 6JW. *01684 833439.* richard.dupont@talk21.com. Mr R Dupont. Six miles west of Tewkesbury on the A438 Ledbury road to site on left. Base for touring Gloucestershire & Worcestershire. Open Easter-October 31.

Ombersley

Holt Fleet Farm, Holt Fleet, Ombersley, Worcestershire WR6 6NW. *01905 620512.* Mr G T Barnett. On A4133 Droitwich to Tenbury road, west off A449 at Ombersley. Turn right 50yd before bridge. 1.5 miles west of Ombersley. Quiet site beside river Severn. Touring centre or overnight stop. Open April-October.

Pershore

Comberton Golf Club, Pershore Road, Great Comberton, Pershore, Worcestershire WR10 3DY. *07774 813381/ 01386 710738.* G L S Hickey. Adjacent to river Avon free fishing (licence needed). Beautiful country pubs and walks over Bredon Hill. New in 1994; 18-hole, par-3, starter golf course adjacent to site plus club room. Clubhouse opened 2002.

Eckington Riverside Caravan Park, Eckington, Pershore, Worcestershire WR10 3DD. *01386 750985.* Eckington Marina's Ltd. By the river Avon with its own fishing. Level ground in pear orchard. Open March 1-October 31..

Stourport-on-Severn

Lickhill Manor Caravan Park, Stourport-on-Severn, Worcestershire DY13 8RL. *01299 871041/01299 877820.* exellent @lickhillmanor.co.uk. www.lickhillmanor.co.uk. Denis Lloyd Jones. Signposted at crossroads with traffic lights on the B4195 Bewdley to Stourport road. Riverside position, level ground. Superb washrooms. Electric, water and drainage hook-ups. Rallies welcome.

Worcester

Lenchford Caravan Park, Shrawley, Worcester, Worcestershire WR6 6TB. *01905 620246.* Mr M A Bendall. 7 miles north of Worcester on A443/B4196, Worcester-Stourport road. Open April-October.

YORK

Acaster Malbis

Chestnut Farm Holiday Park, Acaster Malbis, York YO23 2UQ. *01904 704676.* enquiries@chestnutfarmholidaypark.co.uk. www.chestnutfarmholidaypark.co.uk. S G & A J Smith. Family run site three and half miles from York in pretty village by river Ouse. Modern toilet and shower block. Luxury Rose Award holiday caravans for hire. SAE for terms. Open April-October.

Moor End Farm, Acaster Malbis, York YO2 1UQ. *01904 706727.* moorendfarm@acaster99.fsnet.co.uk. www.ukparks. co.uk/moorend. Mrs G H Hall. Take A64 out of York, turn left at Copmanthorpe for Acaster. 4m S of York. Small park on working farm. Easy reach of river and city. SAE. Graded: 4 stars. Open April-October.

Poplar Farm Caravan Park, Acaster Malbis, York YO23 2UH. *01904 706548.* www.poplarfarmcaravans.co.uk. G Taylor. 4m S of York, turn off A64 at Copmanthorpe junction (A1237) follow signs. Family-run park on banks of river Ouse, riverbus service to York every day. Bar and restaurant. Open end March-end October.

Bishopthorpe

Riverside Caravan & Camping Park, Ferry Lane, Bishopthorpe, York YO23 2SB. *01904 704442/705812.* www.yorkmarine.co.uk. York Marine Services Ltd. From A64 take road to Bishopthorpe. Go down Main St. Right onto Acaster Lane then Ferry Lane. An attractive site alongside river Ouse with moorings, slipways and river bus service. Toilets, showers, H & C. Licensed restaurant. Open Easter to October. Open Easter-October.

Crockley Hill

Wigman Hall, Crockley Hill, York YO1 4SQ. *01904 448221.* Mrs G Duncan. Take the A19 from York turn off for Wheldrake and Thorganby about 4m out of York. 1.5m down this road site is on right. Open March-October.

Naburn

Naburn Lock Caravan Park, Naburn, York YO19 4RU. *01904 728697.* Mr J M Curtis. Open March-November 6.

Strensall

Moorside Caravan Park, Lords Moor Lane, Strensall, York YO32 5XJ. *01904 4912080/1904 491865.* www.moorside caravanpark.co.uk Mr Phil Smith. Take Strensall turn off A1237 and head towards Flaxton. Fishing on site. No children. Open March-October.

York

Acomb Grange, Grange Lane, York YO23 3QZ. *01904 781318.* pbrown@acomb-grange.freeserve.co.uk. www.go.to/ york. C A Brown. Important historical site, moated farmhouse. A residence of kings in the Middle Ages, and the last Royalist stand at the Battle of Marston. Phone for directions.

Rawcliffe Manor Caravan Park, Manor Lane, Shipton Road, York YO3 6TZ. *01904 624422.* Rawcliffe Caravan Co Ltd. On the A19 York to Thirsk road 200yd the York side of the junction of the A1237 (northern York by-pass). A flat well-drained site with all mains services. Large supermarket. 12 screen cinema, bowling alley, within easy walking distance.

The Alders Caravan Park, Home Farm, Alne, York YO61 1RY. *01347 838722.* jdwhiteley@tesco.net. www.alders caravanpark.co.uk. Owner: Mr & Mrs Whiteley. Close to A19 and A1. Level, dry site, tastefully landscaped. Adjoins Village cricket ground. Woodland walk. Ideally located to visit the Yorkshire Moors and Dales and heritage coastline. Open March 1-October 31.

The Old Gate House, Wheldrake Lane, Elvington, York YO41 4AZ. *01904 608225.* Mr G & Mrs L Gatenby. By pass York on A64 turn east on A1079. Then on B1228 Elvington. Aftr about 3 miles turn right opposite garage to Wheldrake. Site is one mile on left. Open March 1-October 31.

WALES

ANGLESEY

Amlwch

Plas Eilian, Llaneilian, Amlwch, Anglesey LL68 9LS. *01407 830323.* Mrs M Owen. 2m E of Amlwch by church in Llaneilian. Off A5025. Signposted with Penysarn. Quiet site with good views. Open April 17-October.

Point Lynas Caravan Park, Llaneilian, Amlwch, Anglesey LL68 9LT. *01407 831130.* peter@pantysaer.freeserve.co.uk. Mr M & P Hoyland. From Anglesey Mowers on A5025, 1.5m seaward direction. 200 metres from Porth Eilian cove. Quiet site overlooking sea by Point Lynas. Slipway for small boats. Graded: 4 stars. Open April 1-October 31.

Tyn Rhos Farm, Penysarn, Amlwch, Anglesey LL69 9YR. *01407 830574.* Mr H P Hughes. 2-acre level site. Dogs allowed on leads. Bookings advisable. 6-berth caravan to let. Takeaway, cafe/restaurant nearby. Open Easter-October.

Beaumaris

Kingsbridge Caravan Park, Llanfaes, Beaumaris, Anglesey LL58 8LR. *01248 490636/0374 842199.* Mr G A Stewart. 1.5 miles north of Beaumaris Castle. At crossroads turn left for 400 yards to site. Quiet, rural surroundings with excellent bird watching, sea fishing, sailing and beaches. Close to many places of historical interest. Fees on application. Open March-October.

Benllech

Ad Astra Caravan Park, Brynteg, Benllech, Anglesey LL78 7JH. *01248 853283.* brian@brynteg.53fsnet.co.uk. www.adastra caravanpark.co.uk. Mrs I Iddon & Mr B Iddon. 2m W of Benllech Bay. At Benllech crossroads, left on B5110. Continue to California Inn, turn left, site 200yd on right. Open March-October.

Bodafon Caravan & Camping Park, Benllech, Anglesey LL74 8RU. *01248 852417.* Mr & Mrs R G Roberts. Through the village of Benllech on the A5025, 50yd after end of 30mph restrictions on left. Quiet family site, near to shops and beaches. Ideal for touring Anglesey and Snowdonia. Open March 1-October 31.

Bwlch Holiday Park, Tynygongl, Benllech, Anglesey LL74 8RF. *01248 852914.* Lloyds Caravan Sales Co Ltd. A5025 Menai Bridge to Benllech (8m), turn left B5108 (1.5m). Open March 1-December 31.

Glan Gors (Tyddyn Llwyd), Brynteg, Benllech, Anglesey LL78 8QA. *01248 853633.* Haulfryn Group Ltd. One mile from Benllech. Take the A5108 at BP petrol station at crossroads. Site is signposted on left after about one mile. Sloping site with hard roads. Faces south quiet rural outlook. Easy access to beaches Graded: 3 stars. Open March-October.

Golden Sunset Holidays, Benllech, Anglesey LL74 8SW. *01248 852345.* Mr J A Hewitt. Site entrance at Benllech Bay on A5025 from Bangor. Well-drained site five minutes walk from sea. Graded: 2 stars. Open Easter-October.

Nant Newydd Park, Brynteg, Benllech, Anglesey LL78 7JH. *01248 852266/852842.* www.nantnewydd.co.uk. Mr & Mrs B W Jones. 3m SW. B5108 off A5025 at Benllech. At crossroads after 2m turn left. Site 1m on right. Hard standings with hook-up points, mains water and waste disposal. Quiet countryside 3m from coast. Dogs allowed. Fees on application. Graded: 4 stars. Open March-October.

Plas-Uchaf Caravan & Camping Park, Benllech, Anglesey LL74 8NU. *01407 763012.* Evans Enterprise. Turn W in square at Benllech on B5108. Site 0.25 miles from signpost on right-hand side. Flat, well-drained and sheltered site. Within 1 mile of beach and easy reach of local amenities. Tarmacadam road with street lighting. Dog walk. Play area. Open Easter-October.

St David's Park, Red Wharf Bay, Benllech, Anglesey LL75 8RJ. *01248 852341.* camp@stdavidspark.com www.stdavidspark. com A Jones & M Bennett. 1m S of Benllech. From Bangor bypass take 2nd slip road after Brittania Bridge (Amlwch to Benllech A5025). 2m from Pentraeth turn right to Red Wharf Bay and to site on right. Holiday site with tavern and beach. Graded: 2 stars. Open March 1-October 31.

Bryngwran

Tyn Llidiart Camping Site, Towan Trewan, Bryngwran, Anglesey LL65 3SW. *01407 810678.* alice@awoolleson. freeserve.co.uk. Mrs A Woolleson. 3m E Rhosneigr A5, sea 3m. Turn left at Bryngwran post office on unclassified road for 1 mile. Turn right at 2nd cross roads at white house. Site at bottom of lane on right.

Brynsiencyn

Fron Caravan & Camping Site, Brynsiencyn, Anglesey LL61 6TX. *01248 430310.* froncaravanpark@brynsiencyn.fsnet.co.uk. Mr & Mrs G Geldard. 6.5m SW of Menai Bridge. Cross Britannia Bridge then first slip road, marked Llanfairpwllgwyn, turn left on A4080 for 6m. Site is on right beyond Brynsiencyn. Flat, rural site 4m from sandy beach. Holiday site with children's play area and swimming pool. Graded: 4 stars. Open April-September.

Brynteg

Garnedd Touring and Camping Site, Lon Bryn Mair, Brynteg, Anglesey LL78 8QA. *01248 853240.* Mrs S Kirk, Mr M McCann. Take A5025 after Britannia bridge. After Pentraeath and derestriction signs turn L on to unclassified road at lay-by signed Llanbedrgoch. In 2 miles turn L at T-junction, then 1st L. Site on right in 0.5 mile at orange signs. Couples preferred. Children by special arrangement. Open March-October.

Dulas

Melin Rhos Farm Caravan & Camping Site, Lligwy Bay, Dulas, Anglesey LL70 9HQ. *01248 852417.* Mr Roberts. 16m from Bangor. A5025 from Bangor. Go through Benllech to Moelfre roundabout, turn left, continue down steep hill, right at bend at top of hill. Continue downhill. Site on left at the dip before bridge. Open Easter-October 31.

Tyddyn Isaf Caravan Park, Lligwy Bay, Dulas, Anglesey LL70 9PQ. *01248 410203.* www.tyddynisaf.demon.co.uk. J E & E W Hunt. A5025 north from Britannia Bridge through Benllech. Third road signposted Lligwy Beach. Five miles south-east of Amlwch. Bar. Private footpath to beach. 'Loo of the Year' winner. Fees on application. Open March-October.

Holyhead

Penrhyn Bay Caravan & Camping Site, Llanfwrog, Holyhead, Anglesey LL65 4YG. *01407 730496/730411.* penrhyn.bay@btinternet.com. www.penrhynbay.com. Mr E T Williams. Via A5025 N from Valley. Through Llanfachraeth, 1st left signposted. Follow signs for Penrhyn. Site next to a sandy beach. Indoor heated swimming pool. Tennis court. Fees on application. Open Easter-October.

Valley of the Rocks Camping & Caravan Park, Porthdafarch Road, Trearddur Bay, Holyhead, Anglesey LL65 2LL. *01407 765787.* Mr D Songhurst. Follow A55 across Anglesey to where the road terminates at the roundabout. Take first left at roundabout then take immediately first right between public houses (The Foresters and The Angel). Follow road for 1m until you see the signpost for Valley of the Rocks caravan park. Turn left into site then fork right. Reception is on the left at site shop. Open March 1-October 31.

Llanbedrgoch

Ty Newydd Caravan Park & Country Club, Llanbedrgoch, Anglesey LL76 8TZ. *01248 450677.* tynewyddcc@aol.com. www.members.aol.com/tynewyddcc. Mr Mike Monger & Mrs Cathi Monger. One mile south west of Benllech. From Britannia bridge take A5025 north. Approx. one mile after Pentraeth village turn left, pass lay by, approx 0.75 mile through village on right hand side. Well-drained site with licensed club. Open March-October.

Llanfairpwllgwyngyll

Plas Coch Caravan & Leisure Park, Llanedwen, Llanfairpwllgwyngyll, Anglesey LL61 6EJ. *01248 714346.* Peerless Leisure Amusements. West on A5 turn left on to A4080 quarter mile after crossing Bridge. Follow signs for Plas Newydd National Trust property, turn left at crossroads about quarter mile. Fully equipped holiday site with pub. 200 acres of park and farmland. Slipway suitable for water-skiing, wind surfing. Sailing and fishing. Dogs allowed. Open March-October.

Llanfwrog

Sandy Beach Touring Park, Porth Tywyn Mawr, Llanfwrog, Anglesey LL65 4YH. *01407 730302.* Ms R Y Jones. A5 to Valley. Right turn on to A5025, first left after Llanfacraeth, left 100 yards past church. First right. Beach side park, ideal base from which to explore Anglesey or just relax. Open April-October.

Lligwy Bay

Creigiau Camping & Touring Site, Dulas, Lligwy Bay, Anglesey. *01248 410897.* Mr & Mrs R P Williams. On the A5025 1.25 miles north of Moelfre roundabout. Sheltered touring site.

Marianglas

Home Farm Caravan Park, Marianglas, Anglesey LL73 8PH. *01248 410614.* enq@homefarm-anglesey.co.uk. www.home farm-anglesey.co.uk. On A5025 road 0.5m left of LLanallgo roundabout. Quiet sheltered site. Graded: 5 stars. Open April-October.

Newborough

Awelfryn Caravan Park, Newborough, Anglesey LL61 6SG. *01248 440230.* Mrs A R Thomas. On A4080 about 15 miles south west of Menai Bridge and 20 miles from Holyhead. Near Llanddwyn Isle and Newborough Warren (noted beauty spots) Fees on application. SAE. Open Easter-September.

Pentraeth

Rhos Caravan Site, Rhos Farm, Pentraeth, Anglesey L75 8DZ. *01248 450214.* Mr Arthur P Owen . After crossing Britannia Bridge on to Anglesey. Take the A5025 Amlwch sliproad, and continue on A5025 through Pentraeth past Bull Hotel on right. Site entrance is 1st left 5m N of Menai Bridge and 0.25m N of Pentraeth. Easy reach of several beaches. Open March-October.

Rhosneigr

Bodfan Farm, Llynfar, Rhosneigr, Anglesey LL64 5XA. *01407 810706.* wap@llynfar.freeserve.co.uk. Mr A Pritchard. A4080 off A5, 9m SE of Holyhead. Close to lake and sea. Fees on application. Open April-September.

Shoreside Camp & Caravan Site, Crigyll View, Station Road, Rhosneigr, Anglesey LL64 5QX. *01407 810279.* shore side@amserve.net. Mr A J Carnall & Son. Site is 0.25m W of Rhosneigr. Turn S off A55 on to A4080, Rhosneigr. Site is opposite golf course. Well-drained site 0.25m from beach. Panoramic views. Good surf, sandy beaches. Riding school on site. Shop, cafe/restaurant available nearby. Open Easter-October.

Valley

Graenafa, Llanfaethlu, Holyhead, Valley, Anglesey LL68 4NI. *01407 730274.* Mr Richard Spencer-Hughes. Five miles north of Valley on the A5025. Touring centre. Open April-September.

Pen y Bont Farm, Holyhead, Valley, Anglesey LL23 7PH. *01407 740481.* Mr E R Parry. From A5 turn S on to B4545 at Valley cross-roads. Site is about 1m at Four Mile Bridge. Fees on application. Open Whitsun-October.

BLAENAU GWENT

Tredegar

Parc Bryn Bach, The Countryside Centre, Merthyr Road, Tredegar, Blaenau Gwent NP22 3AY. *01495 711816.* parcbrynbach@compuserve.com Blaenau Gwent County Borough Council. Signposted with brown tourist signs from the A465 (Heads of Valley Road). Graded: 2 stars. Open all year except Christmas and New Year.

BRIDGEND

Porthcawl

Brodawel Camping Park, Moor Lane, Nottage, Porthcawl, Bridgend CF36 3EJ. *01656 783231.* Mr M Battrick. Leave the M4 at junction 37. Along A4229 for Porthcawl for two miles signposted Moor Lane. Modern, clean site central for touring. One free night on all full weekly bookings. Open April-October.

Happy Valley Caravan Park, Porthcawl, Bridgend CF32 0NG. *01656 782144.* Situated on the A4106 Bridgend to Porthcawl road, two miles east of Porthcawl. Holiday site 0.5 mile from the beach. Fees on application. Open April or Easter-September.

CARMARTHENSHIRE

Carmarthen

Sunrise Bay Holiday Park, Llansteffan, Carmarthen, Carmarthenshire SA33 5LP. *01267 241394.* Dirk & Tracy Rennie. B4312 from Carmarthen for 7 miles. Sharp left on entering Llansteffan to beach. Follow road till end of houses where park entrance is. Friendly, family run park. Ideal for family holidays and touring. Lovely walks and magnificent views. April 1-October 31.

Clynderwen

Grandre Vale Holiday Park, Clynderwen, Carmarthanshire. *01437 563111.* accounts@clarach.fsbusiness.co.uk. Mr T Scarrott. We are situated 2 miles north of Narberth on the A478, just before you enter the village of Clynderwen. Open March-November.

Kidwelly

Carmarthen Bay Touring & Camping Site, Tanylan Farm, Kidwelly, Carmarthenshire SA17 5HJ. *01267 267306.* tanylanfarm@aol.com. www.tanylanfarmholidays.co.uk. Barbara Evans. M4-exit 48 to Kidwelly via Llanelli left at Spar supermarket, coast road to Ferryside 2m. Level site situated on working dairy farm. 200yd from beach. Graded: 3 stars. Open Easter-end-September.

Laugharne

Ants Hill Caravan & Camping Park, Laugharne, Carmarthenshire SA33 4QN. *01994 427293.* antshill caravanpark@tiscali.co.uk. Mrs S Downes. From Carmarthen A40 to St Clears, A4066 to Laugharne. Near historic home town of Dylan Thomas and the famous Pendine sands. Graded: 3 stars. Open Easter-October 31.

Broadway Caravan & Camping Park, Laugharne, Carmarthenshire SA33 4NU. *01994 427272.* Mr Cecil Davies. A4066 south from A40 at St Clears to Laugharne. Continue 1m to Pendine to site. Holiday site on edge of hills, three miles from sea. Dogs on leads allowed. Fees on application. Open March-October.

Llandovery

Black Mountain Caravan Park, Llanddeusant, Llandovery, Carmarthenshire SA19 9YG. *01550 740621.* blackmountain @mapsweet.fetce9.co.uk. www.breconbeacons-holidays.com. MA & PJ Sweet. Glorious views, quiet part of the Brecon Beacons National Park. Unique wildlife, historic interests, good base to tour mid and south Wales. Pets welcome. Caravans for hire. Excellent walking country.

Camping & Caravanning Club Site - Rhandirmwyn, Llandovery, Carmarthenshire SA20 ONT. *01550 760257.* www.campingandcaravanningclub.co.uk. The Camping & Caravanning Club Ltd. 11-acre site with 90 pitches. 320yd frontage to the river Tywi, including exclusive fishing rights. In Rhandirmwyn, turn left down hill opposite post office. Keep to right at church and site is at bottom of hill on left. Caravans, motor caravans and tents accepted. Non-members welcome. Open March-October.

Erwlon Caravan & Camping Park, Llandovery, Carmarthenshire SA20 0RD. *01550 720332.* peter@erwlon.fsnet.co.uk. Messrs C R Rees & Sons. About 1m from town centre on A40 London to Fishguard. Very good fishing and walking. An ideal centre for touring South Wales. Seasonal pitches available. Open April-October.

Galltyberau, Rhandirmwyn, Llandovery, Carmarthenshire. *01550 760218.* Mr I T Williams. 9m N of Llandovery via road to Rhandirmwyn. Site is 2m N of village by concrete bridge. Close to nature and bird reserves. No sanitation. Period of opening and fees on application.

Llanelli

Black Lion Caravan & Camping Park, 78 Black Lion Road, Gorslas, Cross Hands, Llanelli, Carmarthenshire SA14 6RU. *01269 845365.* baz@gorslas.com. www.caravansite.com. Barry Hayes. 1 mile from Cross Hands, off Llandeilo road. follow brown tourist signs from Cross Hands. Close to Cross Hands business park and local shops. Good stop off place when going to and from Ireland. Dogs allowed but must be kept on leash at all times. Licenced bar and club house. Caravan storage available. Open March 30-October 1.

Shoreline Caravan & Chalet Park, Burry Port, Llanelli, Carmarthenshire SA16 0HD. *01554 832657.* S & M Hall & Sons. Popular family park adjoining the sea and harbour. Pembrey Country Park nearby. Open March 1-November 30.

Llangadog

Abermarlais Caravan Park, Llangadog, Carmarthenshire SA19 9NG. *01550 777868/01550 777797.* www.ukparks.co.uk/abermarlais. Juster & Sons. On main A40. 6 miles west of Llandovery. 6 miles east of Llandilo. 8 acres camping, 13 acres woodland walks. Open March 1-November 30.

Blaenau Farm, Llanddeusant, Llangadog, Carmarthenshire SA19 9UN. *01550 740277.* Mr P J Dobbs. 6m SE of Llangadog via A4069 to Pontarllechau. Minor roads through Twynllanan to Llanddeusant. Pass church & continue down valley to site. From A40 follow sign W to Llanddeusant at Trecastle, left to old vicarage, left and left again, continue down valley towards Llyn y Fan. Open Easter-October.

The Pont Aber Inn, Gwynfe, Llanddnesant, Llangadog, Carmarthenshire SA19 9TA. *01550 740202.* S & M Denton. From A40 after Llandovery, turn left to Llangadog. Take Brynaman road for 4 miles.

Llanwrda

Maesbach Caravan Site, Farmers, Pumsaint, Llanwrda, Carmarthenshire SA19 8EX. *01558 650650.* hugh.t.thomas @talk21.com. www.maesbachcaravanpark.co.uk. Mr & Mrs H T Thomas. From A482 2.5m NE of Pumpsaint and 7m SE of Lampeter. Turn N to Farmers. Site is 0.5m from Farmers. Cambrian mountains. Caravans, motor caravans, tents. Gas. Open views. Takeaway meals nearby. Open March-October.

Newcastle Emlyn

Afon Teifi Caravan & Camping Site, Pentre Cagal, Newcastle Emlyn, Carmarthenshire SA38 9HT. *01559 370532.* Mrs S Bishop. Off A484. Quiet riverside site, an ideal touring base for Cardigan Bay. Family run site with playground and games room. Shop, pub and restaurant nearby. All the usual facilities, well-lit and maintained to a high standard. Graded: 3 stars. Open April 1/Easter-October 31.

Dolbryn Farm Camp Site, Capel Iwan Road, Newcastle Emlyn, Carmarthenshire SA38 9LP. *01239 710683.* Mr & Mrs B & MC Gent. 1.75 south of Newcastle Emlyn via minor roads. Signposted for Capel Iwan south off the A484 at signposted leisure centre, turn left at T-junction and over crossroads. Site entrance is first right after garage. Licenced bar. Quiet site in sheltered valley. Conservation area. Open Easter-September.

Pumpsaint

Penlanwen, Llanwrda, Pumpsaint, Carmarthenshire SA19 8RR. *01558 650667.* Mrs R Rees. Eight miles SE of Lampeter on A482. 10m NW of Llandovery. Follow CC signs on right after Bridgend Inn. Rural situation. Old Roman gold mines open to the public. Ideal for families. Good walking country. Open March-October.

St Clears

Afon Lodge Caravan Park, Parciau Bach, St Clears, Carmarthenshire SA33 4LG. *01994 230647.* yvonne@afon lodge.fq.co.uk. www.afonlodge.fq.co.uk. Mr & Mrs W Wiggans. From traffic lights St Clears, take road to Llanboidy, in 100yd fork right, 1.75m turn right, 0.75m turn right continue for 0.25m. Park located on left. Graded: 4 stars. Open March 1-January 10.

CEREDIGION

Aberaeron

Aeron Coast Caravan Park, North Road, Aberaeron, Ceredigion SA46 0JF. *01545 570349.* aeroncoastcaravan park@aberaeron.freeserve.co.uk. Aeron Coast Holidays Ltd. Main coastal road A487. 200 yards from shops and picturesque harbour. 22 acres. of flat, coastal parkland. Filling station at entrance. Owned by same family for 35 years. Families only. Outstanding facilities for children. Advance booking advisable. Graded: 4 stars. Open March 1-October 31.

Aberporth

Dolgelynen, Aberporth, Ceredigion SA43 2HS. *01239 811095.* Mrs H L Thomas. B4333 N off A487 towards Aberporth on main road. Quiet site. Dishwashing facilities available. Dogs allowed on leads. Open Easter-October.

Aberystwyth

Aberystwyth Holiday Village, Penparcau Road, Aberystwyth, Ceredigion SY23 1TH. *01970 624211.* Mr R Ballard. In Borough of Aberystwyth. 0.25m S of town centre on A487. Near sea. River Rheidol alongside. Club, pool and entertainment. Arcade. Ten-pin bowling. Children allowed in nightclub. Big off-season discounts. Fees on application. Open March 1-October 31.

Aeron View Caravan Park, Blaenpennal, Aberystwyth, Ceredigion SY23 4TW *01974 251488.* aeronview@hotmail. com. www.aeronview.com. Mr & Mrs T N Bell. 1 mile west off A485 Aberystwyth to Tregaron Road. 4 miles from Tregaron. High quality but quiet inland site, 15 minutes from sea. Excellent bird watching, fishing, walking or just enjoy the scenery. Open March 1-October 31.

Bryncarnedd Caravan Park, Clarach Road, Aberystwyth, Ceredigion SY23 3DG. *01970 615271.* 1.25 NE of Aberystwyth via A487 for 1m then L on to B4572. Site 0.5m. Overnight stops. Dogs on lead only. Chemical toilet disposal point. Theatre nearby. Motorbikes welcome. Open Easter-October.

Devil's Bridge, Woodlands Caravan Park, Aberystwyth, Ceredigion SY23 3JW. *01970 890 233.*woodlandscp@ btclick.com . R P Davies. A peaceful country site adjoining farm. Ideal for walking, birdwatching, touring and fishing. Beautiful scenery. On A4120, 12m E of Aberystwyth or 3m S of A44 at Ponterwyd. Open Easter-October 31.

Erwbarfe Farm, Devil's Bridge, Ponterwyd, Aberystwyth, Ceredigion SY23 3JR. *01970 890665.* G M & B E Lewis. On A4120,1.5m N of Devil's Bridge and 1.5m S of Ponterwyd. 8m E of Aberystwyth. Scenic situation. Open March-October.

Glan-y-Mor Leisure Park, Clarach Bay, Aberystwyth, Ceredigion SY23 3DT. *01970 828900.* W L Jones Ltd. Showers. Club. Entertainment. Indoor swimming pool. Sauna. Steam room. Whirlpool spa. Sunbeds. Fitness gym. Licensed restaurant. Ten-pin bowling. For brochure write: Freepost, Sunbourne Leisure Ltd. at the above address. Daffodil Award. Graded: 4 stars. Open April-November.

Midfield Holiday & Residential Park, Southgate, Aberystwyth, Ceredigion SY23 4DX. *01970 612542.* enquiries@midfieldcaravanpark.co.uk. www.midfieldcaravan park.co.uk. Mr & Mrs T B Hughes. On A4120 Aberystwyth to Devil's Bridge road. 1.5m SE of Aberystwyth. Children's play area. Panoramic views.Advance bookings for caravans advised. Fees on application SAE. Open Easter-October 31.

Morfa Bychan Holiday Park, Llanfarian, Aberystwyth, Ceredigion SY23 4QQ. *01970 617254.* info@hiccandale.co.uk . www.hiccandale.co.uk . D.& D.Lloyd Jones Securities Ltd. A487 south from Aberystwyth, on

CEREDIGION

outskirts turn right at sign - NB. If towing continue on A487 for two miles to second sign—follow further signs for two miles. Open March 1-January 7.

📞🚐📮♿🅿🔌⊙🅰🍴🔥≈☀🍽🅁🇱♦△🏊🎣🔱〰🔦

Pantmawr Camping Site, Pisgah, Capel Seion, Aberystwyth, Ceredigion SY23 4NF. *01970 880449.* Mr John Griffiths. Three miles west of Devil's Bridge and eight miles from Aberystwyth. Located on the north side of the A4120. A farm site overlooking the Rheidol Valley. Open Easter-October.

📞📮⊙🅰🔥🍴☎🇱♦

Pengarreg Caravan Park, Llanrhystud, Nr Aberystwyth, Ceredigion SY23 5DH. *01974 202247.* iangolfmiller@aol.com. www.utowcaravans.co.uk. Mr C Miller. On A487, 9m S of Aberystwyth, opposite Shell garage. On beach. Two touring fields, two play areas. Slipway for boats. Open March 1-January 1.

📞🚐♿🅿🍴🔥♿🅿✖⊙🅰🔥🗄🍴🔥🏪🇱♦△🎣🔱〰🔦🔱

Rhoslawdden Farm, Moriah, Capel Seion, Aberystwyth, Ceredigion SY23 4EA. *01974 612585.* H Griffiths. From Devil's Bridge 8 miles. 3 miles from Aberystwyth. Dogs allowed under control.

📞📮🔥≈🔱

Riverside Park, Lon Glanfred, Llandre, Borth, Aberystwyth, Ceredigion SY24 5BY. *01970 820070.* Mr Stephen South. A secret place worth finding. Large flat, well sheltered area, where shallow river runs alongside. Judged by the AA to be the most attractive park environment for three consecutive years. Open March 1-October 31.

📞🚐♿🅿🔌⊙🅰🔥🍴🔥🏪≈☎🅁△🎣🔱🔦🔱🅱⊙🔱🔦🔱〰🔦

Woodlands Caravan Park, Llanon, Aberystwyth, Ceredigion SY23 5LX. *01974 202342.* I Lampert. Five miles north of Aberaeron and 11 miles south of Aberystwyth, signposted off the A487. Near beach. Fees on application. Open April-October.

📞🚐📮♿🅿⊙🅰🔥🍴🏪🇱♦△🎣🔦🔱〰🔦🔱

Borth

Cambrian Coast Holiday Park, Borth, Ceredigion SY24 5JU. *01970 871233.* Sunbourne Leisure Ltd. Restaurant and take-away. Indoor swimming pool. Children's activities include fun pool, go-karts, bouncy castle and indoor junior clubroom. Licensed club. Live entertainment. Graded: 4 stars. Open March-October 31.

📞🚐♿🅿🔌⊙🍴♿🅿⊙🅰🔥≈🏪≈🇱♦△🎣🔦🔱〰

Riverside Caravan Park, Lon Glanfred, Llandre, Borth, Ceredigion SY24 5BY. *01970 820070.* S J & J E South. North of Aberystwyth, at Bow Street turn off the A487 at Rhydypennau Garage onto the A4353 (Borth). 200 yards past Llandre Post Office turn right into Lon Glanfred. Site in 500 yards. Quiet, secluded and sheltered Park on banks of the river Leri. Dishwashing and laundrette. Open March 1-October 31.

📞🚐📮♿🅿⊙🅰🔥🍴🔥🏪≈🇱♦🅁🎣🔦🔱〰🔦🔱〰🔦🔱

The Mill House Caravan & Camping Park, Dol-Y-Bont, Borth, Ceredigion SY24 5LX. *01970 871481.* www.ukparks.co.uk/millhousecp. Mr O J Patrick. A quiet site beside trout stream. On the A487. Turn west at Rhydypennau Garage Corner between Talybont and Bow Street, on to B4353, through Llandre. Proceed 1m stop under railway bridge by white railings then fork right into Dolybont village, first right before hump back bridge. Open April-October.

📞🚐📮⊙🅰🔥🍴🏪🇱♦△🎣🔱〰🔦🔱〰🔦🔱

Ty Mawr Caravan Park, Ynyslas, Borth, Ceredigion SY24 5LB. *01970 871327.* P G & C C Beech. 3m N of Borth on B4353, off A487. Quiet, sheltered park. Outstanding views of nature reserve, sand dunes, Dovey estuary and Plynlymon Hills. David Bellamy Gold conservation award winner. Open April-September.

📞🚐📮⊙🅰🔥🍴🔥🗄≈🇱♦🔱〰🔦🔱🔦🔱

Cardigan

Brongwyn Mawr Farm, Brongwyn Mawr, Penparc, Cardigan, Ceredigion SA43 1SA. *01239 613644.* enquiries@cardiganholidays.co.uk. www.cardiganholidays. co.uk. Mrs A M Giles. On A487 Cardigan-Aberystwyth road, 2.5m north of Cardigan. Left at crossroads in Penparc sign-post Ferwig. After half mile turn right into Farm Road. Small peaceful park, 5 minutes from Cardigan and beautiful sandy beaches of Mwnt and Aberporth. Graded: 3 stars. Open March 1-October 31.

📞🚐📮✖⊙🅰🔥🗄♦🍴🔥🏪△🎣🔱〰🔦🔱

Caerfelin Caravan Park, Aberporth, Cardigan, Ceredigion SA43 2BY. *01239 810540.* glyn & Sheila Bright. Turn N off A487 on to B4333 at Blaenannerch to Aberporth. Right at St Cynwyls church to site 200yd on left. Well-sheltered site with made-up roads. About 5 minutes' walk to sandy beach. Safe bathing and boat launching. Cafe/restaurant nearby. Open mid March-October 31.

📞🚐♿🅿🔥🍴♿⊙🅰🔥🍴🔥🇱♦△🎣🔱〰🔦🔱🔦🔱

Camping Blaenwaun, Mwnt, Cardigan, Ceredigion SA43 1QF. *01239 612165.* Mr D J Davies. 4m NW of Cardigan. Take A487 for 0.25m W of Cardigan. Turn N on to B4548 towards Mwnt. After 0.5m turn right at signpost to Mwnt. Follow signs to Mwnt. Site is 300yds from Mwnt beach camp sign. 0.5m from sea. Private coarse fishing lake. Open Easter-September.

📞🚐📮♿🅿⊙🅰🔥🍴🔥🇱♦🎣🔱〰🔦🔱

Ty-Gwyn Farm Caravan Park, Mwnt, Cardigan, Ceredigion SA43 1QH. *01239 614518.* M & M D Evans. 5m NW of Cardigan. Leave A487 at E side of town on B4548. Follow signs to Mwnt. Close to beach. Quiet situation. Fees on application. Open April-October.

📞🚐📮🔌⊙🅰🔥🍴🔥🏪🇱♦△🎣🔱〰🔦🔱

Lampeter

Hafod Brynog Caravan Park, Ystrad Aeron, Felinfach, Lampeter, Ceredigion SA48 8AE. *01570 470084.* Mr & Mrs G Amies. 6m E from Aberaeron off A482. Peaceful site in quiet village. Lovely views. Ideal for touring or relaxing. Pub on site entrance. Open Easter-September 30.

📞🚐📮🔌⊙🅰🔥🗄🍴🔥🔱

Llanarth

Llain Activity Centre, Llain Farm, Llanarth, Ceredigion SA47 0PZ. *01545 580127.* Mr & Mrs D K Thomas. Off A487 on road to Cei Bach beach. Open March-October.

📞🔌📮♿✖🔥≈🏪🍴🔥🏪△🎣🔱〰🔦

Llandysul

Brynawelon Touring and Camping Park, Sarnau, Nr Llangranog, Llandysul, Ceredigion SA44 6RE. *01239 654584.* Mr J & Mrs S Brown. Travelling N turn right at Sarnau Chapel crossroads. Site 0.25m on left down lane. Park is signposted. Small, quiet family site under personal supervision, only two miles from the coast. Dog exercise area. Open April-September.

📞🚐📮🔌⊙🅰🔥🗄🍴🇱♦△🎣🔱〰🔦🔱

Camping & Caravanning Club Site - Cardigan Bay, Llwynhelyg, Cross Inn, Cardigan Bay, Llandysul, Ceredigion SA44 6LW. *01545 560029.* www.campingandcaravanning

club.co.uk. The Camping & Caravanning Club Ltd. 13.5-acre site with 90 pitches. Close to golden beaches, forests and lakes. Leave the A487 at the Synod Inn on to the A486 Newquay road. There are two Cross Inns in the area, please follow the road numbers carefully. Non-members welcome. Caravans, motor caravans and tents accepted. Open March-September.

Maes Glas Caravan Park, Penbryn, Sarnau, Llandysul, Ceredigion SA44 6QE. *01239 654268.* enquiries@maesglas caravanpark.co.uk. www.maesglascaravanpark.co.uk. Mr & Mrs T Hill. Fron main road A487(T), take turning for Penbryn by church in village of Sarnau. Follow road towards Penbryn beach. Park on right after 0.75m. David Bellamy Gold Conservation Award. Open March 1-October 31.

Manorafow Caravan Park, Sarnau, Llandysul, Ceredigion Sa44 6QH. *01239 810564.* manorafow@ukgateway.net. Susan J Jones. 0.75m from Penbryn beach in wooded valley. From A487 at Sarnau take Penbryn beach signs. Cafe/restaurant and takeaway meals available nearby. Open April-October.

Pantgwyn Farm, Synod Inn, Llandysul, Ceredigion SA44 6JN. *01545 580320.* Ms Joan Jones. 6m S of New Quay, between the villages of Plwmp & Synod Inn. On the main A487 Cardigan to Aberystwyth road. Quiet, peaceful farm site 4m from beach. Open Easter-September.

Pilbach Holiday Park, Betws Ifan, Rhydlewis, Llandysul, Ceredigion SA44 5RT. *01239 851434.* heatherdale@fsbdial. co.uk. Mr Barker. Set in nearly 14 acres of land, this award-winning holiday park is surrounded by stunning countryside and close to Newquay with its picturesque harbour. Modern, refurbished club with live entertainment. Freshly prepared bar food. Graded 4 stars. Open March 1-Mid November.

Rhydygalfe Caravan Park, Pontwelli, Llandysul, Ceridigion SA44 5AP. *01559 363211/362738.* L A Davies. 16 miles N from Carmarthen on A484 or S on A487 from Aberystwyth on to A486 to Llandysul. Good salmon fishing close to site. Local pub and late night shop in easy walking distance. Open March-October.

Talywerydd Touring Caravan Park, Penbryn Sands, Sarnau, Cardigan, Llandysul, Ceredigion SA44 6QY. *01239 810322.* R & D Milka. From N or S on A487 take 2nd Penbryn turn, site 500yds on left. Small, friendly site with beautiful sea and country views. Spotlessly clean. Graded: 4 stars. Open March-October.

Treddafydd Caravan Site, Sarnau, Llandysul, Ceredigion SA44. *01239 654551.* G & E Griffiths. Turn off A487 at Sarnau church into Penbryn Road. Then first L and site is farm on left. 0.75m approx Sarnau. Family site about 1m from beach. Open April-October.

New Quay

Brownhill Caravan Park, Synod Inn, Llandysul, New Quay, Ceredigion. *01545 560288.* Mr I L Davies. 3m S of New Quay on A486. 0.5m from Synod Inn. Period of opening and fees on application.

Cei Bach Country Club, Parc-y-Brwcs, Cei Bach, New Quay, Ceredigion SA45 9SL. *01545 580237.* paul@ceibach.freeserve. co.uk. Paul & Stephanie Wynne. Off A487. Take B4342 New

Quay Road for one and half miles. At Cambrian Hotel turn right. Follow signs for Cei Bach, one mile. Coastal walks. Open March-October.

Frondeg Caravan Park, Gilfachreda, New Quay, Ceredigion SA45 9SP. *01545 580444.* Steve Hartley. From A487 at Llanarth take B4342 to New Quay, at Gilfachreda turn left at crossroad after telephone box, right at junction, 200yd on right. Quiet, secluded site half mile from safe, sandy beach. Open April 1-October 31.

Neuadd Caravan Park, Neuadd Farm, New Quay, Ceredigion *01545 560 709.* D R & W M Evans and Son. Quarter mile from New Ruay. Open March 15 - October 31.

Pencnwc Holiday Park, Cross Inn, New Quay, Ceredigion SA44 6NL. *01545 560479.* holidays@pencnwc.co.uk. www.pencnwc.co.uk. Mr I M & Mrs S J Daniels. Signposted outskirts of village Cross Inn within 2m of New Quay on A486. 2m beach. Graded: 3 stars. Open April-September.

Tydu Vale, Cuumtydu, New Quay, Ceredigion SA44 6LH. *01545 560494.* Mr R Reed. 10 miles from Cardigan town, 12 miles from Aberaeron. 3.5 miles from New Quay and Llangranog Beach. Open April-November.

Wern Mill Campsite, Gilfachreda, New Quay, Ceredigion SA45 9SP. *01545 580699.* Mr Hand. From Aberystwyth take A487 Aberaeron to Llanarth road. Gilfachreda is 1.5m from Llanarth on the B4342 to Newquay road. Very sheltered level site near two sandy beaches. Cafe/restaurant available nearby. Ideal centre for touring Mid-Wales. Idyllic walks. Family site. Graded: 3 stars. Open Easter-October 31.

Newcastle Emlyn

Cenarth Falls Holiday Park, Cenarth, Newcastle Emlyn, Ceredigion SA38 9JS. *01239 710345.* enquiries@cenarth-holi park.co.uk. www.cenarth-holipark.co.uk. Mr & Mrs D H G Davies. On A484 Newcastle Emlyn to Cardigan on outskirts of Cenarth. Award winning family run park in beautiful countryside. Newly opened luxurious heated swimming pool and health club, bars and restaurant area. Excellent caravan holiday homes for hire and touring facilities. Graded: 5 stars. Open March 1-January 9.

CONWY

Abergele

Gwrych Towers Camp, Llandulas Road, Abergele, Conwy LL22 8ET. *01745 832109/01829 260210.* M M Dutton. W of Abergele via B5443 and main entrance to Gwrych Castle Park. Privately owned, family site near quiet beach and golf links. Central for touring and coastal resorts. Fees on application. Office in right-hand tower. Open Spring bank holiday. then July- September.

Betws-y-Coed

Hendre Farm, Betws-y-Coed, Conwy LL24 0BN. *01690 710612.* Pierce Bros. On A5, 0.5m W of Betws-y-Coed. Overnight stop, N Wales and Snowdonia. No motorcycles allowed on site. Fees on application. Open March-October.

Riverside Caravan & Camping Park, Old Church Road, Betws-y-Coed, Conwy LL24 0BA. *01690 710310.* R D Harrison & Son. Entering Betws-y-Coed on A5 over Waterloo Bridge. First right after Little Chef. Holiday site. Fees on application. Open March-October.

Rynys Farm Camping Site, Betws-y-Coed, Conwy LL26 0RU. *01690 710218.* Gareth & Carol Williams. Two miles south of Betws-y-Coed on A5, opposite Conway Falls. Peaceful, scenic site in the hill of north Wales, close to the Snowdonia peaks. Excellent clean facilities. Central for touring north Wales. Open Easter-October.

Tyn Rhos Farm, Pentrefoelas, Betws-y-Coed, Conwy LL24 0LN. *01690 770655.* Mr & Mrs T & A Jones. 5m N of Cerrigydrudion via A5. Turn S to Geeler Arms. Keep left after bridge to site. 7m SE of Betws-y-Coed. Flat site within easy reach of Snowdonia and north Wales coast. Restaurant and pub 5 minutes' walk. Open March 1- November 1.

Colwyn Bay

Dinarth Hall, Rhos-on-Sea, Colwyn Bay, Conwy LL28 4PX. *01492 548203.* Messrs. Owen & Parry. 2m NW of Colwyn Bay on B5115 to Dinarth Hall Road (opposite college). Touring centre. Fees on application. Open May-September.

Ty-Ucha Farm Camping Site, Tan-y-Graig Road, Llysfaen, Colwyn Bay, Conwy LL29 8UD. *01492 517051.* Mrs S.A. Hughes. 3m SE of Colwyn Bay via A55 and A547, turn left on to Highlands road near to hotel. Go up hill to junction then right on to Tan-y-Graig road to site on right. Overnight stop London/N Wales, or longer. 2m from beach. 2.5m from Colwyn Bay leisure centre. Open Easter-October.

Conwy

Conwy Touring Park, Trefriw Road, Conwy, Conwy LL32 8UX. *01492 592856.* www.conwytouringpark.com. 1.25m S of Conwy on B5106, large slate-roofed sign on the left. Sheltered wooded site with splendid views. Close to beaches and Snowdonia. Special offers available. Storage facilities. Open Easter-September.

Conwy Valley

Bodnant Caravan Park, Nebo Road, Llanrwst, Conwy Valley, Conwy LL26 0SD. *01492 640248.* ermin@bodnant-caravan-park.co.uk. bodnant-caravan-park.co.uk. Mrs E Kerry Jenkins. South in Llanrwst, opposite Birmingham garage turn off A470 for B5427 signposted Nebo. Site by 30mph sign opposite Leisure Centre. 26 years 'Wales in Bloom' winner. Quiet, relaxed site. For touring caravans, tents and 2 holiday caravans. Ideal for touring the mountains and coast of North Wales. Graded: 4 stars. Open March 1-October 31.

Corwen

Glan Ceirw Caravan Park, Ty Nant, Corwen, Conwy LL21 0RF. *01490 420346.* glanceirwcaravanpark@tinyworld.co.uk. www.ukparks.co.uk/glanceirw. Mrs C Ashford. On A5, 1.25 miles from Cerrigydrudion Corwen side. 1 mile after Country Cooks on left. Picturesque park, gently sloping to river Ceirw. 6 miles from Llyn Brenig for sailing, fishing, and windsurfing. Bordering Snowdonia National Park. Open March 1-October 31.

Penmaenmawr

Trwyn-yr-Wylfa Farm, Conway Old Road, Penmaenmawr, Conwy LL34 6SF. *01492 622357.* Mr E. Lloyd-Hughes. Leave A55 at junction 16A. Left in front of shops. Right at T junction, farm 100yd farther on. Located in National Park. Open Spring bank holiday-September.

Tyddyn Du Touring Park, Conwy Old Road, Penmaenmawr, Conwy LL34 6RE. *01492 622300.* www.ukparks.co.uk/tyddyn-du. Miss P Watson-Jones. Take A55 W from Conwy turn left first roundabout after Little Chef, sharp left again and follow site signs. Open March 21-October 31.

Woodlands Camping Park, Pendyffryn Hall, Penmaenmawr, Conwy LL34 6UF. *01492 623219.* Mr & Mrs K Clarke. Situated off A55 between Conwy and Penmaenmawr. After Conwy tunnel (under river), pass through Penmaenbach Tunnel (through mountain). Take 1st left signposted Dwygyfylchi. 96 acres of private parkland and woods. Situated in Snowdonia National Park. Short walk to beach. Licensed club. Laundry. Showers. Families and couples only. Graded: 2 stars. Open March 1-October 31.

Rhyl

Ty Mawr Holiday Park, Towyn, Abergele, Rhyl, Conwy LL22 9HG. *01745 832079.* Haven Leisure. On A548 Abergele to Rhyl road. 3m W of Rhyl. Family holiday site with indoor pool and licensed clubs. One of Haven's 37 tenting and touring parks around the UK. Free kids' club. Free evening and daytime entertainment for all the family. Open Easter-October.

DENBIGHSHIRE

Corwen

Hendwr Caravan Park, Llandrillo, Corwen, Denbighshire LL21 0SN. *01490 440210.* J & D Hughes. 1m N of Llandrillo on B4401, 4m S of Corwen via A5 and B4401. Site is signposted. Base for touring N Wales. Good walking country. Children's play area. dishwashing room. Restricted services in winter. Open Easter/April 1-October 31.

Llawr Betws Farm, Corwen, Denbighshire LL21 0HD. *01490 460224.* J Gordon Jones & David M Jones. Follow A5 through Corwen to second set of traffic lights. Turn left on to A494. Park signposted in 2 miles. Open April-October 31.

Denbigh

Caer-Mynydd Caravan Park, Saron, Denbigh, Denbighshire LLI6 4TL. *01745 550302.* kathcaermynydd@aol.com. Mrs Kathleen Welch. 4m SW of Denbigh off A525 to Ruthin. Past comprehensive school and pool, turn right to Prion and Saron. Quiet touring centre. Caravan Club and Welsh Tourist Board recommended. Open March 1-October 31.

Llangollen

Wern Isaf Caravan & Camping Park, Wern Isaf Farm, Llangollen, Denbighshire LL20 8DU. *01978 860632.* wernisaf@btopenworld.com. www.wernisaf.supanet.com. Mrs C E Williams. Turn up hill behind Bridge End Hotel, then turn right into Wern road. Site 0.5m. NE of Llangollen. At foot of

DENBIGHSHIRE/GWYNEDD

Castell Dinas Bran (Crow Castle). Quiet, scenic site. Excellent touring centre for coast and Snowdonia. Dogs allowed. Graded: 2 stars. Open Easter-October.

Prestatyn

Nant Mill Family Touring Caravan & Camping Park, Prestatyn, Denbighshire LL19 9LY. *01745 852360.* nantmill touring@aol.com. www.zeropointfive.co.uk/nant_mill. Mr & Mrs K Rowley. On A548 coast road 0.5m E of Prestatyn. Within 1m of beach. Family site. Fees on application. Graded: 4 stars. Open Easter-November.

Rhyl

Henllys Farm, Towyn, Abergele, Rhyl, Denbighshire LL22 9HF. *01745 351208.* Mr G B Kerfoot. On A548 Rhyl to Abergele road. 2m W of Rhyl. Near beach. Graded: 4 stars. Open early April-October.

FLINTSHIRE

Mold

Fron Farm, Hendre, Mold, Flintshire CH7 5QW. *01352 741217.* Mr & Mrs E P Roberts. 4.5m NW of Mold on A541 turn for Rhesycae,1.5m past Hendre. At top of hill turn right, then right again over cattle grid into farm road. Elevated site with good views. Good touring centre for north Wales. Open April-October.

GWYNEDD

Aberdaron

Brynffynnon, Rhoshirwaun, Pwllheli, Aberdaron, Gwynedd. *01758 730643.* Mr & Mrs E W Jones. Take A499 W from Pwllheli, fork on to B4413 at Llanbedrog. About 3m before Aberdaron take road to right signposted 'Whistling Sands'. Near end of Lleyn Peninsula. Easy reach of beaches. Open March 1-October 1.

Mur Melyn, Aberdaron, Gwynedd LL53 8LW. *01758 760522.* Mrs J E Evans. 17m SW of Pwllheli and 2m N of Aberdaron. W on B4413. Fork right signposted 'Whistling Sands' and turn left at Pen-y-Bont House to site 0.5m. Quiet holiday site near end of Lleyn Peninsula. Open Whitsun, July and August.

Abersoch

Beach View Caravan Park, Bwlchtocyn, Pwllheli, Abersoch, Gwynedd LL53 7BT. *01758 712956.* Mr F Weatherby. Through Albersoch continue, Sarnbach over crossroads next left turn sp Bwlchtocyn, Porthtocyn Hotel, continue pass Chapel round S bend first left sp Porthtocyn Hotel, continue beach view on left. Open mid March-mid October.

Bryn Celyn Isaf Camping Site, Bryn Celyn Isaf, Cilan, Abersoch, Gwynedd LL53 7DB. *01758 713583.* Moses J Griffith. Through Abersoch village on the Cilan main road for 2 miles. Pass turning to Bwlchtocyn, then first turning to right. Quiet farm with magnificent views, walking distance to Porth Ceinad and Hell's Mouth beaches. Open Whitsun-September.

Seaside Camping Site, Lon Golff, Abersoch, Gwynedd. *01758 712271.* Mr R T Stubbs. 1m from Abersoch off A499 at Lon Golff. Good views. Safe, sandy beach and golf course 450 yards. Hairdryers. Plugs. Tarmac road from site to village of Sarn Bach.

Seaview, Sarn Bach, Abersoch, Gwynedd LL53 7ET. *01758 712052.* mike.sleigh@tggroup.co.uk. www.tggroup.co.uk. Mr Griffiths. Through Abersoch to Sarn Bach, then sharp left, site 200yd on right. Holiday site. AA approved. Family site. Short walk down quiet lane to beach. Managers: Arwyn and Catherine Williams. Open March-October.

Tan-y-Bryn Farm, Sarn Bach, Abersoch, Gwynedd LL53 7DA. *01758 712093.* Mr Gwilym Hughes. 1m S of Abersoch via Sarn Bach road. Site is first farm on left. Flat, well-drained site, 1m from sea. Fees on application. Shop nearby. Dogs on leads. Open Easter-October.

Tyn-y-Mur Camping & Touring Park, Lon Garmon, Abersoch, Gwynedd LL53 7UL. *01758 712328.* tynymur@abersoch14.fsnet.co.uk. H Roberts & N Harrison. As you drop down to the harbour area of Abersoch, turn sharp right up the hill between Land and Sea Garage and Spinnaker. The park is 0.5mile on the left. It has level ground and panoramic views of Abersoch Bay to the south and Hells Mouth. One dog allowed per unit. Graded: 4 stars. Open Easter-end September.

The Warren Touring Park, Abersoch, Gwynedd LL53 7AY. *01758 712043.* Haulfryn Group Ltd. About 1.5m NE of Abersoch off the A499. First turn on left after passing Llanbedrog Riding School, 100yds before Warren Caravan Site. Near Warren beach. Family site only. Open March-October.

Arthog

Garthyfog Camp Site, Arthog, Gwynedd LL39 IAX. *01341 250338.* garbek@btinternet.com. www.garthyfog.co.uk. Dora Roberts. From Dolgellau, through Arthog then turn left off A493. Turn at end 30mph sign. Site 200yd. Caravans to let on site. Hot water supply to shower only. Mains water, flush toilets and washbasins.

Pant-y-Cae, Arthog, Gwynedd. *01341 250892.* Mr Thomas. From A493 near Arthog turn at Crogennan. Lakes sign to site. Easy reach of sea and mountains.

Bala

Bryn Gwyn Farm Caravan Park, Godre'r Aran, Llanuwchllyn, Bala, Gwynedd LL23 7UB. *01678 540687.* Mr & Mrs A P Roberts. 5m S of Bala. Site is 0.5m W along Trawsfynydd road off A494. 0.5m N of Llanuwchllyn. Approx 1m from the S end of Bala. Lake. Small, peaceful riverside park with fishing. Countryside and hill walks, birdwatching. Exellent cycling centre. Village Inn (good food) within walking distance. Refurbished toilet facilities. Open Easter-October.

Camping & Caravanning Club Site - Bala, Crynierth Caravan Park, Cefn-Ddwysarn, Bala, Gwynedd LL23 7LN. *01678 530324.* www.campingandcaravanningclub.co.uk. The Camping & Caravanning Club Ltd. Three miles to the east of Bala, 0.5m from A494 between Bala and Corwen. Leave the A5 at Druid. Four acres with 50 pitches. Play area. Non-members

120 Camping Sites 2004

welcome. Four miles from Bala Lake in the Snowdonia National Park. Caravans, motor caravans and tents accepted. Open March-October.

Glanllyn-Lakeside Caravan & Camping Park, Glanllyn Farm, Bala, Gwynedd LL23 7ST. 01678 540227/540441. info@glanllyn.com. www.glanllyn.com. E T & M W Pugh. 2.5m SW of Bala on A494 to Dolgellau at end of lake. Holiday centre for sailing and fishing as well as touring. Canoe and sailboard hire available. Dogs allowed. Fees on application. Graded: 3 stars. Open March-October.

Pen-y-Garth Caravan & Camping Park, Bala, Gwynedd LL23 7ES. 01678 520485/07808 198717. stay@penygarth.co.uk. www.penygarth.co.uk. Mr R Baker. 1m from Bala: take B4391, fork right at sign to Rhosygwaliau. Picturesque setting, quiet peaceful surroundings in 20 acres, including areas overlooking lake/town. Flat pitches, clean, modern facilities. Graded: 4 stars. Open March-October.

Penybont Touring & Camping Park, Llangynog Road, Bala, Gwynedd LL23 7PH. 01678 520549. penybont@tinyonline.co.uk. www.penybont-bala.co.uk. David Prince. Half a mile south of Bala, 200 yards from lake on B4391 Bala to Llangynog road. Holiday or overnight stop. Dogs allowed. Fees on application. Graded: 4 stars. Open Easter-October.

Ty-Isaf Farm, Llangynog Road, B4391, Bala, Gwynedd LL23 7PP. 01678 520574. Mr J D & B J Evans. 2.5 miles south-east of Bala. On the B4391 road near telephone kiosk and postbox. Level site with good access comprising of 4 acres. Dogs on lead. Ideal for touring, site alongside stream on working farm. One static for hire. Open April 1 or Easter to October.

Tyn Cornel Camping & Caravanning Park, Frongoch, Bala, Gwynedd LL23 7NU. 01678 520759. www.tyn-cornel.co.uk. Mrs J Franklin. Take A4212 from Bala, drive through Frongoch village. After 1 mile turn sharp left over river bridge (OS map ref 125-895400). Flat site by river Tryweryn, next to the National Whitewater Centre. Access to river for canoeing. Rafting available. Graded: 1 star. Open March-October 31.

Tytandderwen Caravan Park, Bala, Gwynedd LL23 7EP. 01678 520273. Mr R.L. Davies. On B4391 Llangynog road. 3m SE of Bala. Mountain and lake within easy reach. Graded: 3 stars. Open Easter-October.

Barmouth

Bellaport Touring Caravan Site, Talybont, Barmouth, Gwynedd LL43 2BX. 01341 247338. Mrs B Roberts. 4.5m N of Barmouth via A496 to Talybont village. Turn right at 40m sign leaving village. Adults only. Dogs allowed. Mountains and lakes. Open March-September.

Dalar Farm, Tal-y-bont, Barmouth, Gwynedd LL43 2AQ. 01341 247221. Mr M E Wilcox. Five miles north of Barmouth. Leave the A496 at Tal-y-Bont on to beach road. Turn right through green gate near station, follow track to farm. Flat, well-drained site near beaches. Fees on application. Open April-October.

Dyffryn Seaside Estate Co Ltd, Dyffryn Ardudwy, Barmouth, Gwynedd LL44 2HD. 01341 247220. On A496 midway between Barmouth and Harlech. At foot of Ardudwy mountain. 5m N of Barmouth. Large site with facilities for all kinds of camping, including organised parties. Near mountains, alongside beach. Fees on application. Open Easter-September.

Hendre Mynach Caravan & Camping Park, Barmouth, Gwynedd LL42 1YR. 01341 280262. mynach@lineone.net. www.hendremynach.co.uk. Mr A Williams. N on A496 to site on W side of road at outskirts of town. Family holiday site. 100 yards from safe sandy beach. Fees and colour brochure on request. Dogs allowed. Graded: 5 stars. AA Best Campsite in Wales 2001. Open March 1-January 9.

Islawrffordd Caravan & Camping Site, Tal-y-Bont, Barmouth, Gwynedd LL43 2AQ. 01341 247269. info@islawrffordd.co.uk. www.islawrffordd.co.uk. E Evans & Sons. 4m N of Barmouth via A496. Turn left to beach at Tal-y-Bont. Site is second left. Adjoining safe, sandy beach. Touring centre within Snowdonia National Park. Children's rooms. Amusements and licensed premises nearby. Open March-December.

Parc Isaf Farm, Dyffryn Ardudwy, Barmouth, Gwynedd LL44 2RJ. 01341 247447. Mrs Jean Edwards. 5 miles north of Barmouth on A496. Small site situated with a beautiful view of Cardigan Bay, in easy reach of beach and mountain walks. Takeaway meals available nearby. Open March-October.

Trawsdir Touring Caravan & Camping Site, Llanaber, Barmouth, Gwynedd LL42 1RR. 01341 280611/280999. R O Williams & Son. On A496 200yd N from Wayside Inn. Coastal site 2m N of Barmouth. Touring centre and overnight stop. Separate field for caravans. Advance bookings essential (main weeks). Fees on application. Open March-November.

Beddgelert

Beddgelert Caravan & Camping Site, Forestry Commission, Beddgelert, Gwynedd LL55 4UU. 01766 890288. fe.holidays@forestry.gsi.gov.uk. www.forestholidays.co.uk. Forestry Commission (Forest Holidays). 2m N of Beddgelert village on A4085. Brochure request line: 01313 340066. Open December-November.

Blaenau Ffestiniog

Llechrwd Farm, Maentwrog, Blaenau Ffestiniog, Gwynedd LL41 4HF. 01766 590240. Gwen & John Clayton. On A496 N of Maentwrog, 4m W of Ffestiniog. Riverside situation 7m from sea and in Snowdonia National Park. Excellent centre for Ffestiniog railway. Walking, good beaches, climbing, excellent mountain bike area, slate mines, Port Meirion Italianate Village, etc. Open April 1-October 31.

Caernarfon

Bryn Gloch Camping & Caravan Park, Betws Garmon, Caernarfon, Gwynedd LL54 7YY. 01286 650216. eurig@bryngloch.co.uk. www.bryngloch.co.uk. I, B & E Jones. 5m from Caernarfon on A4085 to Beddgelert. Site entrance on right, 1m past village of Waunfawr. 5m SE of Caernarfon. Situated 2m from Mount Snowdon. Award winning site on bank of River Gwyrfai in the Vale of Betws. Cafe/restaurant, takeaway meals available nearby.

GWYNEDD

Challoner Camp Site, Erw Hywel, Llanrug, Caernarfon, Gwynedd LL55 2AJ. *01286 672985.* Mr J B Challoner. On the A4086 three miles east of Caernarfon to Llanberis 3.5 miles. 20 Touring vans and 15 tents. Sheltered small, friendly camp and worling farm site. Ideal for walkers and climbers. Showers. Milk and eggs. Shops nearby. Open March-January 10.

Cwn Cadnant Valley, Llanberis Road, Caernarfon, Gwynedd LL55 2DF. *01286 673196.* camping@cadnantvalley.co.uk. D E & J P Bird. Take A4086 from Caernarfon-Llanberis. Campsite opposite school. Easy distance to Snowdon, Anglesey and many attractions. Well maintained site set in a small peaceful valley. 0.25-mile walk to castle town. Graded: 4 stars. Open March 14-October 31.

Dinlle Park, Dinas Dinlle, Caernarfon, Gwynedd LL54 5TW. *01286 830324.* www.thornleyleisure.co.uk . Thornley Leisure Park. Seven miles south west of Caernarfon. Take the A487-A499 Caernarfon and Pwllheli. After 5.5m Dinas Dinlle is signposted west past AA phone box. Dinlle Park is signposted on beach road. Near sandy beach. Caravans for hire. Views of Snowdonia. Fees on application. Graded: 4 stars. Open March-October.

Glan Gwna Holiday Park, Caeathro, Caernarfon, Gwynedd LL55 2SG. *01286 673456.* touring@glangwna.com. www.glangwna.com. Glan Gwna Estates Ltd. One and half miles from Caernarfon on A4085. Riverside site, landscaped gardens, full time warden. Club house, entertainment, fishing on site-coarse and game. Heated swimming pool, laundrette, take-away, supermarket. Open Easter-October.

Llyn-y-Gele Farm Caravan Park, Pontllyffni, Caernarfon, Gwynedd LL54 5EL. *01286 660289.* William Vaughan Jones. Farm site 7.5m S of Caernarfon on A499 Caernarfon to Pwllheli road, entrance first right by garage in village of Pontllyfni. Beach 7 minutes' walk. Ideal touring site for Snowdonia. Large building for meetings by group camps and wet weather shelter. Open Easter-October.

Plas Gwyn Caravan Park, Llanberis Road, Llanrug, Caernarfon, Gwynedd LL55 2AQ. *01286 672619.* info@plas gwyn.co.uk. www.plasgwyn.co.uk. Len & Jane Hampton. 3m from Caernarfon on A4086. Caravans for hire. Bed and breakfast on request. Open March-October.

Riverside Camping, Seiont Nurseries, Pontrug, Caernarfon, Gwynedd LL55 2BB. *01286 672524.* brenda@riverside camping.freeserve.co.uk. Mrs B E Hummel. 2m from Caernarfon towards Llanberis (on A4086). Small, sheltered site bordered by river. Children's playground. Modern toilet block with separate disabled facilities. New cafe in mill, on site. Ideal touring area. Shops available nearby. Graded: 3 stars. Open Easter-end October.

Twll Clawdd, Llanrug, Caernarfon, Gwynedd LL55 2AZ. *01286 672838.* pwd@twllclawdd.co.uk. www.twllclawdd.co.uk. P W Dodd. On L of A4086 Caernarfon/Llanberis. Central to Snowdonia, places of interest and towns. Easy reach Anglesey. Quiet, grassy rural site. Beach 6 miles. Calor gas stockist, laundrette, showers. Open March 1-October 31.

Tyn-y-Coed Farm Caravan Park, Llanrug, Caernarfon, Gwynedd LL55 2AQ. *01286 673565.* www.hotmail.com-tyn-y-coedfarm. Mr J O Williams. 3m E of Caernarfon via A4086 towards Llanberis. Site is 400yd S of main road. Edge of mountains and easy reach of the sea. Open April-September.

Tyn-yr Onnen Farm, Waunfawr, Caernarfon, Gwynedd LL55 4AX. *01286 650281.* Mr Tom Griffith. 4m SE of Caernarfon via A4085 Beddgelert road Turn left at Waunfawr chip shop to lane with 'No Through Road' sign. 200-acre farm site in good walking area. Within easy reach of beach, Caernarfon Castle and Snowdon. Open May-October.

White Tower Caravan Park, Llandwrog, Caernarfon, Gwynedd LL54 5UH. *01286 830649/07802 562785.* whitetower @supanet.com. www.whitetower.supanet.com. Mrs Lynda Hulme. From Caernarfon follow A487 Porthmadog road for approx 0.25 miles. Past the Tesco supermarket, straight ahead at roundabout and take first right. Park 3 miles on right. Graded: 4 stars. Open March 1-October 31.

Criccieth

Cae-Canol, Criccieth, Gwynedd LL52 0NB. *01766 522351.* Mrs E W Roberts. Approximately 1.5 miles North of Criccieth on B4411. 2 miles South of A487 on B4411. Level pitches. Lovely riverside walk within 300 metres leading to Lloyd George village of Llanystumdwy. Open March-October.

Camping & Caravanning Club Site - Llanystumdwy, Tyddyn Sianel, Llanystumdwy, Criccieth, Gwynedd LL52 0LS. *01766 522855.* www.campingandcaravanningclub.co.uk. The Camping & Caravanning Club Ltd. Immediately off A497, left of road 0.5m west of village of Llanystumdwy. Just outside of the seaside resort Criccieth. 70 pitches. Non-members welcome. Caravans, motor caravans and tents accepted. 4 star rating. Open March-October.

Eisteddfa Caravan & Camping Park, Pentrefelin, Criccieth, Gwynedd LL52 0PT. *01766 522696.* karen@eisteddfa. fsnet.co.uk. www.eisteddfa.fsnet.co.uk. Mr & Mrs A M Leech. On A497 at village of Pentrefelin, between Porthmadog and Criccieth. Swimming pool and takeaway meals nearby. Open March 1-October 31.

Llwyn Bugeilydd Farm, Criccieth, Gwynedd LL52 0PN. *01766 522235.* Mr Robert Roberts. Nearest site on B4411,1m N of Criccieth. Turn S off A487 Porthmadog to Caernarfon road

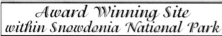

on to B4411, site on left in 3.5m. Level site with sea and mountain views. Quiet family site close to beach and shops. Brand new shower block with free hot water. Graded: 4 stars. Open Easter-October.

Muriau Bach Touring Site, Rhoslan, Criccieth, Gwynedd LL52 0NP. *01766 530642.* William D& Mrs M Roberts. Turn off A487 onto the B4411. Entrance is fourth or fifth over cattle grid. Clean, well kept, level site. Ideal family site, safe for children. Commanding the best views in the area. Convenient for all places of interest. Bowling green nearby. Cycling track one and half miles from site. Also plenty of beaches, mountains, interesting small towns, etc. Open October 31.

Mynydd Du Farm, Criccieth, Gwynedd LL52 0PS. *01766 522533.* Mr R H & E Williams. One mile east of Criccieth and three miles west of Portmadog on A497. On the Criccieth side of Pentrefelin village. Well-drained site with concrete lane and hardcore tracks. Superb views of hill and sea. Beach 1m away. Close to many places of interest. Fees on application. Open March-October.

Tyddyn Cethin, Criccieth, Gwynedd LL52 0NF. *01766 522149.* Mr & Mrs E Cowlishaw. AA 2 pennant site. David Bellamy Conservation Award. Open March-October.

Tyddyn Morthwyl, Criccieth, Gwynedd LL52 0NF. *01766 522115.* Mrs M Trumper. On B4411 Criccieth to Caernarfon road.1.25m N of Criccieth. Sheltered site with good views and convenient for sea and mountains. Fees on application. Open March 1-October 31.

Dolgellau

Dolgamedd, Brithdir, Bontnewydd, Dolgellau, Gwynedd LL40 2DG. *01341 422624.* dolgamedd@ll402dg.fsnet.co.uk. www.midwalesholidays.co.uk. Geraint Thomas Evans. Turn off A494 via B4416, right for Brithdir, site 75 yards on left. 3.5m north east of Dolgellau. Grid ref: 0S (124) SH773202. 8 acres, level sheltered site. On river bank, in good walking country. Camp fires. Barbeques. Fees on application. Open April 1-October 31.

Llwyn-yr-Helm Farm, Brithdir, Dolgellau, Gwynedd LL40 2SA. *01341 450254.* W V Lane. 4m NE of Dolgellau. 0.5m E off B4416, which is loop road between A470 and A494. A quiet and friendly farm site suitable for family holidays. Ideal for country lovers. Coast 10 miles. Limited bus service. Dogs allowed. Open Easter-October.

Tan-y-Fron Caravan & Camping Site, Arran Road, Dolgellau, Gwynedd LL40 2AA. *01341 422638.* rowlands@tanyfron. freeserve.co.uk. Mr E P & D M Rowlands. From Welshpool A470 to Dolgellau, 1st turn left for Dolgellau. Site is 0.5m on left. Small, quiet, sheltered site. Hair-dryers. Water, waste, TV hook ups. Snowdonia National Park Award. Winner of Wales in Bloom 2000. Graded: 5 stars. Open March 1-September 30.

Tyddyn Farm, Islawrdref, Dolgellau, Gwynedd LL40 1TL. *01341 422472.* Mr R D Owen & B M Owen. Three miles from Dolgellau town. 0.25 mile after Gwernan Lake hotel on right.

Dyffryn Ardudwy

Murmur-yr-Afon, Touring Caravan & Camping Park, Dyffryn Ardudwy, Gwynedd LL44 2BE. *01341 247353.* mills@mur muryrafon25.freeserve.co.uk. Mr & Mrs N E Mills. Take A496 coast road from Barmouth towards Harlech. Site entrance is 100 yards from Bentley's garage in Dyffryn village on right-hand side. Set in sheltered and natural surroundings.1 mile from beach. Close to shops and licensed premises. Graded: 4 stars. Open March-October.

Harlech

Barcdy Touring Caravan & Camping Park, Talsarnau, Harlech, Gwynedd LL47 6YG. *01766 770736.* anwen@barcdy. idps.co.uk. www.barcdy.co.uk. Mrs A L Roberts. On A496 midway between Harlech and Porthmadog. Four miles from Harlech. Fees on application. Graded: 4 stars. Open Easter-October 31.

Cae Cethin Farm Camp Site, Llanfair, Harlech, Gwynedd LL46 2SA. *01766 780247.* Mr R G Owen. 1m S of Harlech on E side of A496. Family holiday site. Fees on application. Open March-November.

Min-y-Don Caravan Park, Beach Road, Harlech, Gwynedd LL46 2UG. *01766 780286.* O M Jones & Sons. About one mile from Harlech. Easily accessible off the A496 main road. Turn off opposite Queens Hotel towards beach and proceed for about 400yd. Five minutes walk from Harlech rail station. Nearest park to beach. Open Easter-October.

Llanberis

Snowdon View Caravan Park, Brynrefail, Llanberis, Gwynedd LL55 3PD. *01286 870349.* http://nav.to/snowdonview. Mr T R Mead. Off the main A4086 Caernarfon-Llanberis road, 5m from Caernarfon, 2m from Llanberis take the B4547 for 3/4 mile, park is on right. Open March 1-January 11.

Llwyngwril

Borthowen Bungalow, Llwyngwril, Gwynedd LL37 2JT. *01341 250310.* Mr Griffith Thomas Owen. Off A493. Turn by river bridge on W side of Llanwyngwril. Take Station road to site, 1st to station yard. Enquire at new Borthowen bungalow nearby the railway station.

Machynlleth

Tyn-y-Pwll Camping & Caravan Site, Dinas Mawddwy, Machynlleth, Gwynedd SY20 9JF. *01650 531326.* Mr M. & I. Pugh. 400yd E from Red Lion Inn in Dinas Mawddwy A458 from Welshpool. A470 from Dolgellau or Machynlleth. Well-drained site with caravan to let. Free hot showers. Lovely walks and salmon and trout fishing free. Scenic area.

Nant Peris

Snowdon House, Gwastadnant, Nant Peris, Gwynedd LL55 4UL. *01286 870356.* Mr James M Cumberton. On A4086. 3m SE of Llanberis. Ideal for climbing and rambling. Situated at foot of Llanberis Pass. Convenient for Snowdon, The Horseshoe and Glyders.

GWYNEDD

Penrhyndeudraeth

Blaen Cefn Farm, Penrhyndeudraeth, Gwynedd LL48 6NA. *01766 770981.* Mr Gareth Wyn Jones. On the A487 Porthmadog road, 1m E of Porthmadog. Easy reach of Snowdonia, Ffestiniog and seaside. Bed and breakfast available and caravan for hire. Open Easter-October.

Porthmadog

Black Rock Camping & Touring Park, Morfa Bychan, Porthmadog, Gwynedd LL49 9LD. *01766 513919.* Mrs P Roberts. After coming over toll gate into Porthmadog, turn sharp left by Woolworths. Continue on through Morfa Bychan to the end, the park is opposite Black Rock cafe. Next to beach and close to many places of interest. Excellent facilities plus children's play area. Graded: 3 stars. Open Easter-October.

Garreg Goch Caravan Park, Black Rock Sands, Morfa Bychan, Porthmadog, Gwynedd LL49 9UD. *01766 512210.* Normanhurst Enterprises Ltd. Morfa Bychan road off High Street at Porthmadog Post Office. After 1.5m pass BP filling station then site on lane to left. 2m W of Porthmadog. Mainly caravan park but space for tents. Easy reach of beach. Graded: 4 stars. Open March-October.

Greenacres Holiday Park, Black Rock Sands, Morfa Bychan, Porthmadog, Gwynedd LL49 9YB. *01766 512781.* British Holidays. Off A497. Dogs allowed except in July and August. Club. Heated swimming pool. Tennis. Bowling. Pitch and putt. Kids' club. Access on to Black Rock Sands. Dragon Award. Open Easter-October.

Gwyndy Caravan Park, Black Rock Sands, Morfa Bychan, Porthmadog, Gwynedd LL49 9YB. *01766 512047.* martin@gwyndy.globalnet.co.uk. M S & J Leech. In Porthmadog, turn at Woolworths, sign to Morfa Bychan and Black Rock Sands. Follow road for 2m past Spar, turn 1st left at sign indicating Gwyndy Caravan Park. Turn right after 200yd at Gwyndy sign. Park sited at end of lane. Open March 8-end October.

Tyddyn Adi Touring Caravan & Camping Park, Morfa Bychan, Porthmadog, Gwynedd LL49 9YW. *01766 512933.* Mr I Lewis. 2.5m W to Morfa Bychan village from Portmadog post office. Large white sign at end of village to site. Flat, well-drained site 0.5m from beach. Open April-October.

Tyddyn Llwyn Caravan Park and Campsite, Morfa Bychan Road, Porthmadog, Gwynedd LL49 9UR. *01766 512205.* A G & E E Roberts. 0.5m W of Porthmadog via Black Rock Road to site on right. Beautifully located family park. Level sloping pitches set in 52 acres. 2m from Black Rock beach. Scenic rambles. Licensed bar on site. Dogs allowed. Prices on application. Open March 1-October 31.

Pwllheli

Abererch Sands Holiday Centre, Pwllheli, Gwynedd LL53 6PJ. *01758 612327.* enquiries@abererch-sands.co.uk. www. abererch-sands.co.uk. K J Dunne. On A497 Pwllheli to Criccieth road. 2m east of Pwllheli. Easy access. Adjoining beach with mountain views. Hairdryer points. Heated indoor swimming pool. Fees on application. Open March-October.

Bodwrog, Llanbedrog, Pwllheli, Gwynedd LL53 7RE. *01758 740341.* enq@bodwrog.co.uk. www.bodwrog.co.uk. Mr D Williams. 1m W of Llanbedrog and 5m from Pwllheli on A497. B4413 W for Aberdaron opposite Glyn-y-Weddw Hotel. Continue past Ship Hotel. Site is via third entrance on left going uphill towards Mynytho. Quiet family site. Superb coastal views. Open March-October.

Bolmynydd Touring & Camping Park, Refail, Llanbedrog, Pwllheli, Gwynedd LL53 7NP. *01758 740511.* refail. llanbedrog@ukonline.co.uk. Christine Evans. A499 from Pwllheli to Llanbedrog. Carry on towards Abersoch for half mile. Take first left lane after riding centre. Park half mile on left. Secluded park on Llanbedrog headland with glorious views. Within 10 minutes walk of two beautiful sandy beaches, pub and shop. Essential for tourers and motorhomes to book in advance. Graded: 4 stars. Open Easter to end-September.

Cedfn Caer Ferch, Llangybi, Pwllheli, Gwynedd. *01766 688412.* Mr R E Jones. Remote situation, approached off A499 or B4354. 6m NE of Pwllheli. Fees on application.

Deucoch Camp Site & Touring Caravans, Sarn Bach, Abersoch, Pwllheli, Gwynedd LL53 7LD. *01758 713293.* Mr J I & J M Williams. 1m S of Abersoch via the Sarn Bach road. To Wineshop, then take lane on right for 600yd to site. Flat, well-drained site, 10 mins from beaches. Families only, children's playground. Dogs on leads. Graded: 4 stars. Rail station 10 miles away. Open March 1-October 31.

Pen-y-Bont Bach, Llangwnadl, Pwllheli, Gwynedd LL23 7PH. *01758 770252.* eai@llwyn78.freeserve.co.uk. Mrs Peters. Off B4417 8m SW of Nefyn, NW coast of the Lleyn Peninsula. Approaching from Nefyn, do not take 1st turn signposted to Llangwnnadl, but continue downhill past grocery shop on bridge, to site 1st on left. Small, country site. Open March-September.

Porthysgaden Farm, Tudweiliog, Nefyn, Pwllheli, Gwynedd LL53 8PD. *01758 770206.* Mr J P Owen. 5m SW of Nefyn via B4417 Aberdaron road. Turn right 0.75m beyond Tudweiliog to site 0.75m. Flat, well-drained site 400yds from sea. Good skin-diving area. Slipway for boats. Shops nearby.

Refail Touring & Camping Park, Llanbedrog, Pwllheli, Gwynedd LL53 7NP. *01758 740511.* refail.llanbedrog@ukonline.co.uk. Christine Evans. Follow A499 from Pwllheli. At Llanbedrog turn right on to B4413 (signposted 'Refail'). Site 200 metres on right. Easy access, gravel pitches and super pitches. Beautiful sandy beach, shops, pubs and bistro all within 5 minutes' walk. Graded: 5 stars. Open Easter-September 30.

Sarn Farm, Sarn Bach, Abersoch, Pwllheli, Gwynedd LL53 5BG. *01758 713583.* Mr M J & Mrs E Griffith. Flat, sheltered site. One mile from Abersoch. Families only. Open Easter-October.

Tyddyn Heilyn Farm, Chwilog, Pwllheli, Gwynedd LL53 6SW. *01766 810441.* Mrs L Hughes-Jones & Mr T E Jones. From A497 to B4354 and at village of Chwilog before pub turn right in between houses opposite Povey Butchers. Follow this road for 1.5m, site is 2nd one along. Quiet, level, shady, beautiful family site, easy reach of sea and mountains. Ideal walks. Open 10 months.

Wern Newydd Tourer Park, Llanbedrog, Pwllheli, Gwynedd LL53 7PG *01758 740810/07970 014743 (m).* Owner Mrs M L Valentine. Mobile shop visits in high season. Turn right off A499 (Pwllheli-Abersoch) in Llanbedrog on to B4413 (Sp Aberdaron) continue through village, past the PO on the right then turn right on to unclassified road. Site entrance on right in 700yd. Open March-October.

Tywyn

Cedris Farm, Tal-y-llyn, Tywyn, Gwynedd LL36 9YW. *01654 782280.* Mrs M H Williams. Seven miles NE of Tywyn via B4405. 1st farm on left one mile after Abergynolwyn. Quiet valley 7m from beach and close to narrow-gauge railway and Roman bridge. Rock-climbing and rambling country. Plenty of interesting walks. Stream few yards from site. Bird watching on farm land (Red Kite). One mile to pub with bar meals. Open Whitsun-October.

Cwmrhwyddfor Campsite, Talyllyn, Tywyn, Gwynedd LL36 9AJ. *01654 761286/380.* Mr T D Nutting. On A487 between Dolgellau and Madiyulleth on main road. Site is at white house at the bottom of the pass. In beautiful country at foot of Cader Idris. Shop, cafe/restaurant, bottle gas supply, laundry all available nearby. Terms on application. Caravans, tents and motor caravans accepted. Dogs allowed.

Dol Einion, Tal-y-Llyn, Tywyn, Gwynedd LL36 9AJ. *01654 761312.* M Rees. Situated on the B4405 near junction with A487, at commencement of popular footpath to summit of Cader Idris. A flat 3-acre field with stream near Tal-y-Llyn Lake. Easy access with hard standing. A superb, quiet location in the Snowdonia National Park, ideal for walking and sightseeing. Pub, narrow gauge railway and trout fishing nearby. Dogs allowed.

Llabwst Farm, Rhoslefain, Tywyn, Gwynedd LL36 9NE. *01654 711013.* Mrs D Lewis. Location five miles north of Tywyn. On A493 coast road. Turn opposite white cottage at Rhoslefain village. Quiet, well-sheltered farm site. Open Whitsun-October.

Pall Mall Farm Caravan Park, Tywyn, Gwynedd LL36 9RU. *01654 710384/710591.* Mr & Mrs M L Vaughan & Mr R Vaughan. Site is1st farm on left 400yd W of Tywyn on A493. Flat, well-drained site 1m from beach and close to Talyllyn narrow-gauge railway. Good bird-watching and walking area. Fees on application. Newly-built leisure centre in Tywyn also cinema. Open Easter-October.

Tynllwyn Caravan & Camping Park, Bryncrug, Tywyn, Gwynedd LL36 9RD. *01654 710370.* ppspsmc@aol.com. wwww.tynllwyncaravanpark.co.uk. Mr & Mrs P L McEnvoy. Off the A493. Small family run site, good clean facilities, level site. Talyllyn Narrow Gauge Steam Railway running alongside site. Excellent base for all outdoor activities. Open March-October.

Waenfach Caravan Site, Llanegryn, Tywyn, Gwynedd LL36 9SB. *01654 710375.* W T Davies. 3m N of Tywyn on A493, 3m from sea. Small, friendly site on working farm with beautiful views. Open Easter-end October.

Ynysymaengwyn Caravan Park, Tywyn, Gwynedd LL36 9RY. *01654 710684.* rita@ynysmaengwyn.freeserve.co.uk. www. ynysmaengwyn.co.uk. Tywyn Town Council. 1 mile out of Tywyn on A493 towards Barmouth. This Local Authority owned site, situated in grounds of an old manor house, offers excellent facilities for walking, cycling, climbing, fishing and all water sports. Graded: 4 stars. AA 3 pennants. Open April 1-October 31.

MERTHYR TYDFIL
Merthyr Tydfil

Grawen Caravan & Camping Park, Cwm-Taff, Cefn-Coed, Merthyr Tydfil, Merthyr Tydfil CF48 2HS. *01685 723740.* grawen.touring@virgin.net. www.walescaravanandcamping.com. Mrs F Pugh. On A470 Brecon Beacons road, three miles off A465, known as The Heads of the Valleys. Picturesque forest, mountain and reservoir walks close to site. Four miles to main town and sports complex. Graded: 3 stars. Open April-October.

MONMOUTHSHIRE
Abergavenny

Pysgodlyn Farm, Llanwenarth Citra, Abergavenny, Monmouthshire NP7 7ER. *01873 853271.* pyscodlyn.farm@ virgin.net. www.pyscodlyncaravanpark.com. Mr K T Davies. 2m W of Abergavenny on A40. Easy access to flat, well-drained site in National Park area. Picturesque area, good for walking. Graded: 3 stars. Open April-October.

Rising Sun, Pandy, Abergavenny, Monmouthshire NP7 5RB. *01873 890254.* Owen & Mandy Price. 5m N of Abergavenny on A465 to Hereford at Pandy. Restaurant and bar meals.

Wernddu Farm, Abergavenny, Monmouthshire NP7 8NG. *01873 856223.* Mr G & K Watkins. 1.5m E of Abergavenny on B4521 Old Ross Road. Site is beside road. Peaceful site at gateway to Wales. Open February-November.

Monmouth

Bridge Camping Site, Dingestow, Monmouth, Monmouthshire NP25 4DY. *01600 740241.* info@bridgecaravan park.co.uk. www.bridgecaravanpark.co.uk. S A Holmes. Riverside site with level, sheltered pitches. Signposted from Abergavenny Junction on the A449 trunk road. AA 3 pennant site. Graded: 4 stars. Open Easter-end October.

Glen Trothy Caravan & Camping Park, Mitchel Troy, Monmouth, Monmouthshire NP25 4BD. *01600 712295.* www.glentrothy.co.uk. H & M Y Price. 1.5m SW of Monmouth off A40. Level park in scenic setting. Amenities include showers, toilets, dishwashing, laundry, separate disabled room. Play area. Good road access. Send/phone for free brochure. Open March 1-October 31.

Monnow Bridge Caravan Site, Drybridge Street, Monmouth, Monmouthshire NP25 5AD. *01600 714004.* Mrs M Murray. Small, family run site in town on banks of river. Caravans for hire. Fishing from site on Offa's Dyke path.

PEMBROKESHIRE

PEMBROKESHIRE

Amroth

Little Kings Park, Ludchurch, Amroth, Pembrokeshire SA67 8PG. 01834 831330. www.littlekings.co.uk. R J Blake & C W Blake. Off A477 St Clears-Pembroke, turn left at signpost Amroth, 200yds turn right at crossroads, uphill on left 250 yards. Licensed bar on site. Pitch and putt. Open Easter-September.

🚐🚗📺♿🏪✕☉🏃🏕🏖✿🏪🚰🛒♨💧🏊⚓🏊🎣🎣🔗❓☂❓✔🔗

Cardigan

Allty Coed, St Dogmaels, Cardigan, Pembrokeshire SA43 3LP 01239 612673. G H Biddyr. Grid Ref: 135-495: O.S. sheet 145. Regular visits of dolphins nearby.

🚐📺🛒🏃🏪🚰✿🛒♨💧⚓🎣🔗☂❓✔🔗

Clynderwen

Gower Villa Touring Park, Gower Villa Lane, Clynderwen, Pembrokeshire SA66 7NL. 01437 563859. richard.payler @talk21.com. gowervilla.freewire.co.uk. Mr & Mrs R Payler. From Narbeth A478 towards Cardigan in Clynderwen, turn first right after Farmer Association Store. Recently developed site. Heated toilet block, free hot showers, electric hook-ups. Lots to do in the area. Wales Tourist Board graded: 3 stars. Open March 1-December 20.

🚐🚗📺🏃♿🛒☉🏃🏪🏖🏪🔗✔🔗

Fishguard

Fishguard Bay Caravan & Camping Park, Garn Gelli, Fishguard, Pembrokeshire SA65 9ET. 01348 811415. enquiries@fishguardbay.com. www.fishguardbay.com. C N & L Harries. Brown and white signboard on the A487. Between Fishguard and Dinas Cross, the site can be found one mile along side road. Located three miles east of Fishguard Harbour. Well-appointed family-run holiday park with amenities. Dragon Award. Graded: 4 stars. Open March-December.

🚐🚗📺🏃☉☉🏪🚰🏪🏪🔗🏖🔗⚓🎣🔗☂❓✔🔗

Gwaun Vale Touring Park, Llanychaer, Fishguard, Pembrokeshire SA65 9TA. 01348 874698. Pete & Sheila Duffill. One and a half miles from Fishguard on the B4313 on right-hand side of road. Quiet and peaceful site, ideally situated for walking and water sports. Family run park with a children's play area. Overlooking National Park and Fishguard Bay. Local pub 0.5-mile. Graded: 4 stars. Open March 1-January 10.

🚐🚗📺🛒☉✿🏪🚰🏪🏖🏖⚓🎣🔗🏖⚓🎣🔗☂❓✔

BRANDY BROOK CARAVAN AND CAMPSITE

Rhyndaston Hayscastle Haverford
Pembrokeshire SA62 5PT
Tel: 01348 840 272

This naturally well-drained site is in a secluded unspoiled valley through which runs a trout stream. It is signposted from the A47 Haverfordwest to St Davids Road and is approximately 3 miles from Newgale beach. An ideal spot for those needing a quiet retreat from the stress of every day life.

Tregroes Touring Park, Fishguard, Pembrokeshire SA65 9QF.
01348 872316. Mr Hugh Williams. Site 1 mile south of Fishguard on A40. 1 mile from coast and ferry port. Attractive farm site. Children's play area. Pets welcome. Late arrivals accepted. Some restricted facilities for the disabled. Takeaway meals available nearby. Open Easter-October.

🚐🚗📺🛒☉☉🏪🏪🏪🏖🏪🛒🔗🏖⚓🎣🔗☂❓✔🔗

Haverfordwest

Brandy Brook Caravan & Camping Site, Haverfordwest, Pembrokeshire SA62 5PT. 01348 840272. f.mrowe@btopen world.com. Mr & Mrs Rowe. Secluded, well-drained site in beautiful area, 3m from beach. Signposted from Roch Motel on A427. Open Easter-October.

🚐📺☉☉🏪🏪🏪🔗🔗❓

Broad Haven Holiday Park, Broad Haven, Haverfordwest, Pembrokeshire SA62 3JD. 01437 781277. info@bhhp.co.uk. www.broadhavenholidaypark.co.uk. A & N Mock. 6.5 miles west of Haverfordwest. B4341 to Broad Haven. Site is on the right at bottom of hill leading into village. Close to safe, golden beaches. Fees on application. Open May-September (tents).

📺🏃☉☉🏪🏪🏪🔗🏖⚓🔗☂❓✔🔗

Camping & Caravanning Club Site - St David's, Dwr Cwmdig, Berea, St David's, Haverfordwest, Pembrokeshire SA62 6DW. 01348 831376. www.campingandcaravanning club.co.uk. The Camping & Caravanning Club Ltd. 4 acres with 40 pitches accepting motorcaravans, caravans and tents. Very convenient for the coast, being 0.5m by footpath from Aber-eiddy. From Fishguard on A487, after Croesgoch, fork right. Site is 1m on the right. Non-members welcome. Open May-September.

🚐🚗📺🏃🏪🛒☉🏪🏪🏪🔗🏖⚓🔗✔🔗

Cove Holiday Park, Howelston, Little Haven, Haverfordwest, Pembrokeshire SA62 3UU. 01305 821286/01437 781253. coveholidaypark@onetel.net.uk. Totemplant Ltd. Minor road on coast off B4327 and B4341. From Haverfordwest. Overlooking St Brides Bay and 1 mile from seaside village of Little Haven. 200yd from coastal path. Open April-September.

🚐🚗📺🛒☉☉🏪🏪🏪⚓🎣🔗🔗✔🔗

Creampots Touring Caravan & Camping Park, Broad Haven, Haverfordwest, Pembrokeshire SA62 3TU. 01437 781776. www.creampots.co.uk. R W & C Ashford. From Haverfordwest, take B4341 Broad Haven road. At Broadway turn left (signpost Milford Haven). Creampots is second park on right. Quiet, level park with excellent facilities including free showers. Convenient for touring, beaches, coast path and bird sanctuaries. Surfing and wind-surfing also available nearby. Graded: 4 stars. Open March-October.

🚐🚗📺🏃♿🛒☉☉🏪🏪🏪🔗⚓🔗✔

Dunston Hill Farm, Pelcomb, Haverfordwest, Pembrokeshire SA62 6ED. 01437 710525. Mrs R Jenkins. 3m W of Haverfordwest on A487 St David's road. Touring centre or overnight stop. Peaceful, sheltered site within easy reach of many sandy beaches. Open Easter-October.

🚐🚗📺🏃🛒☉🏪🏪✕🔗🏖⚓🎣🔗☂❓✔☉🔗

East Hook Farm, Marloes, Haverfordwest, Pembrokeshire SA62 3BJ. 01646 636291. Chetwynd Farmers. From Haverfordwest B4327 towards Dale. First right 2m before Dale and through Marloes, about 1m to farm on Pembrokeshire coast path. 15 minutes walk to beaches. Scenic views. Small farm site. Cycle hire. Windsurfing nearby. Open January-December.

🚐📺🛒☉☉🏪🏪🏪✿🏪🔗⚓🎣🔗

PEMBROKESHIRE

Nine Wells Caravan & Camping Park, Nine Wells, Solva, Haverfordwest, Pembrokeshire SA62 6UH. *01437 721809.* N D Bowie. From Haverfordwest, take A487 signposted St David's. Go through Solva. After 0.5-mile signpost to Nine Wells Site. Rural site, 5 minutes walk down National Trust valley to coastal footpath and cove. Bottled gas supply available nearby. Open Easter-October.

Park Hall Caravan Park, Penycwm, Haverfordwest, Pembrokeshire. *01437 721606.* E R & H M Harries. A487 12m from Haverfordwest and 2.5m W of Newgale. Turn north at sign for Royal Signals Cawder Barracks Brawdy, then first left. Site 1m from A487. Pleasant rural and sea area. Open March 1-October 31.

Redlands Touring Caravan & Camping Park, Hasguard Cross, Nr Littlehaven, Haverfordwest, Pembrokeshire SA62 3SJ. *01437 781300.* jenny.flight@virgin.net. Trevor & Jenny Flight. From Haverfordwest take the Dale Road (B4327) for 7 miles. Site on right. 5 acres of open grassland. 64 pitches. Pets welcome. Graded: 4 stars. Convenient base for Pembrokeshire holidays. Immaculate facilities. Open March-January.

South Cockett Touring Caravan & Camping Park, Broadway, Little Haven, Haverfordwest, Pembrokeshire SA62 3TU. *01437 781296/01437 781760.* wjames01@farming. co.uk. www.southcockett.co.uk. Mrs E R James. B4341 from Haverfordwest, turn left at official camping sign site 300yd on right. Centrally situated family-run site with excellent facilities. Open Easter-October.

Tan y Bryn, Whitesands, St David's, Haverfordwest, Pembrokeshire SA62 6PS. *01437 720168.* Situated next to Whitesands Beach. Manager: Mr M Pawlik—contact at Whitesands Beach cafe/shop. Open March 1-December 31.

The Rising Sun Caravan Site, St Davids Road, Pelcomb Bridge, Haverfordwest, Pembrokeshire SA62 6EA. *01437 765171.* Mr & Mrs R Brown. From Haverfordwest take road to St Davids (A487) site is 1.25m on left-hand side. Small, friendly, sheltered site, partly gently sloping to stream. Pub on site with excellent reasonably priced food. Open Easter-end-October.

Kilgetty

Cross Park Holiday Centre, Broadmoor, Kilgetty, Pembrokeshire SA68 0RS. *01834 811244.* reservations@crossparkholidaycentre.co.uk. www.crossparkholidaycentre.co.uk. New Horizons Holidays. One mile west of Kilgetty on A477. Turn right at Cross Inn pub. Site 300 yards along on the left. Showbar with nightly entertainment. Shop. Arcade, diner, indoor pool, etc. Open April 4-October 31.

Masterland Farm Touring Caravan & Tent Site, Broadmoor, Kilgetty, Pembrokeshire SA68 0RH. *01834 813298.* bonser masterland@aol.com. Mr H & M Davies. Tenby 4m, Saundersfoot 2.5m. All mod cons. Children's play area. Pets permitted. SAE for brochure. Graded: 3 stars. Open February 28-January 7.

Maenclochog

Rosebush Caravan & Camping Park, Rosebush, Maenclochog, Pembrokeshire SA66 7QT. *01437 532206.* Mr Gareth Williams. 1.5m north of Maenclochog, midway Narberth to Fishguard on B4313. Flat site with fishing lake. Putting green. Dogs allowed. David Bellamy Gold Conservation Award. Open March 14-October 31.

Mynachlog-ddu

Trefach Country Pub and Caravan Park, Mynachlog-ddu, Pembrokeshire SA66 7RU. *01994 419225.* trefach@bigfoot. com. www.trefach.co.uk. O & D Enterprises Ltd. 4m E of Maenclochog, 9m N of Narbeth via A478 to 1m N of Efailwen, turn left by Cross Inn to site, 1m on right. Well-drained site in good walking area within Preseli National Park. Graded: 2 stars. Open March-January 6.

Narberth

Dingle Farm Caravan Park, Narberth, Pembrokeshire SA67 7DP. *01834 860482.* Mrs R Owen & Sons. Showers. Clubhouse. Play area. Takeaway facilities, laundry and swimming pool all nearby. Open April-October.

Llandissilio Caravan Park, Clynderwen, Narberth, Pembrokeshire SA66 7TT. *01437 563408.* R S & T G Spencer. On the A478 midway between Tenby and Cardigan. Three miles north of Narberth. Countryside site near Preseli Hills. Play area for children. Sauna spa. New pool bar. Open March-October.

New Park Caravan Park, Landshipping, Narberth, Pembrokeshire SA67 8BG. *01834 891369.* E & C A Jones. Seven miles west of Narberth. Turn off the A40 on to A4075. Turn west at Canaston Bowl on to unclassified roads signposted for Landshipping. Quiet, touring centre. Open Easter-October.

Noble Court Caravan Site, Redstone Road, Narberth, Pembrokeshire SA67 7ES. *01834 861191.* Mr A Pritchard. 0.5m north of Narberth on B4313 and 0.5m south of A40. Touring centre and club in the heart of Pembrokeshire. 92 touring pitches all level and some hard standings. Open March-November.

Wood Office Caravan & Tent Park, Cold Blow, Narberth, Pembrokeshire SA67 8RR. *01834 860565.* Mrs Barabara E Morris. 2m S of Narberth. Flat, well-drained site. Oakwood Park, Folly Farm and Heron's Brook all nearby. Open Easter-September.

Woodland Vale Holiday Park, Ludchruch, Narberth, Pembrokeshire SA67 8JE. *01834 831 319.* accounts@clarach.fsbusiness.co.uk. Mr T Scarrott. From Carmarthan head down A40, pass St Clears and follow signs to Ludchurch. Woodland Vale is situated on the left after passing through Ludchurch. Open March-November.

Newport

Morawelon, Parrog, Newport, Pembrokeshire SA42 0RW. *01239 820565.* Mr B Watts. On A487 in Newport turn N on road to Parrog. Site on sea front. Close to sandy beach. Safe bathing. Good sailing, slipway for boat launching ideal for wind surfers. Sheltered site with beautiful sea views. Open end March-end October.

PEMBROKESHIRE

Tredegar House & Park, Newport, Pembrokeshire NP10 8TW. *01633 815600.* www.caravanclub.co.uk. Newport County Borough Council. One mile south of M4 Junction 28 and three miles south west of Newport. Follow signs to Newport, Tredegar House and Park is signposted at first roundabout. Suitable for short stay, on holiday route London to Wales. Tredegar House stately home. Open April-November.

Tycanol Farm Camp Site, Organic, Newport, Pembrokeshire SA42 0ST. *01239 820264.* www.caravan campingsites.co.uk. Mr Hugh Harris. On the A487 near Newport. Sign to Tycanol on milk stand. Level, sheltered pitches, overlooking Newport Bay. By the coastal path. Free hot showers. Bicycle hire nearby. Nature walk for wildlife. Barbecue free nightly.

Newquay

Penlon Caravan Park, Cross Inn, Newquay, Pembrokeshire SA44 6JY. *01545 560620.* Chris & Ele Willis. A486 (signposted Newquay) off the A487 Aberystwyth to Cardigan main road. Managed by Chris and Ele Willis. Open March 1-January 6.

Pembroke

Castle Farm Camping Site, Angle, Pembroke, Pembrokeshire SA71 5AR. *01646 641220.* G.B. Rees & Sons. Enter opposite Globe Hotel in Angle or follow directions to Lifeboat station. Holiday site near entrance of Milford Haven. Limited number of touring vans. Situated directly behind village church. Site overlooking East Angle Bay. Open Easter-October.

Upper Portclew, Freshwater East, Pembroke, Pembrokeshire SA71 5LA. *01646 672112.* Mrr M A Phillips. On B4584 between Lamphey and Freshwater East. Three miles south east Pembroke. Near safe beaches. Open May-September 10.

Saundersfoot

Mill House Caravan Park, Pleasant Valley, Stepaside, Saundersfoot, Pembrokeshire SA67 8LN. *01834 812069.* holiday@millhousecaravan.demon.co.uk. www.mill house caravan.demon.co.uk. Simon and Amanda Wood. Beautiful family site next to old watermill. 15-minute walk to beach and coast path. Pub 5 minutes. Laundry and washing up, some pitches with TV & electricity. 13 miles west St Clears A477. Phone for directions. Open March-October.

Moreton Farm Leisure Park, Moreton, Saundersfoot, Pembrokeshire SA69 9EA. *01834 812016.* moretonfarm@ btconnect.com. www.moretonfarm.co.uk. At junction of Sandy Hill Lane and A478. 2m N of Kilgetty to Tenby. Tenby 3.5m, Saundersfoot 1.5m. Dragon Award pine lodges. Bed linen provided, colour TV, CH. Modern facilities for tents and tourers. Children's play area. Graded: 4 stars. Open March 1-November.

Moysland Farm, Narberth Road, Saundersfoot, Pembrokeshire SA69 9DS. *01834 01 2455.* Mrs V Rawson & M J Humphries. At junction of Sandy Hill Lane and A478. 2m N of Tenby. Quiet family holiday site with sandy beach 0.5m. On site tents for hire Motor cycles welcome. Open July-September.

Sunnyvale Holiday Park, Valley Road, Saundersfoot, Pembrokeshire SA69 9BT. *01348 872462.* www.howells leisure.co.uk. Howells Leisure. On A478 towards Tenby. Three miles from Tenby at Pentlepoir, pass Murco petrol station on right, take next left into Valley Road. Sunnyvale on left, 300 yards down the road. Club. Nightly entertainment, heated indoor pool. Graded 4 stars. Open April-October.

St David's

Caerfai Bay Caravan & Tent Park, St David's, Pembrokeshire SA62 6QT. *01437 720274.* info@caerfaibay.co.uk www.caer faibay.co.uk Mr & Mrs I E Panton. Off A487 at Visitor Centre near Grove Hotel, St David's signposted Caerfai Bay. Entrance to park is at end of road. 0.25m on right overlooking the bay. Launderette. Showers. Bathing beach 200yd. Takeaway, Cafe/restaurant nearby. AA 3 pennant. Graded: 4 stars. Open March-November.

Glan-y-Mor Tent Park, Caerfai Bay Road, St David's, Pembrokeshire SA62 6QT. *01437 721788.* clive@ divewales.com. www.divewales.com. Mr Hayes. Off A487. 5 minutes' walk from beach and St Davids. Open February-October.

Hendre Eynon, St David's, Pembrokeshire SA62 6DB. *01437 720474.* www.ukparks.co.uk/hendreeynon. Mr Ian Jamieson. 2m N of St David's to the right of coast road to Llanrian. Join this road from A487 from St David's. Within easy reach of beaches and coastal paths. Laundry facilities. All facilities are of a high standard. Dogs allowed. Graded: 3 stars. Open May-October.

Porthclais, St David's, Pembrokeshire SA62 6RR. *01437 720256.* Mr Rhys G Morgan. 1m SW of St David's. From Haverfordwest on A487. Keep left at St David's and join Porthclais road. Site is left after 0.5m farm site which adjoins Porthclais Harbour. Open March-October.

Prendergast Caravan & Camping Park, Trefin, Haverfordwest, St David's, Pembrokeshire SA62 5AJ. *01348 831368.* Mr A Jenkins. 8m NE of St Davids via A487 to Trefin signpost. N for 1m to site. 0.25m from beach. Fees on applica-tion. Graded: 3 stars. Open April-October.

Rhos-y-Cribed, St David's, Pembrokeshire SA62 6RR. *01437 720336.* Miss M Lewis. 1m SW via road to Porthclais Harbour. Farm is signposted. Farm touring site. Fees on application. SAE. Special reduction for deaf children. Ice pack freezing available.

Rhosson Farm, St David's, Pembrokeshire. *01437 720335/6.* Mr W D M Lewis. St Justinian road out of St David's. Site is on S side of road, farm identified by Flemish chimney. 1m W of St Davids. Close to good beach and nature survey area. Ice pack freezing service. Fees on application. Special reduction for deaf children. Open Easter-October.

Tretio Caravan & Camping Park, St David's, Pembrokeshire SA62 6DE. *01437 781600/720270.* www.tretio.com. B G & P J Rees. On leaving St David's, keep left at St David's RFC and continue straight for 3 miles until sign pointing right. Park 300 yards. 0.5 miles to coastal path. Panoramic views. 4.5 acre 9-hole pitch and putt course. Takeaway nearby. Dogs on leads allowed. Open Easter-October.

PEMBROKESHIRE

Tenby

Buttyland Touring Caravan & Tent Park, Manorbier, Tenby, Pembrokeshire SA70 7SN. *01834 871278.* buttyland@ tesco.net. www.buttyland.co.uk. Mrs May. 5m W of Tenby via A4139. Pass through Penally and Lydstep. After Lydstep straight over crossroads and after 1m turn right at sign to Manorbier Station. Site is 150yd on right. 1m to beach. Cafe nearby. Fees on application. Open Easter-October.

Kiln Park Holiday Centre, Marsh Road, Tenby, Pembrokeshire SA70 7RB. *01834 844121.* www.british-holidays.co.uk. British Holidays. Outskirts of town on A4139. Kiln Park Petrol Station at site entrance. Near town and beach. Indoor swimming pool, waterslide and jacuzzi. Sports and leisure facilities. Advance booking essential. Welcome Host and David Bellamy Conservation Award. Graded: 3 stars. Open April-September.

Manorbier Country Park, Station Road, Manorbier, Tenby, Pembrokeshire SA70 7SN. *01834 871952.* Mr Bob McHarg. From Tenby, follow A4139 towards Pembroke. Road widens with chapel on right. Take right-hand turn for Manorbier Newton/Station. Park 300yd on left. Open March 1-October.

Meadow House Holiday Park, Amroth, Tenby, Pembrokeshire SA67 8NS. *01834 812438.* Treatcourt Ltd. 6m NE of Tenby. From Tenby take A478. After 3.5m turn right on to A477, turn right again at sign Amroth and Wisemans Bridge. From St Clears A477 for 10m, after 'Stage Coach Inn' turn left at sign. 1m from beach. No dogs July 19-August 31. Open April-September.

Milton Bridge Caravan Park, Milton, Tenby, Pembrokeshire SA70 8PH. *01646 651204.* Kenneth & Joyce Gouldsbrough. A477 St Clear to Pembroke Dock, turn right at Milton. Small, peaceful, family-run park set in the National Park on river estuary. Convenient for visiting Pembroke's numerous attractions. Open Easter-October 1.

Park Farm Caravans, Manorbier, Tenby, Pembrokeshire SA70 7SU. *01646 672583.* Mr G O Thomas. 5m W of Tenby via A4139. Second turning left for Manorbier, turn right 500yd. Private foot path to beach. Quiet family site within Pembrokeshire Coast National Park. Open Easter-October.

Red House Farm, New Hedges, Tenby, Pembrokeshire SA69 9DP. *01834 813918.* Mrs J Marden. Last farm on right side of main roundabout into both Tenby and Saundersfoot. Both 1.5m distant. Very small, family site with easy access to all amenities.

Rowston Holiday Park, New Hedges, Tenby, Pembrokeshire SA70 8TL. *01834 842178.* andrea@rowston-hpfreeserve.co.uk. www.rowston-holiday-park.co.uk. D C Ormond. 1.5m N of Tenby off A478 on to minor road to New Hedges. Slightly sloping, landscaped site with sea views and private path to safe beach. Children's play area. Fees on application. No dogs during Spring bank holiday, July and August. Open April-October.

Rumbleway Caravan & Tent Park, New Hedges, Tenby, Pembrokeshire SA70 8TR. *01834 845155.* Mr V G Lawrence. 1.5 miles north of Tenby via A478. Flat site within easy walking distance of sandy beaches. Play area. Pub. Arcade. New toilet/shower block. Tent hook-ups available. Open April-October.

The Lodge Farm Caravan & Tent Park, New Hedges, Tenby, Pembrokeshire SA70 8TH. *01834 842468.* S J Weaver & A L Williams. 1.5 miles north of Tenby via A478. Open April 1-October 31.

Trevayne, Saundersfoot, Tenby, Pembrokeshire SA69 9DL. *01834 813402.* Mr Dennis L Reed. Three miles north of Tenby. east of Tenby. East off the B4316 one mile south of Saundersfoot Just north of junction with A478. Roomy site adjoining Monkstone Bay and Point. Open Easter to April-October.

Tudor Glen Caravan Park, Jameston, Tenby, Pembrokeshire SA70 7SS. *01834 871417.* info@tudorglencaravanpark.co.uk. www.tudorglencaravanpark.co.uk. V J Stevens & Sons. Halfway between Tenby and Pembroke on A4139, approaching from Tenby Tudor Glen is right-hand side before Jameston village. Family site, no groups. Graded: 3 stars. Open March 1-October 31.

Well Park, New Hedges, Tenby, Pembrokeshire SA70 8TL. *01834 842179.* enquiries@wellparkcaravans.co.uk. www.well parkcaravans.co.uk. Mr D J Nash. On A478, 1m N of Tenby. Convenient for all beaches and places of interest along Pembrokeshire coast. Excellent facilities. Baby room. Private washing facilities. Hair-drying points. Family-run park. Licensed bar. Wales in Bloom award-winning park. Graded: 4 stars. Open March-October.

Whitwell Camping Park, Nr Lydstep Haven Beach, Penally, Tenby, Pembrokeshire SA70 7RY. *01834 842200.* 3m W of Tenby off A4139 Manorbier road. Footpath to beach. Campers bar. Open Easter-September.

Windmills Camping Park, Narberth Road, Tenby, Pembrokeshire SA70 8TJ. *01834 842200.* 0.75m Tenby from town centre. 5 acres well-drained, level grass with lovely sea views. Good walking area. Free hot water. Fees on application. Open Easter-October.

Wood Park Caravans, New Hedges Bypass, Tenby, Pembrokeshire SA70 8TL. *01834 843414.* info@woodpark. co.uk. www.woodpark.co.uk. Mrs E M Hodgkinson & Jill. 1m N of Tenby on W side of A487 on New Hedges bypass. Quiet family park. Caravan and tent site, with licensed bar. No dogs end-July and August. Small dogs other times. Fees on application. Graded: 4 stars. Open Easter-September.

Whitland

Pantglas Farm Caravan Park, Tavernspite, Amroth, Whitland, Pembrokeshire SA34 0NS. *01834 831618.* steve@pantglasfarm.com. www.pantglasfarm.com. Steve & Alison Bolas. A477 to Tenby, turn right at Red Roses to Tavernspite 1.25m, take the middle road at village pump, Pantglas 800 yards on left. Pretty Wales in Bloom award-winning park. Play area. Caravan storage. Graded: 4 stars. Open Easter-October.

South Caravan Caravan Park, Tavernspite, Whitland, Pembrokeshire SA34 0NL. *01834* 831451/651/586. Mrs E James & Mr I James. 5m SW of St Clears and 2.75m S of Whitland. From St Clears take A477 to Red Roses. Turn right for 1.25m to Tavernspite. Sheltered site 3m from beach. Club on site. Play area for children. Open April-October.

▓ ❤ ⬇ ▦ ☉ ♨ ▦ ≋ ⋒ ▯ ≋ 𝐿 𝐽

POWYS

Brecon

Anchorage Caravan Park, Bronllys, Brecon, Powys LD3 0LD. *01874 711246.* J A & B M Powell & Sons. 8m NE of Brecon on A438 in Bronllys. Near Brecon Beacons. Fees on application. Graded: 4 stars. SAE for brochure.

▓ ❤ ▦ ⅆ ⚓ ℒ ☉ ☺ ♨ ▦ ⋒ ✿ 𝐿 𝐽 ∪ ⤳ ९

Bishops Meadow Caravan Park, Hay Road, Brecon, Powys LD3 9SW. *01874 610000.* enquiries@bishops-meadow.co.uk. Mr Howard Perry. From town centre, take B4602 signed Builth Wells. Park has spectacular views of the Brecon Beacons and is 1 mile from Brecon. Open March-October.

▓ ❤ ⬇ ▦ ⅆ ⚓ ℒ ✕ ☉ ☺ ♨ ▦ ⋒ ▯ 𝐿 𝐽 𝐽 ⤳ ९

Brynich Caravan Park, Brecon, Powys LD3 7SH. *01874 623325.* brynich@aol.com . www.brynich.co.uk . Mr & Mrs C R Jones. 1m E of Brecon on A470, 250yd from A40-A470 roundabout. Free hot water. Two showers for disabled. Children's adventure playground. Large pitch areas. Dogs allowed on leads. Ideal centre for touring mid-Wales. AA 4 pennants, Graded: 5 stars. Open March 25-October 27.

▓ ❤ ▦ ⅆ ⚓ ℒ ☉ ☺ ♨ ▦ ⋒ ▯ 𝐿 ♀ ✿ 𝐽 𝐽 ✓ ∪ ⤳ ९ ⤴

Lakeside Caravan & Camping Park, Llangorse, Brecon, Powys LD3 7TR. *01874 658226.* holidays@lakeside.zx3.net. www.lakeside-holiday.net. Mr Ray Davies. 6m E of Brecon via A40 to Bwlch then B4560 to Llangorse. Signposted to Llangorse Lake & Common. Site adjacent 365-acre lake in Brecon Beacons National Park. Well-equipped site. Licensed club. Windsurfing. Fishing. Canoeing. Pony trekking. AA member. Graded: 4 stars. Open April-October.

▓ ❤ ⬇ ▦ ⅆ ℒ ✕ ☉ ☺ ♨ ▦ 𝐿 ♀ ✿ 𝐽 ✿ 𝐽 ∪ ⤴

Llynfi Holiday Park, Llangorse Lake, Brecon, Powys LD3 7TR. *01874 658283.* Brian & Jill Strawford. 6.5m E of Brecon. Quiet, sheltered site near Llangorse Lake.In Brecon Beacons National Park. Fees on application. Graded: 3 stars. Open March-October.

▓ ❤ ▦ ⅆ ⚓ ℒ ☉ ☺ ♨ ▦ ≋ ⋒ ▯ 𝐿 ♀ ✿ 𝐽 𝐽 ✓ ∪ ⤳ ९ ⤴

LLYNFI HOLIDAY PARK
Llangorse Lake, Brecon,
Wales, LD3 7TR

A flat, well-sheltered camping and caravan park at Llangorse Lake in the Brecons National Park. An ideal centre for touring South and Mid-Wales. Own boating facilities. All amenities with bar and heated pool. Seasonal sites available for caravans. Holiday homes for sale.

Write for reservation and brochure
(SAE please) or telephone
Llangorse (01874658) 283
Fax: (01874658) 575
www.llynfi.com
brian.strawford@btinternet.com

Pencelli Castle Caravan & Camping Park, Pencelli, Brecon, Powys LD3 7LX. *01874 665451.* pencelli.castle @virgin.net. www.pencelli-castle.co.uk. Mr & Mrs G Rees. AA Best Campsite in Wales 2002, Calor Gas Best Park in Wales 2001. Peaceful countryside park in heart of Brecon Beacons National Park. Within walking distance of highest peaks. Adjoining Brecon Canal. Good for walking. Luxurious heated shower block. Village pub 150yd. Mountain bike hire, play area, on bus route.

▓ ❤ ▦ ⅆ ⚓ ℒ ☉ ☺ ♨ ▦ ⋒ ✕ ▯ ✿ 𝐿 ✿ 𝐽 𝐽 ✓ ▿ ∪ ⤳ ९ ⤳

Riverside International Caravan & Camping Park, Talgarth, Brecon, Powys LD3 0HL. *01874 711320.* riversideinternational @bronllys1.freeserve.co.uk. D A & A C Gorman. 0.5m W of Talgarth on A479 opposite Bronllys Castle. Touring centre near Brecon Beacons and Wye Valley. In an area of outstanding beauty. Licensed restaurant on site. Recreation and TV room. Fees and brochure on application. SAE. Graded: 4 stars. Open Easter-October 31.

▓ ❤ ⬇ ▦ ⅆ ⚓ ℒ ✕ ☉ ☺ ♨ ▦ ≋ ⋒ ⋒ ✕ ▯ ♀ ✿ 𝐽 𝐽 ✓ ∪ ⤳ ९ ⤴

Upper Genfford Farm, Talgarth, Brecon, Powys LD3 0EN. *01874 711360.* B G M Prosser. 3m S of Talgarth and12m E of Brecon on A497 (Crickhowell). Edge of Black Mountains, 4m from Llangorse Lake, Brecon Beacons. Gliding. Paragliding. Pony trekking. Hot water supplied at house, also use of toilets and bathroom. Leisure centre 8 miles.

▓ ▦ ⅆ ℒ ✕ ☺ ▦ ♨ ♨ ▯ △ ♀ 𝐽 𝐽 ✓ ▿ ∪ ⤳ ९ ⤳ ⤴

Builth Wells

Fforest Fields, Hundred House, Builth Wells, Powys LD1 5RT. *01982 570406.* office@fforestfields.co.uk. www.fforest fields.co.uk. Mr & Mrs G T Barstow. Good access directly off A481, half mile from Hundred House. Delightfully quiet, level mown site, straddling mountain stream. Modern toilets, free hot showers, washing and drying facilities. Lovely forest and moorland walks. Pub and village stores half mile. Open April-October.

▓ ❤ ▦ ⅆ ℒ ✕ ☉ ☺ ♨ ▦ ⋒ ♨ 𝐿 𝐽 ✓ ⤳ ९

Irfon River Caravan Park, Upper Chapel Road, Garth, Builth Wells, Powys LD4 4BH. *01591 620310.* 500yd S of Garth along B4519. 6m W of Builth Wells. Well-equipped site surrounded by mountains, rivers and forest. Situated on the banks of the river Irfon with trout fishing available. Cafe/restaurant nearby. Graded: 4 stars. Open Easter-October.

▓ ❤ ▦ ℒ ☉ ☺ ♨ ▦ ⋒ ≋ 𝐿 ♀ 𝐽 𝐽 ∪ ⤳ ९

Llewelyn Leisure Park, Cilmery, Builth Wells, Powys LD2 3NU. *01982 551090/01982 552838.* deejay1010@aol.com. www.derekjohnson.co.uk. Mr Derek Johnson. 2m W of Builth Wells, on S of A483 behind Prince Llewellyn free house. Panoramic views. Central touring location.

▓ ❤ ▦ ℒ ✕ ☺ ☺ ♨ ▦ ⋒ ♨ ▯ ≋ 𝐿 ▯ △ 𝐽 ✓ ∪ ⤳ ९

Prince Llewelyn Inn, Cilmery, Builth Wells, Powys LD2 3NU. *01982 552694.* Ms L Jennings & Ms L Jones. 2m W of Builth Wells on A483. Pleasant position. Tents only. A pleasant c14th village inn with dining. Children welcome. Also bed and breakfast. Open April-October.

⬇ ✕ ⋒ ≋ 𝐽 ✓ ९

Riverside Caravan Park, Llangammarch Wells, Builth Wells, Powys LD4 4BY. *01591 620 465/629.* www.caravancamping site.co.uk. Barry & Pauline Smith. 8m SW from Builth Wells via A483 to Llandovery. Site is 2nd left in Garth. Flat, well-drained site in beautiful valley. Winter and summer storage. Dogs on leads allowed. Phone on site. Open April-October.

▓ ❤ ⬇ ▦ ⅆ ℒ ✕ ☉ ☺ ♨ ▦ ⋒ ▯ ≋ 𝐿 △ 𝐽 ✓ ∪ ⤴

POWYS

Crickhowell

Cwmdu Camping Site, Crickhowell, Powys NP8 1RU. *01874 730441.* Mrs O M Farr. W of Crickhowell on A40, fork right on to A479. Site is 3m from junction. 4m N of Crickhowell. Edge of Black Mountains. Route to London and N & W Wales. Dogs allowed on leads. Open March-November 1.

Riverside Caravan & Camping Park, New Road, Crickhowell, Powys NP8 1AY. *01873 810397.* Ruth Price. Between A40 and B4588 at Crickhowell. Grassy, level site in National Park. 5 mins walk to town. No large single-sex groups. Over 18's only. Mountain and canal walks. No hang/para gliders. Open March 1-October 31.

Lake Vyrnwy

Fronheulog, Lake Vyrnwy, Powys SY10 0NN. *01691 870662.* Mr Merion Jones. On the B4393 Llanfyllin to Lake Vyrnwy road. Two miles south east of Lake Vyrnwy. On right hand side of road to lake. Booking necessary. Adults only. Open March-October.

Llanbrynmair

Cringoed Caravan & Camping Park, The Birches, Llanbrynmair,Powys SY19 7DR. *01650 521237.* susan.mathers @virgin.nett. Paul & Sue Mathers.Turn off A470 at Llanbrynmair on B4518 for 1m. By river Twymyn. New facilities block and laundry room. Ideal base for touring mid-Wales with many attractions including castles, slate mines and the Alternative Technology Centre. Idyllic location for escaping the pressures of life. Open March 7-January 7.

Llandrindod Wells

Brynithon Caravan & Camping Site, Llanbister, Llandrindod Wells, Powys LD1 6TR. *01597 840231.* Mr G G Hughes. 10m N of Llandridod Wells on A483 to Newtown. 0.5m N Llanbister village, 200yd off main road. Rambling, fishing and pony trekking country. Shop and pub. Dogs allowed. Open March 1-October 31.

Dalmore Caravan Park, Howey, Llandrindod Wells, Powys LD1 5RG. *01597 822483.* peter.speake@freeuk.com. Mr Peter Speake & Mrs Heather Speake. On A483 between Builth Wells and Llandrindod Wells. Small, family run park with panoramic views. Very well maintained with level terraced and fenced pitches. Graded: 3 stars. All facilities. Suitable for retired people. Open March 1-October 31.

Disserth Caravan & Camping Park, Disserth, Howey, Llandrindod Wells, Powys LD1 6NL. *01597 860277.* m.hobbs@virgin.net. Mike Hobbs. 1.5 miles east of Newbridge. From Newbridge B4358 towards Llandrindod Wells. Then fork east to site or 3m south from Llandrindos Wells on A483 towards Builth Wells and turn west to Disserth south of Howey. Small, rural touring centre. Graded: 4 stars. Open March-October.

Park Motel Camping & Caravan Park, Crossgates, Llandrindod Wells, Powys LD1 6RF. *01597 851201.* enquiries@theparkmotel.freeserve.co.uk. www.theparkmotel. freeserve.co.uk. Steve & Laura McNuey. Three miles north of Llandrindod Wells via A483 to Crossgates and W on A44. Family-run park set in 3 acres amid beautiful mid-Wales

countryside. Near the famous Elan valley reservoirs. Ideally situated for touring and sightseeing. Open March-October.

Llanidloes

Dol-llys Farm, Llanidloes, Powys SY16 6JA. *01686 412694.* Mr O S Evans. Sports centre within one mile. 6m from rail station. Dogs on leads welcome. Open April-October.

Llansantffraed Ym Mechain

Bryn Vyrnwy Caravan Park, Bryn Vyrnwy, Llansantffraed Ym Mechain, Powys SY22 6AY. *01691 828252.* D & J Williams. Main A495 at Llynclys, off main A483 Oswestry to Welshpool road, on left just outside of village. Quiet park overlooking river Vyrnwy. Convenient for all mid-Wales beauty spots and National Trust locations. Graded: 3 stars. Open April 1-October 31.

Machynlleth

Celyn Brithion, Dinas Mawddwy, Machynlleth, Powys SY20 9LP. *01650 531344.* celyn.brithion@btopenworld.com. www. celynbrithion.co.uk. Rolland & Isabel Turnbull. 2m N of Mallwyd on A458. Overnight stop and longer up to 28 days. Snowdonia. Dogs allowed if kept under control. Open March 1-October 31.

Dovey Valley Caravan & Camping Park, Llanwrin, Machynlleth, Powys SY20 8QJ. *01650 511501.* Mr C Taylor. 5m NW of Machynlleth on B4404, 0.5m N of junction with A489. Half hour to beach at Aberdovey. Small site, for forest and mountain walking. Open Easter-October.

Morben Isaf Camping Park, Derwenlas, Machynlleth, Powys SY20 8SE. *01654 781473.* Two miles south of Machynlleth, five star park, estuary view. Ideal for walking, fishing, birdwatching. Ten minutes from sandy beach.

Ty Craig Holiday Park, Llancynfelin, Machynlleth, Powys SY20 8PU. *01970 832339.* Mr R J & M B Rhodes. On B4353 1m from junction with A497 at Tre'r-Ddol. Small, sheltered site 3m from Borth less than 2m to beach. Open March 1-January 10.

Tynypwll Camping & Caravan Site, Dinas Mawddwy, Machynlleth, Powys. *01650 531326.* M & I Pugh. Cafe nearby. Caravan to let.

Montgomery

Bacheldre Watermill, Churchstoke, Montgomery, Powys SY15 6TE. *01588 620489.* Mr Tony Jay. About 2.5 miles west of Churchstoke, just off A489. Small, secluded site with 25 grassy, level pitches, most with hook-ups. Shower/toilet facilities all inclusive. Adjacent to 18th century working watermill. Graded: 4 stars. Open Easter-October.

Newtown

Llwyn Celyn Holiday Park, Adfa, Newtown, Powys SY16 3DG. *01938 810720.* Mr & Mrs P Fenton. Off B4390 at New Mills to Adfa. Through village, 1st left, 100yd on left. Peace and quiet. Outstanding views. Excellent walking. Steam railway. 1 hour to coast. Open March 1-January 1.

Tynycwm Camping Site, Aberhafesp, Newtown, Powys SY16 3JF. *01686 688651/0411 497424.* Mr D Richards. 7m NW of Newtown via A489 to Caerws, then B4569 N signposted Aberhafesp, cross B4568 (ignoring sign for Aberhafesp and continue to next crossroads, turn left signposted Bwlch-y-Garreg, farm and site)1 mile on right. Quiet site on hill farm with beautiful views. Open May-October.

Oswestry

Henstent Caravan Park, Llangynog, Oswestry, Powys SY10 0EP. *01691 860479.* David & Angela Rabbetts. Off the B4391 midway between Bala and Oswestry. Ideal walking area. Small site on bank of river Tanat. Heated toilets. Two inns 5 minutes' walk serving food. Open March 1-October 31.

Presteigne

Court Cottage, Walton, Presteigne, Powys LD8 2PY. *01544 350259.* Elwyn Price. On A44, 5m W of Presteigne, opposite Crown Hotel in Walton. Beautiful unspoilt countryside. Fully equipped 6-berth holiday caravan available for hire.

Rockbridge Park, Presteigne, Powys LD8 2NF. *01547 560300.* Mr R M Deakins. 1m W of Presteigne on B4356 towards Whitton and Llanbister. A small site in beautiful surroundings. Close to Offa's Dyke. Open April-October.

Rhayader

Wyeside Caravan & Camping Site, Llangurig Road, Rhayader, Powys LD6 5LB. *01597 810183.* info@wyeside camping.co.uk. www.wyesidecamping.co.uk. Mr K Brumwell. On the bank of river Wye. Adjoining Rhayader to Aberystwyth road (A470). Pleasant riverside situation. 5 minutes' walk to Rhayder town centre. Fees on application. Graded: 4 stars. Open February 1-end November.

Welshpool

Bank Farm, Middletown, Welshpool, Powys SY21 8EJ. *01938 570526.* gill@bankfarmcaravans.fsnet.co.uk. Mrs G Corfield. On A458 13.5m W of Shrewsbury. On Shrewsbury to Welsh coast route. Overnight stop. Fees on application. Caravans for hire. Holiday cottage available. SAE for brochure. Graded: 4 stars. Open March 1-October 31.

Henllan Caravan Park, Llangyniew, Welshpool, Powys SY21 9EJ. *01938 810554.* www.ukparks.com. Ms S Evans. 6 miles west of Welshpool, approached by a lane 0.5 mile off the Welshpool to Dolgellau road. Situated on meadow land adjoining the River Banwy. Pitch and Putt course. Fishing. Open March 1-October 31.

SNOWDONIA

Betws Y Coed

Tan Aeldroch Farm, Nr Pont Y Pant, Betws Y Coed, Snowdonia LL25 0LZ. *01690 750225.* Rebecca Taylorson. From Betws Y Coed follow A470 to Dolwyddelan, pass under railway viaduct, 0.5m turn left at farm sign. Tranquil and spacious riverside site. 3 touring caravans. 1 static and B&B. Open April 1-October 1.

SWANSEA

Gower

Three Cliffs Bay Caravan & Camping Park, North Hills Farm, Penmaen, Gower, Swansea SA3 2HB. *01792 371218.* D G & J M Beynon. Open April 1-October 31.

Llangennith

Hillend Camping Park, Llangennith, Swansea SA3 1JD. *01792 386204.* G Howells. Level 13 acre site adjacent to Rhossili Bay and National Trust land, 15 miles from Swansea on B4295. Britain's first area of outstanding natural beauty. Off licence. Children's play area. Surfing and canoeing nearby. Write or phone for details. Open April-October.

Llanmadoc

Llanmadoc Camping Site, Llanmadoc, Swansea SA3 1DE. *01792 386202.* Mr A C Price. On NW corner of Gower Peninsula.14m from Swansea via Llanrhidian and local roads. Holiday situation near beach and in area of outstanding beauty. Fees on application. Open April-October.

Morriston

Riverside Caravan Park (Feelfree Ltd), Ynysforgan Farm, Morriston, Swansea SA6 6QL. *01792 775587.* Mr & Mrs Brian Parker. Leave M4 at junction 45, direct access from roundabout under motorway in Swansea direction. 200yd from junction 45. No large dogs accepted. Graded: 2 stars.

Oxwich Bay

Greenways Leisure Park, Oxwich BaySwansea SA3 1LY. *01792 390220.* james@whitefordbayleisure.fsbusiness.co.uk. Mr & Mrs M Mead. From Swansea, take the A4118 Gower road for 12m to Oxwich. Follow road for 1.5m, straight over crossroads. Well-drained site is 150yds on right, on gentle slope with tarmac roads. Beach 2min drive away. Couples and families only. Family bar. Swimming pool. Children's play area. Open March 1-December 31.

Oxwich Camping Park, Oxwich, Swansea SA3 1LS. *01792 390777.* Miss C A Short. A4118 from Swansea for 10 miles. Turn left signpost Oxwich, after 1 mile turn right. After 500 yards turn right. A quite, secluded site family site, surrounded by trees in the heart of the beautiful Gower Peninsula. Graded: 3 stars. Open April-September.

Pen-y-cae

Maes-yr-Eglwys Farm, Pen-y-cae, Swansea SA9 1GS. *01639 730849.* Mr Ronald Watts. On A4067 5m NW of Ystradgynlais and 24m from Swansea. Mountain scenery. Entrance next church half mile on Sennybridge side of Dan-yr-Ogof caves. Fees on application. Open May 15-September 30.

Port Eynon

Newpark Holiday Park, Port Eynon, Swansea SA3 1NP. *01792 390292.* Llechwedd Slate Mines. A4118 14m from Swansea approaching Port Eynon. Entrance to site on left. Scenic views over Bristol Channel, beautiful walks, good food at local pubs and restaurants. Graded: 2 stars. Open April-October.

Rhossilli

Pitton Cross Caravan Park, Pitton Cross, Rhossilli, Swansea SA3 1PL. *01792 390593.* enquiries@pittoncross.co.uk. www. pitton cross.co.uk. Mr Roger Button. From Swansea—A4118 to Scurlage 16 miles, turn right signposted Rhossili, site two miles on left. Level site. From £45 per week off-peak season. Open April-October.
🏕🚐⚡📺♨⚓☉⛽🔥🔋🏪🚻🦽🍴♿🚿🍼⛵⚓✈

VALE OF GLAMORGAN

Cowbridge

Llandow Touring Caravan Park, Llandow, Cowbridge, Vale of Glamorgan CF7 7PB. *01446 794527/792462.* enquiries @llandow.com. www.llandowcaravanpark.com. Mr A Evans & Mrs S Evans. Take the M4, leave at junction 33 to Culverhouse Cross to A48. Bypass Cowbridge, follow brown tourist signs off the A48. Secure caravan storage. Open February 1-November 30.
🏕🚐📺♨⚓☉⚓⛽🔥🔋🏪♿🍴✈🚿⛵☉⚓

Llantwit Major

Acorn Camping & Caravanning, Rosedew Farm, Hamlane South, Llantwit Major, Vale of Glamorgan CF61 1RP. *01446 794024.* acorncampsite@aol.com. www.campingand caravansites.co.uk. Mr D & Mrs S D Bradley. From M4 leave at junction 33 and follow signs for Cardiff Airport then Llantwit Major B4265. Camp site is signposted from main road. Graded: 4 stars. Open February 1-December 8.
🏕🚐⚡📺♨⚓☉⚓⛽🔥🔋🏪♿🍴✈🚿⛵☉⚓

Penarth

Lavernock Point Holiday Estate, Fort Road, Penarth, Vale of Glamorgan CF6 2XQ. *029 2070 7310.* 2.5m S of Penarth via B4267 Penarth/Barry road. Fort Road to Lavernock Point. Holiday site near beach. Open May-September.
🏕📺🔋☉⚓🔥🔋♨⚓🏪🍴♿🍴♿🚿⛵☉⚓✈🔋

WREXHAM

Bangor-on-Dee

Camping & Caravanning Club Site - Bangor-on-Dee, c/o Bangor-on-Dee Racecourse, Overton Road, Bangor-on-Dee, Wrexham LL13 0DA. *01978 781009.* www.campingandcara vanningclub.co.uk. The Camping & Caravanning Club Ltd. From Whitchurch take A525 to 'Bangor Is y Coed' signpost. Turn right before bridge and right at racecourse signpost into Bangor village. Keep left into B5069 and under bridge. Site 0.5m on right. 5 acres with 100 pitches. Dogs welcome. Open April-October.
🏕🚐📺♨⚓☉⚓⛽🔥🔋🏪♿🍴✈☉

Ruabon

James Caravan Park, Ruabon, Wrexham LL14 6DW. *01978 820148.* ray@carastay.demon.co.uk. Mr Bailey. 5m SW of Wrexham off A539 near junction with A483. 5m E of Llangollen. Leisure centre nearby. Fees on application. Graded: 3 stars.
🏕🚐📺♨☉⚓⛽🔥🏪🍴♿✿☀

Wrexham

The Plassey Touring Caravan & Leisure Park, Eyton, Wrexham, Wrexham LL13 0SP. *01978 780277.* enquiries@the plassey.co.uk. www.theplassey.co.uk. Mr J S Brookshaw. 4.5m S of Wrexham via A483, turn L on to B5426 follow signs to Plassey, site 1.5m on left. Indoor swimming pool, badminton, sauna, 9 hole golf course, craft centre, unique restaurant, real ale brewery. Graded: 5 stars. Open March-November.
🏕🚐⚡📺♨⚓⚓✖☉⚓⛽🔥🔋⚓🏪🍴♿🍴✈🔋🚿⛵☉⚓✈

SCOTLAND

ABERDEEN

Aberdeen

Hazlehead Caravan Park & Camp Site, Groats Road, Aberdeen, Aberdeen AB1 8BL. *01224 321268.* Aberdeen City Council. From city centre via Union Street, Albyn Place, Queens Road. From ring road A947, turn W at Queens Road (A944). Booking essential at peak periods. Site brochure available. Fees on application. Graded: 3 stars. Open April-September.

Maryculter

Lower Deeside Holiday & Leisure Park, Maryculter, Aberdeen AB12 5FX. *01224 733860.* Mrs A K Mitchell. On the B9077 South Deeside road, 6m from Aberdeen, 10m from Stonehaven and 10m from Banchory. Attractive country site. Ideal for touring Royal Deeside. Graded: 4 stars. Open January-December.

ABERDEENSHIRE

Aboyne

Camping & Caravanning Club Site - Tarland, Tarland, Aboyne, Aberdeenshire AB34 4UP. *01339 881388.* www.campingandcaravanningclub.co.uk. The Camping & Caravanning Club. Approaching Tarland from SW on B9119, bear left before bridge, continue for 600yd. Site on left. Close to the village of Tarland, about 6m from Aboyne. The area is paradise for walkers and anglers. 90 pitches set in 8 acres. Caravans, motor caravans and tents accepted. Non-members welcome. Some caravan holiday homes available for purchase. Open March-October.

Alford

Haughton House Caravan Park, Alford, Aberdeenshire AB33 8NA. *01975 562107.* Aberdeenshire Regional Council. 1m from Alford on Montgarrie Road. Sheltered site. Nature trails. No pets in self-catering accommodation. Graded: 4 stars. Open April-September.

Ballater

Ballater Caravan Site, Anderson Road, Ballater, Aberdeenshire AB3 5QW. *01339 755727/01569 768358.* Aberdeenshire Council. 0.25m from town centre, site is off A93 Aberdeen to Braemar situated by river Dee. Nearby golf course. Bicycle hire from nearby garage. Open April-October.

Banchory

Campfield Caravan Site, Glassel, Banchory, Aberdeenshire AB31 4DN. *01339 882250.* I & P Gray. On A980 5m N of Banchory and 2m S of Torphins. Deeside hills. Fees on application. Graded: 4 stars. Open April-September.

Feughside Caravan Park, Strachan, Banchory, Aberdeenshire AB31 6NT. *01330 850669.* Mr Graham Hay. From Banchory take B974 to Strachan, then B976 for Aboyne, 2 miles on turn right at Feughside Inn. Park is 100yd on. Quiet

family run park in picturesque location. Ideal touring area. Takeaway meals at adjacent pub. Shops 2m. Graded: 4 stars. Open Easter/April 1-mid October.

Silver Ladies Caravan Park, Strachan, Banchory, Aberdeenshire AB31 6NL. *01330 822800.* admin@silver ladies.co.uk. www.silverladies.co.uk. Normanhurst Enterprises Ltd. Approx 2 miles from Banchory on the B974 Fettercairn road. Situated in the lovely valley of the Feugh. Golf course and pony trekking centres nearby. Park provides sports area and games room. Graded: 4 stars. Open April 1-October 31.

Banff

Banff Links Caravan Site, Airnavaig, Boyndie Road, Banff, Aberdeenshire AB4 2JD. *01261 812228.* Banff & Buchan District Council.1m W of Banff. Turn N off A98 on to B9139. 150yds turn right to site. By sandy beach. Graded: 3 stars. Open Last Friday March-4th Monday October.

Wester Bonnyton Farm Park, Gamrie , Banff, Aberdeenshire AB45 3EP. *01261 832470.* Ms Clare Doyle. On Moray Firth, 2m E of Banff/Macduff on B9031, about 1 mile from the A98, main Banff/Fraserburgh road. Small site. Facilities for children. Dogs allowed. Graded: 2 stars. Open March-October.

Fraserburgh

Esplanade Site, Harbour Road, Fraserburgh, Aberdeenshire AB42 1NS. *01463 510041.* B B D C, Leisure & Recreation Department. Near S entrance to Fraserburgh right at roundabout to Harbour road. Site entrance on right. Fees on application. Graded: 2 stars.

Huntly

Huntly Castle Caravan Park, The Meadows, Huntly, Aberdeenshire AB54 4UJ. *01466 794999.* enquiries@huntly castle.co.uk. www.huntlycastle.co.uk. Mr & Mrs Hugh Ballantyne. Follow sign on A96 Huntly bypass. Cooking shelters, 5 minute walk to town. Large indoor activity centre with children's playground. Ideal touring base for whisky, castle and coastal trails. Open March 21-November 2.

McRobert Park Caravan Site, Aberchirder, Huntly, Aberdeenshire. *01466 780510.* W Bremner. Open June 1-September 30.

Johnshaven

Wairds Park Caravan Site, Montrose, Johnshaven, Aberdeenshire DD10 0HD. *01561 362395.* Mrs E Adam. Signposted on A92 at Johnshaven. Three miles north of St Cyrus. Nine miles north of Montrose. Overnight stop, Edinburgh and north, or touring centre near sea. Graded: 4 stars. Open April-October.

Kintore

Hillhead Caravan Park, Kintore, Aberdeenshire AB51 0YX. *01467 632809.* enquiries@hillheadcaravan.co.uk. www.hillhead caravan.co.uk. Mr D G Smith & Mr A Ainge. From south leave A96 at Broomhill roundabout 3rd exit. From north stay on A96 past Kintore (Do not enter Kintore). Leave at Broomhill roundabout 1st exit. follow brown/white caravan signs on to B994. In 0.25m turn left B994 signposted Kemnay. In 2m turn right signpost Kintore. Park 1m on right. Graded: 4 stars. Caravan storage. AA 3 pennant. RAC approved. Thistle Award.

🚐🚲📺♿⚓☺☻♨🔥🔥🔋▥🏠🗖🏊✿❀♀♂♪♪✓🌙↺↝🔍

Laurencekirk

Brownmuir Caravan Park, Fordoun, Laurencekirk, Aberdeenshire AB30 1SJ. *01561 320786.* brownmuircaravanpark @talk21.com. www.brownmuircaravanpark.co.uk. Mr M Bowers & Mrs J Bowers. Off A90 4m N of Laurencekirk, 9m S of Stonehaven, turn right at village of Fourdon, from Laurencekirk turn left at village, site on right after 1m. Quiet, sheltered site. Graded: 3 stars. 3 pennant AA. Open April-October.

🚐🚲📺♿⚓☺☻♨🔥🔥🗖🏠🗖♪✓🌙

Dovecot Caravan Park, Northwaterbridge, Laurencekirk, Aberdeenshire AB30 1QL. *01674 840630.* info@dovecotcaravan park.com. www.dovecotcaravanpark.com. Mrs A Mowatt. Off A90, 5 miles north of Brechin. Turn left at RAF Edzell road. Site is 500yd on left. Well-maintained, sheltered park. Excellent base for touring. Graded: 4 stars. Open April-mid October.

🚐🚲📺♿⚓✗☺☻♨🔥🔋🗖🏠🗖♪🌙✓

Macduff

Myrus Caravan Site, Macduff, Aberdeenshire AB45 3QP. *01261 812845.* Mr & Mrs J Garden. On A947 1m S of Macduff. Overnight stop for tents. Fees on application. Open April-October.

🚐🚲📺⚓✗☺☻♨🔥🔋♠🏠🗖♬🎗♪♪🌙↺🔍

Montrose

East Bowstrips Caravan Park, St Cyrus, Montrose, Aberdeenshire DD10 0DE. *01674 850328.* tully@bowstrips. freeserve.co.uk. www.ukparks.co.uk/eastbowtrips. P M & G Tully. Approx 6m N of Montrose on A92. From S (Montrose) enter St Cyrus, pass hotel, 1st left, 2nd right. From N (Aberdeen) enter St Cyrus 1st right, 2nd right. Quiet, family park about 1m from beach and nature reserve. Excellent facilities. Ideal touring base. AA 4 pennants. Graded: 5 stars. Open April-October.

🚐🚲📺♿⚓🔋⚓☺☻♨🔥🔥🗖🏠♪🌙♪↺

Peterhead

Aden Country Park Caravan Park, Mintlaw, Peterhead, Aberdeenshire AB42 8FQ. *01771 623460.* Banff & Buchan District Council. Access to site is 9m W of Peterhead off A950 at Mintlaw stn. Attractive woodland site set in 230-acre country park. Graded: 5 stars. Open Last Friday March-4th Monday October.

🚐🚲📺♿⚓🔋⚓✗☺☻♨🔥🔥🗖🏠♪🌙↺

Portsoy

Portsoy Links Park, Portsoy, Aberdeenshire. *01261 42695.* Banff & Buchan District Council. Within Portsoy town boundary. In Portsoy turn N off A98 on to Church Street. After l00yd turn right onto Institute Street. Fees on application. Graded: 4 stars. Open Last Friday March-4th Monday October.

🚐🚲📺⚓🔋✗☺☻♨🔥🔥🗖🏠♪🌙✓

Sandend Caravan Park, Sandend, Portsoy, Aberdeenshire AB4. *01261 842660.* Mrs J Winfield. 3m W of Portsoy on the A98 Aberdeen to Inverness road. Ideally situated next to the safe sandy beach of Sandend with magnificent views over the Moray Firth. Graded: 4 stars. Open April 1-October 31.

🚐🚲📺♿⚓🔋⚓☺☻♨🔥🔥🗖🏠🗖♪🕏♀🔋♪♪🌙↺♀

Stonehaven

Queen Elizabeth Caravan Park, Queen Elizabeth Park, Stonehaven, Aberdeenshire AB39 2RD. *01569 764041.* Aberdeenshire Council. Follow beach signs off main Aberdeen road at north end of town. Large family site, holiday statics, caravan and camping pitches. Graded: 3 stars. Open April-October.

🚐🚲📺♿⚓🔋⚓☺☻♨🔥🔥🗖🏠🗖🏊♨▲🎗♂♪🌙↺🔍

Turriff

Turriff Caravan Park, Station Road, Turriff, Aberdeenshire AB53 7ER. *01888 562205.* Aberdeenshire Council. 0.5m from Turriff town centre off A947 Aberdeen to Banff road 9m S of Banff. Site is adjacent to attractive park with children's play area, crazy golf, bowling and boating pond. Sports centre. Dogs on leads allowed. Graded: 4 stars. Open April-October.

🚐🚲📺♿🔋⚓✗☺☻♨🔥🔥♠🏠🗖♪♪🌙↺🔍

ANGUS

Brechin

Glenesk Caravan Park, By Edzell, Brechin, Angus DD9 7YP. *01356 648565.* Mr J K Gray. From A90, Aberdeen to Dundee, B966 to Edzell. 1.5m N of Edzell, signposted Glenesk. Park 1m from junction. Attractive woodland site, small fishing lake. Many local attractions and outdoor activities. Graded: 3 stars. Open April-October.

🚐🚲📺♿⚓☺☻♨♨🔥🔋♠🏠🗖🔲♪♪🌙✓↺🔍

Forfar

Drumshademuir Caravan Park, Roundyhill, By Glamis, Forfar, Angus DD8 1QT. *01575 573284.* easson@uku.co.uk. Ian & Pat Easson. On A928 between Glamis and Kirriemuir. Licensed bar with food. Gliding. AA 4 pennant. Graded: 4 stars. 🚐🚲♨📺♿⚓ 🔋✗☺☻♨🔥🔋♠🏠🗖♨♪🎗♪🌙↺🔍

ARGYLL & BUTE

ARGYLL

Barcaldine by Connel

Camping & Caravanning Club Site - Oban, Barcaldine by Connel, Argyll PA37 1SG. *01631 720348*. www.campingandcaravanningclub.co.uk. The Camping & Caravanning Club Ltd. On main A828 Oban to Fort William road. 6m N of Connel Bridge. All units accepted. Non-members welcome. Well located for Highlands and islands. Caravans, motor caravans and tents accepted. 75 pitches set in 4.5 acres. Open April-October.

Morvern

Fiunary Caravan & Camping Park, Morvern, Argyll PA34 5XX. *01967 421 225*. Philip & Joanne Herderson. Leave A82 8m S of Fort William. Cross Corran-Ardgour car ferry. Follow s/p to Lochaline (A884) 31m, turn R on B849. 4.5m to site. Open May-September.

Mull of Kintyre

The Machrihanish Caravan & Camping Park, East Trodigal, Machrihanish, Campbeltown, Mull of Kintyre, Argyll PA28 6PT. *01586 810366*. steveandjacquie@mullcamp.freeserve.co.uk. www.mullcamp.com. Steve & Jacquie Boyles. A82 Glasgow to Tarbet along Loch Lomond. At Tarbet take A83 through Inveraray, Lochgilphead to Campbeltown. In town centre take B843 to Machrihanish, entrance R, 200yd past chimney. 7 acres 95 pitches motorhomes, caravans, tents. Open March 30-October 31.

ARGYLL & BUTE

Ardlui

Ardlui Camping Site, Ardlui, Argyll & Bute G83 7EB. *01301 704243*. Mrs A Squires. Site is at Ardlui on A82. On the shores of Loch Lomond. Graded: 3 stars.

Argyll

Glendaruel Caravan Park, Argyll, Argyll & Bute PA22 3AB. *01369 820267*. Quin & Anne Craig. Off A886. Near Kyles of Bute. Peaceful small park within 22-acre country estate. Campers' kitchen and shelter. Enjoy walking and bird watching. Sea trout and salmon fishing. Sea 5m. Adults only. Bicycles for hire. Thistle Award. David Bellamy Silver Conservation Award. Graded: 5 stars. Open April-October.

Arrochar

Ardgartan Caravan & Camping Site, (Forestry Commission), Arrochar, Argyll & Bute G83 7AL. *01301 702293*. fe.holidays@forestry.gsi.gov.uk. www.forestholidays.co.uk. Forestry Commission (Forest Holidays). On A83 Inverary to Arrochar, (2m W of Arrochar). On shores of Loch Long, surrounded by magnificent mountain scenery of Argyll Forest Park. Brochure line: 01313 340066. Graded: 3 stars. Open March-November.

Campbeltown

Machribeg Caravan Site, Southend, Campbeltown, Argyll & Bute PA28 6RW. *01586 830249*. Mr J Barbour. 10m S of Campbeltown on B842. Dogs allowed on leads. Beside safe, sandy beach and 18-hole golf course. No booking required. Open Easter-September.

Carradale

Carradale Bay Caravan Site, Carradale, Argyll & Bute PA28 6QG. *01583 431665*. sales@carradalebay.abelgratis.com. Thomas Watson. Well-signposted site from Carradale village. Situated on a mile of golden sands, in an area of outstanding natural beauty. STB grading. Graded: 4 stars. Open Easter-September 30.

Dunoon

Gairletter Caravan Park, Blairmore, Dunoon, Argyll & Bute PA23 8TP. *01475 520794*. James Stirrat. On A880. 2 miles south of Ardentinny. Open March-October.

Stratheck Country Park, Loch Eck, Dunoon, Argyll & Bute PA23 8SG. *01369 840472*. enquiries@stratheck.com. www.stratheck.com. Dain Enterprises Ltd. 7m N of Dunoon on A815, on left 500 yards past Younger Botanic Gardens. Touring centre with licensed bar. Pets corner. Children's play area. Adventure playground. Scenic riverside location. Open March-October.

Inveraray

Argyll Caravan & Camping Park, Inveraray, Argyll & Bute PA32 8XT. *01499 302285*. Trustees of the Tenth Duke of Argyll. In a secluded position on the shores of Loch Fyne 2.5m from Inveraray. Ideal for touring many places of interest and excellent facilities on site. Fees on application. Graded: 4 stars. Open April 1-October 31.

Isle of Mull

Shieling Holidays, Craignure, Isle of Mull, Argyll & Bute PA65 6AY. *01680 812496*. www.shielingholidays.co.uk. David & Moira Gracie. From ferry pier at Craignure turn S on A849 (Bunessan). In 0.25m by church turn left into lane to site. Peaceful, by the sea. A short walk to ferry, shop, pub, castles and steam railway. Self-catering Shielings, hostel beds. Boats for hire. Laundry. Graded: 5 stars. Open April-October.

Lochgilphead

Lochgilphead Caravan Park, Bank Park, Lochgilphead, Argyll & Bute PA31 8MX. *01546 602003*. Mr I M Macdonald. At junction of A83 and A816. Set in area of outstanding scenic beauty. Sports centre nearby. Graded: 4 stars. Open April 1-October 31.

Luss

Inverbeg Holiday Park, Inverbeg, Luss, Argyll & Bute G83 8PD. *01436 860267*. Luss Estates. On A82, 4m N of Luss, on Loch Lomond with large beach, good boat launching. Excellent fishing from shore. Site is very clean and tidy. Restaurant nearby. Boat trips on loch nearby. Graded: 3 stars. Open March 1-October 31.

Oban

Arduaine Caravan & Camping Park, Arduaine, Kilmelford, Oban, Argyll & Bute PA34 4XA. *01852 200331*. Mr & Mrs John Rentoul. 4m S of Kilmelford via A816. On sea front. 20 miles S Oban. 20 miles N of Lochgilphead. Graded: 2 stars. Open March-October.

Crunachy Caravan & Camping Site, Taynuilt, Oban, Argyll & Bute PA35 1HT. *01866 822612.* Mr Angus Douglas. 14m E of Oban on A85 and 2m E of Taynuilt village. Touring centre or overnight stop. Dogs welcome. Fees on application. 9 acres at level grass site with 400 acres of rough woodland available for walking. Open March-November.

Oban Caravan & Camping Park, Gallanachmore Farm, Gallanach Road, Oban, Argyll & Bute PA34 4QH. *01631 562425.* info@obancaravanpark.com. www.obancaravanpark.com. Howard & Judy Jones. From N take A85 from S A816, follow signs to Gallanach from town centre roundabout. 2.5m from Oban. Set in an area of outstanding scenic beauty with excellent facilities. Childrens play area. Children under 5 years free. Pets welcome. Colour brochure available. Graded: 4 stars. Open April-October.

Oban Divers Caravan Park, Glenshellach Road, Oban, Argyll & Bute PA34 4QJ. *01631 562755.* obandivers@tesco.net. www.obandivers.co.uk. David Tye. A quiet park for caravans, motor caravans and tents in a beautiful setting developed over the last 15 years. Undercover facilities for cooking and barbeque. Large children's play area. Graded: 4 stars. Open mid March-November.

Tarbert

Killegruer, Woodend, Glenbarr, Tarbert, Argyll & Bute PA29 6XB. *01583 421241.* anne@littleson.fsnet.co.uk. Mr N Littleson. Minor road off A83 1n S of village. 12m N of Campbeltown. Site adjoins beach. Quadbiking nearby. Good touring centre. Site situated on west coast of Kintyre with views of Inner Hebrides and Northern Ireland. Open April-September.

Point Sands Caravan Park, Tayinloan, Tarbert, Argyll & Bute PA29 6XG. *01583 441263.* Point Sands Ltd. On A83 17m S of Tarbert, Loch Fyne. Beautiful seaside caravan park on edge of the Atlantic opposite Isle of Gigha. CCC listed. Graded: 3 stars.

Port Ban, Kilberry, Tarbert, Argyll & Bute PA29 6YD. *01880 770224.* portban@aol.com www.portban.com. Mrs J Sheldrick and Family. 15m SW of Ardrishaig off B8024,1m N of Kilberry. Beautiful, secluded seaside site with commanding views to Island of Jura. Scenic touring area and good hill walking, birdwatching and wildlife. Good facilities on site. Graded: 3 stars. Open April-October.

BORDERS

Coldingham

Scoutscroft Holiday Centre, St Abbs Road, Coldingham, Borders TD14 5NB. *01890 771338.* holidays@scoutscroft.co.uk. www.scoutscroft.co.uk. Mr & Mrs D & M Hamilton. Off A1 on to A1107 to Eyemouth. Follow signs to Coldingham, B6438 to St Abbs. Site signposted. Graded: 5 stars. Open March 1-October 31.

Galashiels

Kilknowe Caravan Site, Galashiels, Borders TD1 1QS. *01896 2124.* John Tait & Sons. 1m W of Galashiels to the right of A72 Peebles road. Fees on application. Open April-September.

Greenlaw Duns

Blackadder Touring Park, Greenlaw Caravan Park, Bank Street, Greenlaw, Duns, Borders TD10 6XX. *01361 810341.* www.scottishcampsite.com. Mr C Gregg. On the A697. 37 miles south of Edinburgh. Nine miles north of Coldstream in village of Greenlaw. Free fishing. Licensed bowling club. Open countryside views. Open March 1-November 30.

Hawick

Hawick Riverside Caravan Park, Hornshole Bridge, Hawick, Borders TD9 8SY. *01450 373785.* Mr & Mrs K Green. 2.5 miles north east of Hawick on A698 to Jedburgh. Riverside site with free fishing. Quiet, privately owned, 8-acre site. Leisure centre nearby. Dogs allowed. Fees on application. Open March-October 31.

Jedburgh

Camping & Caravanning Club Site - Jedburgh, Elliot Park, Edinburgh Road, Jedburgh, Borders TD8 6EF. *01835 863393.* www.campingandcaravanningclub.co.uk. The Camping & Caravanning Club Ltd. 3-acre site with 60 pitches accepting all units. On the northern outskirts of Jedburgh just off the A68, within walking distance of the town centre. Non-members welcome. Graded: 3 stars. Quiet and secluded site boundered by the river Jed. Caravans, motor caravans and tents accepted. Open May-October.

Jedwater Caravan Park, Jedburgh, Borders TD8 6PJ. *01835 869595.* jedwater@clara.co.uk. www.jedwater.co.uk. Mr Neil Gibson. Four miles south of Jedburgh off A68. Flat site with tarmac roads. On banks of river Jed. Graded: 4 stars. Open Easter-October.

Lilliardsedge Park, Jedburgh, Borders TD8 6TZ. *01835 830271.* Six miles north of Jedburgh on the A68. Sheltered touring centre. Fees on application Graded: 3 stars. Open April-October.

Kelso

Springwood Caravan Park, Kelso, Borders TD5 8LS. *01573 224596.* admin@spingwood.biz. www.springwood.biz. Mr Elliot. On A699. Privately owned park one mile from Kelso. Situated in wooded parkland in unspoilt Border countryside. No dogs allowed in tents. Graded: 4 stars. David Bellamy Gold Conservation Award. Open late March-late October.

Lauder

Camping & Caravanning Club Site - Lauder, Carfraemill, Oxton, Lauder, Borders TD2 6RA. *01578 750697.* www.campingandcaravanningclub.co.uk. Camping & Caravanning Club. From the town of Lauder, turn right at roundabout onto the A697, then left turn at the Carfraemill Hotel. Situated 24 miles south of Edinburgh, close to Thirlstane Castle and a good fishing area. Timber chalets available for holiday lets. 70 pitches available. Open March-October.

Thirlestane Castle Caravan & Camping Park, Lauder, Borders TD2 6RU. *07976 231032.* maitland-carew@compuserve.com. The Hon G. Maitland-Carew. Signposted just off the A68 and A697 28 miles south of Edinburgh. Park is set in beautiful parkland of an historical castle.

Just five minutes walk from Royal Burgh of Lauder, which has excellent shops and pub. Takeaway meals, cafe/restaurant and bottle gas supply all available nearby. Graded: 4 stars. Open April-October.

📞🅿️📷⊙🔥🛁📻⛽🅗 L ◢ ✓ ⚲

Melrose

Gibson Park Caravan Club Site, High Street, Melrose, Borders TD6 9RY. 01896 822969. www.caravanclub.co.uk. The Caravan Club. Scenic site close to centre of town. Separate WC/shower room for disabled. Fully redeveloped in 1998. 60 pitches. Non-members and tent campers admitted. Graded: 5 stars.

📞🅿️📷📶♿🛒⊙🔥🛁📻⛽🅗❄️ L ◢ ✓

Peebles

Crossburn Caravan Park, Edinburgh Road, Peebles, Borders EH45 8ED. 01721 720501. enquiries@crossburncaravans.co.uk. Crossburn Caravans. 0.5m N of Peebles on A703. AA sign at entrance. Overnight stop on route England to Edinburgh. Ideal touring base/night halt. AA 4 Pennants. Graded: 4 stars. Open April 1-October 31.

📞🅿️📷♿🛒⊙🔥🛁📻⛽🅗 L ◢ ◢ ✓ ∪ ⟲ ⚲

Rosetta Caravan & Camping Park, Rosetta Road, Peebles, Borders EH45 8PG. 01721 720770. The Clay family. Park is well signposted from Peebles. Graded: 4 stars. Open April-end October.

📞🅿️📷🛒⊙🔥🛒♜🅗 L ♀ ◢ ✓ ∪ ⟲ ⚲

Selkirk

Angecroft Caravan Park, Ettrick Valley, Selkirk, Borders TD7 5HY. 01750 62355. kevin@ettrickhall.com. www.angecroftpark.com. Kevin Newton. On B709 3m S of Tushielaw Inn. 26m from main A74 at Lockerbie. A warm welcome awaits at this quiet, peaceful, high-quality holiday park in the heart of the Scottish Borders. Graded: 3 stars. Open February 15-January 15.

📞🅿️📷♿🛒⊙🔥🛒📻 L ♀ 🛁 ◢ ∪

Honey Cottage Caravan Park, Hopehouise, Ettrick Valley, Selkirk, Borders TD7 5HU. 01750 62246/01539 531291. www.honeycottagecaravanpark.co.uk. C A & S Woof. 17 miles west of Hawick via the B711. From Selkirk take the B7009. Or from Langholm the B709. On the banks of Ettrick Water. Quiet site, shop on site. Pub and restaurant one mile away. Reduced facilities October to April. Graded: 3 stars.

📞🅿️📷📶⊙🔥🛒♜🅗❄️ L ♀ 🍴 🛁 ◢ ✓

Victoria Park Caravan & Camping Site, Buccleuch Road, Selkirk, Borders TD7 5DN. 01750 20897. Scottish Borders Council. By river Ettrick on edge of town, signposted from A7. Play area on site. Limited facilities in winter. Graded: 3 stars. Open April-October.

📞🅿️📷📶♿🛒✕⊙🔥🛒≋♜🅗🅣 ◢ ✓ ∪ ⟲ ⚲

CLACKMANNAN

Dollar

Riverside Caravan Park, Dollar, Clackmannan FK14 7LX. 01259 742896. info@riverside-caravanpark.co.uk. www.riverside-caravanpark.co.uk. Mr & Mrs A Small. 0.75m S of Dollar on B913 Dollar/Dunfermline road. Foot of Ochil Hills. Dollar Glen, Castle Campbell and Knockhill Racing Circuit nearby. Fees on application. 7 nights for 6 all season. Discounted rates OAPs. Open April-September.

📞🅿️📷🛒⊙🔥🛒♜🅗 L ◢ ✱ ◢ ✓ ⚲

DUMFRIES & GALLOWAY

Annan

Galabank Camping Site, Annan, Dumfries & Galloway DG12 5BQ. 01556 503806. Dumfries & Galloway Council. 0.5m N on B722 from junction with Main Street, Annan. Via Lady St, Thomas St and North St to site. A74 and A75 from Carlisle. Beside river Annan. Fees on application. Graded: 2 stars. Open May-September.

📞🅿️📷🛒✕⊙🔥♜🅗⇌ ◢ ✓ ⟲ ⚲

Castle Douglas

Auchenlarie Holiday Park, Gatehouse of Fleet, Castle Douglas, Dumfries & Galloway DG7 2EX. 01557 840251. Mr & Mrs Swalwell. Main A75, 4 miles west of Gatehouse of Fleet. Family caravan park overlooking the bay with extensive amenities. Families welcome. Graded: 4 stars. Open March 1-October 31.

📞🅿️➕📷♿🛒🛒✕⊙🔥🛒📻♜🅗 L ♀🍴🛁 ◢ ✓ ⟲

Barlochan Caravan Park, Palnackie, Castle Douglas, Dumfries & Galloway DG7 1PF. 01556 600256/01557 870267. ipc@barlochan.co.uk. www.gillespie-leisure.co.uk. Gillespie Leisure Ltd. Located on the A711 Dumfries to Kirkcudbright road. Advance bookings on 01557 870267. Friendly park overlooking Urr Estuary with coarse fishing loch (free). Mini golf. Playground. Pub nearby. Ideal touring base. Graded: 4 stars. Open April-October.

📞🅿️📷♿🛒⊙🔥🛒≋♜🅗 L ◢ ✓

Loch Ken Holiday Park, Parton, Castle Douglas, Dumfries & Galloway DG7 3NE. 01644 470282. office@lochkenholiday park.co.uk. www.lochkenholidaypark.co.uk. Mr & Mrs Mungo Bryson. 7m N of Castle Douglas on A713 just past village of Parton. Quiet site in an area of outstanding natural beauty. Boat, canoe and cycle hire on site. Direct access to the water from the park. Sandy beach and fishing. Pike, perch and roach. Barbecues allowed. Thistle Award. David Bellamy Gold Conservation Award. Graded: 4 stars. Open all year for tourers; open March-October for hire and holiday homes.

📞🅿️📷♿🛒⊙🔥🛒📻♜🅗 L ♀🛁 ◢ ✓ ∪ ⟲ ⚓ 🛥️

Lochside Park Caravan & Camping Site, Castle Douglas, Dumfries & Galloway DG7 1EZ. 01556 502949. Dumfries & Galloway Council. Just of A75. Site is located by Carlingwalk Loch, Castle Douglas. Fees on application. Graded: 3 stars. Open Easter-late October.

📞🅿️📷♿🛒✕⊙🔥🛒📻🅗🛁 ◢ ✓ ⟲ ⚲

Mossyard Caravan Site, Gatehouse-of-Fleet, Castle Douglas, Dumfries & Galloway DG7 2ET. 01557 840226. J McConchie & Sons. Located on the A75 four miles west of Gatehouse-of-Fleet. A quiet site near safe sandy beaches. Ideal for bathing and sailing. Graded: 4 stars. Open Easter-October.

📞🅿️📷📶⊙🔥🛒📻♜🅗🛥️ L ♀🍴🛁 ⟲

Dalbeattie

Castle Point Caravan Park, Rockcliffe, Dalbeattie, Dumfries & Galloway DG5 4QL. 01556 630248. kce22@dial.pipex.com Messrs J & J Bigham. From Dalbeattie take A710, after 5m turn right to Rockcliffe then left after 1m. Food shop one and half miles. Very quiet and clean. Overlooking sea and lovely estuary. Attractive walks and sheltered coves nearby. Open Easter to early-October.

📞🅿️📷📶♿🛒✕⊙🔥🛒📻♜🅗🛥️🛁 ◢ ✓ ∪ ⟲

DUMFRIES & GALLOWAY

Islecroft Caravan & Camping Site, Mill Street, Dalbeattie, Dumfries & Galloway DG5 4HE. *01556 610012.* Dumfries & Galloway Council. Site is in Dalbeattie. From A711 E on to B793 in Dalbeattie. Take first left at the Cross, along Mill Street into Islecroft Park. Family site within public park, easy access to town. No advance bookings. Fees on application. Graded: 3 stars. Open Easter to end-September.

🚐 🏠 🚾 🕭 ⚷ ⊙ 🔥 🅿 🚻 ⚓ ♪ ✓ ∪ ⚲

Kippford Holiday Park, Kippford, Dalbeattie, Dumfries & Galloway DG5 4LF. *01556 620636.* www.kippford holidaypark.co.uk. C R Aston. 3m S of Dalbeattie on A710 towards Kippford (seaside village). David Bellamy Conservation Gold Award. Graded: 5 stars. Hilly, part wooded setting, grassy. Level, sheltered. Cycle hire, shop, golf, walking, fishing, sailing nearby. Open March 1-October 31.

🚐 🏠 🚾 🕭🅻 🅻 ⊙ 🅲 🔥 🛢 🚻 🅿 🚻 ✿ 🅻 ⚓ ♪ ✓ ∪

Sandyhills Bay Leisure Park, Sandyhills, Dalbeattie, Dumfries & Galloway DG5 4 NY. *01387 780257/01557 870267.* camping@sandyhills-bay.co.uk. www.gillespie-leisure. co.uk. Gillespie Leisure Ltd. On A170 Dumfries to Dalbeattie. Award-winning park next finest beach in area. Spectacular coastal walks. Smugglers' caves. Fishing, riding and eating out within walking distance. Family camping. Graded: 4 stars. Open March 21-October 31.

🏠 ⚓ 🚾 🕭🅻 ⊙ 🅲 🔥 🛢 🚻 🅿 🅻 ♪ ✓ ∪ ⚲ ⚲

Dumfries

Lighthouse Leisure, Southerness, Dumfries, Dumfries & Galloway DG2 8AZ. *01387 880277.* Sylvia Robertson. A710 from Dumfries, via New Abbey. Southerness signposted on left. First house and office on right in village. Fully grassed, level site. Sweeping, sandy beaches. Golf course. Children's toytown. Leisure centre, heated pool, Mermaid bar. Sauna. 10-pin bowling. Graded: 3 stars. Open March 1-October 31.

🚐 🏠 ⚓ 🚾 🕭🅻🅻 ✕ ⊙ ⊘ 🔥 🛢 🚻 ⚓ 🅿 🅻 ♪ ✓

Mossband Caravan Park, Kirkgunzeon, Dumfries, Dumfries & Galloway DG2 8JP. *01387 760 208.* Mr & Mrs M Dempster. 8m from Dumfries on the A711. Ideal touring base. Children's play area. Graded: 2 stars. Open Easter-October.

🚐 🏠 🚾 🕭🅻 ✕ ⊙ ⊘ 🔥 🛢 ⚓ 🅿 🅻 ⚓ ♪ ✓ ∪ ⚲ ⚲ ⚲

Mouswald Caravan Park, Dumfries, Dumfries & Galloway DG1 4JS. *01387 83226.* Mr & Mrs S Walker. 6m S of Dumfries via A75 from Annan. Follow international caravan signs. Opening period on application. Graded: 2 stars.

🚐 🏠 🚾 ⊙ 🅲 🔥 🛢 🅿 🅻 ♪ ✓ ∪ ⚲

Park of Brandedleys, Crocketford, Dumfries, Dumfries & Galloway DG2 8RG. *01556 690250.* Mr A W McDonald. At SW end of village 200yd off A75, 9m SW of Dumfries. Fees on application. Graded: 4 stars.

🚐 🏠 ⚓ 🚾 🕭🅻 ✕ ⊙ 🅲 🔥 🛢 🚻 ⚓ 🅿 🚻 ✿ 🅻 🅿 ⚓ ♪ ✓ ∪ ⚲ ⚲ ⚲

Gretna

The Braids Caravan Park, Gretna, Dumfries & Galloway DG16 5DQ. *01461 337409.* Mr & Mrs H Copeland & Mr J Dalgliesh. On B721. Overnight stop. Easy access from M74, north and south. A75 west. Touring advice given. Graded: 4 stars.

🚐 🏠 ⚓ 🚾 🕭🅻 ✕ ⊙ 🅲 🔥 🛢 🚻 🅿 🚻 ≈ ✿ 🅻 🅿 🛢 ♪ ✓ ⚲ ⚲

Kirkbean

Southerness Holiday Village, Kirkbean, Dumfries & Galloway DG2 8AZ. *01387 880256/880281.* enquiries@souter ness.co.uk. www.southerness.co.uk. A710 south from Dumfries through New Abbey and Kirkbean. 1m through Kirkbean turn S on minor road to Southerness. Holiday site with good beaches. Full family facilities. Fees on application. Graded: 4 stars. Open March 1-October 31.

🚐 🏠 ⚓ 🚾 🕭🅻 ⚓ ✕ ⊙ 🅲 🔥 🛢 🚻 ⚓ 🅿 🅻 ♪ 🅣 🛢 ♪ ✓ ∪ ⚲ ⚲ ⚲

Kirkcudbright

Brighouse Bay Holiday Park, Borgue, Kirkcudbright, Dumfries & Galloway DG6 4TS. *01557 870267.* ipc@brig-house-bay.co.uk. www.gillespie-leisure.co.uk. Gillespie Leisure Ltd. Off B727 Kirkcudbright/Borgue. Hidden away within 1200 acres next to beach and bluebell woods. Exceptional amenities: indoor pool, 18 and 9-hole driving range golf. Clubhouse and Bistro. Slipway, pony trekking, mountain bikes. Quad bikes. 10-pin bowling. Lodges and caravans for sale and hire. Graded: 5 stars.

🚐 🏠 ⚓ 🚾 🕭🅻 ⚓ ✕ ⊙ 🅲 🔥 🛢 🚻 ⚓ 🅿 🚻 ✿ ⚲ 🅻 ⚓ ♪ ✓ ∪ ⚲

Seaward Caravan Park, Dhoon Bay, Kirkcudbright, Dumfries & Galloway DG6 4TS. *01557 331079/870267.* ipc@seaward-park.co.uk. www.gillespie-leisure.co.uk. Gillespie Leisure Ltd. On B727 Kirkcudbright/Borgue. Beautifully situated with panoramic views over bay. TV-hook ups. New leisure building. 9-hole golf. Sea angling. Beach picnic area nearby. Graded: 4 stars. Open March-October.

🚐 🏠 🚾 🕭🅻 ⚓ ⊙ 🅲 🔥 🛢 🚻 ⚓ 🅿 🅻 ♪ ✓ ∪ ⚲

Silvercraigs Caravan & Camping Site, Silvercraigs Road, Kirkcudbright, Dumfries & Galloway DG6 4BT. *01557 330123.* Dumfries & Galloway Council. In Kirkcudbright overlooking the town. Approach via silvercraigs Road. Fees on application. No advance booking. Graded: 4 stars. Open Easter to late October.

🚐 🏠 🚾 🕭🅻 ✕ ⊙ 🔥 🅿 🚻 🅿 ♪ ✓ ∪ ⚲ ⚲

Lochmaben

Kirk Loch Brae Caravan Site, Lochmaben, Dumfries & Galloway DG12 6AQ. *01556 503806.* Dumfries & Galloway Council. In Lochmaben, enter via Kirkloch Brae. Graded: 3 stars. Open Easter-October.

🚐 🏠 🚾 🕭 ✕ ⊙ 🅿 🚻 🛢 ♪ ✓ ⚲

Lockerbie

Cressfield Caravan Park, Ecclefechan, Nr Lockerbie, Dumfries & Galloway DG11 3DR. *01576 300702.* Mr R Thomas-Evelyn. Leave A74(M) junction 19 at Ecclefechan. Follow B7076 for half mile to south side of village, signposted. 10 miles north of Gretna, 5 miles south of Lockerbie. Peaceful country park. Good touring base and night halt. Superb facilities, free showers. Level tent field. Putting green. Children's play area. Cafe/restaurant nearby. Graded: 5 stars.

🚐 🏠 🚾 🕭🅻 ⚓🅻 ⊙ 🅲 🔥 🛢 🚻 🅿 ✿ 🅻 ♪ ✓

Halleaths Caravan Park, Halleaths, Lockerbie, Dumfries & Galloway DG11 1NA. *01387 810630.* halleathscaravanpark @btopenworld.com. www.caravansitefinder.co.uk/sites. Gordon Hoey. From Lockerbie on A74 take A709 to Lochmaben. Park is 0.5m to right after crossing river Annan. Kitchen area with microwave oven. Graded: 4 stars. Open March 15-November 15.

🚐 🏠 🚾 🕭🅻 ⚓🅻 ⊙ 🅲 🔥 🛢 🚻 ⚓ ≈ 🅿 ♪ 🛢 ♪ ✓ ⚲

Hoddom Castle & Caravan Park, Hoddom, Lockerbie, Dumfries & Galloway DG11 1AS. *01576 300251.* hoddom-castle@aol.com www.hoddomcastle.co.uk. The Factor Hoddom & Kinmount Estates. Exit A74M (junction 19) follow signs. Peaceful site. Bar, restaurant, golf, tennis, fishing, nature trails. AA Best Scottish Campsite 1996/97. Graded: 5

stars. Calor Gas 2000 Best Park in Great Britain. Open April 1-October 31.

King Robert the Bruce's Cave Camping & Caravan Site, Cove Farm, Kirkpatrick Fleming, Lockerbie, Dumfries & Galloway DG11 3AT. *01461 800285.* enquiries@brucescave. co.uk. www.brucescave.co.uk. Mr Andrew Ritchie & Mrs Jan Ritchie. Site is on W outskirts of town. Leave A74 at sign to Kirkpatrick. Then follow all signs to Bruce's Cave. Ancient monument of King Robert the Bruce's Cave in site grounds. Restricted facilities October-March. BMX bikes on site. Quad riding, clay pigeon shooting and paintball available nearby.

Moffat

Camping & Caravanning Club Site - Moffat, Hammerlands Farm, Moffat, Dumfries & Galloway DG10 9QL. *01683 220436.* www.campingandcaravanningclub.co.uk. The Camping & Caravanning Club Ltd. 10-acre site with 180 pitches. On entering the town of Moffat turn right on to the A708 to Selkirk. The site approach is on the right just before the Weave Inn. Dogs welcome. Non-members welcome. Caravans, motor caravans and tents accepted. Open March-October.

Craiglands Country Park, Beattock, Moffat, Dumfries & Galloway DG10 9RB. *01683 300591.* C Harrison. M74, J15. Wild life and loch. Walks. Dogs on leads.

Newton Stewart

Burrowhead Holiday Village, Isle of Whithorn, Newton Stewart, Dumfries & Galloway DG8 8JB. *01988 500252.* admin@burrowhead.co.uk. www.cinque-portsleisure.com. Cinque Ports Leisure. A714 and A746 S from Newton Stewart to Isle of Whithorn. Beside sea. Graded: 3 stars. Open March 1-October 31.

Castle Cary Holiday Park, Creetown, Newton Stewart, Dumfries & Galloway DG8 7DQ. *01671 820 264.* Mr A P Henryson-Caird. Olde worlde country inn and sun patio. Restaurant. Bar meals. Dish-washing area. Indoor and outdoor heated pools. Games room. Snooker room. Mountain bikes.

Castlewigg Caravan Park, Whithorn, Newton Stewart, Dumfries & Galloway DG8 8DL. *01988 500616.* eastlewigg.park@btconnect.com. www.ukparks.co.uk/ castlewigg. Mr Ted & Mrs Kath Reeder. Between Sorbie & Whithorn on A746. Real Scotland, real close with gulf stream climate. Tranquil countryside setting. Excellent for walking, cycling, bird watching, golf and relaxation. Holiday home hire also available. Open 1 March-31 October.

Cock Inn Caravan Park, Auchenmaig, Newton Stewart, Dumfries & Galloway DG8 0JT. *01581 500227.* Mr P Snowden. 5m from Glenluce. From A75 at Glenluce take A747 to Port William. Graded: 3 stars. Open March 1-October 31.

Creebridge Caravan Park, Newton Stewart, Dumfries & Galloway DG8 6AJ. *01671 402324.* Mr & Mrs J Sharples. 0.25m E of Newton Stewart off A75. Bowling nearby. Short walk to town centre. Graded: 3 stars. Open March-November.

Glenluce Caravan Park, Glenluce, Newton Stewart, Dumfries & Galloway DG8 0QR. *01581 300412.* www.glen lucecaravan.freeserve.uk. J & P Marsden. 10m E of Stranraer on A75. Site entrance is at the phone kiosk in centre of Glenluce village. Secluded touring site 1m from sea. Ideal for walking, bowling and trekking. Fees on application. Graded: 4 stars. Open March-October.

Glentrool Holiday Park, Bargrennan, Newton Stewart, Dumfries & Galloway DG8 6RN. *01671 840280.* enquiries@glentroolholidaypark.co.uk. www.glentroolholiday.co.uk. Mr & Mrs Moore. Off A714. Ideal for touring and exploring Galloway Forest and hills. Graded: 4 stars. AA 3 pennant. Trout fishing pond on site. Well-behaved dogs welcome. Holiday homes for hire. Cafe/restaurant nearby. Open March-October.

Knock School Caravan Park, Monreith, Newton Stewart, Dumfries & Galloway DG8 8NJ. *01988 700414/409.* www.knockschool.com. Mrs P R Heywood. On A747 3m south of Port William. Very small, peaceful touring park. Hard standing pitches. Entrance by golf course and beaches. Bird-watching, archaeology and gardens locally. Open Easter-September.

Whitecairn Farm Caravan Park, Glenluce, Newton Stewart, Dumfries & Galloway DG8 0NZ. *01581 300267.* enquiries@whitecairncaravans.co.uk. www.whitecairncaravans.co.uk. Mr & Mrs Robert Rankin. 1.5m N of Glenluce village and 2m from A75. Small family-run park within easy reach of many local attractions. Caravans for hire or sale. Fully serviced pitches for touring caravans and campers. Dogs welcome. Graded: 4 stars.

Port William

Monreith Sands Holiday Park, Monreith, Port William, Dumfries & Galloway DG8 9LJ. *01988 700218.* A714 from Newton Stewart to Port William. 2m S on A747 to Monreith. 300yd to sandy beach. 0.75m to golf course. Open April-October.

West Barr Farm Caravan Park, Port William, Dumfries & Galloway DG8 9QS. *01988 700367.* Mr J Stewart. On the A747 coast road 2m N of Port William. Holiday site with farm interest and historic centres. Open April-October.

Portpatrick

Castle Bay Caravan Park, Portpatrick, Dumfries & Galloway DG9 9AA. *01776 810462.* Mr R Vautrinot. Enter Portpatrick on A77 past War Memorial. Left opposite Old Mill Restaurant for 0.75m under old railway bridge. 22 acres extending to Irish Sea. Studio cinema on the park. Graded: 3 stars. Open March 1-October 31.

Stranraer

Aird Donald Caravan Park, Stranraer, Dumfries & Galloway DG9 8RN. *01776 702025.* aird@minnamu-net.com www.aird. donald.co.uk. Mr H Cassie. On A75 in town. Small, sheltered, level holiday site. Dogs welcome. Leisure centre with swimming pool half mile from site. Near to ferries for Ireland. Graded: 4 stars. Open March-October.

Cairnryan Caravan Park, Cairnryan, Stranraer, Dumfries & Galloway DG9 8QX. *01581 200231.* Charles Dobson. 5 miles north of Stranraer on the A77, directly opposite the P & O ferry terminal for Larne. Family-run park with licensed club. Graded: 4 stars. Open April 1-October 31.

Clashwhannon Caravan Site & Public House, Drummore, Stranraer, Dumfries & Galloway DG9 9QE. *01776 840632/840474.* Mr P Griffiths. 0.75m N of Drummore to the E of A716. Site is on edge of beach. 2m from Logan Botanical Gardens and within easy reach of Mull of Galloway lighthouse. All hire fleet fully serviced. Seasonal nightclub on site. Fees on application. Open March-October.

Galloway Point Holiday Park, Portree Farm, Portpatrick, Stranraer, Dumfries & Galloway DG9 9AA. *01776 810561.* www.gallowaypointholidaypark.co.uk. Adam & Elizabeth Mackie. 75m from Dumfries. A77 south from Glasgow on entering Port Patrick. Take 1st left quarter mile. Park on right. AA 3 pennant. AA Environment Award. RAC. David Bellamy Silver Conservation Award. Open Easter-mid October.

Sandhead Caravan Park, Sandhead, Stranraer, Dumfries & Galloway DG9 9JN. *01776 830296.* Mr A McLean. Off A716. Open April 1-October 31.

Sands of Luce Caravan Park, Sandhead, Stranraer, Dumfries & Galloway DG9 9JR. *01776 830456.* Mr & Mrs J W Sime. At junction of A716-B7084 6 miles south of Stranraer, beside sandy beach. Dogs allowed on leads. Graded: 4 stars. Open March 15-October 31.

Sunnymeade Caravan Park, Portpatrick, Stranraer, Dumfries & Galloway DG9 8LN. *01776 810293.* info@sunny meade98.freeserve.co.uk. Mr & Mrs E Gray. A77 Stranraer to Portpatrick. Turn left on entering Portpatrick. Park 100yd on left. Centre for touring about 0.5m from coast. Graded: 3 stars. Open April-October.

Wig Bay Holiday Park, Loch Ryan, Stranraer, Dumfries & Galloway DG9 0PS. *01776 853233.* Mr J B Wilson. 4m N of Stranraer via A718 Kirkcolm road. Flat, close to sea. Graded: 3 stars. Open March-October.

Thornhill

Penpont (Floors) Caravan Park, Penpont, Thornhill, Dumfries & Galloway DG3 4BH. *01848 330470.* penpont. caravan.park@ukgateway.net. Mr & Mrs Van Der Wielen. At north end of Thornhill take the A702 to Penpont (2 miles). Park is on the left just before Penpont Village. Quiet riverside site in beautiful country. Fees on application. Open Easter or April-October.

DUNBARTONSHIRE

Arrochar

Camping & Caravanning Club Site - Ardgartan, Coilessan Road, Arrochar, Dunbartonshire G83 7AR. *01301 702253.* www.campingandcaravanningclub.co.uk. The Camping & Caravanning Club Ltd. A83 Inverary road to Arrochar around the head of Loch Long and after one mile go past Forestry Commission campsite, take next road on left and then over bridge. Go past Caravan Club site, fork right, site entrance 0.5 mile on left. Members only. Caravans, motor caravans and tents accepted. 55 pitches set in 3.5 acres. Open April-September.

Loch Lomond

Lomond Woods Holiday Park, Tullichewan, Balloch, Loch Lomond, Dunbartonshire G83 8QP. *01389 755000.* lomond woods@holiday-parks.co.uk. www.holiday-parks.co.uk. Colin & Margaret Wood. From Erskine bridge take the A82 Crainlarich road to Balloch road. Turn right at roundabout for Balloch A811 and first left following international camping sign. Excellent touring facilities, leisure suite, mountain bikes. Next to 'Lomond Shores' visitor attraction and gateway to Scotland's first national park. (Free colour brochure). Graded: 5 stars.

EAST LOTHIAN

Dunbar

Belhaven Bay Caravan & Camping Park, Balhaven Bay, Dunbar, East Lothian EH42 1TU. *01368 865956.* belhaven @meadowhead.com. www.meadowhead.co.uk/belhaven. Meadowhead Ltd. From A1 North or South exit at Beltonford roundabout east of Dunbar. The park is approximately 0.5m down on the A1087 on the left hand side of the road. Thistle award. David Bellamy Conservation Silver Conservation Award. Graded: 4 star. Open March-January.

Camping & Caravanning Club Site - Barns Ness, Dunbar, East Lothian EH42 IQP. *01368 863536.* www.campingand caravanningclub.co.uk. The Camping & Caravanning Club Ltd. 9.75-acre site with 80 pitches. From the A1 turn off at power station for East Barns. Note that Barns Ness is a lighthouse and East Barns is the village. Non-members welcome. Caravans, motor caravans and tents accepted. Open March-October.

Thurston Manor Holiday Home Park, Innerwick, Dunbar, East Lothian EH42 1SA. *01368 840643.* Dunham Leisure Ltd. From Edinburgh head south on A1 past Dunbar and follow signs for Innerwick, Crowhill and Thurston Manor. From Berwick head north on A1 turn left at second sign for Innerwick etc. Leisure facilities on site, clubhouse and family room. Phone for brochure. Graded: 5 stars. Open March 1-January 8 (October 31 for tourers).

Edinburgh

Drum Mohr Caravan Park, Levenhall, Musselburgh, Edinburgh, East Lothian EH21 8JS. *01316 656867.* bookings @drummohr.org. www.drummohr.org. Mr W Melville & A M Brodie. A premier park situated 1.5 miles east of Musselburgh, between the B1348 and B1361. Overlooking the Firth of Forth with an excellent bus service to Edinburgh. Graded: 5 stars. Open March 1-October 31.

Little France Caravan & Camping Park, Old Dalkeith Road, Edinburgh, East Lothian EH16 4SE. Little France Caravan Co. On A7 (formerly A68). Dish-washing facilities. Period of opening and fees on application.

Mortonhall Caravan Park, 38 Mortonhall Gate, Frogston Road East, Edinburgh, East Lothian EH16 6TJ. *01316 641533.* mortonhall@meadowhead.co.uk. www.meadowhead.co.uk. Meadowhead Ltd. From north or south Mortonhall is just 5mins from city by-pass. Exit at Straiton or Lothianburn junctions, follow signs for Mortonhall. Graded: 4 stars. Open March 15-January.

Haddington

The Monks' Muir, Haddington, East Lothian EH41 3SB. *01620 860340.* www.monksmuir.com. Douglas & Deirdre Macfarlane. On A1 2.5 miles east of Haddington. One of Scotland's best camping grounds, sheltered, 'green'. Only 15 mins from fringes of Edinburgh. Licensed shop/eatery. Free hot water and showers. Bus service at gate. 'Green Apple' Environmental Award 1996, 'Most Improved Park in Scotland' 1996. Graded: 4 stars.

Longniddry

Seton Sands Holiday Centre, Longniddry, East Lothian EH22 0QF. *01875 813333.* Graded: 3 stars.

North Berwick

Tantallon Caravan & Camping Park, North Berwick, East Lothian EH39 5NJ. *01620 893348.* tantallon@meadowhead. co.uk. www.meadowhead.co.uk. Meadowhead Ltd. On A198 immediately east of North Berwick. Great facilities include footpath straight to beach. Internet access available on park. Adjacent to Glen Golf Course. Cafe/restaurant and takeaway meals nearby. Graded: 5 star. Open March-January.

FIFE

Crail

Ashburn House Caravan Site, St Andrews Road, Crail, Fife KY10 3UL. *01333 450314.* A & M Ireland & Sons. On A917 coast road. Quiet family-run site. High standard of amentities. Walking distance of town and beach. Open March 1-October 31.

Sauchope Links Caravan Park, Crail, Fife KY10 3XL. *01333 450460.* Largo Leisure Parks Ltd. 1m E of Crail off A917. Adjacent to beach. Fees on application. Graded: 5 stars. Open March-October 31.

Glenrothes

Balbirnie Park Caravan Club Site, Markinch, Glenrothes, Fife KY7 6NR. *01592 759130.* www.caravanclub.co.uk. The Caravan Club. Off A92, follow international signs. Dogs on lead. Although the site is rural, the sporting facilities in nearby Glenrothes make this a good base for families. Ice rink nearby. Non-members welcome. Graded: 4 stars. Open April-October.

Kinghorn

Pettycur Bay Caravan & Holiday Park, Kinghorn, Fife KY3 9YE. *01592 892200.* Mr T Wallace. 0.5m W of Kinghorn. Terraced site with panoramic views of Firth of Forth. Prime tourist area, close to Edinburgh. Open March 1-October 31.

Lundin Links

Woodland Gardens Caravan & Camping Site, Blindwell Road, Lundin Links, Fife KY8 5QG. *01333 360319.* wood landgardens@lineone.net. www.woodland-gardens.co.uk. Mr & Mrs J D Anderson. Three miles east of Leven. Site is 0.5 mile off the A915 at the east end of Lundin Links. Beautiful country. Ideal centre for St Andrews and East Neuk. One mile from sands. Suitable for adults only. Graded: 4 stars. Open April-October.

Pittenweem

Grangemuir Woodland Park, Grangemuir, Pittenweem, Fife KY10 2RB. *01333 311213.* A & M Ireland & Sons. Park is situated half a mile north of Pittenweem along an unclassified road and in a woodland site. One mile from the sea and nine miles from the historic city of St Andrews. Open March-October.

St Andrews

Cairnsmill Caravan Park, Largo Road, St Andrews, Fife KY16 8NN. *01334 473604.* cairnsmill@aol.com. www.ukparks. co.uk/cairnsmill. The Kirkaldy Family. Park is located on the A915 approximately one mile from St Andrews. On level grass. Indoor heated pool and games room. Graded: 4 stars. Open April 1-October 28.

Craigtoun Meadows Holiday Park, Mount Melville, St Andrews, Fife KY16 8PQ. *01334 475959.* craigtoun @aol.com. www.craigtounmeadows.co.uk. From St Andrews leave by West Port. Argyle Street and Hepburn Gardens. Bear left at university playing fields near west end of Hepburn Gardens, and the site is after 1.25 miles. Graded: 5 stars.

St Monans

St Monans Caravan Site, The Common, St Monans, Fife KY10 2DN. *01333 730778.* Abbeyford Caravans (Scotland) Ltd. On E boundary of St Monans on A917. Level site with made-up roads. Adjacent to beach. Graded: 3 stars. Open March 21-October 31.

Tayport

Tayport Caravan Park, Tayport, Fife DD6 9ES. *01382 552334.* www.caravancampingsites.co.uk. Mr & Mrs R B Baillie. On southern outskirts of Tayport off the B945. Level site with made-up roads. 0.75m from beach. Fees on application. Quiet and attractive park near shops and harbour. Open March-October.

GLASGOW

Alexandria

Camping & Caravanning Club Site - Luss, Loch Lomond, Luss, Alexandria Glasgow G83 8NT. *01436 860658.* www.campingandcaravanningclub.co.uk. The Camping & Caravanning Club Ltd. Site on Lochside on A82 Glasgow to Fort William road. 90 pitches set in 12 acres. Non-member tents welcome. Members-only caravans and motor caravans. The site is suitable for watersports enthusiasts. Open March-October.

Drymen

Camping & Caravanning Club Site - Milarrochy Bay, Balmaha, Drymen, Glasgow G63 0AL. *01360 870236.* www.campingandcaravanningclub.co.uk. The Camping & Caravanning Club Ltd. 12 acres on the shores of Loch Lomond with 150 pitches. Fishing permits available. Beach with landing stage. A811 from Drymen, then B837 through Pass of Balmaha (uphill 1 in 6 for 100yds). Road then decends to loch at Milarro. Caravans, motorcaravans and tents accepted. Non-members welcome. Backpacker facility available. Open March-October.

HIGHLAND

Acharacle

Glenview Caravan Park, Strontian, Loch Sunart, Acharacle, Highland PH36 4JD. *01967 402123.* Syd & Shirley Farnell. On A861, turn right at Strontian police station, follow road round green, then signposted to right. Hard standings, electric h/ups, separate camping field with picnic tables and campsites.

Resipole Farm, Loch Sunart, Acharacle, Highland PH36 4HX. *01967 431235.* info@resipole.co.uk. www.resipole.co.uk. Mr Peter Sinclair. Site is on A861 between Strontian and Salen. On N shore of Loch Sunart. Good touring centre near shore of loch. Grassy, level site with beautiful views. Graded: 4 stars. Open Easter-October.

Achnasheen

Camping & Caravanning Club Site - Inverewe Gardens, Poolewe, Achnasheen, Highland IV22 2LF. *01445 781249.* www.campingandcaravanningclub.co.uk. The Camping & Caravanning Club Ltd. In Poolewe by the BP petrol station. Close to famous sub-tropical Inverewe Gardens and Loch Ewe. Non-members welcome. 55 pitches in 3 acres. Caravans, motor caravans and tents accepted. This site nestles in spectacular mountain scenery. Open May-October.

Arisaig

Gorten Sands Caravan Site, Gorten Farm, Arisaig, Highland PH39 4NS. *01687 450283.* Mr A MacDonald. 2m W of Arisaig, turn off A830 at signpost 'Back of Keppoch' left across cattle grid at road end. On sandy beach. Traditional working farm. Excellent views and abundant wildlife. Graded: 3 stars. Open April-September 30.

Aviemore

Dalraddy Holiday Park, Aviemore, Highland PH22 1QB. *01479 810330.* 3.5m S of Aviemore off B9152 (old A9). Well-drained pitches. Half-wooded site in area of natural beauty. Near Aviemore Centre. Good touring base for Highland region. Graded: 2 stars.

Glenmore Caravan & Camping Site, (Forestry Commission), Glenmore, Aviemore, Highland PH22 1QU. *01479 861271.* fe.holidays@forestry.gsi.gov.uk. www.forestholidays.co.uk. Forestry Commission (Forest Holidays). From the A9 turn on to B9152 S of Aviemore. At Aviemore take the B970 to Coylumbridge then take road signposted 'Cairngorm' for 5m. Advance bookings recommended. Brochure request line: 01313 340066. Open early December-end November.

Rothiemurchus Camp & Caravan Park, Coylumbridge, Aviemore, Highland PH22 1QU. *01479 812800.* lizsangster @rothiemurchus.freeserve.co.uk. www.caravan-sitefinder. co.uk. Mrs E Sangster. Coylumbridge Park provides individual pitches in pine forest setting. Good base for touring the Highlands. Cabins for hire. Winner 'Most Improved Park in Scotland' 1995 and 1999. Graded: 5 stars. David Bellamy Gold Conservation Award, Green Tourist Business Scheme Gold Award.

Rothiemurchus Camping & Caravan Park, Coylumbridge, Aviemore, Highland PH22 1QU. *01479 812800.* lizsangster@ rothiemurchus.frsserve.co.uk. www.ukparks.com. Mrs Liz Sangster. From Aviemore take B970 'Ski road'- in one mile park on right.

Beauly

Lovat Bridge Camping Site, Lovat Bridge, Beauly, Highland IV4 7AY. *01463 782374.* allanlymburn@beauly782.fsnet.co.uk. Mr Allan Lymburn. 11m N of Inverness on A862 at Lovat Bridge, 1m S of Beauly. Open March-October.

Boat of Garten

Campgrounds of Scotland, Nr Aviemore, Boat of Garten, Highland PH24 3BN. *01479 831652.* From the A9 take A95 signposted Grantown on Spey then follow signs for Boat of Garten. Situated in the centre of the village. Thistle Award Park. Graded: 4 stars.

Loch Garten Lodges & Caravan Park, Loch Garten Road, Boat of Garten, Highland PH24 3BY. *01479 831769.* David Steer. Follow 'AA' Osprey signs or leave A9 north of Aviemore and follow A95 towards Grantown on Spey, through Boat of Garten village towards Loch Garten. Family run park adjacent to RSPB Reserve. Graded: 3 stars. Open all year.

Dingwall

Camping & Caravanning Club Site - Dingwall, Jubilee Park, Dingwall, Highland IV15 9QZ. *01349 862236.* www.camping andcaravanningclub.co.uk. Camping & Caravanning Club Ltd. 85 pitches set in 6.5 acres. Caravans, motor caravans and tents accepted. Off the A862 on the shores of Cromarty Firth close by the junction with the A835. Site within easy reach of beautiful lochs. Non-members welcome. Open April-October.

Dornoch

Dornoch Caravan & Camping Site, The Links, Dornoch, Highland IV25 3LX. *01862 810423.* info@dornochcaravans. co.uk. www.dornochcaravans.co.uk. W MacRae. From Tain take A9 for 6 miles. Then turn right off A9 on to A949 E for 2m. Adjacent to beach and golf course. Graded: 4 stars. Open April-October.

Grannie's Heilan Hame Holiday Park, Embo, Dornoch, Highland IV25 3QP. *01862 810383.* parkdeanenquiries@ parkdean.com. www.parkdean.com. Parkdean Holidays Plc. Take A9 from Inverness northwards to Dornoch. Free indoor pool and spa bath. Solarium, sauna, bar and clubhouse. Entertainment, meals tennis courts and shop. Children's playground, games room, bowleasy mini bowling and pool. Caravans for sale. Graded: 4 stars. Open March-October.

Pitgrudy Caravan Park, Poles Road, Dornoch, Highland IV25 3HY. *01862 821253.* G N R Sutherland. 1.5m N of town. From B9168 turn off at war memorial. 1m to site. Quiet scenic touring centre with first class amenities. Superb touring pitches. Caravans for hire. Holiday caravans for sale. Graded: 5 stars. Open May-September.

Seaview Farm Caravan Park, Hilton, Dornoch, Highland IV25 3PW. *01862 810294.* Mr T R Preston. Approaching from S turn left at square. After 1.25m turn right at road junction by telephone box. Small sheltered site near beach. Dogs allowed on leads. Tents - Camping Sites members only. Graded: 2 stars. Open mid April-October.

Dunbeath

Inver Caravan Site, Dunbeath, Highland KW6 6EH. *01593 731441.* kgwillim@aol.com. Rhona & Keith Gwillim. Adjacent A9 just north of Dunbeath, 21m SW of Wick. Gently sloping, smooth grassy site. Some shelter. Beautiful views over Dunbeath Bay. Convenient location for Caithness and Orkney crossings.

Durness

Sango Sands Caravan & Camping Site, Durness, Highland IV27 4PP. *01971 511262/511222.* Mr F R Keith. On main A838 Durness-Tongue. Between only two shops in the village. Overlooking good clean beach, safe bathing. Beautiful scenery. Open April 1-October 15.

Evanton

Black Rock Caravan & Camping Park, Evanton, Highland IV16 9UN. *01349 830917.* relax@blackrockscot.fsnet.co.uk. www.sites.ecosse.net/blackrock. Mr & Mrs K Petley. A9 from Inverness for 15 miles, turn left for Evanton B 817, proceed for 0.75 miles. Wooded glen, banks of river Glass. Thistle Award caravans for hire. Graded: 4 stars. Open April-October.

Fort Augustus

Fort Augustus Caravan & Camping Site, Fort Augustus, Highland PH32 4DH. *01320 366618.* Mr B Clark. Half mile S of Fort Augustus off A82 Inverness-Glasgow road. Flat, well-drained site, half mile from Loch Ness. Open end April-September.

Fort William

Corran Caravan Site, Moss Cottage, Onich, Fort William, Highland PH33 6SE. *01855 821208.* Mr J & Mrs T Legg. On the A82. Lochside. Small, friendly, family site. Breathtaking lochside location with panoramic views of Loch Linnhe and surrounding mountains. Graded: 3 stars. Open March 14-October 14.

Glen Nevis Caravan & Camping Park, Glen Nevis, Fort William, Highland PH33 6SX. *01397 702191.* camping@glen-nevis.co.uk. www.glen-nevis.co.uk. Glen Nevis Holidays Ltd. Into Glen Nevis off A82 at Fort William for 2m. Beauty spot. At foot of Ben Nevis. Good touring centre. Graded: 5 stars. Open March-October.

Linnhe Lochside Holidays, Corpach, Fort William, Highland PH33 7NL. *01397 772376.* holidays@linnhe.demon.co.uk. www.linnhe-lochside-holidays.co.uk. On A380, 1.5m west of Corpach village. 5m from Fort William. One of the best and most beautiful lochside parks in Scotland. Pine chalets and holiday caravans for hire. Camping for small tents only. Park open December 15 to October 31. Graded: 5 stars. Open Easter-October 31 for tents.

Lochy Caravan Park Ltd, Fort William, Highland PH33 7NF. *01397 703446.* Mr Ian C Brown. 2.5m N of Fort William. Turn off A82 0n to A830 Mallaig road. Site signposted on Camaghael road. Touring centre for north Scotland. Grassy, gently-sloping site. Graded: 4 stars.

Fortrose

Camping & Caravanning Club Site - Rosemarkie, Ness Roadeast, Rosemarkie, Fortrose, Highland IV10 8SE. *01381 621117.* www.campingandcaravanningclub.co.uk. The Camping & Caravanning Club Ltd. One mile north of Fortrose on the A832. On the shores of the Black Isle overlooking the Moray and Cromarty Firths. 60 pitches accepting all units. Non-members welcome. Graded: 4 stars. The spectacular coastline is famous for its bottlenose dolphins. Open April-September.

Gairloch

Gairloch Caravan & Camping Site, Strath, Wester Ross, Gairloch, Highland IV21 2BX. *01445 712373.* Mr Robert Forbes. At Gairloch turn W off A382 on B8021. Turn right for site entrance close to Millcroft Hotel. Flat site with magnificent views over bay and mountains. Handy for all village amenities. Graded: 4 stars. Open Easter-October.

Sands Holiday Centre, Gairloch, Highland IV21 2DL. *01445 712152.* Mr W & M Cameron. Off A832 at junction of B8021 on Melvaig road for 4m. Very large, picturesque site adjoining sandy beach. Full facilities from May 20-Sept 15. Fees on application. SAE. Graded: 4 stars. Open April-September.

Glencoe

Invercoe Caravan & Camping Park, Glencoe, Highland PH49 4HP. *01855 811210.* invercoe@sol.co.uk. www.invercoe.co.uk. Iain & Lynn Brown. On B863 0.25m from Glencoe crossroads, beside loch. Holiday touring centre. Advance bookings for electric hook-ups. Graded: 5 stars.

Red Squirrel Camping Site, Glencoe, Glencoe, Highland PA49 4HX. *01855 811256/811912.* squirrels@amserve.com. Mr Hugh MacColl. 12m S of Fort William. On the old Glencoe road. 1.5m through Glencoe village over hump bridge. Parallel with A82. An easy going, hill farm site on the river Coe. Fishing, climbing, walking country. Appeals to naturalists. Graded: 2 stars. Open all year.

Grantown-on-Spey

Grantown-on-Spey Caravan Club Park, Seafield Avenue, Grantown-on-Spey, Highland PH26 3JQ. *01479 872474.* Sandra McKelvie & John Fleming. Site 0.5m from centre of town. Turn at The Bank of Scotland. Touring centre. Set in heart of Highlands, quiet and peaceful off peak. Open March 31-end October.

HIGHLAND

Invergarry

Faichem Park, Faichem, Invergarry, Highland PH35 4HG. 01809 501226. ardgarry.farm@lineone.net. www.scottish-high landholidays.glo.cc. MrJ Fleming. Cycle hire available. Graded: 4 stars. Open April-October.

Faichemard Farm, Invergarry, Highland PH35 4HG. 01809 501314. dgrant@fabdial.co.uk. www.host.co.uk. A & D Grant. Leave A87 one mile west from junction with A82, turn right, go past Ardgarry Farm and Faichem Park camp site then turn right at sign A & D Grant. All pitches with picnic tables. Cafe/restaurant nearby. Graded: 3 stars. Open April-October.

Invermoriston

Loch Ness Caravan & Camping Park, Easter Port Clair, Invermoriston, Highland IV3 6YE. 01320 351207. bob@ girvan7904freeserve.co.uk. Mr Bob Girvan. On A82, 1.5m S of Invermoriston. 8-acre park in the Highlands with more than 0.5m frontage to Loch Ness. Forest and mountain walks with magnificent scenery. Private beach. Children's play area with models of Loch Ness monster. Fees on application. Graded: 4 stars. Open 11 months.

Inverness

Auchnahillin Caravan & Camping Centre, Daviot East, Inverness, Highland IV2 5XQ. 01463 772286. info@auch nahillin.co.uk. www.auchnahillin.co.uk. The Graham Family. 7m SE of Inverness on B9154 (Moy Road) off A9. Beautiful location surrounded by hills and forests. Graded: 4 stars. Open Easter-October 31.

Borlum Farm Caravan Park, Drumnadrochit, Inverness, Highland IV63 6XN. 01456 450220. info@borlum.com. www.borlum.com. AD & Mrs MacDonald-Haig. 1m S of Drumnadrochit on right of main road. 16m S of Inverness towards Fort William. Overlooking Loch Ness. Graded: 3 stars. Open all year.

Bught Caravan & Camping Site, Inverness, Highland IV3 5JR. 01463 239111/236920. The Highland Council. Site is within S boundary of Inverness. 4m from S shores of Loch Ness. Well-equipped site. Children's play area and many sports facilities available. Walking distance to town. Graded: 3 stars. Open Easter-October.

Bunchrew Caravan Park, Bunchrew, Inverness, Highland IV3 6TD. 01463 237802. 3m W of Inverness on A862 to Beauly. Site on right. Touring centre, sheltered but with good views over Beauly Firth. Graded: 3 stars. Open mid March-end December.

Cannich Caravan & Camping Park, Cannich, by Beauly, Inverness, Highland IV4 7LN. 01456 415364. enquiries@high landcamping.co.uk. www.highlandcamping.co.uk. Matthew & Fay Jones. Out of Inverness on A82. At Drumnadrochit, take A831 to Cannich. Quiet, family-run park, ideal for touring the Highlands. Dogs allowed on lead. Open March-October.

Culloden Moor Caravan Club Site, Newlands, Culloden Moor, Inverness, Highland IV2 5EF. 01463 790625. www. caravanclub.co.uk. The Caravan Club. On B9006. Dogs on lead. Glorious views with many local attractions—indoors and outdoors. Non-members and tent campers welcome. Ideal family

site. Graded: 5 stars. Open late March-late October.

Dochgarroch Caravan Site, Dochgarroch, Inverness, Highland IV3 6SY. 01463 861333. Gordon Charles. Quiet, pleasant site situated alongside the Caledonian Canal and River Ness. 1.5 miles to Loch Ness. 4 miles west of Inverness to Fort William road. Access road is by Dochgarroch shop and Post Office. Loch Ness cruises. Open Easter-mid October.

Scaniport Caravan & Camping Park, Inverness, Highland IV1 2DL. 01463 751351. The Factor for Baillie 1987 Trust. Small select site 5m from Inverness S on A862. Right side of road opposite telephone box, 3.5 miles from Dodes and Loch Ness. No advance booking. Graded: 2 stars. Open Easter-September.

Isle of Skye

'Coolin View' Caravan & Camping Site, 3 Upper Breakish, Isle of Skye, Highland IV42 8PY. 01471 822248. Mr A Campbell. 2m E of Broadford on A850 towards bridge at Kyleakin. Overlooking bay and near beach. Fees on application.

Glenbrittle Beach Site, Glenbrittle, Isle of Skye, Highland. 01478 640404. info@dunvegancastle.com. www.dunvegancastle. com. Macleod Estates. Leave A850 at Sligachan and take A863 W for 5m. B8009 2.5m to Merkadale. Turn S on to road for 8m to site. Safe swimming and sandy beach at site. The centre for the Cuillins. Open April-October.

Loch Greshonish Caravan & Camping Site, Borve Arnisort, Edinbane, Isle of Skye, Highland IV51 9PS. 01470 582230. info@skyecamp.com. www.skyecamp.com. Ben & Rhonda Palmer. 12m from Portree on the A850 Portree to Dunvegan road. Open April 1-October 15.

Staffin Caravan & Camping Site, Staffin, Isle of Skye, Highland IV51 9JX. 01470 562213. staffin@namacleod. freeserve.co. Mr A Macleod. 16m N of Portree on A855. Peaceful situation, excellent location for touring island. Birdwatching, fishing and walking abundant in the locality. Free hot showers. Dogs welcome. Graded: 2 stars. Open April-September.

Torvaig Caravan & Camping Site, Portree, Isle of Skye, Highland IV51 9HU. 01478 612209. John Maclean. On main Staffin road, A855. 1m N of Portree ideal centre for touring. Graded: 3 stars. Open April-October.

Uig Bay Camping & Caravan Site, 10 Idrigill, Uig, Isle of Skye, Highland IV51 9XU. 01470 542714. Mr & Mrs M Madigan. Drive past pub at pier approx. 150yd along shore road. Grass and hard standing pitches. Footpath to beach. Ideal base for hillwalking. Cycle hire on site. Open February 21-October 31.

John O'Groats

John O' Groats Caravan & Camping Site, John O'Groats, Highland KW1 4YS. 01955 611329. Mr William Steven. At end of A99 on sea front beside the Last House in Scotland. Dogs on lead only. Booking office for day trips to Orkney Isles on site. Harbour 150yd. Magnificent cliffs 2m. Hotel and restaurant 200yds. Dogs allowed. Fees on application. Graded: 3 stars. Open April-September.

HIGHLAND

Kinlochbervie

Oldshoremore Caravan Site, 152 Oldshoremore, by Lairg, Kinlochbervie, Highland IV27 4RS. *01971 521281.* Mr J P Mackenzie. A838 over Laxford Bridge to Rhiconich, B801 to Oldshoremore. Site 200yds off road 200yds past Oldshoremore sign. 2m N of Kinlochbervie. 50m N of Lairg. Sheltered. Good sands. Fees on application. Open April-September.

꿈 🖭 ⊕ ᣃ 🅟 ⓗ 🄻 ♿ ⤺ ↗ ↘

Kinlochleven

Caolasnacon Caravan & Camping Park, Kinlochleven, Highland PA50 4RJ. *01855 831279.* Mrs P Cameron. On S shore of Loch Leven between Kinlochleven and Glencoe. Lochside, well-drained site with mountain scenery. Good hill walking area. Open April-October.

꿈 🖭 ⊙ ⓒ ᣃ 🄵 🅟 ᖰ ♿ 🄻 ↗ ↓ ⤓

Kyle of Lochalsh

Ardelve, Dornie, Kyle of Lochalsh, Highland. *01599 555231.* Mr M Macrae. Beside the A87 0.5m NW of Dornie. Open May-September.

꿈 🖭 ⊙ ᣃ 🅟 ⓗ 🄵

Lairg

Woodend Caravan & Camping Site, Achnairn, Lairg, Highland IV27 4DN. *01549 402248.* Mrs C M Ross. A836 from Lairg onto A838 beside Loch Shin. Signposted from Lairg. Highland touring centre or overnight stop. Gold award for quality and service, AA 3 pennants. Open April 1-September 30.

꿈 🖭 ⓛ ⊙ ⓒ ᣃ 🅟 ᖰ 🄻 ↗ ↘ ⤺ ⤓

Nairn

Delnies Woods Caravan Park, Delnies Wood, Nairn, Highland IV12 5NX. *01667 455281.* G M Munro. 2m W of Nairn on A96 Aberdeen to Inverness road. Secluded site 3m from beach. Attractive scenery and historic countryside abounding in sporting activities. Dogs welcome. Graded: 3 stars. Open Easter-October.

꿈 🖭 ⊙ ⓒ ᣃ 🄵 🅟 ᖰ 🄻 ↗ ↓ ⤺ ⤓

Nairn Lochloy Holiday Park, East Beach, Nairn, Highland IV12 4PH. *01667 453764.* parkdeanenquiries@parkdean.co.uk. www.parkdean.com. Parkdean Holidays Plc. 5 minutes from Nairn town between sandy beach and 18-hole golf course. Free indoor pool. Sauna and solarium. Restaurant, lounge bar, family entertainment and takeaway. Games room, children's play area. Free kids' club for 5-11 year olds. Open March-October.

꿈 ♨ 🖭 ⓛ ✕ ᣃ 🄵 ≋ 🅟 ᖰ 🄻 ⤓ ⤺ ↘

Old Mill Caravan Park, Brodie, Nr Forres, Nairn, Highland IV36 0TD. *01309 641244.* admin@theoldmillbrodie.com. www.theoldmillbrodie.com/oldmillcaravanpark.htm. M Jamisson. On main A96 trunk road between Forres and Nairn, at village of Brodie. Quiet, level, sheltered sight with all amenities on site, including traditional pub and restaurant. Graded: 4 stars. Open April-October.

꿈 ♨ 🖭 ⓛ ✕ ⊙ ⓒ ᣃ 🄵 🅟 🄻 ↗ ↓ ⤺ ⤓

Spindrift Caravan & Camping Park, Little Kildrummie, Nairn, Highland IV12 5QU. *01667 453992.* camping@spindrift caravanpark.freeserve.co.uk. Mr B J Guillot. Take B9090 Nairn to Cawdor road for about 1.5m, turn right on sharp left-hand bend direction Little Kildrummie, site 300 yds on left. Overlooking the river Nairn, salmon and sea trout fishing. Quiet, secluded site with free showers, laundrette and dish-washing facilities. Graded: 4 stars. Open April 1-October 31.

꿈 🖭 ⓛ ⊙ ⓒ ᣃ 🅟 ᖰ 🄻 ↗ ↓ ⤺ ⤓

Newtonmore

Invernahavon Caravan Site, Glentruim, Newtonmore, Highland PH20 1BE. *01540 673534/219.* enquiry@inverna havon.com. Mr & Mrs K W Knox. S of Newtonmore off A9. Level site close to river Truim. Surrounded by woods and mountains. Non members and tent campers welcome. Ideal family site. Good area for walking. Graded: 3 stars. Open March-October.

꿈 🖭 ⓛ ᣃ ⓒ ᣃ 🄵 🅟 ᖰ 🄻 ↗ ↓ ⤺ ⤓

Ross-shire

Dornoch Firth Caravan & Camping Park, Meikle Ferry South, Tain, Ross-shire, Highland IV19 1JX. *01862 892292.* will@dornochfirth.co.uk www.dornochfirth.co.uk. Will Porter. A9 north from Inverness, past Tain to Meikle Ferry roundabout, A836: Dornoch Firth scenic route, 1st right Meikle Ferry South. Beautiful scenic location, ideal for touring Highlands. STB 4 stars. Takeaway meals, shops, cafe/restaurant adjacent to park. Open January-December.

꿈 🖭 ⓛ ⊙ ⓒ ᣃ 🄵 🅟 ᖰ ✿ 🄻 ↗ ↓ ⤺ ⤓

Roy Bridge

Bunroy Camping & Caravanning Park, Roy Bridge, Highland PH31 4AG. *01397 712332.* info@bunroycamping.co.uk. www.bunroycamping.co.uk. Gail & Andy Markham. A82 from Fort William, A86 at Spean Bridge to Roy Bridge. At Stronlossit Hotel turn right. Site is 300yd at end of lane. Peaceful riverside location. Good centre for touring. Open March-October 30.

꿈 🖭 ⓛ ⊙ ⓒ ᣃ 🅟 ᖰ 🄻 ↗ ↓

Scourie

Scourie Caravan & Camping Park, Harbour Road, Scourie, Highland IV27 4TG. *01971 502060.* Mr A MacKenzie. Near Scourie village. Overlooking Scourie Bay. At junction of Harbour Road and A894. 20m S of Cape Wrath. Holiday site. Hill walking. Handa Island birdwatching. No bookings except by phone on morning of intended arrival. Fees on application SAE. Open Easter-September.

꿈 🖭 ♨ ⓛ ✕ ⊙ ⓒ ᣃ 🅟 🄻 🄻 ↗ ↓ ⤺

Shiel Bridge

Shiel Bridge, By Kyle, Shiel Bridge, Highland IV40 8HW. *01599 511221.* Take road from Shiel Bridge shop and filling station. At S end of Loch Duich, 15m E of Kyle via A87. Flat site within reach of Kintail Hills. Proprietors: John & Lynne Metclafe. Open May-September.

꿈 🖭 ⓛ ✕ ⊙ ᣃ 🅟 🄻 ↗ ↓

Spean Bridge

Gairlochy Holiday Park, Old Station, Gairlochy Road, Spean Bridge, Highland PE34 4EO. *01397 712711.* theghp@ talk21.com. www.theghp.co.uk. Mr J Anderson. From Spean Bridge go 1m NW on A82 towards Inverness, turn on to B8004 at Commando Memorial, signposted Gairlochy. Site 1m on left. Near Ben Nevis, amid beautiful scenery. Shop, bus stop and station 2m. Fees on application. Graded: 4 stars. Open April-October.

꿈 🖭 ⓛ ⊙ ᣃ 🅟 ᖰ 🄻 ↗ ↓

Stronaba Caravan & Camping Site, Spean Bridge, Highland PH34 4DX. *01397 712259.* Mrs MacDonald. 2.5m N of Spean Bridge and 12m N of Fort William on A82. Beside AA telephone box. Quiet with view of Ben Nevis, central for touring. Well kept site and we welcome tents, caravans and dormobiles. Conveniently situated with very good entrance. Graded: 2 stars. Open April-October.

꿈 🖭 ⓛ ✕ ⊙ ᣃ 🅟 ✕ 🄻 ↗ ↓ ⤺ ⤓

Strathcarron

Applecross Camp Site, Applecross, Strathcarron, Highland IV54 8ND. *01520 744284/268.* Mr A C Goldthorpe. Remote site in Applecross Forest, opposite island of Raasay. 8m N of Lochcarron on A896, turn left on to Applecross road, the Bealach-Na-Bo (the Pass of the Cattle). Site is signposted. Caravans N along A896 for 8m, then turn left. E.Mail applecross@sol.co.uk Open April-October.

🚐🏕️📶✉️🔌⚡✖️⊙🚿🚻🅿️☕📮🛒♿🚸🎣🐟🚶🏊

Strathpeffer

Riverside Caravan Site, Contin, Strathpeffer, Highland IV14 9ES. *01997 421351.* Mr R Finnie. 5m W of Maryburgh on A835. Site in Contin village. 2m from Strathpeffer. Touring centre for west coast of Scotland.

🚐🏕️♿✉️⚡✖️⊙🚿🛒📮☕❀🚸🎣🐟🚶🚲⊙🚻🎣

Sutherland

Craigdhu Caravan & Camping Site, Betty Hill, By Thurso, Sutherland, Highland KW14 7SP. *01641 521273.* Donald M Mackenzie. On main A836 Thurso-Tongue road. 30 miles west of Thurso. Picturesque scenery on sheltered site. Golden beaches. Trout fishing. Swimming pool nearby. Geologists, botanists and ornithologists welcome. Open April 1-October 1.

🚐🏕️♿✉️⚡✖️⊙🚻🛒📮🌿🎣🚶🚲⚓🚸🎣

Kincraig Caravan & Camping Site, Tongue, Sutherland, Highland IV27 4XF. *01847 55218.* Open: May-October.

🚐🏕️📶⚡⊙🚻🛒📮⚡🚶🎣

Thurso

Dunnet Bay Caravan Club Site, Dunnet, Thurso, Highland KW14 8XD. *01847 821319.* The Caravan Club. Off A836. Operator: The Caravan Club. Dogs on lead. The ideal seaside spot overlooking the clean sands of the Caithness coast. Non-members welcome. Non-members and tent campers welcome. Ideal family site. Open late April-late September.

🚐🏕️📶⚡⊙☕🛒📮🐕♿🎣

Thurso Camping & Caravan Site, Smith Terrace, Scrabster Road, Thurso, Highland KW14 7JY. *01847 894631.* Highland Council. Outskirts of town on A9 Thurso to Scrabster road. Opposite Smith Terrace. 0.5m from town centre. Touring stop on north coast road. Dogs accepted. Fees on application. Graded: 3 stars. Open May 3-September 30.

🚐🏕️📶♿🛒✖️⊙🚿🛒📮🐕🚻⚓🎣📞♿🚶🎣🚲🚶⊙🚸🎣🚸

Ullapool

Ardmair Point Caravan Site, Ardmair Point, Ullapool, Highland IV26 2TN. *01854 612054.* Mr P J Fraser. 3.5m N of Ullapool. Boat hire facilities on site. Beautiful coastal location overlooking 'Summer Isles'. Graded: 4 stars. Open Easter-September.

🚐🏕️♿🛒♿✖️⊙♿🚿🛒📮⚡🚻⚓🎣🚶🚲🚶⊙🚸🎣🚸

Broomfield Holiday Park, Ullapool, Highland IV26 2SX. *01854 612020/612664.* Mr S M Ross. Superb seaside site within village of Ullapool. Graded: 3 stars. Open Easter-end September.

🚐🏕️📶♿🛒🚿✖️⊙🛒📮🚻📮🐕♿🎣🚶🚲🚶⊙🚸🎣🚸

Wester Ross

Gruinard Bay Caravan Park, Laide, Wester Ross, Highland IV22 2ND. *01445 731225.* Tony & Ann Davis. On A832 just east of the village of Laide. Unspoilt beachside park on beautiful Gruinard Bay. Magnificent views of mountains and islands. Graded: 4 stars. Open April 1-October 31.

🚐🏕️📶♿🛒✖️⊙🚿🛒📮✖️🚻📮⚡♿🚸🎣🚶🚲🚶🎣🚸🎣

Wick

Riverside Caravan Club Site, Janetstown, Wick, Highland KW1 5SR. *01955 605420.* www.caravanclub.co.uk. The Caravan Club. Off A882 into Riverside Drive. Dogs on lead. Lovely walks along beautiful white, sandy beaches with seabirds and seal colonies off coast. Fees on application. Non-members welcome. Tent campers welcome. Graded: 4 stars. Open late April-late September.

🚐🏕️📶♿🛒⚡⊙☕🛒📮🐕🚶

Stroma View Caravan & Camping Park, Huna, John O' Groats, Wick, Highland KW1 4YL. *01955 611313.* stroma dundas@aol.com. www.google.com. Mr & Mrs R G Dundas. Follow A99 to John O'Groats and turn left at Sea View Hotel, follow A836 Thurso Road for 1.5m. Site is on the left opposite the Islands of Stroma. Open April-October.

🚐🏕️📶♿🛒⊙🛒📮🐕🚶🎣⚓🚶🚲🚸🎣🎣

MORAY

Aberlour

Camping & Caravanning Club Site - Elchies By Craigellachie, Speyside, Elchies By Craigellachie, Aberlour, Moray AB38 9SL. *01340 810414.* www.camping andcaravanningclub.co.uk. The Camping & Caravanning Club Ltd. 75-pitch site set among rolling hills within 7 acres. Salmon and whiskey the specialities of the Spey valley. 2.5m from junc. of A941. Dogs allowed. Non- members welcome. Caravans, motor caravans and tents accepted. Cafe/restaurant 300yd. Open March-October.

🚐🏕️📶♿⊙☕🛒📮🚻📮🐕📺🎣🚶🎣

Aberlour-on-Spey

Aberlour Gardens Caravan Park, Aberlour-on-Spey, Moray AB38 9LD. *01340 871586.* abergard@compuserve.com. www.aberlour.gardens.co.uk. John & Pauline Moss. Midway between Aberlour and Craigellachie off A95. Vehicles over 10'6" high use A941. Quiet site close to river Spey and Speyside Way on the Malt Whisky Trail. Hot showers. Graded: 5 stars. Open March-October.

🚐🏕️📶♿🛒⊙☕🛒📮🚻📮⚡🎣🚶🚲🚶⊙🚸🎣🚸

Buckie

Strathlene Caravan Site, Strathlene, Buckie, Moray. *01542 834851.* Kris Fraser. From Buckie 1.5m E of town centre on A942. Private caravan site situated by sea on Eastern outskirts of Buckie. Graded: 4 stars. Open Easter-October.

🚐🏕️📶♿🛒⚡♿🛒📮🚻📮♿🚶🎣🚶⊙🚸🎣🎣

Elgin

North Alves Caravan Park, Alves, Elgin, Moray IV30 3XD. *01343 850223.* Mr A V Gomez. Turn N to site at Alves village, by the filling station. Between Elgin and Forres on A96. Alves is 6m W of Elgin. Very fully-equipped holiday site. Open April-October.

📞🔌♨🏧♿⚡✕⊙♨♨🔋🛢🐕🚲🐾♨🚿▲♨🍴🚽⚷♨⚓⛵🎣

Riverside Caravan Park, Elgin, Moray IV30 8UN. *01343 542813.* Christine & John Mitchell. On A96 0.5m W of Elgin. Local touring or overnight stop. Fees on application. Graded: 4 stars. Open April-October.

📞🔌♨♿⚡⊙🔋♨🛢🐕🚽♨🍴⚷⛵🎣

Station Caravan Park, West Beach, Hopeman, Elgin, Moray IV30 5RU. *01343 830880.* stationcaravanpark@talk21.com. www.stationcaravanpark.co.uk. David & Angie Steer. On coast road B9040, 6 miles from elgin. Family-run park adjacent to sandy beach. Open March-November.

📞🔌♨⊙⚡🔋🛢🐕♨⚷🚽▲♨🍴🚿⚓⛵🎣

Findochty

Findochty Caravan Park, Jubilee Terrace, Findochty, Moray AB56 4QA. *01542 835303.* moiramain@aol.com. www.findochty caravanpark.co.uk. Moira & Dennis Main. From Buckie 3m E on A942 in centre of village by harbour. Delightful small family caravan site close to the rocks, seashore and harbour where many small craft operate. Fees on application. Open March-October.

📞🔌♨⊙♨🔋🛢🐕♨▲♨⚷⚓🎣

Fochabers

Burnside Caravan Site, Fochabers, Moray IV32 7PF. *01343 820511.* Christies (Fochabers) Ltd. On the outskirts of Fochabers. Fees on application. Open April-October.

📞🔌♨⚡✕⊙🔋♨≋♨🐕♨⚷⚓

Spey Bay Caravan Site, Spey Bay, Fochabers, Moray IV32 7PJ. *01343 820424.* Christies (Fochabers) Ltd. 4.5m W of Buckie and 9m E of Elgin. From Buckie take A942. Take A98 E at Fochabers turn N on to B9104 for 4m to Spey Bay and site. Flat, well-drained site adjacent to golf course and hotel. Very close to sea. Graded: 3 stars. Open April-September.

📞🔌♨♿⚡⊙🔋♨🐕🐾✕♨⚷🚽⚷⊙⚓⛵

Forres

Findhorn Sands Caravan Park, Findhorn , Forres, Moray IV36 0YZ. *01309 690324.* Mr C MacCallum. On main Aberdeen to Inverness road, at Forres roundabout take Kinloss road, at Kinloss turn left. Park entrance after 3 miles. Takeaway neaby. Dogsd allowed. Graded: 5 stars. Open April 1-October 31.

📞🔌♨♿⚡✕⊙🔋♨🐕♨×♨≋▲♨⚷⚓🎣

Inverness

Camping & Caravanning Club Site - Nairn, Delnies Wood, Nairn, Inverness, Moray IV12 5NX. *01667 455281.* www.campingandcaravanningclub.co.uk. Camping & Caravanning Club. 75 pitches set in 14 acres. Non-members welcome. Off the main A96 Inverness to Aberdeen road, 2 miles of the town of Nairn. Situated in a wooded setting close to the beach. Open March-October.

📞🔌♨⊙🔋♨🐕♨≋⚷⚓

Lossiemouth

Seatown Caravan Site, Lossiemouth, Moray IV31 6JJ. *01343 813980.* Moray Council. 6.25m N of Elgin off A941 (Lossiemouth). Site overlooks river Lossie and extensive stretches of white sandy beaches. Open April-September.

📞🔌♨✕⊙🔋♨🐕♨⚷⚓🎣

Silver Sands Leisure Park, Covesea, West Beach, Lossiemouth, Moray IV31 6SP. *01343 813262.* President Leisure Ltd. 6m N of Elgin, 1.5m W of Lossiemouth. From Elgin take a941 N for 4m, turn left on B9135 left again on B9040. Site is 1m on right. Good family site with direct access to beautiful beach. Essential amenities and attractions. Graded: 4 stars. Open March-October.

📞🔌🚻♨🏧✕⊙♨🔋🛢🐕♨🍴⚷♨🚽▲♨🚿⚓⊙⚓🎣

NORTH AYRSHIRE

Irvine

Cunninghamhead Estate Caravan Park, Kilmarnock, Irvine, North Ayrshire KA3 2PE. *01294 850238.* Mr John Sims. From Irvine via Glasgow road (A736). At Stanecastle roundabout turn E on to B769 Stewarton road. Park is on the left. Three miles north east of Irvine. Secluded site in pleasant country. Good centre for touring Burns country and Clyde resorts. Open April-September.

📞🔌♨⊙🔋♨🛢🐕♨⚷

Isle of Arran

Lochranza Golf Caravan & Camping Site, Lochranza, Isle of Arran, North Ayrshire KA27 8HL. *01770 830273.* office@lochgolf.demon.co.uk. www.arran.net/lochranza. I M Robertson. In the v illage at N end of island, beside superb golf course. Ideal for golfers, birdwatchers and walkers. Climbing, hill walking, canoeing etc. close by. Ask for details of ferry inclusive packages. Open April 1-October 20.

📞🔌♨♿⚡⊙🔋♨🐕♨⚷🚽♨🍴⚓♨⚷⊙⚓

Lamlash

Middleton Caravan & Camping Park, Lamlash, North Ayrshire KA27 8NN. *01770 600255/251.* Mr R J Middleton. 0.25m from centre of Lamlash. Flat, grassy site. 5 min from beach. Night lighting. Graded: 3 stars. Open April-October.

📞🔌♨⚡✕⊙🔋♨🛢🐕♨▲♨⚷🚽⚷⊙⚓⛵🎣

Skelmorlie

Mains Caravan Park, Skelmorlie Mains, Skelmorlie, North Ayrshire PA17 5EU. *01475 520794.* mainscaravanpark.co.uk. T A James Stirrat & Norman Stirrat. A78 from Largs. Site is signposted. Four miles north of Largs. Turn off A78 behind Skelmorlie Castle. Near Wemyss Bay and Largs for all Clyde sailings. Fees on application. Graded: 3 stars. Open April-September.

📞🔌♨♨⊙🐕♨≋🐾▲♨⚷⊙⚓

NORTH LANARKSHIRE

Motherwell

Strathclyde Country Park Caravan Site, 366 Hamilton Road, Motherwell, North Lanarkshire ML1 3ED. *01698 266155.* strathcydepark@northlan.gov.uk. www.northlan.gov.uk. North Lanarkshire Council. M74 Junction 5 to park. Set in 2000 acres with watersports facilities in an area of outstanding natural beauty. Graded: 4 stars. Open Easter-mid October.

📞🔌🚻♨♿♨⊙🔋♨🛢🐕♨▲♨⚷⚓♨⚓🎣

ORKNEY

Kirkwall

Pickaquoy Caravan & Camping Site, Kirkwall, Orkney KW15 1NY. *01856 873535.* Orkney Islands Council, Recreation Services Department. 100yd SW of the foot of the hill leading into Kirkwall. On the A965 to Stromness. Holiday centre. Area of archaeological interest. Graded: 3 stars. Open May-September.

🚐📺♿⚡☺◍🔥🏃🍴×🏠⌗🍳↻🏇🚲

Stromness

Point of Ness Camping Site, Stromness, Orkney KW16 3DL. *01856 873535.* Orkney Islands Council, Recreation Services Sector. Follow main street through Stromness to South End. On shore. Graded: 3 stars. Open mid-May to mid-September.

🚐📺☺◍🔥🏃🍴×🏠⌗🍳🏇

PERTHSHIRE & KINROSS

Aberfeldy

Aberfeldy Caravan Park, Dunkeld Road, Aberfeldy, Perthshire & Kinross PH15 2AQ. *01887 820662.* Perth & Kinross Council. E side of town on A827. Beautiful scenery. Ideal for touring. Fees and free leaflet on application. Advance bookings.Sports and retail discount card for stays of 2 days or more. Senior citizens off-peak discount. AA 3 pennant. Graded: 4 stars. Open end March-end October.

🚐📞♿⚡☺◍🔥🏠🍳🍴🏃🚲↻🏇

Kenmore Caravan & Camping Park, Taymouth Holiday Centre, Kenmore, Aberfeldy, Perthshire & Kinross PH15 2HN. *01887 830226.* info@taymouth.co.uk. www.taymouth.co.uk D Menzies & Partners. A9 to Ballinluig, A827 to Kenmore (15 miles), through village and over bridge on right-hand side. Family-run site with magnificent scenery in highland Perthshire. Bar and restaurant. Excellent golf course on site. Ideal location for walking and cycling. Graded: 4 stars. Open March-October.

🚐📞♨📺♿⚡🍽×☺◍🔥🏃🏠⌗🍳🍴🔥×🏇🚲↻🏇🚲

Blairgowrie

Blairgowrie Holiday Park, Rattray, Blairgowrie, Perthshire & Kinross PH10 7AL. *01250 872941.* Colin & Margaret Wood. 0.5m N of Blairgowrie town centre via A93 Braemar road. Friendly, family-run park. Putting green. Play area. Heated facilities. Caravan holiday homes and superb pine lodges for hire. Graded: 4 stars.

🚐📞♨📺🍽♿⚡×☺◍🔥🏠🍳🍴🏃🚲↻🏇🚲

Corriefodly Holiday Park, Bridge of Cally, Blairgowrie, Perthshire PH10 7JG.*01250 886236.* Colin & Margaret Wood. Follow A93, 6 miles North of Blairgowrie to Bridge of Cally. Turn left on Pitlochry Road, at bridge and post office. Corriefodly is 100yd on left.

🚐📞♨📺🍽♿⚡×☺◍🔥🔥🏠❄🍴🏃🍳

Nether Craig Caravan Park, Nether Craig, By Alyth, Blairgowrie, Perthshire & Kinross PH11 8HN. *01575 560204.* nethercraig@lineone.net. www.nethercraigcaravanpark.co.uk. Peter & Pat Channon. At roundabout south of Alyth, join B954 signposted Glenisla. Follow caravan/tent signs for 4 miles. Peaceful family-run park with views of the Strathmore valley. Graded: 5 stars. Open March 15-December 14.

🚐📞♨♿⚡☺◍🔥🏠🍴🍳🏃

Bridge of Cally

Ballintuim Caravan Park, Ballintuim, Bridge of Cally, Perthshire & Kinross PH10 7NH. *01250 886276.* Phil & Karen Clark. 9m from Blairgowrie. A93 to Bridge of Cally then A924

midway betwwen Bridge of Cally and Kirkmichael. Good toilet facilities. Graded: 3 stars.

🚐📞📺☺◍🔥🏠🍳🏃🌸↻

Comrie

West Lodge Caravan Park, Comrie, Perthshire PH6 2LS. *01764 670354.* Mr P J & E L Gill. A85 Crieff to Comrie road. One mile east of Comrie. Quiet site. Good touring centre. Holiday caravans for hire. Good facilties. Free Showers and electric. Bowling nearby. Calor gas and camping gaz for sale. Dogs allowed. Golf, walking and fishing all nearby. Graded: 4 stars. Open April-October.

🚐📞♨📺♿☺◍🔥🏠⌗🍳🏃🍳🍴🏃🚲↻🏇🚲

Crieff

Crieff Holiday Village, Turret Bank, Crieff, Perthshire & Kinross PH7 4JN. *01764 653513.* info@crieff.holidayvillage. co.uk. www.crieff-holidayvillage.co.uk. D M & C P T Sloan. 0.5m W of Crieff on A85. Site is 300yds on left. Attractively situated touring site bordering river Turret and public parks. Easy walking distance from town. Graded: 4 stars.

🚐📞♨🍴🍽♿⚡×☺◍🔥🔥🏠🍳🌸🏃🍳🍴🍳🏃🚲↻🏇🚲

Thornhill Lodge Tenting Park, 'Monzievaird', Crieff, Perthshire & Kinross PH7 4JU. *01764 655382.* Jennifer & Ian Morrison. 3m W of Crieff on A85 turn S at telephone box, 1st house on left. Restaurant and swimming pool nearby. Open Easter-October 31.

🚐📺♨🍴☺◍🔥🏠⌗🍳🏃🍴🍳🏃🚲↻🏇🚲

Dunkeld

The Erigmore Estate, Birnham, Dunkeld, Perthshire PH8 9XX. *01350 727236.* President Leisure Ltd. Signposted. On B898, off A9 in Birnham village. 12m N of Perth. Overnight Perth to Inverness or touring centre. Restaurant, dancing, entertainment, bar, family room. No tents. Graded: 3 stars. Open March-October.

🚐📞♨📺♿🍴×☺◍🔥🏠❄≋🔥🏠⌗≋🍳🍳🏃🏇🚲↻🏇

Killin

Cruachan Caravan & Camping Park, Cruachan, Killin, Perthshire & Kinross FK21 8TY. *01567 820302.* Mr J Campbell. 3 miles east of Killin on A827. Peaceful, family-run park. Good situation for touring Central Highlands. Good walks from site. Licensed coffe shop/restaurant. Takeaway meals/packed lunches. Graded: 2 stars. Open mid March-end October.

🚐📞♨📺🍴×☺◍🔥🏠🍳🍴🏃🍳🍴🏃🚲↻🏇🚲

Kinross

Gairney Bridge Farm Ltd, Gairney Bridge Caravan Site, Kinross, Perthshire & Kinross KY13 7JZ. *01577 862336.* Mr & Mrs G T King. Off B996 by monument, 14m N of Forth road bridge. 2m S of Kinross (leave M90 jct 5) NE towards Kinross. Route Edinburgh to Perth. Touring site. Fees on application. Graded: 1 star.

Perth

Beech Hedge Caravan Park, Cargill, Perth, Perthshire & Kinross PH2 6DU. *01250 883249.* Mr & Mrs Rowan. 10 miles north of Perth on the A93. Small quiet site, wonderful views. Central for touring Perthshire. Open mid-March to end-October.

Cleeve Caravan Park, Glasgow Road, Perth, Perthshire PH2 0PH. *01738 639521.* Perth & Kinross Council. On A93, 0.25m E of A9-M90 bypass roundabout. A pleasant, friendly, quiet, woodland park close to Perth and ideal for touring loch, river coast and glen. Discount card for stays of two days or more and Senior Citizens off-peak reductions. AA 4 Pennant De-Luxe. Graded: 4 stars. Open mid March-October 31.

Pitlochry

Blair Castle Caravan Park, Blair Atholl, Pitlochry, Perthshire PH18 5SR. *01796 481263.* mail@blaircastlecaravanpark.co.uk. www.blaircastlecaravanpark.co.uk. Blair Castle Estates Ltd. Site is in centre of Blair Atholl 7m NW of Pitlochry. Flat, grassy site in good hill-walking and climbing area. Open March 1- November 30.

Faskally Home Farm, Pitlochry, Perthshire & Kinross PH16 5LA. *01796 472007.* Mr E M R Hay. 2m N of Pitlochry on B8019 Killiecrankie Road. Roomy farm site. Touring centre. Graded: 3 stars. Open March-October.

Glengoulandie Farm Site & Deer Park, Foss, Pitlochry, Perthshire & Kinross PH15 6NL. *01887 830261.* Mr H S & J E McAdam. From Aberfeldy B846 to Kinloch Rannoch. Site is beside road. 9m from Aberfeldy. Deer and animal park beside site, which is amid mountains. Open April-October.

Milton of Fonab Caravan Site, Bridge Road, Pitlochry, Perthshire & Kinross PH16 5NA. *01796 472882.* info@fonab.co.uk. www.fonab.co.uk. Mr Michael Stewart. Signposted on A9, 0.5m S of Pitlochry. Holiday site. Mountain bike hire. Free trout fishing. Dogs allowed. Fees on application. Graded: 4 stars. Open March-October.

River Tilt Caravan Park, Blair Atholl, Pitlochry, Perthshire & Kinross PH18 5TE. *01796 481467.* Mr Stuart I Richardson. Take B8079 off A9, signposted to Blair Atholl. On banks of River Tilt, next to golf course and 100yds from town. New showers. Calor Gas and Camping Gaz. Calor Best Park of Scotland. New indoor heated pool. Sauna. Solarium. Steam room. Gym. Restaurant. David Bellamy Conservation Award. Graded: 5 stars.

Tummel Valley Holiday Park, Tummel Bridge, Pitlochry, Perthshire & Kinross PH16 5SA. *01882 634221.* parkdeanenquiries@parkdean.com. www.parkdean.com. Parkdean Holidays Plc. 12 miles west of Pitlochry on B8019. Free indoor pool and paddling pool. Entertainment, lounge bar, restaurant and takeaway meals. Children's play area, crazy golf, solarium and supermarket. Fishing in the grounds. Caravans for sale. Graded: 4 stars. Open March-January.

Stirling

Balquhidder Braes Caravan & Camping Park , Balquhidder Station, Lochearnhead, Stirling, Perthshire FK19 8NX. *01567 830293.* balquhidderbraes@onetel.net.uk. www.balquhidderbraes.co.uk. Mr J & Mrs C Cooper. On A84, 2m S of Lochearnhead. Situated in First National Park for Scotland. Level site ideal base for touring, hill walking etc. Excellent facilities for 2003. Good restaurant next to site Graded: 4 stars. Open March-January.

SHETLAND

Lerwick

Clickimin Camp Site, Lochside, Lerwick, Shetland ZE 1 0PJ. *01595 741000.* Shetland Recreational Trust. Large sports hall. Fitness suite. Sauna, solarium. Indoor bowling hall and leisure pools. Graded: 4 stars. Open May 1-September 30.

Levenwick

Levenwick Camp Site, Levenwick, Shetland ZE2 9HX. *01950 422207.* Situated on A970,18m S of Lerwick, 7m N of Sumburgh Airport signposted. Warden: J G Jamieson. Open May 1-September 30.

SOUTH AYRSHIRE

Ayr

Carskeoch Caravan Park, Patna, Ayr, South Ayrshire KA6 7NR. *01292 531205.* Mr & Mrs W H Proctor. Take A713 S from Ayr for 10m to Patna. Follow caravan park signs for 0.5m to site. Flat, well-drained site in Burns country. Good hill walking area. Licensed clubhouse. Open March 1-October 31.

Crofthead Caravan Park, Ayr, South Ayrshire KA6 6EN. *01292 263516.* Mr & Mrs Borland. 2m E of Ayr off A70.

Sundrum Castle Holiday Park, Coylton, Ayr, South Ayrshire KA6 6HX. *01292 570057.* parkdeanenquiries@parkdean.com. www.parkdean.com. Parkdean Holidays Plc. 4m E of Ayr, off A70-signposted. Indoor pool, Games room and amusement arcade. Restaurant & bars. Tennis and putting green. Free kids' club. Free family entertainment. Graded: 3 stars. Open March-October.

Girvan

Laggan House Leisure Park, Ballantrae, Girvan, South Ayrshire KA26 0LL. *01465 831229.* Mr & Mrs R B Finch. A77 to Ballentrae, from north go through village, cross river and take 1st left. Follow road for 2 miles to T-junction, turn left. Park on left after 0.5 miles. Quiet, family run park in beautiful wooded valley. Enjoy walking, river and sea fishing, sightseeing or a day trip to Northern Ireland. Sauna and solarium. Graded 4 stars. Open March-October.

SOUTH AYRSHIRE/STIRLING

Windsor Holiday Park, Barrhill, Girvan, South Ayrshire KA26 0PZ. *01465 821355.* bookings@windsor-park. freeserve.co.uk. www.windsor-park.freeserve.co.uk. Mr & Mrs D Martin. On the A714, nine miles south of Girvan on Girvan to Newton Stewart road. Site is well signed and lies between Pinwherry and Barrhill, off main road. Level site with all-weather and grass pitches. Graded: 3 stars. Open March 1-October 31.

Maybole

Camping & Caravanning Club Site - Culzean Castle, Glenside, Culzean Castle, Maybole, Strathclyde, South Ayrshire KA19 8JX. *01655 760627.* www.campingand caravanningclub.co.uk . The Camping & Caravanning Club Ltd. Off the A719. In grounds of Culzean Castle on the west coast of Scotland. The Site entrance is same as entrance to the Castle. 90 pitches—caravans, motor caravans and tents accepted. Play area. Non-members welcome. Open March-October.

The Walled Garden Caravan & Camping Park, Kilkerran, Maybole, South Ayrshire KAI9 7SL. *01655 740323.* walled gardencp@clara.co.uk. www.walledgardencp.clara.co.uk. Jim McCosh. 4-acre site with 80 pitches accepting all units. On B741 to Girvan look for Kilkerran sign. About 45m from Glasgow. Senior citizen concessions. Non-members welcome. Open April-October.

SOUTH LANARKSHIRE

Lanark

Clyde Valley Caravan Park, Kirkfieldbank, Lanark, South Lanarkshire ML11 9JW. *01698 357684.* Mr James McWhinnie. One mile north west of Lanark off the A72 or A73. Riverside site for touring or overnight route from Edinburgh to Glasgow. Fees on application. Open April-October.

Newhouse Caravan & Camping Park, Ravenstruther, Lanark, South Lanarkshire ML11 8NP. *01555 870228.* new housepark@btinternet.com. www.ukparks.co.uk/newhouse. Mrs J Seed. 3m E of Lanark via A743 and A70. 0.5m W of Carstairs. Within easy reach of Glasgow, Edinburgh and motor-way network. Flat, grassy site. Graded: 4 stars. Open mid March-mid October.

STIRLING

Aberfoyle

Cobleland Caravan & Camping Site, Forestry Commission, Aberfoyle, Stirling FK8 3UX. *01877 382392.* fe.holidays@ forestry.gsi.gov.uk. www.forestholidays.co.uk. Forestry Commission (Forest Holidays). Off A81 Glasgow to Aberfoyle. In heart of Trossachs, ideal for walking, cycling and sightseeing. Brochure request line: 0131 3340066. Open end March-end September.

Trossachs Holiday Park, Aberfoyle, Stirling FK8 3SA. *01877 382614.* info@trossachsholidays.co.uk. www.trossachsholi-days.co.uk . Joe & Hazel Norman. 3m S of Aberfoyle on A81. Mountain bike hire. Thistle Award. David Bellamy Gold

Conseration Award. Graded: 5 stars. Open March -October 31.

Balmaha

Cashel Caravan & Camping Site, (Forestry Commission), Rowardennan, Balmaha, Stirling G63 0AW. *01360 870234.* fe.holidays@forestry.gsi.gov.uk. www.forestholidays.co.uk. Forestry Commission (Forest Holidays). Off B837 Drymen-Rowardennan road, 3m N of Balmaha. On shores of Loch Lomond. Ideal for watersports. Brochure request line: 0131 3340066. Open March-October.

Blairlogie

Witches Craig, Blairlogie, Stirling FK9 5PX. *01786 474947.* witchescraig7545@aol.com. Mr A & V Stephen. On A91 St Andrews road 3m E of Stirling. Grassy and flat. Well-drained site within easy reach of Wallace Monument and Stirling Castle. Cafe and restaurant nearby. National winner 'Loo of the Year' 1999. Graded: 5 stars. Open April-October.

Callander

Keltie Bridge Caravan Park, Callander, Stirling FK17 8LQ. *01877 330606.* stay@keltiebridge.co.uk. Cambusmore Estate. On A84 between Doune and Callander. Quiet riverside location close to the town of Callander, in the scenic Trossachs area. Top quality shower block. Takeaway meals, store, cafe/restaurant all available nearby. Graded: 4 stars. Open April 1-October 31.

Fintry

Balgair Castle Caravan Park, Fintry, Stirling G63 0LP. *01360 860283.* Limited facilities for disabled people. Graded: 4 stars. Open March 1-October 31.

Killin

High Creagan Caravan Site, High Creagan, Killin, Stirling FK21 8TX. *01567 820449.* A Kennedy. 2m E of Killin on A827. Site overlooks Loch Tay. Open March-October.

Stirling

Auchenbowie Caravan Site, Stirling, Stirling FK7 8HE. *01324 822142.* Mr Robert Forsyth. 3.5m S of Stirling. Leave M80-M9 at exit 9. Take A872 towards Denny for 0.5m. Turn right, site is 0.5m. Fees on application. Graded: 2 stars. Open April-October.

Mains Farm, Thornhill, Stirling, Stirling FK8 3QR. *01786 850605.* gsteedman@lineone.net. MrJohn Steedman. 6 miles south of Callander on B822 through Thornhill. Site is on right. In Trossachs National Forest Park. Swimming pool, cafe/restaurant available nearby. Open April 1-October 31.

Strathyre

Immervoulin Caravan and Camping Park, Strathyre, Stirling FK18 8NJ. *01877 384285.* Mr T R Lloyds. 8m N of Callander. Easy and clearly marked access from the A84. Situated in an area of picturesque beauty alongside the river Balvaig, the site provides facilities for the tourer and camper. Within easy walking distance of the village. Graded: 2 stars. Open Easter-end September.

TAYSIDE

Scone

Camping & Caravanning Club Site - Scone, Scone Palace Caravan Park, Scone, Tayside PH2 6BB. *01738 552323.* www.campingandcaravanningclub.co.uk. The Camping & Caravanning Club Ltd. Site lies 2m north of Perth on A93 adjacent to racecourse. Turn left on to Stormontfield Road. 0.5m later turn left onto drive to racecourse. 150 pitches. Caravans, motor caravans and tents accepted. Play area. Non-members welcome. David Bellamy Gold Conservation Award. Open March-October.

WEST LOTHIAN

Linlithgow

Loch House Farm Site, Linlithgow, West Lothian EH49 7RG. *01506 842144.* dotandonj@aol.com. Mrs Dorothy Johnston. From Linlithgow take A706 towards Bo'ness, take first left after motorway bridge. Dogs allowed. Graded: 1 star.

WESTERN ISLES

Benbecula

Shell Bay Holiday Park, Liniclate, Benbecula, Western Isles HS7 5PJ *01870 602447.* Allan Buchanan. site 23 miles from Lochboisdale on A865/B892. 21 miles from Lochmaddy. Near beaches and community school. Dogs allowed. Graded: 2 stars.

Harris

Laig House Caravan Site, 10 Drinishadder, Harris, Western Isles HS3 3DX. *01859 511207.* Mr Angus Macdonald. From car ferry in Tarbert left at all junctions. S on A859 4.5m to site. Coastal site with access to beaches. Dogs welcome. Open April-October.

Isle of Lewis

Laxdale Holiday Park, 6 Laxdale Lane, Stornaway, Isle of Lewis, Western Isles HS86 0DR. *01851 703234/706966.* gordon@laxdaleholidaypark.force9.co.uk. Gordon Macleod. From Stornaway ferry terminal take A857 for 1.5 miles, turn left just before the Laxdale river. Park is 100yd on left-hand side. Quiet, family run park in peaceful tree-lined surroundings. All modern facilities including bunkhouse. Ideal base for touring the Isles. Graded: 4 stars. Open March 31-October 31.

> **Please mention *Camping Sites 2004* when contacting sites in this guide**

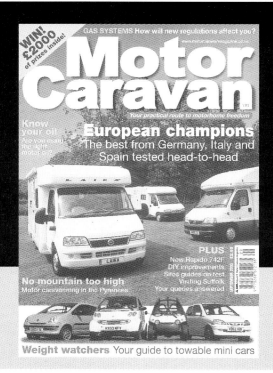

NORTHERN IRELAND

ANTRIM

Antrim

Sixmilewater Caravan Park, Antrim Forum, Lough Road, Antrim, Co Antrim BT41 4DQ. *028 9446 3113/4131.* info@antrim.gov.uk. www.antrim.gov.uk. Antrim Borough Council. Situated close to the shores of Lough Neagh—an area steeped in history and natural beauty with many attractions and activities for the holidaymaker to enjoy. Ideal for accommodating tents, touring caravans and motorcaravans. Open Easter-end September.

Ballycastle

Silvercliffs Holiday Village, 21 Clare Road, Ballycastle, Co Antrim BT54 6DB. *028 2076 2550.* Hagans Leisure Group. Close to the Glens of Antrim and the Giants Causeway. Wide range of facilities including sunbed and sauna. Adventure playground. Lounge bar with live entertainment.

Ballymoney

Drumaheglis Marina & Caravan Park, 36 Glenstall Road, Ballymoney, Co Antrim BT53 7QN. *028 2766 6466/028 27660227.* info@ballymoney.gov.uk. www.ballymoney.gov.uk. Ballymoney Borough Council. Situated about 4 miles from Ballymoney, off the A26 Ballymoney to Coleraine road—well signposted. Rural location on Lower River Bann. Marina, Boat park, Slipway, Jetty, Volleyball, Table tennis, Childrens' play area. Nature walk. Open April-October.

Bushmills

Portballintrae Holiday Home Park, Ballaghmore Avenue, Bushmills, Co Antrim BT57 8RX. *028 2073 1478/028 7082 4644.* Rubane Investments Ltd. B17 to Bushmills, B145 to Portballintrae. Also signposted A2-B145 junction in Portballintrae. Quiet family touring and static site. Reservations required for July and August. Open March-November.

Cushendun

Cushendun Caravan Park, 14 Glendun Road, Cushendun, Co Antrim BT44 0PX. *028 2176 1254*Moyle District Council. Open Easter-end September.

Larne

Carnfunnock Country Park, Coast Road, Drain's Bay, Larne, Co Antrim BT40 2QG. *02828 270541/02828 260088.* larne tourism@btconnect.com. www.larne.gov.uk. Larne Borough Council. Situated on A2 coast road, 3.5m north of Larne within 473 acres of parkland. Attractions include: walled garden, miniature railway, orienteering, outdoor adventure playground, golf, maze, woodland walks and visitor centre. Open Easter-October.

Curran Court Caravan Park, 131 Curran Road, Larne, Co Antrim BT40 1XB. *028 28273797/3203.* From town centre take signs for leisure centre. Half mile from ferry terminal and amenities. Near leisure centre, hotel, bowling green and putting green. Open April-September.

Portrush

Hilltop Holiday Park, 60 Loguestown Road, Portrush, Co Antrim BT56 8PD. *01265 322760.* Blairs Caravans Ltd. 0.5m S of Portrush on A29 just off main road to Coleraine. Holiday site. Open Easter-September.

Skerries Holiday Park, 126 Dunluce Road, Portrush, Co Antrim BT56 8NB. *028 70822531.* D J Locuhart Ltd. 1m E of Portrush on coast road to Giant's Causeway. Near Giant's Causeway. Holiday site, 1m from beach. Children's play area. Tennis courts. Open April-September.

ARMAGH

Lurgan

Kinnego Marina Caravan Park, Kinnego Marina, Oxford Island, Lurgan, Co Armagh BT66 6WJ. *028 3832 7573/028 3831 2400.* kinnego.marina@craigavon.gov.uk. Craigavon Borough Council, Leisure Services. Off N1 motorway, Lurgan roundabout, junction 10. Follow signs from N1 to Oxford Island. Open April 1-October 31.

Markethill

Gosford Forest Park, 7 Gosford Demesne, Gosford Forest Park, Markethill, Co Armagh BT60 1GD. *028 3755 1277/028 3755 2154.* Department of Agriculture. From Armagh A28 to Newry. 10 miles from Newry City. Conservation forest. Walks. Picnic sites. Barbecue sites. Collection of rare breeds of farm animals. Deer park. Collection heritage poultry. 7 miles from Armagh City. Guided walks available, please book in advance.

DOWN

Banbridge

Banbridge Tourist Information Centre, 200 Newry Road, Banbridge, Co Down BT32 3NB. *028 4062 3322.* banbridge @nitic.net. www.banbridge.com. Situated on the main A1/N1 Belfast/Dublin Euroroute. Convenient for ferry ports at Larne, Belfast and Dublin. Electricity included in site fees. Children's play area.

Castlewellan

Castlewellan Forest Park, The Grange, Castlewellan, Co Down BT31 9BU. *028 4377 8664.* Dept of Agriculture. 30m S of Belfast signposted off the Belfast-Newcastle route. Game fishing on site. Families only. Open Easter-end October.

Cloughy

Kirkistown Caravan Park, 55 Main Road, Cloughy, Co Down BT22 1JB. *02842 771183.* umex@zetnet.co.uk. Peter Marsden. Travelling south on the A2 from Portavogie, the park is on the northern end of Cloughy. Free draining, level pitches overlooking the sea. Centrally heated toilet block. Direct access to safe, sandy beach. Open March 17-October 31.

Kilkeel

Chestnutt Caravan Park, 3 Grange Road, Cranfield West, Kilkeel, Co Down BT34 4LJ. *028 4176 2653.* Chestnutt Caravans. 3m S of Kilkeel to Greencastle Post Office. Follow signposts for Cranfield West. Cranfield is signposted and site is on left. Ideal overnight stop on Dublin to Belfast coastal route or touring centre. Terms on application. Open March-October.

Killy Leagh

Camping & Caravanning Club Site - Delamont Country Park, Down Patrick Road, Killy Leagh, Co Down BT30 9TZ. *028 4482 1833* www.campingandcaravanningclub.co.uk. The Camping & Caravanning Club. Off A22 one mile south of Killyleagh and 4 miles north of Down Patrick. The park, 64 pitches, is located in an area of outstanding natural beauty. Features to attract all kinds of visitors: walks, picnic areas, birdwatching, Victorian walled garden, children's playground. Non-members welcome. Caravans, motor caravans and tents accepted. Open March-November.

Millisle

Rathlin Caravan Park, 43-45 Moss Road, Millisle, Co Down BT22 2DS. *028 9186 1386* Seven acres of riverside meadows within the village of Millisle. 500yd from the beach. Close to local pubs and hostelries. Open Easter-end October.

Newcastle

Greenhill YMCA National Centre, Donard Park, Newcastle, Co Down BT33 0GR. *013967 23172.* National Council of YMCA's of Ireland. Down Newcastle Main Street, turn right Brynsford road, first left (YMCA Greenhill sign), first left again, left into park and follow through park into woods to Greenhill site. Organised groups only are welcome.

Tollymore Forest Park, 176 Tullybranigan Road, Newcastle, Co Down BT33 0PW. *023 4372 2428* Department of Agriculture. 2m from Newcastle, 0.25m from Bryansford. Woods and parklands. Fees on application. Inquiries to Head Forester. Dogs must be kept under control.

Newtownards

Ballywhiskin Caravan & Camping Park, 216 Ballywalter Road, Millisle, Newtownards, Co Down BT21 2LY. *01247 862262.* Roy & Hilda Butler. From Newtownards take B172 east to Millisle. Turn R on the A2 towards Ballywalter. Site on right hand side. 18 acre site with sea view. Small animal farm for children. Open April-October. Also open weekends from October to April.

Portaferry

Silver Bay Caravan Park, 15 Ardminnan Road, Portaferry, Co Down BT22 1QJ. *028 42771321.* info@ardminnan.com. James Gowan. On A20. From Belfast to Newtownards, Grey Abbey, Kircubbin and take B173 to Cloughey. Approx. 1 mile on coast road. Safe beach. Bar/restaurant. Open one week before Easter -October 31.

Rostevor

Kilbroney Caravan Park, Shore Road, Rostevor, Co Down BT34 3DQ. *028 4173 8134/028 4176 5411* Newry & Mourne District Council. Approx. half mile from Rostrevor on main A2 road to Kilkeel. Large areas of open space, riverside walks and arboretum. Open April-end October.

FERMANAGH

Enniskillen

Blaney Caravan Park, Blaney, Enniskillen, Co Fermanagh. *00 353 2868641634.* info@blaneycaravanpark.com. www.blaney-caravanpark.com. 8 miles from historical town of Enniskillen (off main A46 road to Belleek). 5-star park with all amenities on site. Unspoilt countryside.

Lakeland Canoe Centre Campsite, Castle Island, Enniskillen, Co Fermanagh BT74 5HH. *01365 324250.* Gary Mitten. From local Visitors Centre, head for the Lakeland Forum, then to jetty behind Forum; ferry will pick you up. In a unique setting on an island yet just a stone's throw from Enniskillen. The centre is the focus for activity holidays with a difference. Open Easter-October.

Irvinestown

Castle Archdale Caravan Park & Camp Site Ltd, Castle Archdale, Lisnarick, Irvinestown, Co Fermanagh BT94 1PP. *01365 621333.* David Mahon. Sited on the shores of Lower Lough Erne within a Country Park of beautiful mixed woodlands. Pony trekking, boat trips and cycle hire. Located off B82 Enniskillen to Kesh Road. Open April 1/Easter-October 31.

Kesh

Lakeland Caravan Park, Boa Island Road, Kesh, Co Fermanagh BT93 1AD. *028 6863 1578.* mail@drumrush.co.uk. www.drumrush.co.uk. Joan & Lisa Armstrong. This multi-facility complex offers picturesque views over Lough Erne as well as a fully licensed bar and restaurant with entertainment throughout the summer months.

Lisnakea

Share Holiday Village, Smith's Strand, Shanaghy, Lisnakea, Co Fermanagh BT92 0EQ. *028 6772 2122.* share@dnet.co.uk. www.sharevillage.org. Discovery 80 Ltd (Share). Main Belfast to Enniskillen road (A4) take turn off for Maguires bridge go through towards Lisnaskea, in Lisnaskea take B127 towards Derrylin, centre is 4m on right. Water activities on site. Sauna, steam room and fitness room on site. Open Easter-end October.

LONDONDERRY

Castlerock

Castlerock Holiday Park, 24 Sea Road, Castlerock, Co Londonderry BT51 4TN. *028 7084 8381.* Bonalston Caravans Ltd. Take the A2 from Coleraine to Castlerock for 5m. Turn right at thatched cottage, turn right at railway crossing on B119 into Castlerock village. Park signposted. Close to magnificent Benevenagh mountain with spectacular views. Close to many places of interest. Open Easter-October 31.

LONDONDERRY/CLARE

Coleraine

Tullans Farm Caravan Park, 46 Newmills Road, Coleraine, Co Londonderry BT5 2JB. *028 7034 2309.* tullansfarm@hot mail.com. Diana McClelland. One mile from Coleraine. Cinema, skating rink and swimming pool within 6m. Large children's play area. Snooker pool, table tennis (indoors) TV room. Country ambience yet just one mile from Coleraine. Open March-end October.

🚐🛉📺♨🛁🚿🔌⊙🔥🔵🛒🍴🚻🅿 🔥📞ℓ🎱♿🏊🚶⊙🔍🏹🚵

Limavady

Benone Tourist Complex, 53 Benone Avenue, Magilligan, Limavady, Co Londonderry BT49 0LQ. *028 7775 0555.* Limavady Borough Council. On A2 coast road about 12m from Limavady and 9m from Coleraine. Beside Benone Strand. European Blue Flag Winner. 9-hole golf course, tennis courts, 2 outdoor heated splash pools, children's play area, practice range and natural history exhibition.

🚐🛉📺♨🛁🚿🔌⊙🔥🔵🍴🚻🅿☀♿ℓ🎱🏊⊙🔍🏹

Golden Sands Caravan Parks, 26A Benone Avenue, Magilligan, Limavady, Co Londonderry BT49 0LQ. *028 7775 0324* John & Stanley Walls. 9m N of Limavady on coast road to Coleraine. Beside extensive sandy beach on north coast. Open March-end October.

🚐🛉♨🛁🚿🔌⊙🔥🔵🍴🚻🅿☀ℓ🎱📞☀🏹🏊⊙🔍🏹🚵

Portstewart

Portstewart Holiday Park, 80 Mill Road, Portstewart, Co Londonderry BT55 7SW. *012870 833308.* Stephen & Terry O'Neill (Bonaslton Caravans Ltd). On approach to Portstewart from Coleraine, A2 turn right at roundabout into Mill Road. Park on right. Level ground. Close to beaches and Portstewart Promenade. Open Easter-October 31.

🚐🛉📺♨🛁⊙⊙🔥🔵🍴🚻☀ℓ🎱♿🏊⊙🔍🏹🚵

TYRONE

Clogher

Clogher Valley Country Caravan Park, 9 Fardross Forest, Clogher, Co Tyrone BT76 0HG. *028 8554 8932* Sydney Somerville. Signposted off main A4 between Clogher and Fivemiletown. Forest walks. Bird-watching. Bicycles for hire. Dogs allowed. Open mid March-end October.

🚐🛉📺♨⊙⊙🔥🔵🍴🚻ℓ🎱♿

Dungannon

Dungannon Park, Moy Road, Dungannon, Co Tyrone BT71 6DY. *028 8772 7327/028 8772 9196* dungannonpark@utuinter net.com. Dungannon District Council. Signposted off A29, one mile from Dungannon. Site overlooks Park lake. Barbecue area. Fishing, walks. New visitor centre. Open March 1-October 31.

🚐🛉📺♨🛁⊙🔵🍴🚻🅿🔍🏊⊙🔍

Killymaddy Centre, Ballygawley Road, Dungannon, Co Tyrone BT70 1TF. *028 87767259* killymaddy@nitic.net. Dungannon & South Tyrone Borough Council. From end of M1, 6 miles along A4 in Enniskillen direction on left.

🚐🛉♨♨🛁🚿✕⊙🔥🔵🍴☀ℓ🎱🏊⊙🔍🏹

Fivemiletown

Round Lake Caravan Park, Murley Road, Fivemiletown, Co Tyrone BT75 0QS. *028 8776 7529/028 8772 0300.* killymaddy @nitic.net. Dungannon District Council. 0.5m outside Fivemiletown on Fintona road. Visitor centre, games room, toilets, tuck shop. Lakeside walks, playpark, paddling pool.

🚐🛉📺♨🛁✕⊙🔥🔵🍴🚻☀ℓ🎱🏊⊙🔍

IRELAND

CAVAN

Virginia

Lough Ramor Caravan & Camping Park, Ryefield, Virginia, Co Cavan. *00 353 1 837 1717.* Located 0.5km off N3 route, 5km south of Virginia, on the scenic shores of Lough Ramor. Facilities include a toilet block and hard standing sites with electrical supply poins. Close to shops, pubs and restaurants. Open May-September.

🚐♿⊙🔥🍴🔵🏊🏹

CLARE

Corofin

Corofin Village Caravan and Camping Park, Main Street, Corofin, Co Clare. *00 353 65 6837683.* corohost@iol.ie. Neylon Family. Corofin is located at entrance to the Burren. From Ennis follow N85 and R476. Campsite is in village centre behind the Hostel. Comfortable campers kitchen/dining room with free gas and free hot water. Open April-September.

🚐🛉♨🔵🍴🔥🏹

Doolin

Nagles Doolin Caravan and Camping Park, Doolin, Co Clare. *00 353 65 7074458.* ken@doolincamping.com. www.doolin camping.com. Ken Nagle. From Lisdoonvarna go towards Cliff of Moher, turn right for Doolin and follow signs to Doolin Pier. Located beside Doolin Pier. Close to excellent restaurants and famous pubs with traditional music nightly. Shop open June Bank Holiday-end of August. Open April-September.

🚐🛉📺♨🛁🚿⊙⊙🔥🔵🍴🚻ℓ☀🏹🏊⊙🔍🏹🚵

O'Connors Riverside Camping & Caravan Park, Doolin, Co Clare. *00 353 65 7074314.* joan@oconnorsdoolin.com. www.oconnorsdoolin.com. Joan & Pat O'Connor. From Lisdoonvarna go towards Cliffs of Moher (N67), turn right for Doolin. Go straight at main cross-roads in centre of Doolin. Park is situated over the Aille River Bridge on the left hand side behind O'Connors farmhouse bed and breakfast. Well sheltered and supervised. Open April-September.

🚐🛉♨🛁🚿⊙⊙🔥🔵🍴🚻🔍🏹🏊⊙🔍🏹

Killaloe

Lough Derg Holiday Park, Killaloe, Co Clare. *00 353 61376329.* From Dublin, Limerick Road, N7, North from Nenagh, follow signs for Killaloe/Ballina. 4.5 acres. Family owned and run, situated in the very scenie Shannon Valley, on the shores of Lough Derg, well sheltered. Open May-September.

🚐🛉♨🛁✕⊙🔵🍴🔥🏹🏊⊙🔍

Lahinch

Lahinch Camping & Caravan Park, Lahinch, Co Clare. *00 353 65 81424* In the village of Lahinch 300yd from excellent beach. Rocky coastline. Good touring centre for Burren country, Cliffs of Moher, Aran Islands. Good fishing nearby. Pony trekking. Fees on application. Open May-September.

🚐🛉📺♨🛁✕⊙⊙🔥🔵🍴🚻ℓ☀🏹🏊⊙🔍🏹🚵

CORK

Ballymacoda

Sonas Caravan Park, Ballymacoda, Co Cork. *00 353 24 98132/00 353 24 98960.* sonas-camping@yahoo.co.uk. www. sonascamping.ie. C Riordon. From Cork N25 to Castlemartyr, just over the birdge in the village, take R632 to Ladysbridge. Turn left in middle of village for Ballymacoda. Follow direction signs from Ballymacoda to Sonas. Park set in unspoilt rural birdwatching area, with direct access to the beach. Open May 1- mid September.

Bantry

Eagle Point Camping, Ballylickey, Bantry, Co Cork. *00 353 2750630.* eaglepointcamping@eircom.net. www.eaglepoint camping.com. Elizabeth Sullivan. On N71 Bantry to Glengarriff. Situated on a peninsula with direct access to the sea and suitable for all kinds of water activities. Covering over 20 acres and providing top standard facilities. Open April 26-September 30.

Blarney

Blarney Caravan & Camping Park, Stone View, Blarney, Co Cork. *00 353 214385167.* con.quill@camping-ireland.ie. From N71 at Cork City follow signs for Blarney. Signposted from Blarney Esso filling station. Family-run touring park set in 3 acres of countryside. Sheltered and well landscaped overlooking Blarney Castle and Stone. Large campers kitchen dining area. Shops, restaurants, pubs available in Blarney, 1.5m. Open February-November.

Clonakilty

Desert House Caravan & Camping Park, Coast Road, Clonakilty, Co Cork. *00 353 23 33331.* The Jennings family. From Cork N71 to Bandon and Clonakilty. Park is signposted at roundabout in Clonakilty. Small park situated on a dairy farm overlooking Clonakilty Bay. Sandy beaches, bird watching. Model village nearby. Restaurants, music in pubs close by. Open Easter and May 1-September 30.

Glengarriff

Dowlings Caravan & Camping Park, Castletownbere Road, Glengarriff, Co Cork. *00 353 2763154.* James F Dowling. 2km on Castletownbere road R572 out of Glengarriff. Open Easter-October.

Kinsale

Garrettstown House Holiday Park, Kinsale, Co Cork. *00 353 21 4778156.* 6 miles from Kinsale R600. Through Ballinspittle village, past school and football pitch on main road to beach. Set in the grounds of an 18th C. estate, the park provides numberous top class facilities for families. Blue flag beach 1km. Open May-September.

Skibbereen

Barleycove Holiday Park, Crookhaven, Skibbereen, Co Cork. *00 353 2835302/00 353 214346466.* Kenneally's Caravans Ltd. N71 from Cork to Bandon, R589 Bandon to Bantry. R591 to Crookhaven just before Bantry. Excellent restaurants, and scenic boat trips nearby. BBQ, Children's club, baby-sitting, bicycles for hire, pitch and putt, tennis courts available on site. Open Easter and May-September.

The Hideaway Camping & Caravan Park, Skibbereen, Co Cork. *00 353 28 22254/33280.* the_hideaway@oceanfree.net. Stephen Keohane. 1km from Skibbereen Town Centre on R596 to Castletownsend. Family-run park, ideally located for touring the southwest. Rural setting 10 minutes' walk to Skibbereen town. Open Easter-end September.

DONEGAL

Portnoo

Dunmore Caravans, Strand Road, Portnoo, Co Donegal. *00 353 75 45121.* Mr John Gillespie. Flat, sandy site near beach. 9-hole putting green. 18-hole golf course. Open March 10-November 1.

Portsalon

Knockalla Caravan & Camping Park, Portsalon, Co Donegal. *00 353 74 59108/53213.* Situated near Portsalon on the beautiful Knockalla Coast Road, overlooking Ballymastocker Bay. Campers kitchen, children's outdoor play area. Open March-September.

DUBLIN

Camac Valley Tourist Caravan & Camping Park, Naas Road, Clondalkin, Dublin 22, Co Dublin. *00 353 1 4640644.* camac morriscastle@eircom.net. www.irishcamping.com. M50, exit junction 9 take N7 South (direction Cork). Groups and rallies well catered for in the spacious park with individual hard standings. Children's playground. Helpful staff, information room and 24hr security.

Dublin

Shankill Caravan & Camping Park, Shankill, Dublin, Co Dublin. *00 353 12820011.* shankillcaravan@eircom.net. Nearest camp site/caravan park to Stena Line and HSS fast ferry with lovely view of the Dublin mountains. 8km from Dun Laoghaire car ferry terminal, 16km from Dublin and 3km from Bray and sea. Contact Mrs M Hutchinson. Pre bookings not taken. Please note our rates will be in Euros for 2002.

GALWAY

Connemara

Actons Beachside Caravanning & Camping, Grallagh Streamstown Point, Clifden, Connemara, Co Galway. *00 353 9544036.* Christopher Acton. Located six miles west of Clifden, adjacent Omey Island, near Claddaghduff village. Majestically set on a peninsula within a natural heritage area. 300 degrees of sea and beach frontage. Private setting. Dolphin watching, beach walking. Open April-October.

Galway

Barna House Caravan Park, Barna Road, Galway, Co Galway. *00 353 1915 92469.* Co-operative Enterprises Society. 3m W of Galway on Spiddal road. Beautifully positioned site.

GALWAY/KERRY

0.5m from sandy beach. Well-equipped family site. Boat trips from Galway and many holiday attractions at Salthill. Open May-September.

Galway City

Ballyloughane Caravan & Camping Park, Ballyloughane Beach, Renmore, Galway City, Co Galway. *00 353 91755338/752029*. galwcamp@iol.ie. Situated beside sandy beach with panoramic views of Galway Bay and less than 5km from city centre. Leisure centre with 25m swimming pool within walking distance. Supermarket, laundrette and newsagents within 200yd. Open mid April-mid September.

Renvyle

Renvyle Beach Caravan & Camping Site, Tullybeg, Renvyle, Co Galway. *00 353 9543462*. renvylebeach@circom.net. Mrs Pauline Mortimer. 12m N of Clifden. Site signposted at Letterfrack. Turn to coast and site at Renvyle. Beside sandy beach. Dishwashing facility. Campers kitchen. Dogs welcome if on lead. Graded: 2 stars. Open Easter-September.

Spiddal

Spiddal Caravan & Camping Park, Spiddal, Co Galway. *00 353 91553372/558960*. paircsaoire@eircom.net. 1.6km from Spiddal village in Connemara Gaeltacht. Turn right at signpost in centre of village. Gaelic speaking park, nearest to the Aran Islands. Modern toilet block, fully serviced hard standings, playground, kitchen and cooking facility, indoor play area. Groups/buses welcome by prior arrangement. Open mid March-mid October.

KERRY

Ballyheigue

Casey's Caravan & Camping Park, Main Street, Ballyheigue, Co Kerry. *00 353 667133195*. Family-run park situated in the centre of Ballyheigue village. All amenities. Exit to Main Street with shops, supermarket, post office, take-away food and pubs, hotel. Water sports on beach. Hill walking. Open May-September.

Caherdaniel

Glenbeg Caravan & Camping Park, Caherdaniel, Co Kerry. *00 353 669475182*. glenbeg@eircom.net. Located on the Ring of Kerry Road, and adjacent to a fine sandy beach. Restaurants, hotel and pubs within walking distance. Open April-October.

Wave Crest Caravan Park, Caherdaniel, Co Kerry. *00 353 669475188*wavecrest@eircom.net. www.wavecrestcamping. com. Sean & Patricia O'Shea. 8m S of Waterville on Ring of Kerry road. Between Kenmare and Cahersiveen. On sea shore. Trips to Skellings Island and close to archaeological sites. Spacious site offering mountain walks, sandy beaches and surfing. Sitting room with open fire. Open March-October.

Dingle

Ballintaggart House Budget Accommodation, Racecourse Road, Dingle, Co Kerry. *00 353 669151454*. info@dingle accommodation.com. www.dingleaccommodation.com. Mr Paddy Fenton. Located on the right as you approach Dingle Town by the Tralee to Dingle Road, N86. Site is situated in the

grounds of a 1703 hunting lodge overlooking the bay with easy access to beaches. Self-catering kitchen available on site. Open May-September.

Glenbeigh

Falvey's Camping Site, Caherciveen Road, Glenbeigh, Co Kerry. *00 353 669768238*. Mr John Falvey. Take the Caherciveen Road in Glenbeigh village. Site is on main ring of Kerry Road. 0.25m from sea. Well-equipped site with poolroom and children's entertainment. Walking and pony trekking area nearby. Dogs allowed on leads. Open Easter-October.

Kenmare

Ring of Kerry Caravan & Camping Park, Kenmare, Co Kerry. *00 353 6441648*. info@kerrycamping.com. www.kerrycamping. com. Catherine Gibbons. N70 Sneem/Ring of Kerry road. 3.5 miles West of Kenmare. Park established over 20 years ago—suitable base for touring the Ring of Kerry, Beara and Dingle peninsulas. Open April-September.

Killarney

Fleming's White Bridge Caravan & Camping Park, White Bridge, Ballycasheen Road, Killarney, Co Kerry. *00 353 6431590*. fwbcamping@eircom.net. www.killarneycamping. com. Moira & Hillary Fleming. Unique location nestled on the banks of the river Flesk, away from busy and noisy roads yet only 1km east of Killarney centre. Family-run, friendly and helpful staff. Camper's kitchen, sports field, bicycle hire and dog walks. Tours available from site. Open mid March-end October.

Flesk Muckross Caravan & Camping Park, Muckross Road, Killarney, Co Kerry. *00 353 6431704*. killarneylakes@eircom. net. J & S Courtney. 1.5km from Killarney town centre, on N71 road to Kenmare. Next door to Glen Eagle Hotel. At the start of the Kerry way walk/cycle path from Caravan Park to National Park and Lakes. Open end March-end September.

Fossa Caravan & Camping Park, Fossa, Killarney, Co Kerry. *00 353 6431497*. fossaholidays@eircom.net. www.camping-holidaysireland.com. The Brosnan Family. Park is set in wooded area, in the village of Fossa, overlooking the MacGillycuddy Reeks and 5 mins walk from Lough Leane. Open end March-end September.

White Villa Farm Camping & Caravan Park, Cork Road, N22, Killarney, Co Kerry. *00 353 6420671/6432456*. killarneycamping @eircom.net. www.killarneycaravanpark.com. The O'Donoghue Family. 2m E on N22 Killarney road to Cork, 500 yards from N22 and N72 road junction. TV room. Camper kitchen with tables and chairs. Ice pack freezing. Takeaway meals, shops, cafe/restaurant and bottled gas supply all available nearby. Touring centre. National Park and Killarney lakes only 3 miles. Coach tours from park daily. Self-catering holiday apartments to rent. Open March-October.

Ring of Kerry

Glenross Caravan & Camping Park, Glenbeigh Village, Ring of Kerry, Co Kerry. *00 353 669768451/6431590*. fwb camping@eircom.net. www.killarneycamping.com. From Killarney/Killorglin take the N70 towards Glenbeigh. Park is on the right just before entering Glenbeigh village. Associate site

KERRY/MAYO

of Fleming's White Bridge, Killarney, discount for staying at both parks. Open May-September.

Goosey Island Campsite, Sneem, Ring of Kerry, Co Kerry. *00 353 6445577.* washer@oceanfree.net. Park is a new development located in the centre of Sneem village, on the Ring of Kerry. Open mid April-mid October.

West's Caravan Park, Killarney Road, Killorglin, Ring of Kerry, Co Kerry. *00 353 669761240.* reservations@west caravans.com. www.westcaravans.com. From Killorglin take main Killarney Road, after 1.6km park will be on your right hand side. Ideal touring centre. Park overlooked by Ireland's highest mountain, on Riverbank. On Ring of Kerry, close to Gap of Dunloe, Dingle peninsula. Open Easter-end October.

Ring of Kerry Coast

Mortimer's Mannix Point Camping & Caravan Park, Cahirciveen, Ring of Kerry Coast, Co Kerry. *00 353 669472806.* mannixpoint@mail.com. www.campingkerry.rural-biznet.com. Mr Mortimer Moriarty. Located on the coast, 300 meters off N70 Ring of Kerry road. 15 mins walk to restaurants, pubs, shops, cybercafe, cycle hire, etc. Impeccably clean on site facilities include a cosy campers' sitting room renowned for impromptu music sessions. No dogs from July 15 to August 15. Open March-October.

Tralee

Woodlands Caravan & Camping Park, Dan Spring Road, Tralee, Co Kerry. *00 353 667121235.* wdlands@eircom.net. Mike & Martina McDonnell. N21 then N22, turn left at roundabout after McDonalds and follow signs. Designed by campers this family run park is located on a 16 acre parkland setting just 10 mins walk from the centre of Tralee town. Washrooms, shower block. Campers kitchen. Hard standings, 10amp electric hook-ups, mains water and drains. Open March 15-end September.

KILDARE

Athy

Forest Farm Caravan & Camping Park, Dublin Road, Athy, Co Kildare. *00 353 50731231.* forestfarm@eircom.net. Mary & Michael McManus. Three miles from Athy Heritage town on Dublin road (N78) 38 miles from Dublin. Family run park on 140 acre working farm, surrounded by mature trees, beech and evergreen. Campers kitchen, large lounge and laundry. Quiet park well back from road.

KILKENNY

Bennettsbridge

Nore Valley Caravan & Camping Park, Bennettsbridge,Co Kilkenny. *00 353 5627229.* norevalleypark@eircom.net. www.norevalleypark.tripod.com. Samuel & Isobel Harper. From Kilkenny take the R700 to Bennettsbridge, just before bridge turn right at sign. Situated on an open farm, patrons have free access to the farm and the children are encouraged to assist in animal feeding. Open March-October.

Kilkenny

Tree Grove Caravan & Camping Park, Danville House, Kilkenny, Co Kilkenny. *00 353 5670302.* treecc@iol.ie. 1.5km from Kilkenny City centre after roundabout on R700 in the direction of New Ross. Free and unlimited hot showers, sheltered eating area, campers kitchen and laundry, bike hire on site. Open March-mid November.

LIMERICK

Adare

Adare Camping & Caravan Park, Adare, Co Limerick. *00 353 61395376.* dohertycampingadare@eircom.net. Hugh & Marie Doherty. From Limerick N20/N21 for Tralee. Stay on N21 through Adare, take left for R519 for Ballingarry and follow camp signs. Play area for children separate from parking area. Relaxing atmosphere, sheltered bounderies. Open March-September/October-February by appointment.

Kilcornan

Curragh Chase Caravan & Camping Park, Coillte Forest Park, Kilcornan, Co Limerick. *00 353 61396349.* okeeffe_e@coillte.ie. www.coillte.ie. From Limerick City take N69 coast road for 25km south-west towards Foynes. Park is located in a 242 hectare Coillte Forest Park of exceptional beauty. Open May-September.

LOUTH

Dundalk

Gyles Quay Caravan & Camping Park, Dundalk, Co Louth. *00 353 429376262.* Travel 3.2km on the Dundalk/Newry Road. Turn right on to the coast road, travel 7 miles and turn right at signpost for Gyles Quay. Open May-September.

Omeath

Tain Holiday Village, Ballyoonan, Omeath, Co Louth. *00 353 429375385.* www.tainvillage.com. On coastal road from Newry to Dundalk. Go through Omeath for 1m, park on left as you drive towards Carlingford. 40,000 sq feet of indoor leisure facilities including indoor and outdoor play areas and licensed bar and restaurant. Open March-November.

MAYO

Achill Island

Keel Sandybanks Caravan & Camping Park, Keel, Achill Island, Co Mayo. *00 353 9432054/9843211.* post@mayoholidays.com. www.mayoholidays.com. Bridged-linked to mainland Mayo, Achill Island offers a variety of scenic beauty and a range of holiday opportunities unequalled anywhere. On site: campers kitchen, assembly area, TV room, hot showers and plenty of outdoor playing space. Cafe/restaurant 200 metres away. Open May-September.

Seal Caves Caravan & Camping Park, The Strand, Dugort, Achill Island, Co Mayo. *00 353 9843262.* Mr Patrick J Gallagher. 7.5m north west of Achill Sound. Turn right off R319

MAYO/SLIGO

at Bunnacurry junction. Sheltered site near beach. Then on to valley and roads, turn left on for 4km to Dugort Beach. Open April-September.

Ballina

Belleek Caravan & Camping Park, Ballina, Co Mayo. *00 353 9671533.* lenahan@indigo.ie. www.indigo.ie. Joe & Phil Lenahan. 300 metres off the Ballina to Killala road. Just 2.5km from Ballina Town. Family-run park, sheltered and tranquil location with excellent facilities and guaranteed high standards. Open all year by arrangement.

Castlebar

Carra Caravan & Camping Park, Belcarra, Castlebar, Co Mayo. *00 353 9432054.* post@mayoholidays.com. www.horsedrawn.mayonet.com. From Castlebar follow the N84 towards Ballinrobe. Cross the railway bridge and turn left for Belcarra (8km). Horse-drawn caravan holidays and country walks are a speciality from this quiet family-run park. Shops, pubs, meals, are all within 200 metres. Open June-September.

Carrowkeel Camping & Caravan Park, Ballyvary, Castlebar, Co Mayo. *00 353 949031264.* carrowkeelpark@eircom.net. Alex Peters. Take N5 from Castlebar to Dublin. Carrowkeel Park is signposted on your left, 7 miles from Castlebar. Children's games room and outdoor play area. Campers kitchen, clubhouse, live entertainment in high season. Open April-September.

Cong

Cong Caravan & Camping Park, Lisloughrey, Quay Road, Cong, Co Mayo. *00 353 9246089.* quiet.man.cong@iol.ie. www.quietman-cong.com. Located 0.5m from Lough Corrib between Lough Mask and Lough Corrib, 1m from Cong village.

Knock

Knock Caravan & Camping Park, Claremorris Road, Knock, Co Mayo. *00 353 9488100.* info@knock-shrine.ie. www.knock-shrine.ie. At Knock roundabout take (N17) Claremorris/Galway road for one mile, the park is located on the left. Open March-October.

Louisburgh

Old Head Forest Caravan & Camping Park, Old Head, Louisburgh, Co Mayo. *00 353 876486885.* N60 to Westport, R335 to Louisburgh. Old Head 12m from Westport. Turn right at Old Head crossroad, park is 300 metres to left. Situated in woodland surroundings, sited at the edge of Old Head prehistoric woods on the shores of Clew Bay. Open June-September.

Westport

Parkland Caravan & Camping Park, Westport House and Country Park, Westport, Co Mayo. *00 353 9827766.* camping@westporthouse.ie. www.westporthouse.ie. On main Westport/Louisburgh Road R335, 2m from Westport. Turn right at Westport Quay. Open May-September.

OFFALY

Clonmacnoise

The Glebe Caravan & Camping Park, Clonfanlough, Clonmacnoise, Co Offaly. *00 353 0906430277.* joanna holmes@eircom.net. www.glebecaravanpark.ie. Noel & Vivienne Holmes. 3m east of Clonmacnoise, approx. half way between Ballinahown and Shannonbridge. Signposted turning off Clonmacnoise road. Award winning, friendly, family-run park offering modern facilities in an unspoilt rural setting. Open Easter-mid October.

Tullamore

Green Gables Caravan & Camping Park, Geashill, Tullamore, Co Offaly. *00 353 50643760.* ggcp@iol.ie . Geashill is on R420 between Tullamore and Portarlington. Quiet family run park in Geashill village, pubs and shops alongside, offering a good base for touring. Open Easter-September.

ROSCOMMON

Athlone

Hodson Bay Caravan & Camping Park, Athlone, Co Roscommon. *00 353 90292448.* On N61 from the western part of Athlone travel north for 3m, turn right at sign for Hodson Bay. Open June-September.

Ballaghderreen

Willowbrook Caravan & Camping Park, Kiltybranks, Ballaghderreen, Co Roscommon. *00 353 90761307.* willowbrook@eircom.net. www.willowbookpark.com. Dave & Lin Whitfield. R293 from Ballaghderreen towards Castlerea/Ballyhaunis, then R325 over bridge and bear left, one mile on turn right at signpost, park is 500yd. On site activities include walking, archery, kayaking and coarse fishing.

Boyle

Lough Key Caravan & Camping Park, Lough Key Forest Park, Boyle, Co Roscommon. *00 353 7962212/7962363.* Lough Key is 3km east of Boyle on N4. Park is set in the breathtaking surroundings of the 800 acre Lough Key Forest Park on the shores of Lough Key. Boyle provides a range of entertainment including restaurants, bars, traditional music, arts, craft shopping and much more. Open March-September.

Knockcroghery

Gailey Bay Caravan & Camping Park, Knockcroghery, Co Roscommon. *00 353 90361058.* From Knockcroghery village, past village take left turn nearest Railway station. Family-run self contained holiday park on the shores of Lough Rea. Campers kitchen, TV and games room. Open April-October.

SLIGO

Easkey

Atlantic 'n' Riverside Caravan & Camping Park, Easkey, Co Sligo. *00353 9649001.* atlanticriverside@yahoo.com. Mr Louis Smith. On T40 coast road 20m west of Sligo. Quiet scenic area, rugged coastline. Salmon trout river bordering site. Holiday caravan site. Some space for tents. Pool room. TV room and playground. Camper kitchen with all facilities. Wheelchair accessible toilet/shower suite. Fees and dates of opening on application. Open March-September.

Enniscrone

Atlantic Caravan Park, Enniscrone, Co Sligo. *00 353 9636132.* A long established family holiday resort with its famous 3-mile golden beach. Open April-October.

Rosses Point

Greenlands Caravan & Camping Park, Rosses Point, Co Sligo. *00 353 7177113.* Rosses Point is 8km west of Sligo on R29 off N15. Site is beside golf club. Direct access to two safe beaches. Shops, restaurants, pubs 500yd. Open March-September.

Sligo

Gateway Caravan & Camping Park, Ballinode, Sligo, Co Sligo. *00 353 7145618.* gateway@oceanfree.net. Carrie & Phil Maguire. Located on N16 Sligo/Belfast road, 1.2km from Sligo City centre at Ballinode traffic lights. Excellent on site facilities. Shop, pub/pub food across the road. Takeaway deliveries to site. Open January 15-December 15.

Strandhill

Strandhill Caravan & Camping Park, Strandhill, Co Sligo. *00 353 7168111.* Strandhill is 8km west of Sligo on N59, site is on airport road. Shops, pubs and restaurants within 100 metres. Open Easter, end April-end September.

TIPPERARY

Cahir

The Apple Caravan & Camping Park, Moorstown, Cahir, Co Tipperary. *00 353 5241459.* con.traas@theapplefarm.com. www.theapplefarm.com. Park is 300yd off the main Waterford/Limerick road (N24), between Clonmel (5.5m) and Cahir (4m). Friendly site located on award winning fruit farm. Free access to tennis court and rackets. Open May-September.

Glen of Aherlow

Ballinacourty House Caravan & Camping Park, Glen of Aherlow, Co Tipperary. *00 353 6256000.* info@ballina courtyhse.com. www.ballinacourtyhse.com. In Tipperary town turn left and follow signs for Glen Hotel, pass Glen Hotel, 1km next right. Watch out for hairpin bends and steep incline. On-site facilities include campers kitchen, table tennis, mini golf, children's playground. Open March-September.

Glogheen

Parsons Green Caravan & Camping Park, Glogheen, Co Tipperary. *00 353 5265290.* kathleennoonan@oceanfree.net. www.clogheen.com. Small, family-run park centrally situated for touring the whole of the south of Ireland. Excellent on-site facilities include: garden and river walks, pet field, farm museum, playground, pony, boat rides, picnic area, tennis and basketball court, TV and function rooms.

Roscrea

Streamstown Caravan & Camping Park, Streamstown, Roscrea, Co Tipperary. *00 353 50521519.* streamstown caravanpark@eircom.net. www.elyocarroll.com. From Roscrea, take the R491 to Shinrone for 2.5km. The Park is signposted. A family run tourist park set on a dairy farm in quiet surroundings. Hikers can be collected from Roscrea bus or train station by telephoning the park on arrival. Open April-November.

WATERFORD

Dungarvan

Bayview Caravan & Camping Park, Ballinacourty, Dungarvan, Co Waterford. *00 353 5845345/5842296.* bayview@cablesurf.com. From Dungarvan turn south off N25 onto Gold Coast Road and follow signs to park. Open April-October.

Casey's Caravan & Camping Park, Clonea, Dungarvan, Co Waterford. *00 353 5841919.* Follow signpost off the N25. From Dungarvan town take the R675 coast road and follow signpost. Family run park. Shop adjacent to park. Direct access to the beach. Open April-September.

Tramore

Newtown Cove Caravan & Camping Park, Tramore, Co Waterford. *00 353 51381979.* newtown_cove@iol.ie. From Tramore on the R675 Coast Road to Dungarvan, 1km from town turn left at the top of the second hill, opposite golf course. Family-run park, in a peaceful setting, well sheltered. Kitchen and all weather camping facilities. Open May-September.

WESTMEATH

Multyfarnham

Lough Derravaragh Caravan & Camping Park, Multyfarnham, Co Westmeath. *00 353 4471500.* camping @iol.ie. Paul Smith. Park is located on the N4 between Mullingar and Longford, take road to Multyfarnham and follow signs to Derravaragh/Donore. Facilities include campers kitchen, children's playground, bike hire, TV and pool table. Dog racing, forest walks, historic sites, castles and pubs are all nearby. Open March-September, rest of year by appointment.

WEXFORD

Ballaghkeen

The Trading Post, Ballaghkeen, Co Wexford. *00 353 5327368.* thetradingpost@eircom.net. www.tradingpostireland. com. Patrick Power. R741 out of Wexford, across the new bridge, continue for 14km. The Trading Post Service Station and Camper Park is on your left. Wexford's first privately owned specialist camper park where the tourer gets priority. Open April-September.

WEXFORD/WICKLOW

Ferrybank

Ferrybank Camping & Caravan Park, Ferrybank, Co Wexford.
00 353 5344378/43274. wexfordcorporation@wexfordcorp.
ie. www.wexfordcorp.ie. Five minutes' walk across the
bridge on seafront on the R741. Open Easter-September.
🚐🅿♿🔌💻≋🔥🎣♨↘⚲⛵

Kilmuckridge

**Morriscastle Strand Farmily Caravan & Camping Park,
Kilmuckridge, Co Wexford.** *00 353 5330124/30212.* camacmorris
castle@eircom.net. www.irishcamping.com. From Wexford,
N11 then after 4km take the right turn off for Castlebridge and
R741. Stay on this road till right turn for Kilmuckridge Village,
follow signs for Morriscastle Strand, then park. On-site security
at night is one of our priorities. Dogs permitted with caravans/
campervans in certain areas. Open May-September.
🚐🅿♿🔌💻🅿🛒🔥♨↗⚲⛵

New Ross

**Ocean Island Caravan & Camping Park, Fethard On Sea,
New Ross, Co Wexford.** *00 353 51397148.* Set in a tranquil
setting, easy walking distance of sandy beaches. Open Easter-
September.
🚐🅿♿🔌🛒💻🔥♨↘⚲↻⚲

Rosslare

**St Margarets Beach Caravan & Camping Park, Our Lady's
Island, Rosslare, Co Wexford.** *00 353 5331169.* stmarg@indigo.
ie. Kathryn Traynor. 9km from Rosslare Ferry Port, well suited to
those beginning or ending their holiday in Ireland. Family-run
park. Shop open from June to August only. Open April-October.
🚐🅿💻🔌🛒☉♨🔥🔥🎣♨↘⚲⚲

WICKLOW

Donard

Moat Farm Caravan & Camping Park, Donard, Co Wicklow.
00 353 45404727. moatfarm@ireland.com. Edward & Nuala Allen.
15kms south of Blessington on N81, turn left at the Old Toll House
Pub. Signposted to park. Small, quiet, family-run park in rural setting, within walking distance to village. Open March-September.
🚐🅿💻🔌♿🛒☉♨🔥🔥🎣♨🔥♨↘⚲↻

Rathdrum

**Avonmore Riverside Caravan & Camping Park, Rathdrum,
Co Wicklow.** *00 353 40446080.* avonmoreriverside@eircom.net.
From Dublin N11 to Rathnew, then R742. Quiet site on the banks
of the Avonmore River and on the edge of the Wicklow Mountains.
Village 10 minutes' walk. Open Easter-end September.
🚐🅿🔌♨☉🔥🎣♨≋↺♨

Redcross Village

**River Valley Caravan & Camping Park, Redcross Village, Co
Wicklow.** *00 353 40441647.* info@rivervalleypark.ie. www.river
valleypark.ie. 36m South of Dublin within easy reach of two
ferry ports, Rosslare and Dun Laoghaire. No dogs during July
and August. Open March-September.
🚐🅿♿♨🔌✕☉🛒🔥🎣♨↘⚲↻⚲

Roundwood

**Roundwood Caravan & Camping Park, Roundwood, Co
Wicklow.** *00 353 12818163.* roundwoodcaravancamp@yahoo.co.uk.
Mr Nigel Dickson. On Bray (12m)-Glendalough road, 6m from
Glendalough. 8 m from sea. Open March-September.
🚐🅿💻🔌♨☉♨🔥🔥🎣♨↺♨↘⚲↻⚲

TO SUBSCRIBE TO

camping sites

Caravan and Motor Caravan

www.caravanmagazine.co.uk   www.motorcaravanmagazine.co.u

PARK HOME
& HOLIDAY CARAVAN
www.phhc.co.uk

INDEX TO ADVERTISERS